Market-Valuation Methods in Life and Pension Insurance

In classical life insurance mathematics, the obligations of the insurance company towards the policy holders were calculated on artificial conservative assumptions on mortality and interest rates. However, the classical approach is being superseded by developments in international accounting and solvency standards coupled with theoretical advances in the understanding of the principles and methods for a more market-based valuation of risk, i.e. its price if traded in a free market.

The book describes these new approaches, and is the first to explain them in conjunction with more traditional methods. The exposition integrates methods and results from financial and insurance mathematics, and is based on the entries in a life insurance company's market accounting scheme. With-profit insurance contracts are described in a classical actuarial model with a deterministic interest rate and no investment alternatives. The classical valuation based on conservative valuation assumptions is explained and an alternative market-valuation approach is introduced and generalized to stochastic interest rates and risky investment alternatives. The problem of incompleteness in insurance markets is addressed using a variety of methods, for example risk minimization, mean-variance hedging and utility optimization. The application of mathematical finance to unit-linked life insurance is unified with the theory of distribution of surplus in life and pension insurance. The final chapter provides an introduction to interest rate derivatives and their use in life insurance.

The book will be of great interest and use to students and practitioners who need an introduction to this area, and who seek a practical yet sound guide to life insurance accounting and product development.

International Series on Actuarial Science

Mark Davis, Imperial College London
John Hylands, Standard Life
John McCutcheon, Heriot-Watt University
Ragnar Norberg, London School of Economics
H. Panjer, Waterloo University
Andrew Wilson, Watson Wyatt

The International Series on Actuarial Science, published by Cambridge University Press in conjunction with the Institute of Actuaries and the Faculty of Actuaries, will contain textbooks for students taking courses in or related to actuarial science, as well as more advanced works designed for continuing professional development or for describing and synthesising research. The series will be a vehicle for publishing books that reflect changes and developments in the curriculum, that encourage the introduction of courses on actuarial science in universities, and that show how actuarial science can be used in all areas where there is long-term financial risk.

Market-Valuation Methods in Life and Pension Insurance

THOMAS MØLLER
PFA Pension, Copenhagen

MOGENS STEFFENSEN
Institute for Mathematical Sciences, University of Copenhagen

Library
University of Texas
at San Antonio

CAMBRIDGE UNIVERSITY PRESS
Cambridge, New York, Melbourne, Madrid, Cape Town, Singapore, São Paulo

Cambridge University Press
The Edinburgh Building, Cambridge CB2 2RU, UK

Published in the United States of America by Cambridge University Press, New York

www.cambridge.org
Information on this title: www.cambridge.org/9780521868778

First published 2007

Printed in the United Kingdom at the University Press, Cambridge

A catalog record for this publication is available from the British Library

ISBN-13 978-0-521-86877-8 hardback
ISBN-10 0-521-86877-7 hardback

Contents

Preface

Insurance mathematics and financial mathematics have converged during the last few decades of the twentieth century and this convergence is expected to continue in the future. New valuation methods are added to the traditional valuation methods of insurance mathematics. Valuation and decision making on the asset side and the liability side of the insurance companies are, to an increasing extent, being considered as two sides of the same story.

The development has two consequences. Demands are made on practising actuaries, whose education dates back to when financial mathematics was not considered as an integrated part of insurance mathematics. By considering the convergence as it applies to their daily work, such actuaries should be kept abreast of this convergence. From this starting point, the ideas, concepts and results of finance should be brought together to construct a path between classical actuarial deterministic patterns of thinking and modern actuarial mathematics. This is where stochastic processes are brought to the surface in payment streams as well as in investment possibilities.

At the same time, present students of actuarial mathematics need to apply financial mathematics to classical insurance valuation problems. These students will typically, and should, meet financial mathematics in textbooks on pure finance. However, to receive the full benefit of financial mathematical skills, these skills need to be integrated and proven beneficial for classical problems of insurance mathematics already on a student level.

International accounting standards have developed over the years. Denmark has been at the forefront, implementing new accounting methods to replace (assumed to be) conservative book values with real values based on market information. Although the international accounting standards have not yet been settled, the Danish approach to market valuation seems to be an important step in the right direction. Many aspects of this approach are underpinned by methods taken from mathematical finance.

The rationale for this book is that practising actuaries need an exposition of financial methods and their applications to life insurance from the point of view of a practitioner. Methods and applications are discussed in terms of the Danish approach to market valuation. As a by-product, the book explains to present students how financial methods known to them can be applied to valuation problems in the life insurance market.

In 1995 and 1996, Tomas Björk and Ragnar Norberg gave courses in financial mathematics and applications to life insurance at the University of Copenhagen. These courses aroused our interest in the interplay between finance and insurance. We studied the topics in our master theses, finished in 1996 (T.M.) and 1997 (M.S.), and continued our studies in our Ph.D. theses, finished in 2000 and 2001, respectively.

Parts of the book (Chapter 2–5) are based on material which was developed for a course on market valuation in life and pension insurance. This course was organized by the Danish Actuarial Association in 2001. Each chapter was the material for one course module and was written more or less independently of the others. The material was originally written in Danish. In 2002 the material was developed further and translated into English, and Chapter 1 was added. In 2003, Chapters 6 and 7 were added on the occasion of The First Nordic summer school in insurance mathematics, entitled "New Financial Products in Insurance." In 2004, the material was made consistent for notation and terminology. However, it is still our intention that each chapter should be readable more or less independently of the others. Therefore, some definitions and introductions of quantities are repeated throughout the book.

The book suggests approaches to life insurance market-valuation problems. The starting point is the version of with-profit insurance provided by Danish life insurance companies. In order to help the reader follow the mathematical description of this type of product, Chapter 1, written by Mogens Steffensen, provides a non-mathematical introduction to life insurance practise in general.

In Chapter 2, also written by Mogens Steffensen, the with-profit insurance contract is described at first in a classical actuarial model with a deterministic interest rate and no investment alternatives. The classical valuation based on conservative valuation assumptions is explained, and an alternative market-valuation approach is introduced. Here, the partition of future payments in guaranteed payments and non-guaranteed payments is important. Particular attention is paid to the intervention options held by the policy holder, i.e. the surrender and free policy (paid-up policy) options. Various approaches to these options are suggested.

The market-valuation method introduced in Chapter 2 is generalized to a stochastic interest rate in Chapter 3. Both discrete-time and continuous-time bond market theory are introduced to a level such that the reader can follow the reasoning behind replacing the discount factor in the market-valuation formulas for guaranteed payments by zero coupon bond prices. Fundamental financial concepts, such as arbitrage and market completeness, are introduced in a bond market framework. Difference and differential equations for the market value of guaranteed payments are derived. Chapter 3 is written by Thomas Møller.

In Chapter 4 the market-valuation method introduced in Chapter 2 is generalized to a situation with one risky investment alternative to the deterministic interest rate. Both discrete-time and continuous-time stock market theory are introduced to a level such that the reader can follow calculations of market valuations of non-guaranteed payments in the case of two investment alternatives. Fundamental financial concepts, such as arbitrage and market completeness, are repeated in a stock market framework. Difference and differential equations for the market value of the total payments, including the non-guaranteed payments, are derived. Finally, the stock market is connected to the stochastic bond market introduced in Chapter 3. Chapter 4 is written by Mogens Steffensen.

The usual outline of introductory financial mathematics is to introduce the fundamental financial concepts in a discrete and/or continuous stock market model. Afterwards these are repeated in a discrete- and/or continuous-time bond market model. In our exposition, the cut is different and is based on entries in a life insurance company's market accounting scheme. Valuating the guaranteed payments, the important stochastic generalization of the classical actuarial deterministic financial market lies at the introduction of a stochastic bond market. A stochastic stock market comes into play when valuating the non-guaranteed payments.

An alternative class of insurance contracts to with-profit insurance is unit-linked insurance contracts, which are studied in Chapter 5, written by Thomas Møller. This class of contracts and their market values are analyzed on the basis of the stochastic financial markets introduced in Chapters 3 and 4. The problem of genuine incompleteness in insurance markets is addressed. The incompleteness in insurance markets stemming, for example, from mortality risk is often taken care of in the literature by assuming risk neutrality of the insurance company with respect to such a risk. Relaxing this assumption, we suggest various approaches to incomplete market valuation. In particular, valuation and optimal investment methods based on risk minimization, mean-variance hedging and utility optimization are introduced and exemplified in the case of unit-linked insurance.

In Chapter 6, the application of mathematical finance to unit-linked life insurance is unified with the theory of distribution of surplus in life and pension insurance. The unification is based on a consideration of distribution of surplus as an integrated part of the insurance contract. The notion of surplus and various dividend and bonus schemes linked to this surplus are studied. In particular, explicit results are obtained in the case where dividends and bonus payments are linear in the surplus. Chapter 6 is written by Mogens Steffensen.

Typically, insurance companies are faced by insurance liabilities that extend up to sixty years into the future, whereas the financial markets typically do not offer bonds that extend more than thirty years into the future. With market-based valuation methods, the value of both assets and liabilities are affected by changes in the economic environment. Here, interest rate derivatives seem to have become an important risk-management tool for life insurance companies. An introduction to certain concepts and instruments from the area of interest rate derivatives is therefore given in Chapter 7, written by Thomas Møller. Examples are swap rates, swaps, floors, caps, swaptions and CMS options. Various pricing methods are discussed, and it is demonstrated how the financial impact on a life insurance company of these instruments could be assessed.

The book studies approaches for market valuation of life insurance liabilities. The various chapters address specific aspects of market-based valuation and contain introductions to theoretical results from financial mathematics and stochastic calculus that are necessary for the applications. A brief discussion of the relation to existing books on financial mathematics and insurance mathematics is given in the following list.

- Björk, T. (2004). *Arbitrage Theory in Continuous Time*, 2nd edn (Oxford: Oxford University Press). Most of the theoretical results related to financial mathematics presented here can be found in this book by Tomas Björk. To some extent, the notation suggested by Björk is considered as "standard" and is therefore used in the present book. Even the structural exposition of certain topics of financial mathematics is inspired by Björk's book.
- Briys, E. and de Varenne, F. (2001). *Insurance: From Underwriting to Derivatives: Asset Liability Management in Insurance Companies* (Chichester, UK: Wiley). The book discusses the convergence between the insurance industry and the capital markets. It is less mathematical than the current book and focuses on institutional aspects of the interplay between the two fields. In contrast, the current book investigates the convergence of the theories of financial mathematics and insurance mathematics and their applications to market-based valuation.

- Gerber, H.U. (1997). *Life Insurance Mathematics* (Berlin: Springer). This provides an introduction to classical life insurance mathematics and can be viewed as a necessary prerequisite for the current book. The concepts and techniques discussed in Gerber's book (for example, present values, specific life insurance contracts, decrement series, Thiele's differential equation) are also used and explained in the present book. However, the current manuscript has a completely different goal and goes considerably beyond the introductory presentation in Gerber's book.

- Koller, M. (2000). *Stochastische Modelle in der Lebensversicherung* (Berlin: Springer). The book presents a framework where the underlying insurance contracts are modeled by Markov chains and where stochastic interest rates are allowed. The main difference between Koller's book and the current manuscript is that we focus more on market values and the application of theories from financial mathematics in the area of life insurance; Koller's book deals more with the underlying Markov chains and on deriving differential equations for the corresponding reserves (based on the work by Hoem, Norberg and others).

We expect our readership to fall into two categories. Firstly, practising life insurance actuaries who need an update of the mathematics of life insurance, an introduction to financial mathematics in an insurance context and an approach to market valuation in life insurance. Indeed, the book takes the point of view of a practising actuary. Chapter 1 on life insurance practice will provide the reader with sufficient insight into this practice.

Secondly, it is expected that the book will be read by students in actuarial science, who have prerequisites in both life insurance mathematics and mathematical finance, but want to see how these disciplines can and will be combined in both theory and practice. By taking the viewpoint of a practising actuary as a starting point, the student also sees how aspects of the classical life insurance mathematics are implemented in practice.

The level is advanced. Basic knowledge of life insurance mathematics (such as in Gerber's book) is required. In addition, basic probability theory is required, such that the reader can follow the introduction of filtrations, martingales, stochastic differential equations, etc. No previous knowledge of financial mathematics is required. However, the theoretical results are at times developed quickly in order to get to the applications, and at some points the reader would probably benefit from studying textbooks on financial mathematics for more details and more background information; for example, Björk (2004).

We would like to thank Tomas Björk and Ragnar Norberg for arousing our curiosity and for sharpening our understanding of the mathematics of life insurance and finance. The combination of basic knowledge in both areas and a provoked curiosity made our studies of the interplay between these fields possible, challenging and interesting. In addition, we wish to thank Ragnar Norberg, Christian Hipp and Martin Schweizer for their guidance and support during our Ph.D. studies. We would also like to thank Vibeke Thinggard and Mikkel Jarbøl for valuable comments and discussions on earlier versions of this material: in 2001 they were members of the Continued Professional Development Committee under the Danish Actuarial Association and were deeply involved in the organization of the course given in 2001.

1

Introduction and life insurance practice

1.1 Introduction

This chapter provides an introduction to life insurance practice with focus on with-profit life insurance. The purpose is to give the reader sufficient insight to benefit from the remaining chapters. In life insurance, one party, the policy holder, exchanges a stream of payments with another party, the insurance company. The exchanged streams of payments form, in a sense, the basis of the insurance contract and the corresponding legal obligations. When speaking of life insurance practice, we think of the way this exchange of payments is handled and settled by the insurer. We take as our starting point the idea of the policy holder's account. This account can be interpreted as the policy holder's reserve in the insurance company and accumulates on the basis of the so-called Thiele's differential equation. Its formulation as a forward differential equation plays a crucial role, and this chapter explains in words the construction and the elements of this equation and its role in accounting. Note, however, that the policy holder's account is not in general a capital right held by the insured but a key quantity in the insurer's handling of his obligations.

1.2 The life insurance market

In this section we explain the most typical environments for negotiation and contractual formulations for a life insurance policy. We distinguish between *defined benefits* and what we choose to call *defined contributions with partly defined benefits*.

Defined contributions with partly defined benefits cover the majority of life insurance policies. The policy holder agrees with the insurance company about a certain premium to cover a basket of benefits with, for example, a

life insurance sum paid out upon death before the termination of the contract
and/or a pension sum paid out upon survival until the termination of the
contract. The benefits agreed upon at issuance are set systematically low by
basing them on conservative assumptions on interest rates, insurance risk
and expenses. As the market interest rates, the market insurance risk and the
market costs evolve, a surplus emerges, and this surplus is to be paid back to
the policy holder. This typically happens by increasing one or more benefits.
This combination of known premiums reflected in guaranteed benefits, which
may be increased depending on the development in the market, categorizes
the contracts as defined contributions with partly defined benefits.

One construction is to increase all benefits proportionally such that the
ratio between, for example, the death sum and the pension sum is maintained.
Another construction is to keep the death sum constant or regulated with
some price index while residually increasing the pension sum. Only very
rarely is the surplus paid out in cash or used to decrease the premium instead
of increasing the benefits. Such rare constructions should in principle be
categorized as defined benefits with partly defined contributions since then a
basket of known benefits is combined with guaranteed premiums which may
be decreased depending on the development in the market.

The policies with defined contributions with partly defined benefits are
naturally classified as *private, firm-based*, or *labor-based*.

A *private* policy is agreed upon by a private person and the company.
The private person is the policy holder and negotiates the conditions in the
contract.

A *firm-based* policy is a contract which is part of an agreement between
an employer and an insurance company. The employer typically pays a part
of the premium but receives no benefits. The total premium paid is typically
a percentage of the salary. Although the terms of the contract are typically
negotiated between the employer and the company, the employees are still the
policy holders. The agreement between the employer and the company may
either be compulsory, in which case all employees are forced to participate,
or optional, in which case it is up to the employees to decide whether or not
to participate. Since the employer has no claims and no obligations besides
paying the premium, this premium can in many respects be interpreted as
salary.

A *labor-based* policy works in many respects as a firm-based policy except
for the fact that the employer and the employees are represented at the negotiation by organizations rather than the employers and employees themselves.
These organizations typically take care of people employed in the uniformed
services or education. The result is an agreement where the employer is

obliged to participate in the employees' policy on terms agreed upon by the organizations. The policy is then issued by a company taking care of all the employees in a particular organization. Once the agreement has been made and the contract has been issued, it works basically as a firm-based policy with the employer and the employees as payers of premiums and the employees as receivers of benefits. The total premium paid is typically a percentage of the salary. The employees are the policy holders. The labor-based policy is often part of a compulsory agreement, both the employer and the employed are obliged for which to agree to minimum conditions. The premium part paid by the employer can in many respects be interpreted as salary.

The *defined benefit* policies are usually a part of an agreement between a firm and an insurance company, are therefore and comparable with the firm-linked policy described above. The contract is negotiated indirectly by settlement of the agreement. However, instead of sharing the premium defined as a percentage of the salary between the employer and the employees, only the employees' part of the premium is defined as a percentage of the salary. On the other hand, the benefits are also defined as a percentage of the salary. This leaves a risk on the premium side. This risk is split between the employer and the insurance company according to the agreement. If the risk is left to the insurance company exclusively, then neither the employer nor the policy holder participates in the development in the market but leaves all risk to the insurance company. In contrast, if the risk is left to the employer exclusively, the insurance company is pure administrator and takes no risk. As mentioned above, a certain part of the defined contribution policies, where the surplus is redistributed as cash or used to decrease the premiums, can actually be considered as defined benefit policies with partly defined contributions.

The classification given above is fairly broad. When discussing details, there may be a lot of differences in the concrete formulations of the various agreements and contracts. Policies belonging to different classes may also be mixed within an agreement and within a contract. In the following, we concentrate on defined contributions with partly defined benefits. Although most of the ideas presented in Chapters 2–5 may be applied to defined benefits as well, all examples and interpretations take the defined contributions with partly defined benefits policy as a starting point. as:eksist It should be mentioned that in addition to the life insurance market described above, there may exist a set of public insurance schemes. For instance, in Denmark the national pension scheme is a pay-as-you-go scheme where present retirement pensioners are covered by present tax payers. In addition, the Danish state regulates a couple of particular funded pension schemes for people who work.

1.3 The policy holder's account

In our setting, the policy holder's account or the technical reserve and its dynamics are the technical elements in the handling and administration of life insurance contract. We classify the changes of the technical reserve in two different ways. The first way classifies the changes of income and outgo. The other way classifies the changes in what was agreed beforehand in a particular sense and additional changes made by the insurance company at the discretion of the company.

The technical reserve can in certain respects be interpreted as a bank account. The income on a bank account consists of capital injections and capital return provided by the bank from capital gains on investment of the account. The outgo on a bank account consists of capital withdrawals. Correspondingly, the income on an insurance account consists of premiums paid by the policy holder and return provided by the insurance company from capital gains on investment of the account. And, correspondingly, the outgo on an insurance account consists of the benefits paid to the policy holder. However, two additional terms add to the change of the account. One term is an outgo and covers the expense to the insurance company to administrate the policy. Administration expenses on the bank account must also be paid, but these are charged indirectly by a reduction of the return. The other additional term which adds to the change of the account is the so-called risk premium, which can be considered as an income or an outgo depending on its sign.

The risk premium is a premium that the policy holder pays from their account; it may be positive, in which case it can be considered as an outgo, or negative, in which case it can be considered as an income. The risk premium is paid to cover the loss to the insurance company in case an insurance event takes place in some small time interval. The amount of the potential loss is also spoken of as the sum at risk. The premium for this coverage is set to the expected value of this loss. Considering a so-called term insurance paying out a sum upon death, the loss to the insurance company in case of death equals the death sum which has to be paid out minus the technical reserve which, on the other hand, can be cashed. The expected value of that loss is the difference between the death sum and the technical reserve times the probability of dying in some small time interval. The death sum exceeds the technical reserve such that the risk premium is positive and can be considered as an outgo. Considering instead a pure endowment insurance, the insurance company cashes the technical reserve upon death and has no obligations. The expected value of this gain is the technical reserve times the probability of dying in a small interval. This results in a negative risk premium, and the risk premium may be considered as an income. In addition, the bank account can be interpreted as an insurance contract where the technical reserve is simply paid out upon death. This gives a potential loss upon death of the technical reserve paid out minus the technical reserve cashed, whereby the risk premium equals zero.

The term insurance and the pure endowment insurance are simple insurance contracts. If we introduce such things as disability annuities, premium waiver and deferred benefits, the picture becomes more blurred, but the underlying idea is basically the same. Apart from the real incomes and outgoes in form of premiums, returns and benefits, the policy holder pays or gains, depending on the sign of the risk premium, for the risk imposed on the insurance company.

Another way of classifying the changes of the technical reserve is firstly to identify the technical change which conforms with the guaranteed payments and then identify the additional changes made by the insurance company at the discretion of the company. When an insurance company issues an insurance policy, it guarantees a minimum benefit which is based on a technical return. Furthermore, the minimum benefit is based on a certain technical probability of the insurance event, for example the probability of dying in a small time interval. Finally, it is based on a technical amount for administration expenses. Basically, it simply guarantees to pay out a benefit which is "fair" under a certain set of assumptions on return, insurance risk and expenses. However, this set of assumptions is meant to be set so conservatively that a surplus emerges over time. This surplus is provided by the policy holder due to conservatism in assumptions and has to be paid back as the real market conditions evolve. This is achieved by adding dividends to the policy holder's account.

The law states that the surplus must be paid back to those who created it. The usual way of allocating the dividends is to change the account, not in correspondence with the technical assumptions, but in correspondence with a set of assumptions that is more favorable to the policy holder. Then, we can classify, element by element, the technical change and the additional change. Concerning the return, the insurance company firstly pays the technical return. Secondly, it pays the difference between the more favorable return and the technical return. Concerning the mortality, the insurance company firstly collects a risk premium in correspondence with the technical probability of death. Secondly, it pays back the difference between the risk premiums in correspondence with the more favorable probability and the technical probability. Concerning the expenses, the insurance company firstly withdraws the technical amount for expenses. Secondly, it pays back the difference between the more favorable amount and the technical amount for expenses. The use of the favorable assumption is that, element by element, the policy holder should not be put into a worse position than if the technical assumption had been used.

The favorable development of the account including dividends may be used to reach a higher value to be paid out as a pension sum at the termination of the contract. However, the policy holder may also wish that this favorable development provides capital for an increase of benefits and/or a decrease of premiums throughout the term of the policy. This has a feedback effect on the dynamics of the account, since premiums, benefits and risk premiums need to be adjusted in the light of such a change of payments. One construction is to let the death sum and the pension sum increase proportionally, such that the ratio between the two benefits is constant. However, the most typical constructions are to let the death sum be constant or regulated by some price index and then use the residual dividends to increase the pension sum.

We should mention an alternative application of dividends which has gained ground in recent years. Instead of increasing benefits and/or decreasing premiums, one may keep the guaranteed payments and instead change the underlying technical assumptions. In this way, dividends are added to the policy holder's account without changing the guaranteed payments. One may then ask: where did the money go and does allocation of dividends really put the policy holder in a better position? The point is that paying out dividends leads to what seems to be less favorable technical conditions. However, the guaranteed payments are not changed and can therefore not be less favorable. Furthermore, the consequence of less favorable technical conditions is higher surplus contributions in the future. And since these surplus contributions eventually have to be redistributed and reflected in payments, the position is indeed favorable. By this construction, allocation of dividends in a way postpone the increment of guaranteed benefits without postponing the increment of the account.

1.4 Dividends and bonus

The premiums agreed upon at the time of issuance of an insurance policy are "too high" compared with the benefits that are guaranteed at the time of issuance. This disproportion is the source of surplus, and it is stated by law that this surplus should be paid back to those policy holders who created it. In practice, this happens in two steps. Firstly, the surplus is distributed among the owners of the insurance company and the group of policy holders, and, secondly, the surplus distributed to the policy holders is distributed among the policy holders.

So, why should the owners of the company take part in the surplus that was created by policy holders? The problem is that "too high" may not be high enough. The insurance company is allowed to invest not only in fixed income assets, but also in stocks. Investment in stocks is, however, a risky business, and the insurance company may end up in a situation where it is not possible to increase the policy holder's account by the technical interest rate by means of capital gains. In that situation the owners of the insurance company must still provide capital for the technical increments of the technical reserve. Also, concerning mortality and expenses the insurance company may experience a situation worse than that considered as the worst possible case at the time of issuance. Concerning mortality and other kinds of insurance risk, medical, sociological and demographic uncertainties play a different role. The insurance company may need to help by injecting capital in the technical reserve in order to live up to the technical conditions. The owners of the insurance company must eventually cover the loss on the insurance portfolio.

The risk that things may go wrong, leading to the owners having to pay, is the reason why they, when things go right, deserve a share in the surplus created by the insurance portfolio. However, the distribution of surplus between owners and policy holders has to be fair in some sense. One of the purposes of this book is to provide the insurance companies with tools and ideas to make distributions that, to an increasing extent, are fair.

The part of the surplus distributed to the policy holders is deposited in the so-called undistributed reserve. That is, this reserve is distributed to the policy holders as a group but is not yet distributed among the policy holders. The distribution among policy holders takes place by deciding on the favorable set of assumptions introduced above. This mechanism transfers money from the undistributed reserve to the individual policy holder's account. As was required from the distribution between owners and policy holders, the mutual distribution between policy holders is also required to be fair. Fairness is here given by the statement that the surplus should be redistributed to those who earned it. A redistribution of the surplus to those who earned it has two consequences.

The first consequence is that the insurance company is not allowed to grow "large" undistributed reserves. This would systematically redistribute surplus from the past and present policy holders to the future policy holders. Thus, the insurance company needs to assign the undistributed reserve to the individual technical reserves "in due time." Here, "due time" is, of course, closely connected to the risk of the insurance company owners to eventually suffer a loss on the portfolio, which again connects to the owner's share in the surplus. If the undistributed reserve is high, then this reserve can take a big loss before the owners have to take over. Then the insurance portfolio pays a small, possibly zero, premium to the owners for taking risk. If the undistributed reserve is low, then this reserve may easily run out, and the insurance portfolio must pay a larger premium to the owners. This shows that the solution to a fair distribution of the surplus between the owners and the policy holders interacts substantially with the solution to a fair mutual redistribution amongst policy holders over time.

The second consequence is that, given a redistribution to the present policy holders, this must happen in a way that reflects which present policy holders have contributed a lot to the surplus and which have contributed less. Such a mechanism can be imposed by favorable assumptions on interest rates, mortality and expenses. The return is proportional to the technical reserve, the risk premium is proportional to the sum at risk, and the expense is typically formalized as a part of the premium. Therefore the individual technical reserve, the sum at risk and the premium determine the individual share in the total distribution. Once a redistribution from the undistributed reserve among the policy holders is elected to happen now instead of later, the set of favorable assumptions must to some extent reflect the present policy holder's contributions to the undistributed reserves.

Depending on the bonus scheme, the policy holder may experience the redistribution in different ways. The typical construction is to increase the benefits proportionally or to increase the pension sum residually, for example, after a price index regulation of the death sum. The redistribution may also be paid out as cash.

The redistribution of the surplus between the owners of the company and the policy holders and the mutual redistribution between policy holders are regulated by law and overseen by the supervisory authorities. Thus, they are not directly specified in the contract. However, they make up a part of the legislative environment in which the contract has been agreed upon, and therefore they can be considered, in many respects, as part of the contract itself. On the other hand, the conversion of dividends into payments on the individual policy is a part of the individual policy conditions. Therefore, this conversion is directly negotiable between the insurance company and the policy holder or, in the case of a firm-linked or labor-linked contract, between the company and the firm or labor organization, respectively. It is important to realize how the legislative environment and the contract, in combination, make up the conditions for all changes that are made over time by the insurance company to the premiums and benefits agreed upon at issuance. Firstly, the distribution between owners and policy holders (regulated by law);

secondly, the distribution mutually among policy holders (regulated by law); and thirdly, by changing the terms in the individual policy (regulated by the contract).

1.5 Unit-linked insurance and beyond

Several features characterize the participating policy as explained above. The policy holder participates in a mutual fund, so to speak, together with the other policy holders and together with the owners of the insurance company. The legislative environment sets the conditions for this cooperation. However, it may be difficult for the individual policy holder to understand whether the conditions are followed, in particular concerning the several layers of fair distributions. Even by representation of their ambassadors in the cooperation in the form of the supervisory authorities, this may be a difficult task. One way of avoiding the problems with fair distribution is that each and every single policy holder forms their own individual fund. This is what happens in unit-linked insurance.

In a unit-linked insurance contract, the policy holder does not participate in a mutual fund but decides on their own investments to some extent. The participating policies hold a very strong position in many countries and the unit-linked market has been long in coming, but since the beginning of the twenty-first century life insurance companies in these countries have started to offer unit-linked insurance contracts. The unit-linked insurance contract can be decorated with many different kinds of guarantees, and insurance companies have shown some creativity on that point. However, the market is still young, and there is still a lot of space for new developments and improvements.

When giving up the investment cooperation and entering into unit-linked contracts, policy holders typically also give up certain features of the participating policy. By working with an undistributed reserve, one achieves a smoothing effect of the market conditions. The undistributed reserve protects the underlying technical reserves, and hereby the guaranteed payments, from shocks in the market conditions. The technical reserves then only experience a smoothed effect from such shocks. However, it is important to realize that these smoothing effects do not rely particularly on the policy holders' participation in an investment cooperation. There is, in principle, no problem in maintaining the smoothing effect in a unit-linked insurance policy. This is only a matter of a proper definition of the unit to which the payments of the contract are linked. Some insurance companies have introduced advanced unit-linked products which maintain the smoothing effect. When speaking of such products as unit-linked contracts, our characterization of unit-linked products is that the investment game is an individual matter. If the investment game is individualized, then the unit-linked contract stays unit-linked, no matter the complexity of the unit, even when including any kind of smoothing effect.

One may argue that a unit-linked insurance contract endowed appropriately with smoothing effects and guarantees is close, both in spirit and in payments, to a participating policy. On the other hand, one may also argue that it makes a huge difference whether the conditions for smoothing effects and the guarantees are stated in the contract and individualized or are given in the legislative environment by somewhat more vague statements on fairness. One challenge is to incorporate the participating policies in an environment of finance theory, as has successfully been achieved for unit-linked policies. However, a proper description of unit-linked products in terms of finance theory requires an enlargement of this environment. Furthermore, an appropriate enlargement of this environment is definitely needed to deal with the complex nature of participating contracts and the special conditions of the life and pension insurance market in general. One of the aims of the remaining chapters of this book is to provide the reader with a box of tools that can be applied for working with this challenge with theoretical substantiation.

2

Technical reserves and market values

2.1 Introduction

This chapter deals with some aspects of valuation in life and pension insurance that are relevant for accounting at market values. The purpose of the chapter is to demonstrate the retrospective accumulation of the technical reserve and to formalize an approach to prospective market valuation. We explain and discuss the principles underpinning this approach.

The exposition of the material distinguishes itself from scientific expositions of the same subject, see, for example, Norberg (2000) or Steffensen (2001). By considering firstly the retrospective accumulation of technical reserves, secondly the prospective approach to market valuation and thirdly the underpinning principles, things are turned somewhat upside down here. The aim is to meet the practical reader at a starting point with which he is familiar.

The terms *prospective* and *retrospective* play an important role. The idea of a liability as a retrospectively calculated quantity needs revision when going from the traditional composition of the liability to a market-based composition of the liability. This is an important step towards comprehending both the market-valuation approach presented here and the generalization and improvement hereof, taking into consideration more realistic actuarial and financial modeling.

Throughout the chapter, we consider all calculations pertaining to the primary example of an insurance contract. This primary example is an endowment insurance with premium intensity π, pension sum guaranteed at time 0, $b^a(0)$, and guaranteed death sum, b^{ad}. Bonus is paid out by increasing the pension sum. The insurance contract is issued at time 0 when the insured is x years old and with a term of n years. Generalizations to other insurance contracts are left to the reader. Throughout the chapter expenses are disregarded.

Assume that death occurs with a deterministic mortality intensity $\mu(s)$ at age $x + s$, keeping in mind that this $\mu(s)$ of course depends on x then, and assume that discounting is based on a deterministic interest rate r. An important quantity is the discount factor from $u \geq t$ to t, $\exp\left(-\int_t^u r(s)\,ds\right)$, which we abbreviate by $\exp\left(-\int_t^u r\right)$. If the interest rate is constant, this discount factor equals $\exp\left(-r(u-t)\right) = v^{u-t}$, where $v = \exp(-r)$. Another important quantity is the survival probability from time t to u corresponding to age $x + t$ to age $x + u$, $\exp\left(-\int_t^u \mu(s)\,ds\right)$, which we abbreviate by $\exp\left(-\int_t^u \mu\right)$. The actuarial notation for such a survival probability is $_{u-t}p_{x+t}$.

We remind the reader about the following notation for the capital value at time t of one unit of a pure endowment insurance, a temporary term insurance and a temporary life annuity also used as a premium payment annuity:

$$_{n-t}E_{x+t} = v^{n-t}{}_{n-t}p_{x+t} = e^{-\int_t^n r+\mu},$$

$$A^1_{x+t\overline{n-t}|} = \int_t^n v^{s-t}{}_{s-t}p_{x+t}\mu(s)\,ds = \int_t^n e^{-\int_t^s r+\mu}\mu(s)\,ds,$$

$$a_{x+t\overline{n-t}|} = \int_t^n v^{s-t}{}_{s-t}p_{x+t}\,ds = \int_t^n e^{-\int_t^s r+\mu}\,ds.$$

In principle, the quantities $a_{x+t\overline{n-t}|}$ and $A^1_{x+t\overline{n-t}|}$ should be decorated with a bar, but since only continuous-time versions appear in this chapter, this notation is omitted. All quantities appear, on the other hand, with the decorations $*$ and δ, for example $_{n-t}E^*_{x+t}$ and $a^\delta_{x+t\overline{n-t}|}$. These refer to the corresponding fundamental quantities r and μ and the contents are obvious from the context.

2.2 The traditional composition of the liability

2.2.1 The technical reserve and the second order basis

In this section we study the technical reserve and how it arises from the second order basis. The *second order basis* is a pair (r^δ, μ^δ) containing the *second order interest rate* and the *second order mortality rate* by which the technical reserve accumulates.

We consider an accumulation of the technical reserve by the second order basis. This corresponds to a difference equation with initial condition as follows:

$$\Delta V^*(t) = r^\delta(t) V^*(t) \Delta t + \pi \Delta t - \mu^\delta(t) R^*(t) \Delta t, \qquad (2.1)$$

$$V^*(0) = 0,$$

where R^* is the sum at risk given by

$$R^*(t) = b^{\text{ad}} - V^*(t),$$

and where Δt is the time unit chosen for the accumulation. Actually, Equation (2.1) is a discrete-time version of a corresponding differential equation which can be obtained by dividing the difference equation by Δt and letting Δt go to zero. The corresponding differential equation with initial condition reads as follows:

$$\frac{\mathrm{d}}{\mathrm{d}t} V^*(t) = r^\delta(t) V^*(t) + \pi - \mu^\delta(t) R^*(t), \qquad (2.2)$$

$$V^*(0) = 0.$$

This differential equation can be solved over the time interval $(0, t]$ and the initial condition leads to the retrospective form:

$$V^*(t) = \int_0^t e^{\int_s^t r^\delta + \mu^\delta} \left(\pi - b^{\text{ad}} \mu^\delta(s) \right) \mathrm{d}s. \qquad (2.3)$$

The differential equation, Equation (2.2), solved over the time interval $(t, n]$ leads to the prospective form,

$$V^*(t) = b^{\text{ad}} A^{1\delta}_{x+t\,\overline{n-t}|} + V^*(n)\,_{n-t}E^\delta_{x+t} - \pi a^\delta_{x+t\,\overline{n-t}|}, \qquad (2.4)$$

where $V^*(n)$ is the terminal value of the technical reserve.

The second order basis is a decision variable held by the insurer that is to be chosen within certain legislative constraints and market conditions. One notes that in the prospective form, Equation (2.4), the second order basis over $(t, n]$ appears together with the terminal value of the technical reserve $V^*(n)$. Since these may be unknown at time t, Equation (2.4) is a representation of the solution to Equation (2.2), but not a constructive tool for calculation of the technical reserve. Nevertheless, if the terminal value $V^*(n)$ is interpreted as a terminal benefit, the prospective form expresses the technical reserve as a prospective value of all payments valuated under the future second order basis.

2.2.2 The technical reserve and the first order basis

In this section we study the technical reserve and how it arises from the first order basis. The *first order basis* is a pair (r^*, μ^*) containing the *first order interest rate* and the *first order mortality rate* under which the guaranteed benefits are set according to the equivalence principle.

We consider an accumulation of the technical reserve by the first order basis. This corresponds to a differential equation with initial condition as follows:

$$\frac{d}{dt}V^*(t) = r^*(t)V^*(t) + \pi - \mu^*(t)R^*(t) + \delta(t),\tag{2.5}$$

$$V^*(0) = 0,$$

where the dividend rate δ is given by

$$\delta(t) = \left(r^\delta(t) - r^*(t)\right)V^*(t) + \left(\mu^*(t) - \mu^\delta(t)\right)R^*(t).\tag{2.6}$$

The rate of dividends is determined such that the technical reserve in Section 2.2.1 coincides with the technical reserve in this section. Given a second order basis the rate of dividends is determined by Equation (2.6). On the other hand, given a rate of dividends δ, any pair $\left(r^\delta, \mu^\delta\right)$ conforming with Equation (2.6) is a candidate for the second order basis.

The differential equation, Equation (2.5), solved over $[0, t]$ leads to the retrospective form,

$$V^*(t) = \int_0^t e^{\int_s^t r^* + \mu^*}\left(\pi - b^{ad}\mu^*(s) + \delta(s)\right)ds.\tag{2.7}$$

On the basis of the technical reserve, the pension sum guaranteed at time t is calculated in accordance with the equivalence principle,

$$b^a(t) = \frac{V^*(t) + \pi a^*_{x+t\,\overline{n-t}|} - b^{ad}A^{1*}_{x+t\,\overline{n-t}|}}{{}_{n-t}E^*_{x+t}}.\tag{2.8}$$

Hereafter, we can write the prospective form as follows:

$$V^*(t) = b^{ad}A^{1*}_{x+t\,\overline{n-t}|} + b^a(t)\,{}_{n-t}E^*_{x+t} - \pi a^*_{x+t\,\overline{n-t}|}.\tag{2.9}$$

Note that from Equation (2.8) we get $b^a(n) = V^*(n)$ such that the technical reserve at the terminal time n coincides with the pension sum at that time. This motivates the interpretation of the technical reserve $V^*(n)$ as the terminal benefit at the end of the Section 2.2.1. In the following, we write $b^a(n)$ instead of $V^*(n)$ when it is appropriate to think of $V^*(n)$ as the pension sum. Note that Equation (2.8) also sets the guaranteed pension sum at time 0:

$$b^a(0) = \frac{\pi a^*_{x\,\overline{n}|} - b^{ad}A^{1*}_{x\,\overline{n}|}}{{}_nE^*_x}.$$

Since $b^a(t)$ is calculated on the basis of the retrospectively derived technical reserve, we see that Equation (2.9) is a representation of $V^*(t)$ but not a constructive tool for its derivation. Nevertheless, the prospective form expresses the technical reserve as a prospective value of the payments guaranteed at time t valuated under the first order basis.

The technical reserve at time t covers payments guaranteed at time t. Later, we use a technical reserve at time $u \geq t$ for payments guaranteed at time t. We choose to introduce this quantity now and denote it by $V^*(t, u)$. Then

$$V^*(t, u) = b^{\mathrm{ad}} A^{1*}_{x+u\overline{n-u}|} + b^{\mathrm{a}}(t)_{n-u}E^*_{x+u} - \pi a^*_{x+u\overline{n-u}|},$$

and for $u \geq t$ we have a differential equation with initial and terminal conditions, respectively, as follows:

$$\frac{\partial}{\partial u} V^*(t, u) = r^*(u) V^*(t, u) + \pi - \mu^*(u) R^*(t, u), \qquad (2.10)$$

$$V^*(t, t) = V^*(t),$$

$$V^*(t, n) = b^a(t),$$

where $R^*(t, u)$ is the sum at risk, given by

$$R^*(t, u) = b^{\mathrm{ad}} - V^*(t, u).$$

2.2.3 The undistributed reserve and the real basis

In this section we study the undistributed reserve and discuss how the undistributed reserve arises from the real basis. The *real* or *third order basis* is the pair (r, μ) containing the *real* or *third order interest rate* and the *real* or *third order mortality rate* by which the total reserve accumulates.

We consider an accumulation of the total reserve by the real basis. This corresponds to the differential equation with initial condition as follows:

$$\frac{\mathrm{d}}{\mathrm{d}t} U(t) = r(t) U(t) + \pi - \mu(t) R(t), \qquad (2.11)$$

$$U(0) = 0,$$

where R is the sum at risk, given by

$$R(t) = b^{\mathrm{ad}} - U(t).$$

The differential equation, Equation (2.11), solved over $[0, t]$ leads to the retrospective form:

$$U(t) = \int_0^t e^{\int_s^t r+\mu} \left(\pi - b^{\mathrm{ad}} \mu(s) \right) \mathrm{d}s. \qquad (2.12)$$

The differential equation, Equation (2.11), solved over $(t, n]$ leads to the prospective form:

$$U(t) = b^{\mathrm{ad}} A^1_{x+t\,\overline{n-t|}} + U(n)_{n-t}E_{x+t} - \pi a_{x+t\,\overline{n-t|}}, \tag{2.13}$$

where $U(n)$ is the terminal value of the total reserve.

The undistributed reserve X is calculated residually as the difference between the total reserve and the technical reserve:

$$X(t) = U(t) - V^*(t). \tag{2.14}$$

By differentiation, we obtain the retrospective form:

$$X(t) = \int_0^t e^{\int_s^t r+\mu} (c(s) - \delta(s))\,\mathrm{d}s, \tag{2.15}$$

where the contribution rate c is defined by

$$c(t) = (r(t) - r^*(t))V^*(t) + (\mu^*(t) - \mu(t))R^*(t). \tag{2.16}$$

The retrospective form given in Equation (2.15) shows how the undistributed reserve consists of past contributions minus past dividends.

Now we put up the following condition on the second order basis:

$$X(n) = U(n) - V^*(n) = 0. \tag{2.17}$$

Under this condition we have the following prospective form for the undistributed reserve:

$$X(t) = \int_t^n e^{-\int_t^s r+\mu} (\delta(s) - c(s))\,\mathrm{d}s. \tag{2.18}$$

This can be verified by differentiation of Equations (2.15) and (2.18) with respect to t. Equation (2.18) shows how the undistributed reserve is consumed in the future by letting the dividend rate differ from the contribution rate. Furthermore, with $V(t)$ defined as the prospective value of future payments as follows:

$$V(t) \equiv b^{\mathrm{ad}} A^1_{x+t\,\overline{n-t|}} + b^{\mathrm{a}}(n)_{n-t}E_{x+t} - \pi a_{x+t\,\overline{n-t|}}, \tag{2.19}$$

the condition on the second order basis, Equation (2.17), implies that

$$U(t) = V(t). \tag{2.20}$$

This is obtained by replacing $U(n)$ in Equation (2.13) by $V^*(n) = b^{\mathrm{a}}(n)$. In this chapter, we work under the assumption from Equation (2.17) such that Equation (2.20) holds. We therefore switch between U and V, in accordance with Equation (2.20), from situation to situation depending on whether it is beneficial to think of the quantity as retrospective or prospective.

Note that the future second order basis appears in Equations (2.18) and (2.19) through dividends and the terminal pension sum, respectively. This means that Equations (2.18) and (2.19) are representations, following from the condition $X(n) = 0$, of the total and the undistributed reserves but are not constructive tools for their derivation. Nevertheless, these forms express the total and the undistributed reserves as prospective values of different future payments depending on the future second order basis valuated under the real basis. The total reserve is a value of the total payments and the undistributed reserve is a value of dividends minus contributions.

Equations (2.12) and (2.15) are definitions of U and X whereas Equations (2.18) and (2.20) are representations of the same quantities based on the condition $X(n) = 0$. However, one may also start out with these representations as definitions, hereby including the future second order basis in the definition of U and X. If we then restrict the second order basis to obey $X(n) = 0$ with X defined by Equation (2.15), the formulas above show that further specification of the future second order basis is redundant. The quantities are hereafter given simply by the retrospective formulas, Equations (2.12) and (2.15).

The condition $U(n) - b^a(n) = 0$ can, by multiplication of $e^{-\int_0^n r + \mu}$, be written as follows:

$$b^a(n)\,_nE_r + b^{ad} A^1_{x\overline{n}|} - \pi a_{r\overline{n}|} = 0.$$

This shows that the condition $X(n) = 0$ is the same as performing the equivalence principle on the total payments under the real basis.

It is important to understand that it is the condition $X(n) = 0$ that spares us from discussing the future second order basis further. If, for one reason or another, the condition X is not to be fulfilled, the future second order basis is inevitably brought into the quantity V.

Traditionally, one would, in addition to the terminal condition $X(n) = 0$, impose a solvency condition in the following form:

$$X(t) \geq 0, \qquad 0 \leq t \leq n. \tag{2.21}$$

In practice, the undistributed reserve must, together with other sources of capital, excess a value based on the technical reserve, the sum at risk and the premium. The purpose of Equation (2.21) is to secure that U at any point in time covers the technical reserve interpreted as the value of guaranteed payments valuated by the first order basis, including the safety margins this may contain. Thus, in the traditional composition of the liability, one would not accept that $U \leq V^*$. One of the potentials of accounting at market value is to set up alternative solvency rules in terms of market values. As we shall see, solvency rules such as $U \geq V^*$ are, in principle, not necessary in the market-based composition of the liabilities.

2.3 The market-based composition of the liability

2.3.1 Guaranteed payments and the market reserve

In this section we introduce the market reserve for the guaranteed payments. The *guaranteed payments* at time t are given by the premium rate π, the death sum b^{ad} and the pension sum $b^{\text{a}}(t)$. The *market reserve* at time t is given by the prospective formula,

$$V^{\text{g}}(t) = b^{\text{ad}} A^{1}_{x+t\,\overline{n-t}|} + b^{\text{a}}(t)\,_{n-t}E_{x+t} - \pi a_{x+t\,\overline{n-t}|}. \qquad (2.22)$$

Thus, $V^{\text{g}}(t)$ is a prospective value of the guaranteed payments under the real basis.

The market reserve at time t, $V^{\text{g}}(t)$, covers payments guaranteed at time t. Later, we use a market reserve at time $u \geq t$ for the payments guaranteed at time t. We choose to introduce this quantity now and denote it by $V^{\text{g}}(t, u)$. Then

$$V^{\text{g}}(t, u) = b^{\text{ad}} A^{1}_{x+u\,\overline{n-u}|} + b^{\text{a}}(t)\,_{n-u}E_{x+u} - \pi a_{x+u\,\overline{n-u}|},$$

and for $u \geq t$ we have a differential equation with initial and terminal conditions, respectively, as follows:

$$\frac{\text{d}}{\text{d}u} V^{\text{g}}(t, u) = r(u) V^{\text{g}}(t, u) + \pi - \mu(u) R^{\text{g}}(t, u), \qquad (2.23)$$

$$V^{\text{g}}(t, t) = V^{\text{g}}(t),$$

$$V^{\text{g}}(t, n) = b^{\text{a}}(t),$$

where $R^{\text{g}}(t, u)$ is the sum at risk, given by

$$R^{\text{g}}(t, u) = b^{\text{ad}} - V^{\text{g}}(t, u).$$

2.3.2 Bonus payments and the bonus potential

In this section we introduce the bonus payments, the bonus potential, the individual bonus potential and the collective bonus potential. In Section 2.2.3 we introduced U and X and we concluded that the retrospective quantities were constructive tools for the calculation of the prospective quantities given by Equations (2.18) and (2.20), given the condition on the second order basis, $X(n) = 0$. Also in this section we define prospective values based on the future payments. As we shall see, the condition $X(n) = 0$, with X given by Equation (2.15), again leads to retrospective calculation formulas.

The *bonus payments* at time t are the payments which are not guaranteed at time t. The guaranteed payments at time t are given by the premium π, the death sum b^{ad} and the pension sum $b^{\mathrm{a}}(t)$. The real payments differ from these payments by the pension sum $b^{\mathrm{a}}(n)$ only. The difference is exactly the pension sum $b^{\mathrm{a}}(n) - b^{\mathrm{a}}(t)$ making up the bonus payments. This bonus payment has the following market value:

$$V^{b}(t) = (b^{\mathrm{a}}(n) - b^{\mathrm{a}}(t))\,_{n-t}E_{x+t}. \tag{2.24}$$

Thus, $V^{b}(t)$ is a prospective value under the real basis of the payments not guaranteed. We also speak of $V^{b}(t)$ as the *bonus potential* at time t.

The bonus potential at time t, $V^{b}(t)$, covers payments not guaranteed at time t. Later, we use a market-based reserve at time $u \geq t$ for the payments not guaranteed at time t. We choose to introduce this quantity now and denote this by $V^{b}(t, u)$. Then

$$V^{b}(t, u) = (b^{\mathrm{a}}(n) - b^{\mathrm{a}}(t))\,_{n-u}E_{x+u},$$

and for $u \geq t$ we have a differential equation with initial and terminal conditions, respectively, as follows:

$$\frac{\partial}{\partial u} V^{b}(t, u) = (r(u) + \mu(u)) V^{b}(t, u),$$

$$V^{b}(t, t) = V^{b}(t), \tag{2.25}$$

$$V^{b}(t, n) = b^{a}(n) - b^{a}(t).$$

Now, we include the condition on the second order basis that $X(n) = 0$ with X given by Equation (2.15). By means of the differential equations (2.11) and (2.23), it can now be shown that $V^{b}(t, u) = U(u) - V^{g}(t, u)$, from which it follows that

$$V^{b}(t) = U(t) - V^{g}(t). \tag{2.26}$$

We note that the bonus potential at time 0 equals the negative market reserve, $-V^{g}(0)$, since $U(0) = 0$.

In general, the quantity V^{b} defined by Equation (2.24) depends on the future second order basis through the terminal pension sum. However, as in Section 2.2.3, the condition $X(n) = 0$ saves us from further specifications since we have the representation in Equation (2.26).

It turns out to be informative to decompose the bonus potential into two reserves: the *individual bonus potential* V^{ib} and the *collective bonus potential* V^{cb} .

We consider the situation

$$V \geq V^* \geq V^g. \tag{2.27}$$

Then V^b is decomposed as follows:

$$V^b = V^{cb} + V^{ib} = (V - V^*) + (V^* - V^g).$$

Firstly, consider the individual bonus potential. From the differential equations (2.10) and (2.23) and the terminal condition $V^*(n, t) - V^g(n, t) = b^a(t) - b^a(t) = 0$, one obtains the prospective form,

$$V^{ib}(t) = V^*(t) - V^g(t) = \int_t^n e^{-\int_t^s r+\mu} c(t, s) \, ds, \tag{2.28}$$

where

$$c(t, s) = (r(s) - r^*(s)) V^*(t, s) + (\mu^*(s) - \mu(s)) R^*(t, s). \tag{2.29}$$

Thus, the individual bonus potential is simply the market value of the safety margins in the guaranteed payments. This explains the term individual bonus potential. We note that the individual bonus potential at time 0 equals the negative market reserve, $-V^g(0)$, since $V^*(0) = 0$.

Secondly, we consider the collective bonus potential,

$$V^{cb}(t) = V(t) - V^*(t) = X(t). \tag{2.30}$$

The collective bonus potential can also be calculated residually as the bonus potential minus the individual bonus potential. This explains the term collective bonus potential. We note that the collective bonus potential at time 0 equals zero since $U(0) = V^*(0) = 0$.

We now turn to the general case where Equation (2.27) does not necessarily hold. If $V^* < V^g$, we set the individual bonus potential to zero using the following formula:

$$V^{ib} = (V^* - V^g)^+$$

$$= \max(V^*, V^g) - V^g, \tag{2.31}$$

where $(a)^+$ equals a if $a \geq 0$ and 0 if $a < 0$. This is equivalent to

$$V^{ib}(t) = \left(\int_t^n e^{-\int_t^s r+\mu} c(t, s) \, ds \right)^+. \tag{2.32}$$

In Sections 2.5.1 and 2.6.3, we discuss alternative definitions of the individual bonus potential.

If we do not have the solvency constraint $X(t) \geq 0$, it may also happen that $V < V^*$. In that case we set the collective bonus potential to zero. Taking into account all possible relations between V, V^* and V^g, the collective and the individual bonus potential are formalized by the following general formulas:

$$V^{cb} = \left(V - V^g - (V^* - V^g)^+ \right)^+ ,$$

$$V^{ib} = V - V^g - \left(V - V^g - (V^* - V^g)^+ \right)^+ .$$

From these formulas we easily see that V^{cb} and V^{ib} are positive and sum up V^b.

2.4 The liabilities and principles for valuation

In this section we interpret the liabilities put up in the previous sections. We represent these liabilities as conditional expected values and discuss the principles underpinning this representation.

In Section 2.2 we presented formulas of both retrospective (Equations (2.3), (2.7), (2.12), (2.15)) and prospective (Equations (2.4), (2.9), (2.18), (2.20)) type, and in Section 2.3 we presented primarily prospective formulas (Equations (2.22), (2.24), (2.28), (2.30)). We now discuss the elements in these prospective formulas. This enables us to generalize these formulas to other types of insurance. This also helps us in the search for theoretically substantiated methods for calculation of values in the case where we do not require from the second order basis that $X(n) = 0$.

We remind the reader that a liability is a value set aside by the insurer in order to be able to meet certain obligations in the future. Elementary examples of such payments are the benefits of a pure endowment insurance, a temporary term insurance or a temporary life annuity. These benefits appear as building blocks in a number of insurance types, for example the level premium paid endowment insurance, which is the main example given in this chapter.

Assume that Z is a process measuring whether death has occurred. A process is here defined as a continuum of stochastic variables, indexed by time, such that Z at time t assumes a certain value $Z(t)$. Then

$$Z(t) = \begin{cases} 0, & \text{if death has not occurred at time } t, \\ 1, & \text{if death has occurred at time } t. \end{cases} \tag{2.33}$$

Such a process, assuming the values 0 or 1, is called an indicator process for the condition which has to be fulfilled for the process to assume the value 1. Thus, Z is an indicator process for the insured to be dead.

We introduce another process N counting the number of deaths, i.e. $N(t) =$ number of deaths until time t, and in this situation, of course, $Z = N$.

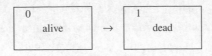

Figure 2.1. Survival model.

The process I is defined by $I(t) = 1 - Z(t) = 1 - N(t)$, and I is thus an indicator process for the insured to be alive. The process Z is illustrated in Figure 2.1. The underlying stochastic variable, determining all the stochastic processes Z, N and I at any point in time is the remaining lifetime at time 0 corresponding to age x, which we denote by T_x.

Now the elements of the prospective formulas can be written as follows:

$$_{n-t}E_{x+t} = E_t \left[e^{-\int_t^n r} I(n) \right],$$

$$a_{x+t\overline{n-t}|} = E_t \left[\int_t^n e^{-\int_t^s r} I(s) \, ds \right], \qquad (2.34)$$

$$A^1_{x+t\overline{n-t}|} = E_t \left[\int_t^n e^{-\int_t^s r} \, dN(s) \right],$$

where E_t denotes an expectation conditional on $Z(t) = 0$. We now interpret the elements in the square brackets in Equations (2.34).

$_{n-t}E_{x+t}$. This is the conditional expectation of the discounted benefit $I(n)$.

$a_{x+t\overline{n-t}|}$. The integral is interpreted as follows:

$$\int_t^n e^{-\int_t^s r} I(s) \, ds = I(t) \int_t^{\min(T_x, n)} e^{-\int_t^s r} \, ds. \qquad (2.35)$$

On the left hand side of Equation (2.35) the value is written as the discounted benefits since $I(s) \, ds$ is exactly the benefit over the time interval $(s, s+ds]$.

$A^1_{x+t\overline{n-t}|}$. The quantity $dN(s)$ is the change in N at time s, such that $dN(s) = 0$ if $s \neq T_x$ and $dN(s) = 1$ if $s = T_x$. If the insured survives until time n, $dN(s) = 0$ for $t \leq s \leq n$. Thus, $dN(s)$ is the benefit at time s from one unit of a term insurance. The integral now becomes a sum of infinitely many zeros plus one discount factor from T_x to t if death occurs before time n, i.e.

$$\int_t^n e^{-\int_t^s r} \, dN(s) = I(t)(1 - I(n)) e^{-\int_t^{T_x} r}.$$

The fundamental elements in Equations (2.34) are discounting ($e^{-\int_t^s r}$), conditional expectation ($E_t^0 [\cdot]$) and the elementary payments ($I(n)$, $I(s) \, ds$ and $dN(s)$). Whereas the elementary payments are just what we want to valuate, the other elements, discounting and the conditional expectation are based on some principal considerations about what a value is and how it is determined.

2.4.1 Absence of arbitrage

In this section we introduce the principle of no arbitrage and discuss how discounting connects to this principle.

We assume that payments to the insurer are deposited in a bank account with continuously accrued interest. Negative payments in the form of benefits are withdrawn from the bank account. We denote by $S^0(t)$ the value at time t of one unit deposited in the account at time 0, and we find that the value at time t of one unit deposited at time s equals $S^0(t)/S^0(s)$. We assume that there exists a short rate of interest r such that

$$\frac{\mathrm{d}}{\mathrm{d}t}S^0(t) = r(t)S^0(t), S^0(0) = 1, \tag{2.36}$$

i.e.

$$S^0(t) = e^{\int_0^t r}.$$

Instead of rushing to insert a corresponding discount factor appropriately, we hesitate and discuss the real content of S^0. What we are really doing here is mathematical finance dealing with arbitrage-free prices and investment strategies in a particular financial market. By introducing S^0 we have started the specification of this market. We have specified an asset in which the insurer can invest. On the other hand, we have not specified any investment alternatives. Hereby, we have specified a financial market containing only one asset S^0 in which the insurer invests all payments.

If S^0 is deterministic, i.e. if r is deterministic, we can easily valuate deterministic payments, and bond prices and prices of options on bonds etc. are easily found. A zero coupon bond is an asset which pays one unit at the terminal time n, and we denote by $P(t, n)$ its value at time t. If S^0 is deterministic, we have that

$$P(t, n) = e^{-\int_t^n r}.$$

Even if this may seem obvious, it is a good idea to underpin the result by a so-called arbitrage argument as follows. Assume that $P(t, n) = \exp\left(-\int_t^n r\right) + \varepsilon$. Now assume that we sell the bond and invest its price, $P(t, n)$, in S^0, i.e. we buy $P(t, n)/S^0(t)$ units of the asset S^0. At time n the value of our investments, after fulfillment of the obligation to pay one unit to the owner of the bond, is given by

$$P(t, n) S^0(n) / S^0(t) - 1 = \varepsilon e^{\int_t^n r}.$$

If $\varepsilon \neq 0$ this value is created without any risk. We do not accept the possibility of creating value without risk and conclude that $\varepsilon = 0$.

Thus, an arbitrage argument deals with prices and investment strategies avoiding the possibility of risk-free capital gains beyond the interest rate. This is the *principle of no arbitrage*.

If S^0 is not deterministic, it is by no means clear what can be said about $P(t, n)$. Certain areas of mathematical finance deal with questions such as: Given a stochastic model for r, what can be said about $P(t, n)$ in general and about its relation to $P(t, u)$, $t < u < n$, in particular? Such considerations typically take the principle of no arbitrage as the theoretical starting point.

Throughout this chapter r is assumed to be deterministic. Chapter 3 deals with stochastic interest rates.

2.4.2 Diversification

In this section we introduce the principle of diversification and discuss how conditional expectation connects to this principle.

In Section 2.4.1 we stated that valuation of deterministic payments is simple if $S^0(t)$ is assumed to be deterministic. If, for example, the payment $I(n)$, which is the benefit at time n, is known at time 0, we simply obtain the value

$$e^{-\int_0^n r} I(n).$$

However, the time of death and other conditions which may determine a payment in general are not known at time 0. Thus, $\exp\left(-\int_0^n r\right) I(n)$ cannot be interpreted as a value but as a stochastic present value. The question is, what can be said about the value of a stochastic present value?

A special situation arises if the insurer issues, or can issue, contracts to a "large" number m of insured with independent and identically distributed payments. Denote by $I^i(t)$ the function indicating that insured number i is alive at time t. Then the law of large numbers comes into force and we conclude that the total present value per insured converges towards the expected present value of a single contract as the number of contracts is increased, i.e.

$$\frac{1}{m}\sum_{i=1}^{m} e^{-\int_0^n r} I^i(n) \to e^{-\int_0^n r} E[I(n)] \text{ as } m \to \infty.$$

This result can be generalized to a situation when the insurance contracts do not have the same terminal time n. If death is assumed to occur with intensity μ, we obtain the following candidate to the value of $I(n)$ at time 0:

$$e^{-\int_0^n r} E[I(n)] = e^{-\int_0^n r+\mu} = {}_nE_x, \tag{2.37}$$

giving the liability at time 0 of a pure endowment insurance issued to an insured who at time 0 is x years old. We say that the value in Equation (2.37) builds on the principles of no arbitrage and diversification.

It is important to note that none of the presented principles, no arbitrage and diversification, solve the valuation problem by itself. We mention that the mathematical financial term for the combination of the principles is the principle of no asymptotic arbitrage, and particular asymptotic arbitrage arguments lead exactly to the value given in Equation (2.37).

The value in Equation (2.37) is a good candidate for the value at time 0 of $I(n)$ paid at time n. For various reasons, one is interested in evaluating future payments at any point in time during the term of the contract. If one wishes to sell the obligation of the payments, one needs to set a price. But even if one does not want to sell, various institutions may be interested in the value of future payments. The owners of the insurance company and other investors are interested in the value of the payments for the purpose of assessing the value of the insurance company itself; regulatory authorities are interested in securing that the insurer can meet these payments with a large probability and put up solvency rules which are to be met; the tax authorities are interested in the surplus of the insurer as a basis for taxation. All these institutions are interested in the value of future obligations.

By repeating the reasoning leading to the value ${}_nE_x$, we can put up the liability at time t. Assuming that the insurer knows that the insured is alive at time t, we obtain the following value:

$$e^{-\int_t^n r} E_t[I(n)] = e^{-\int_t^n r+\mu} = {}_{n-t}E_{x+t},$$

giving the liability at time t of an insurance contract issued to an insured who was x years old at time 0 and who is alive at time t.

2.4.3 The market-based liability revisited

In this section we show how the principles of no arbitrage and diversification underpin the market-based composition of the liability.

By a simple rewriting of the prospective market-based liabilities, we unveil the principles on which these are based. From Equations (2.22), (2.24), (2.28) and (2.30) we obtain with help from Equation (2.34), the following:

$$V^{g}(t) = E_t \left[\int_t^n e^{-\int_t^s r} \left(b^{ad} \, dN(s) - I(s) \, \pi \, ds \right) \right.$$

$$\left. + b^{a}(t) \, e^{-\int_t^n r} I(n) \right], \tag{2.38}$$

$$V^{b}(t) = E_t \left[\left(b^{a}(n) - b^{a}(t) \right) e^{-\int_t^n r} I(n) \right], \tag{2.39}$$

$$V^{*}(t) - V^{g}(t) = E_t \left[\int_t^n e^{-\int_t^s r} I(s) \, c(t,s) \, ds \right], \tag{2.40}$$

$$V(t) - V^{*}(t) = E_t \left[\int_t^n e^{-\int_t^s r} \left(\delta(s) - c(s) \right) I(s) \, ds \right]. \tag{2.41}$$

All these quantities are seen to build on the *principles of no arbitrage and diversification*. The principles leave tracks in terms of discount factors and conditional expectations, respectively. We recall the interpretation of the elements. Compared with the elementary payments in Equation (2.34) we see that the death sum b^{ad}, the pension sum $b^{a}(t)$ and the premium π appear in $V^{g}(t)$. The bonus payment $b^{a}(n) - b^{a}(t)$ appears in $V^{b}(t)$. In $V^{*}(t) - V^{g}(t)$ the payment process can be interpreted as continuous payments of a life annuity with time dependent annuity rates where the safety margin $c(t,s)$ makes up the annuity rate at time $s \geq t$. The rate $(\delta(s) - c(s))$ plays a corresponding role in the quantity $V(t) - V^{*}(t)$.

Now consider the prospective versions of the technical reserve, as follows:

$$V^{*}(t) = E_t^{\delta} \left[\int_t^n e^{-\int_t^s r^{\delta}} \left(b^{ad} \, dN(s) - I(s) \, \pi \, ds \right) + e^{-\int_t^n r^{\delta}} b^{a}(n) I(n) \right],$$

$$V^{*}(t) = E_t^{*} \left[\int_t^n e^{-\int_t^s r^{*}} \left(b^{ad} \, dN(s) - I(s) \, \pi \, ds \right) + e^{-\int_t^n r^{*}} b^{a}(t) I(n) \right],$$

where the superscipts δ and $*$ on E denote that N under these expectations has the intensities μ^{δ}, the second order mortality rate, and μ^{*}, the first order mortality rate, respectively. We see that these quantities do not build on the principles of no arbitrage and diversification. Indeed, we can trace both discount factors and conditional expectations, but since the discount factor is not based on the bank account interest rate and since the intensity of N in the conditional expectation is not μ, these quantities can only be said to build on suitable imitations of the principles.

2.5 The liability and the payments

In this section we introduce the idea of a payment process and discuss how the market-based composition is built from payment processes of guaranteed payments and payments which are not guaranteed.

The *payments* are the elements of the total payments in an insurance contract. In our example, the payments are the elements of Equations (2.38) and (2.39),

$$b^{\mathrm{ad}}\,\mathrm{d}N\,(s)\,,\,b^{\mathrm{a}}\,(t)\,I\,(n)\,,\,-\pi I\,(s)\,\mathrm{d}s \text{ and } (b^{\mathrm{a}}\,(n)-b^{\mathrm{a}}\,(t))\,I\,(n)\,.$$

The first task in connection with a precise description of the payments is to identify the stochastic phenomena on which the claims depend. For certain elementary insurances the time of death plays an important role. It turns out to be beneficial to introduce the stochastic process Z based on the stochastic time of death, given by Equation (2.33). The time of death is modeled by a probability distribution of the counting process N, for example by the introduction of a deterministic intensity μ.

To formalize claims we introduce a *payment process* B such that $B(t)$ represents the accumulated payments from the insurer to the insured over $[0, t]$. This means that payments from the insured to the insurer appear in B as negative payments. We specify the payments in continuous time, although in practice the payments are discrete, for example monthly premiums. Fixing the time horizon n for the insurance contract, we can describe the claims in our example by collecting them in the payment process in the following form:

$$B(t) = \int_0^t \mathrm{d}B(s)\,, \qquad 0 \leq t \leq n, \tag{2.42}$$

where

$$\mathrm{d}B(t) = b^{\mathrm{ad}}\,\mathrm{d}N(t) + b^{\mathrm{a}}(t)\,I(t)\,\mathrm{d}\epsilon(t, n) - \pi I(t)\,\mathrm{d}t. \tag{2.43}$$

Here, $\epsilon(t, n)$ is an indicator process for $t \geq n$. In Equation (2.42), the integration sums up the infinitesimal changes $\mathrm{d}B$, and Equation (2.43) shows the elements of these changes. We also speak of B as a *payment stream*, since it describes payments floating between two parties.

The process Z serves to describe precisely a number of elementary claims and payment processes in life and pension insurance, but there are many

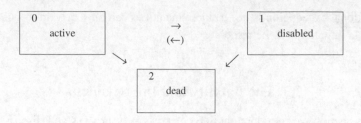

Figure 2.2. Disability model with recovery.

situations which are not described by such a process. One example is premium waiver. Premium waiver and other types of disability assurances can be described by extending the state space of Z with a third state, "disabled." One can, in general, let Z be a process moving around in a finite number of states J. The situation with a disability state is illustrated in Figure 2.2.

Corresponding to a general J-state process Z, one can introduce a J-dimensional counting process where the jth entry N^j counts the number of jumps into state j. The disability model is a three-state model, i.e. $J = 3$. Models with more states are relevant for other types of insurances, for example contracts on two lives where each member of a couple is covered against the death of the other.

We mention this to give an idea of how the construction of payment processes generalizes to various forms of disability payment processes etc. All generalizations of liability formulas are left to the reader. An important reference is Norberg (2000).

With the collection of claims in a payment process, we search for the present value and the market value of a payment process. The principle of no arbitrage determines the present value as a sum of present values of the single elements of the payment process, and we get the present value at time t of the payment process B over $(t, n]$ as follows:

$$\int_t^n e^{-\int_t^s r} \, dB(s).$$

Combining the principles of no arbitrage and diversification, we obtain the market value at time t of a payment process as follows:

$$E_t\left[\int_t^n e^{-\int_t^s r} \, dB(s)\right]. \tag{2.44}$$

2.5.1 The market-based liability revisited

In this section we identify the payment processes in the market-based composition of the liabilities.

In Equations (2.38)–(2.41) we wrote the entries in the market-based composition of the liability in terms of claims. We now collect these claims in payment processes such that all entries can be written as market values of payment processes. It is suitable to characterize the entries in the balance sheet by different payment processes. This makes it easy to generalize the entries to other insurances by simply specifying the generalized payment processes. We also have in mind the situation where the condition $X(n) = 0$ cannot be fulfilled.

We introduce now the *guaranteed payment process* at time t, which we denote by $B(t, \cdot)$. Then for $s \geq t$,

$$dB(t, s) = -\pi I(s)\, ds + b^{\mathrm{ad}}\, dN(s) + b^{\mathrm{a}}(t) I(s)\, d\epsilon(s, n),$$

$$V^{\mathrm{g}}(t) = E_t \left[\int_t^n e^{-\int_t^s r}\, dB(t, s) \right].$$

Correspondingly, we denote by $B^{\mathrm{b}}(t, \cdot)$ the *payment process not guaranteed* at time t, and, for $s \geq t$,

$$dB^{\mathrm{b}}(t, s) = (b^{\mathrm{a}}(s) - b^{\mathrm{a}}(t)) I(s)\, d\epsilon(s, n),$$

$$V^{\mathrm{b}}(t) = E_t \left[\int_t^n e^{-\int_t^s r}\, dB^{\mathrm{b}}(t, s) \right].$$

The difference $V^*(t) - V^{\mathrm{g}}(t)$ stems from the accumulated safety margins in the guaranteed payments, denoted by $C(t, \cdot)$, such that for $s \geq t$ we have

$$dC(t, s) = I(s) c(t, s)\, ds,$$

$$V^*(t) - V^{\mathrm{g}}(t) = E_t \left[\int_t^n e^{-\int_t^s r}\, dC(t, s) \right]. \tag{2.45}$$

We remind ourselves that this constitutes the individual bonus potential if $U(t) \geq V^*(t) \geq V(t)$.

We end this section by repeating, for the case $U(t) \geq V^*(t)$, the suggested definition of the individual bonus potential in Equation (2.32), since Equation

(2.45) inspires us naturally to suggest two alternative definitions. Of course, we have the following inequalities:

$$V^{\mathrm{ib}}(t) = \left(E_t \left[\int_t^n e^{-\int_t^s r} \, dC(t,s) \right] \right)^+ \tag{2.46}$$

$$\leq E_t \left[\left(\int_t^n e^{-\int_t^s r} \, dC(t,s) \right)^+ \right] \tag{2.47}$$

$$\leq E_t \left[\int_t^n e^{-\int_t^s r} \, dC^+(t,s) \right]. \tag{2.48}$$

Here, the quantities in Equations (2.47) and (2.48) comprise alternatives to the definition given in Equation (2.46). The two alternatives coincide with the first definition if $c(t,s)$ (see Equation (2.29)) is either positive or negative for all s. The definition of the individual bonus potential could be based on a more precise description of how the safety margins are used for bonus. In Section 2.6.3 we suggest a third alternative to Equation (2.46) which is not based on the future safety margins.

The quantities in Equations (2.47) and (2.48) are closely connected to the discussion about what an interest rate guarantee is worth. Whereas Equation (2.47) is connected to a terminal bonus, Equation (2.48) is connected to a certain interpretation of the contribution principle. Values similar to Equation (2.48) are the basis for calculation of prices on interest rate guarantee options.

2.6 The surrender option

2.6.1 Intensity-based surrender option valuation

In this section, we approach the value of the surrender option by the three-state Markov model illustrated in Figure 2.3. Thus, we introduce a state of

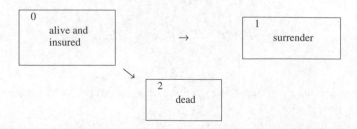

Figure 2.3. Survival model with surrender option.

surrender, which at time t is reached by a surrender intensity ν and leads to a payment of a surrender value $G(t)$. Using a version of Thiele's differential equation for a three-state model, we can write the differential equation with terminal condition for the total reserve V^{sur} including the surrender option as follows:

$$
\frac{\mathrm{d}}{\mathrm{d}t} V^{\mathrm{sur}}(t) = r(t) V^{\mathrm{sur}}(t) + \pi - \mu(t) \left(b^{\mathrm{ad}} - V^{\mathrm{sur}}(t) \right) \tag{2.49}
$$

$$
- \nu(t) \left(G(t) - V^{\mathrm{sur}}(t) \right),
$$

$$
V^{\mathrm{sur}}(n) = b^{\mathrm{a}}(n).
$$

We require an explicit expression for the value of the surrender option, i.e. $V^{\mathrm{sur}} - V$. It can be verified that this additional reserve can be written in the following form:

$$
V^{\mathrm{sur}}(t) - V(t) = \int_t^n \mathrm{e}^{-\int_t^s r + \mu + \nu} \nu(s) \left(G(s) - V(s) \right) \mathrm{d}s. \tag{2.50}
$$

The calculation of $V^{\mathrm{sur}}(t) - V(t)$ involves the future second order basis through future values of G and V. Therefore, one is interested in a simplified estimate of the value of the surrender option. We consider the case where the surrender value equals the technical reserve, i.e. $G(t) = V^*(t)$, such that

$$
V^{\mathrm{sur}}(t) - V(t) = \int_t^n \mathrm{e}^{-\int_t^s r + \mu + \nu} \nu(s) \left(V^*(s) - V(s) \right) \mathrm{d}s. \tag{2.51}
$$

Firstly, we consider the case where $V(t) < V^*(t)$, i.e. $X(t) < 0$. We assume that the future second order basis is settled such that $\delta(s) \leq c(s)$ for $s > t$. One now obtains the following:

$$
V^{\mathrm{sur}}(t) - V(t) = \int_t^n \mathrm{e}^{-\int_t^s r + \mu + \nu} \nu(s) \, \mathrm{e}^{\int_t^s r + \mu} \left(V^*(t) - V(t) \right) \mathrm{d}s
$$

$$
+ \int_t^n \mathrm{e}^{-\int_t^s r + \mu + \nu} \nu(s) \int_t^s \mathrm{e}^{\int_\tau^s r + \mu} \left(\delta(\tau) - c(\tau) \right) \mathrm{d}\tau \, \mathrm{d}s
$$

$$
\leq \left(V^*(t) - V(t) \right) p(t), \tag{2.52}
$$

where

$$
p(t) = \int_t^n \mathrm{e}^{-\int_t^s \nu} \nu(s) \, \mathrm{d}s.
$$

Secondly, we consider the case where $V(t) \geq V^*(t)$, i.e. $X(t) \geq 0$. We assume that the future second order basis is settled such that $X(s) \geq 0$ for

$s > t$. We then obtain the following inequality:

$$V^{\mathrm{sur}}(t) - V(t) = \int_t^n e^{-\int_t^s r + \mu + \nu} \nu(s) \left(V^*(s) - V(s)\right) \mathrm{d}s$$

$$\leq 0. \tag{2.53}$$

We conclude that, given the constraints on the future second order basis leading to Equations (2.52) and (2.53), we have the following inequality:

$$V^{\mathrm{sur}}(t) - V(t) \leq \max\left(p(t)\left(G(t) - V(t)\right), 0\right).$$

2.6.2 Intervention-based surrender option valuation

In this section, we approach the value of the surrender option by considering the idea that the insured surrenders "if it is worth it." Hereby we take into consideration the fundamental difference between transitions between the states in the model illustrated in Figure 2.3. One can certainly criticize the approach taken in this section. One problematic circumstance is that there seems to be only weak historical evidence from situations where surrender was optimal. Another circumstance is that, given a situation where surrender is optimal, the insurer or the regulatory authorities will probably put up a protection against systematic surrender. This can happen by either not allowing surrender or by making surrender less attractive by introducing costs. Will we in practice allow for a situation where the insured gains on surrender? In this section the starting point is that the insured surrenders immediately if it is advantageous to do so.

Optimal strategies of the insured provide a starting point for a detailed study of the problem and a derivation of the corresponding deterministic differential systems given by Steffensen (2002), which should be consulted for a generalization of the payment processes, the ideas and the results in this section.

Consider a general payment process B. By introducing the surrender option, an arbitrage argument gives the market value including the surrender option as follows:

$$V^{\mathrm{sur}}(t) = \max_{t \leq \tau \leq n} E_t\left[\int_t^\tau e^{-\int_t^s r}\, \mathrm{d}B(s) + e^{-\int_t^\tau r} I(\tau) G(\tau)\right], \tag{2.54}$$

where we put $G(n) = 0$. Here, we can think of B as the payment process for the example given by Equation (2.43), and τ is the time of surrender or the terminal time, depending on what occurs first. Obviously the insured must decide on surrender at time t based on the information available. One speaks of τ as a stopping time. We recall that $I(t)$ indicates whether the insured is alive at time t and that $G(t)$ is the surrender value at time t.

In order to say something general about the quantity $V^{\text{sur}}(t)$, we consider a process $Y^{\text{sur}}(t, u)$ defined by

$$Y^{\text{sur}}(t, u) = \int_t^u e^{-\int_t^s r}\, dB(s) + e^{-\int_t^u r} I(u) G(u).$$

Thus, $Y^{\text{sur}}(t, u)$ is the present value of the payments to the insured including the surrender value, given that the contract is surrendered at time u.

In the following, we use the notions of a super-martingale and a sub-martingale, and we explain briefly these notions in the Markovian case. A super-martingale describes the process that over time is expected to decrease in value compared to where it is. Formally, the condition for Y to be a super-martingale is that, for $u \geq t$,

$$E_{t,y}[Y(u)] \leq y,$$

where the subscript t, y denotes that an expectation is conditional on $\{Y(t) = y\}$. Correspondingly, a sub-martingale describes a process expected to increase in value. Formally, Y is a sub-martingale if, for $u \geq t$,

$$E_{t,y}[Y(u)] \geq y.$$

Finally, a martingale is defined as a process which is both a sub-martingale and a super-martingale, i.e. a process which is expected to maintain its value over time. Formally, Y is a martingale if, for $u \geq t$,

$$E_{t,y}[Y(u)] = y.$$

Proposition 2.1 *(1) If*

$$V(t) \geq G(t)$$

for all t, it is optimal never to surrender and

$$V^{\text{sur}}(t) = V(t).$$

Intuition: if the total liability exceeds the surrender value, the company gains by surrender the value $V - G$. Thus, it cannot be beneficial to surrender and the company should set aside V, corresponding to the situation without surrender option. If $G \leq V^*$, we see that the classical solvency rule $U \geq V^*$ exactly prevents the policy holder from making gains on surrender.

(2) If $Y^{sur}(t, u)$ is a sub-martingale, it is never optimal to surrender, and

$$V^{sur}(t) = V(t).$$

Intuition: that $Y^{sur}(t, u)$ is a submartingale means that the present value of payments to the policy holder is expected to increase as a function of the time to surrender. Thus, the policy holder should at any point in time postpone the surrender in order to increase the expected present value of the contract.

(3) If $Y^{sur}(t, u)$ is a super-martingale, it is optimal to surrender immediately and

$$V^{sur}(t) = G(t).$$

Intuition: that $Y^{sur}(t, u)$ is a super-martingale means that the present value of payments to the policy holder is expected to decrease as a function of the time to surrender. Thus, the policy holder should surrender immediately in order to obtain the highest possible expected present value of the contract.

Given a value of the total payment process, for example given by Equation (2.54), the question is how to decompose this total reserve into a reserve for the guaranteed payments, $V^{g,sur}$, and a reserve for the payments which are not guaranteed, $V^{b,sur}$. One idea is to define $V^{g,sur}$ as follows:

$$V^{g,sur}(t) = \max_{t \le \tau \le n} E_t \left[\int_t^\tau e^{-\int_t^s r} \, dB(t, s) + e^{-\int_t^\tau r} I(\tau) G(t, \tau) \right], \quad (2.55)$$

and then determine $V^{b,sur}$ residually as $V^{sur} - V^{g,sur}$. In Equation (2.55), $G(t, \tau)$ is the surrender value at time τ given that no dividends are distributed over $(t, \tau]$. We introduce the process $Y^{g,sur}(t, u)$ as follows:

$$Y^{g,sur}(t, u) = \int_t^u e^{-\int_t^s r} \, dB(t, s) + e^{-\int_t^u r} I(u) G(t, u).$$

Thus, $Y^{g,sur}(t, u)$ is the present value of the guaranteed payments to the insured including the surrender value given that the contract is surrendered at time u.

Now we can state Proposition 2.1 with $V^{sur}(t)$, $V(t)$ and $Y^{sur}(t, u)$ replaced by $V^{g,sur}(t)$, $V^g(t)$, and $Y^{g,sur}(t, u)$. In order to apply this result, we need to identify whether $Y^{g,sur}(t, u)$ is a super-martingale or a sub-martingale, respectively. We use a result stating that if a process can be written as the sum of a decreasing or increasing process and a martingale, then the process itself is a super-martingale or a sub-martingale, respectively. This result is applicable once we have established the following lemma.

Lemma 2.2 *Assume that* $G(t, u) = V^*(t, u)$. *Then it is possible to write* $Y^{g, sur}(t, u)$ *as follows:*

$$Y^{g, sur}(t, u) = V^*(t) - \int_t^u e^{-\int_t^s r} I(s) c(t, s) \, ds + M^{sur}(t, u),$$

where $M^{sur}(t, s)$ *is a martingale.*

We can now conclude the following for the case $G(t, u) = V^*(t, u)$ as follows.

Corollary 2.3 *(1) If* $c(t, s) \geq 0$, *we have that*

$$V^{g, sur}(t) = V^*(t).$$

Intuition: the policy holder loses the future positive safety margins by keeping the contract. This can be avoided by immediate surrender such that the value of the guaranteed payments simply becomes the surrender value.

(2) If $c(t, s) \leq 0$, *we have that*

$$V^{g, sur}(t) = V^g(t).$$

Intuition: the policy holder has the negative safety margins covered by keeping the insurance contract since we disregard all bonus payments. The policy holder gains maximally in expectation by keeping the policy until termination, such that the value of the guaranteed payments simply becomes the corresponding value without the surrender option.

In Proposition 2.1 and Corollary 2.3 we put up specific conditions under which it is relatively easy to calculate the relevant maximum. Nevertheless, it is possible to derive a deterministic differential system, comparable with Thiele's differential equation, for calculation of the general market values V^{sur} and $V^{g, sur}$. Even though this goes beyond the scope of this chapter, we give, out of interest, the result for $V^{\mathrm{g,sur}}$. We have that $V^{\mathrm{g,sur}}(t) = V^{\mathrm{g,sur}}(t, t)$, where

$$\frac{\partial}{\partial u} V^{\mathrm{g,sur}}(t, u) \leq \pi + r(u) V^{\mathrm{g,sur}}(t, u) - \mu(u) \left(b^{\mathrm{ad}} - V^{\mathrm{g,sur}}(t, u) \right),$$

$$V^{\mathrm{g,sur}}(t, t) \geq G(t),$$

$$0 = \left(-\frac{\partial}{\partial u} V^{\mathrm{g,sur}}(t, u) + \pi + r(u) V^{\mathrm{g,sur}}(t, u) \right.$$

$$\left. - \mu(u) \left(b^{\mathrm{ad}} - V^{\mathrm{g,sur}}(t, u) \right) \right) \times \left(G(t, u) - V^{\mathrm{g,sur}}(t, u) \right),$$

$$V^{\mathrm{g,sur}}(t, n) = b^{\mathrm{a}}(t).$$

The reader should recognize several elements in this system. The first inequality, together with the terminal condition, only differs from Thiele's differential equation by containing an inequality instead of an equality. The second inequality simply states that the sum at risk connected to the transition to the state surrender is always negative. The equality in the third line is the formalization of the following statement: at any point in the state space, one of the two inequalities is an equality.

2.6.3 The market-based liability revisited

Corollary 2.3 is closely connected to the market-based composition of the liabilities. We repeat the definition of the individual bonus potential given in Equation (2.31) for the case $V \geq V^*$, since the studies in Section 2.6.2 lead us, quite naturally, to an alternative definition. We have the following inequality:

$$V^{\mathrm{ib}} = \max\left(V^*, V^{\mathrm{g}}\right) - V^{\mathrm{g}}$$

$$\leq V^{\mathrm{g,sur}} - V^{\mathrm{g}}, \tag{2.56}$$

with $G(t, u) = V^*(t, u)$. Corollary 2.3 shows us that the alternative definition in Equation (2.56) coincides with the definition in Equation (2.31) if $c(s, t)$ is either positive or negative for all s. In Equations (2.47) and (2.48) we gave alternatives to the definition in Equation (2.31) in connection with a discussion of how the safety margins are redistributed as dividends. In Equation (2.56) we suggest an alternative which does not contain this subjectivity of the dividend distribution.

Actually, it is the inequality in Equation (2.56) which motivates us to suggest the alternative definition, $V^{\text{g,sur}} - V^{\text{g}}$, for the individual bonus potential. The inequality in Equation (2.56) follows from

$$\max\left(V^*, V^{\text{g}}\right) \leq V^{\text{g,sur}},$$

which is true since the left hand side corresponds to Equation (2.55), where the maximum is taken over only two possible points in time, t and n. On the right hand side, the maximum is taken over all points in time between t and n.

2.7 The free policy option

2.7.1 A simple free policy option value

The starting point for the value of the free policy option is a model with three states as illustrated in Figure 2.4. However, the idea is not to introduce a free policy intensity in the same way as we introduced a surrender intensity in Section 2.6.1. We recall that

$$V^*\left(t\right) - V^{\text{g}}\left(t\right) = \int_t^n \mathrm{e}^{-\int_t^s r + \mu} c\left(t, s\right) \mathrm{d}s.$$

A part of the safety margin in the guaranteed payments can be said to stem from future premiums. One can argue that if we take into account the future premiums we should also, given the free policy option, put up a reserve for the bonus based on these premiums.

The liability concerning bonus stemming from the future premiums is given by the bonus potential on a contract with premium π issued at time t with a deposit equal to zero. We now calculate this bonus potential and start

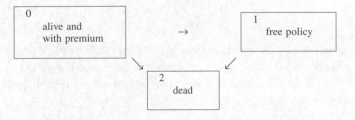

Figure 2.4. Survival model with free policy option.

out by finding the benefits on the issued contract. We introduce the following notation:

$$V^{*+}(t) = b^{ad} A^{1*}_{x+t\overline{n-t|}} + b^a(t)\,_{n-t}E^*_{x+t},\qquad(2.57)$$

$$V^{g+}(t) = b^{ad} A^{1}_{x+t\overline{n-t|}} + b^a(t)\,_{n-t}E_{x+t},\qquad(2.58)$$

i.e. the superscript $+$ denotes here that only the benefits are included. Then we can, from Equations (2.9) and (2.22), write the life annuities $a^*_{x+t\overline{n-t|}}$ and $a_{x+t\overline{n-t|}}$ in the following way:

$$a^*_{x+t\overline{n-t|}} = \frac{V^{*+}(t) - V^*(t)}{\pi},\qquad(2.59)$$

$$a_{x+t\overline{n-t|}} = \frac{V^{g+}(t) - V^g(t)}{\pi}.\qquad(2.60)$$

The number of units of guaranteed benefits, $\beta(t)$, that can be bought from the future premiums at time t are defined simply by the equivalence principle:

$$\beta(t)\left(b^{ad} A^{1*}_{x+t\overline{n-t|}} + b^a(t)\,_{n-t}E^*_{x+t}\right) = \pi a^*_{x+t\overline{n-t|}},$$

which, by Equations (2.57) and (2.59), yields

$$\beta(t) = \frac{V^{*+}(t) - V^*(t)}{V^{*+}(t)}.\qquad(2.61)$$

In Section 2.3.2 we noted that the bonus potential on an insurance contract at the time of issuance simply equals the negative market value of the guaranteed payments stipulated in the contract. We see that the bonus potential on the new insurance is given by

$$-\beta(t)\left(b^{ad} A^{1}_{x+t\overline{n-t|}} + b^a(t)\,_{n-t}E_{x+t}\right) + \pi a_{x+t\overline{n-t|}},$$

which by Equations (2.58), (2.60) and (2.61) equals

$$\frac{V^*(t) V^{g+}(t)}{V^{*+}(t)} - V^g(t).$$

This quantity is now our candidate for the value of the free policy option. This value must be added to the market value of the guaranteed original payments in order to obtain the value of the guaranteed payments including the free policy option. We reach the following:

$$\left(\frac{V^*(t) V^{g+}(t)}{V^{*+}(t)} - V^g(t)\right) + V^g(t) = \frac{V^*(t) V^{g+}(t)}{V^{*+}(t)} \equiv V^f(t).$$

Note that V^f is also the market value of the guaranteed free policy benefits since the guaranteed benefits upon conversion into a free policy are exactly reduced by the factor $V^*(t)/V^{*+}(t)$.

It turns out to be informative to decompose the individual bonus potential into the bonus potential on premiums V^{bp} and the bonus potential on the free policy V^{bf}. Firstly, we consider the situation

$$V \geq V^* \geq V^f \geq V^g.$$

Then $V^{ib} = V^* - V^g$ decomposes into

$$V^{ib} = V^{bf} + V^{bp}$$
$$= \left(V^* - V^f\right) + \left(V^f - V^g\right).$$

The market value of guaranteed payments on a contract issued at time t, $V^{bp}(t)$, can also be expressed as the market value of the safety margins in these payments. A situation can arise where these safety margins are negative. Since negative safety margins cannot be distributed as bonus, the bonus potential on premiums is in this case set to zero. For the case $V \geq V^*$ we obtain an expression for V^{bp} which is similar to Equation (2.31):

$$V^{bp} = \max\left(V^f, V^g\right) - V^g. \qquad (2.62)$$

If, at one time, we want to take into consideration all possible relations between V, V^*, V^f and V^g, the bonus potential on premiums and the bonus potential on the free policy can be formalized as follows:

$$V^{bf} = \left(V - V^g - \left(V^f - V^g\right)^+\right)^+ - \left(V - V^g - \left(V^* - V^g\right)^+\right)^+,$$

$$V^{bp} = V - V^g - \left(V - V^g - \left(V^f - V^g\right)^+\right)^+.$$

2.7.2 Intervention-based free policy option valuation

In this section the free policy option is dealt with in the same way as the surrender option was dealt with in Section 2.6.2. Even though the intuitive interpretations on this background could be left to the reader, we keep them here and follow Section 2.6.2 closely.

We now take the logical starting point that the insured converts into free policy "if it is worth it." Hereby we take into consideration the fundamental difference between transitions between the states in the model illustrated in Figure 2.4. One can certainly criticize the approach taken in this section. One problem is that we have no historical evidence from a situation where conversion into a free policy was optimal. Another is that, given a situation where conversion into free policy is optimal, the insurer or the regulatory authorities will probably put up a protection against systematic conversion. This can happen by making conversion less attractive by introducing costs. In opposition to the surrender option, however, one cannot stop conversions into free policy. This would involve difficult considerations about credit risk. Thus, will one in practice allow for a situation where the insured gains on conversion? In this section the starting point is that the insured converts immediately if it is advantageous to do so.

Optimal strategies of the insured provide a starting point for a detailed study of the problem and a derivation of the corresponding deterministic differential systems given by Steffensen (2002), which should be consulted for a generalization of the payment processes, the ideas and the results in this section.

Consider a general payment process B. By introducing the free policy option, an arbitrage argument gives the market value including the free policy option as follows:

$$V^{\text{free}}(t) = \max_{t \leq \tau \leq n} E_t \left[\int_t^{\tau} e^{-\int_t^s r} \, dB(s) + e^{-\int_t^{\tau} r} I(\tau) \left(V^{\text{f}}(\tau) + X^{\text{f}}(\tau) \right) \right], \quad (2.63)$$

where V^{free} corresponds to V^{sur} with the surrender value $G(t)$ replaced by the reserve $V^{\text{f}}(\tau) + X^{\text{f}}(\tau)$. We think of B as the payment process for the example given by Equation (2.43), and τ is the time of conversion or the terminal time depending on what occurs first. Obviously the insured must decide on conversion at time t based on the information existing at that time. Thereby, τ is a stopping time. The quantity $X^{\text{f}}(\tau)$ is the undistributed reserve upon conversion, i.e. if the full undistributed reserve is carried over upon conversion, $X^{\text{f}} = X$.

In order to say something general about the quantity $V^{\text{free}}(t)$, we consider a process $Y^{\text{free}}(t, u)$ as a function of u, which we define by

$$Y^{\text{free}}(t, u) = \int_t^u e^{-\int_t^s r} \, dB(s) + e^{-\int_t^u r} I(u) \left(V^{\text{f}}(u) + X^{\text{f}}(u) \right),$$

where

$$V^{\text{f}}(t) = \frac{V^*(t) \, V^{\text{g}+}(t)}{V^{*+}(t)}.$$

Thus, $Y^{\text{free}}(t, u)$ is the present value of the payments to the insured, including the liability to cover free policy benefits and benefits which are not guaranteed from the time of conversion, given that conversion happens at time u.

Proposition 2.4 *(1) If*

$$V(t) \geq V^{\mathrm{f}}(t) + X^{\mathrm{f}}(t)$$

for all t, it is optimal never to convert and

$$V^{\mathrm{free}}(t) = V(t).$$

Intuition: if the total liability exceeds the market value of payments at conversion, the company gains by conversion the value $V - \left(V^{\mathrm{f}}(t) + X^{\mathrm{f}}(t)\right)$. Thus, it cannot be beneficial to convert and the company should set aside V, corresponding to the situation without free policy option. If $V^{\mathrm{f}} + X^{\mathrm{f}} \leq V^*$, we see that the classical solvency rule $U \geq V^*$ exactly prevents the policy holder from making gains on conversion.

(2) If $Y^{\mathrm{free}}(t, u)$ is a sub-martingale, it is never optimal to convert and

$$V^{\mathrm{free}}(t) = V(t).$$

Intuition: that $Y^{\mathrm{free}}(t, u)$ is a sub-martingale means that the present value of payments to the policy holder is expected to increase as a function of the time to conversion. Thus, the policy holder should at any point in time postpone the conversion in order to increase the expected present value of the contract.

(3) If $Y^{\mathrm{free}}(t, u)$ is a super-martingale, it is optimal to convert immediately and

$$V^{\mathrm{free}}(t) = V^{\mathrm{f}}(t) + X^{\mathrm{f}}(t).$$

Intuition: that $Y^{\mathrm{free}}(t, u)$ is a super-martingale means that the present value of payments to the policy holder is expected to decrease as a function of the time to conversion. Thus, the policy holder should convert immediately in order to obtain the highest possible expected present value of the contract.

Given a value of the total payment process, for example given by Equation (2.63), the question is how to decompose this total reserve into a reserve for the guaranteed payments, $V^{\mathrm{g,free}}$, and a reserve for the payments which are not guaranteed, $V^{\mathrm{b,free}}$. We suggest the definition

$$V^{\mathrm{g,free}}(t) = \max_{t \leq \tau \leq n} E_t\left[\int_t^\tau \mathrm{e}^{-\int_t^s r}\, \mathrm{d}B(t, s) + \mathrm{e}^{-\int_t^\tau r} I(\tau) V^{\mathrm{f}}(t, \tau)\right], \qquad (2.64)$$

where

$$V^{\mathrm{f}}(t, \tau) = \frac{V^{*}(t, \tau) \, V^{\mathrm{g}+}(t, \tau)}{V^{*+}(t, \tau)}.$$

Then one could choose to define $V^{\mathrm{b,free}}$ residually by $V^{\mathrm{b,free}} = V^{\mathrm{free}} - V^{\mathrm{g,free}}$. We introduce the process $Y^{\mathrm{g,free}}(t, u)$ given by

$$Y^{\mathrm{g,free}}(t, u) = \int_{t}^{u} \mathrm{e}^{-\int_{t}^{s} r} \, \mathrm{d}B(t, s) + \mathrm{e}^{-\int_{t}^{u} r} I(u) \, V^{\mathrm{f}}(t, u).$$

Thus, $Y^{\mathrm{g,free}}(t, u)$ is the present value of the guaranteed payments to the insured, including the liability for future free policy benefits, given that the contract is converted at time u.

Now we can state Proposition 2.4 with $V^{\mathrm{free}}(t)$, $V^{\mathrm{f}}(t) + X^{\mathrm{f}}(t)$ and $Y^{\mathrm{free}}(t, u)$ replaced by $V^{\mathrm{g,free}}(t)$, $V^{\mathrm{g}}(t)$ and $Y^{\mathrm{g,free}}(t, u)$. In order to apply this result, we need to identify when $Y^{\mathrm{g,free}}(t, u)$ is a super-martingale or a sub-martingale, respectively. We use a result stating that if a process can be written as the sum of a decreasing or increasing process and a martingale, then the process itself is a super-martingale or a sub-martingale, respectively. This result is applicable once we have established the following lemma.

Lemma 2.5 *It is possible to write $Y^{\mathrm{free}}(t, u)$ as follows:*

$$Y^{\mathrm{free}}(t, u) = V^{\mathrm{f}}(t) - \int_{t}^{u} \mathrm{e}^{-\int_{t}^{s} r} I(s) c^{\mathrm{free}}(t, s) \, \mathrm{d}s + M^{\mathrm{free}}(t, u),$$

where $M^{\mathrm{free}}(t, u)$ is a martingale and $c^{\mathrm{free}}(t, u)$ is a rather involved function of $V^{*}(t)$, $V^{*+}(t)$, $V^{\mathrm{g}}(t)$, $V^{\mathrm{g}+}(t)$ and the first order and real bases. See Steffensen (2002) for details of the function $c^{\mathrm{free}}(t, u)$.

We can now conclude the following.

Corollary 2.6 *(1) If $c^{\mathrm{free}}(t, u) \geq 0$, we have that*

$$V^{\mathrm{g,free}}(t) = V^{\mathrm{f}}(t).$$

Intuition: the policy holder loses the future positive safety margins on the future premiums by continuing to pay the premiums on the contract since we disregard all future bonus payments. This can be avoided by immediate conversion such that the value of the guaranteed payments simply becomes the market value of the free policy benefits.

(2) If $c^{\text{free}}(t, u) \leq 0$, *we have that*

$$V^{\text{g,free}}(t) = V^{\text{g}}(t).$$

Intuition: the policy holder has the negative safety margins on future premiums covered by continuing to pay the premiums on the insurance contract since we disregard all bonus payments. The policy holder gains maximally in expectation by continuing to pay the premium on the policy until termination, such that the value of the guaranteed payments simply becomes the corresponding value without the free policy option.

In Proposition 2.4 and Corollary 2.6 we put up specific conditions under which it is relatively easy to calculate the relevant maximum. Nevertheless, it is possible to derive a deterministic differential system, comparable with Thiele's differential equation, for calculation of the general market values V^{free} and $V^{\text{g,free}}$. Even though this goes beyond the scope of this chapter, we give, out of interest, the result for $V^{\text{g,free}}$. We have that $V^{\text{g,free}}(t) = V^{\text{g,free}}(t, t)$, where

$$\frac{\partial}{\partial u} V^{\text{g,free}}(t, u) \leq \pi + r(u) V^{\text{g,free}}(t, u) - \mu(u) \left(b^{\text{ad}} - V^{\text{g,free}}(t, u)\right),$$

$$V^{\text{g,free}}(t, t) \geq V^{\text{f}}(t),$$

$$0 = \left(-\frac{\partial}{\partial u} V^{\text{g,free}}(t, u) + \pi + r(u) V^{\text{g,free}}(t, u)\right.$$

$$\left. - \mu(u)\left(b^{\text{ad}} - V^{\text{g,free}}(t, u)\right)\right) \times \left(V^{\text{f}}(t, u) - V^{\text{g,free}}(t, u)\right),$$

$$V^{\text{g,free}}(t, n) = b^{\text{a}}(t).$$

The reader should recognize several elements in this system. The first inequality together with the terminal condition, only differs from Thiele's differential equation by containing an inequality instead of an equality. The second inequality simply states that the sum at risk connected to the transition to the free policy state is always negative. The equality in the third line is the formalization of the following statement: at any point in the state space, one of the two inequalities is an equality.

2.7.3 The market-based liability revisited

Corollary 2.6 is closely connected to the market-based composition of the liabilities. We repeat the definition of the individual bonus potential on premiums given in Equation (2.31) for the case $V \geq V^*$, since the studies in

Section 2.7.2 lead us, quite naturally, to suggest an alternative definition. We have the following inequality:

$$V^{\mathrm{bp}} = \max \left(V^{\mathrm{f}}, V^{\mathrm{g}} \right) - V^{\mathrm{g}}$$

$$\leq V^{\mathrm{g,free}} - V^{\mathrm{g}}. \tag{2.65}$$

Corollary 2.6 shows us that the alternative definition in Equation (2.65) coincides with the definition in Equation (2.62) if $c^{\mathrm{free}}(t, s)$ is either positive or negative for all s.

Actually, it is the inequality in Equation (2.65) which motivates us to suggest the alternative definition, $V^{\mathrm{g,free}} - V^{\mathrm{g}}$, for the bonus potential on premiums. The inequality in Equation (2.65) follows from

$$\max \left(V^{\mathrm{f}}, V^{\mathrm{g}} \right) \leq V^{\mathrm{g,free}},$$

which is true since the left hand side corresponds to Equation (2.64), where the maximum is taken over only two possible points in time, t and n. On the right hand side, the maximum is taken over all points in time between t and n.

3

Interest rate theory in insurance

3.1 Introduction

This chapter provides a brief introduction to some basic concepts from interest rate theory and financial mathematics and applies these theories for the calculation of market values of life insurance liabilities. There exists a huge amount of literature on financial mathematics and interest rate theory, and we shall not mention all work of importance within this area. Some basic introductions are Baxter and Rennie (1996) and Hull (2005). Readers interested in more mathematical aspects of these theories are referred to Lamberton and Lapeyre (1996) and Nielsen (1999). Finally we mention Björk (1997, 2004) and Cairns (2004).

The present chapter is organized as follows. Section 3.2 demonstrates how the traditional actuarial principle of equivalence can be modified in order to deal with situations with random changes in the future interest rate, i.e. to the case of stochastic interest rates. This argument, which involves hedging via so-called zero coupon bonds, leads to new insights into the problem of determining the market value for the guaranteed payments on a life insurance contract. Section 3.3 gives a more systematic treatment of topics such as zero coupon bonds, the term structure of interest rates and forward rates. In addition, this section demonstrates how versions of Thiele's differential equation can be derived for the market value of the guaranteed payments. In these equations, forward rates now appear instead of the interest rates. In Section 3.5, we mention more general bonds and relations to zero coupon bonds, and in Section 3.6 we briefly turn to the estimation of forward rates. Section 3.7 presents an introduction to arbitrage pricing theory in models, where trading is possible at fixed discrete time points. This discussion leads to formulas for market values involving so-called martingale measures. In addition, the analysis provides a basis for an integrated description of the liabilities and assets of the insurance company which can be used for assessment of the company's total financial situation under various economic scenarios. Essential elements are stochastic models for the future interest rate, bond prices and stock prices. The importance of this analysis is increased by the introduction of market-based accounting in life insurance, since in this case the market value of the liabilities is also affected by the financial situation.

3.2 Valuation by diversification revisited

How are life insurance contracts traditionally valuated? What is the reasoning behind these methods? What is diversification? To answer these questions, let us first recall the traditional actuarial law of large number considerations and see how these can be modified for the most simple life insurance contracts in the presence of financial uncertainty. In particular, we consider situations with stochastic interest.

3.2.1 The law of large numbers

A first version of the law of large numbers was formulated by the Swiss mathematician Jakob Bernoulli. The law of large numbers states that the average from some experiment (for example, the average number of heads from tossing the same coin m times) will converge to some number as the number of experiments increases. In the coin-tossing example, we could let X^i be the outcome from the ith toss, by taking $X^i = 1$ if the coin shows a "head" and $X^i = 0$ if it shows a "tail." We can write this in a more compact form using the indicator function $X^i = 1_{A^i}$, where A^i is the event that the ith toss leads to a "head," i.e. $A^i = \{i\text{th coin head}\}$. Then the law of large numbers states that

$$\frac{1}{m} \sum_{i=1}^{m} 1_{A^i} \to E[1_{A^1}], \qquad (3.1)$$

as m increases to infinity. Since the expected value of the indicator function 1_{A^1} is equal to the probability of the event A^1, we see that the average of heads converges to the probability of observing a head, which for most coins should be $\frac{1}{2}$.

3.2.2 A portfolio of insured

Consider now a portfolio of l_x, say, identical n-year pure endowment contracts with sum insured 1. For $t \geq 0$ we denote by l_{x+t} the expected number of survivors at age $x + t$. We impose here the following standard assumptions.

- The l_x policy holders are all of age x at time 0 with remaining lifetimes given by $T^1, \ldots, T^{l_x}$ with the same survival probability,

$$_tp_x = \frac{l_{x+t}}{l_x} = \exp\left(-\int_0^t \mu(x+u)\,du\right), \qquad (3.2)$$

where the mortality intensity μ is a deterministic function, and where we have used standard actuarial notation. For example, μ could be a Gompertz–Makeham intensity of the form

$$\mu(x+t) = \alpha + \beta\, c^{x+t}.$$

- The contracts are paid by a single premium $\pi(0)$ at time 0.

Of course, we cannot predict exactly the number of policy holders, l_x, who actually survive until time n, at which time each survivor receives one unit. However, we know that if the portfolio is large, the actual number of survivors at time n is in some sense close to the expected number l_{x+n}. Mathematically, this is a consequence of the law of large numbers. To see this, introduce the indicator $1_{\{T^i>n\}}$ that the ith policy holder survives. The ratio between the actual (unknown) number of survivors at time n and the number of policy holders l_x entering the contract at time 0 can now be written as follows:

$$\frac{1}{l_x}\sum_{i=1}^{l_x} 1_{\{T^i>n\}}. \qquad (3.3)$$

The situation is now almost identical to the coin-tossing example, and, by the law of large numbers, Equation (3.3) converges to

$$E[1_{\{T^1>n\}}] = P(T^1 > n) = {}_np_x = \frac{l_{x+n}}{l_x}$$

as the number of policy holders l_x increases to infinity, provided that the lifetimes of the policy holders are independent. This shows that the actual number of survivors is indeed close to the number predicted by the decrement series l_{x+n} if l_x is "big," i.e.

$$\sum_{i=1}^{l_x} 1_{\{T^i>n\}} \approx l_x\, {}_np_x = l_{x+n}.$$

In a sufficiently large insurance portfolio, the actual number of survivors at a given fixed time is hence relatively close to the expected number of survivors. Similar arguments can be applied in situations where several time points or even payment processes are considered.

We emphasize that the assumed independence is crucial in order to obtain this convergence. In more realistic models, where the future mortality intensity μ is unknown (stochastic), the law of large numbers does not imply that the quantity (3.3) converges to a constant. Here, one distinguishes between *unsystematic* and *systematic mortality risk*. The systematic risk is associated with the consequences of random changes in the underlying mortality intensity, and the unsystematic risk is the risk associated with the insured lifetimes given the underlying mortality intensity. It is the unsystematic risk, which is diversifiable and can be eliminated by increasing the size of the portfolio, whereas the systematic is undiversifiable and remains with the insurer. This problem is addressed further in Section 5.5.

3.2.3 Interest, accumulation and discount factors

What is the relation between yearly interest rate and the force of interest? How do we handle interest rates that are not constant during the term of the contracts? In this section, we recall these and other basic concepts.

In the traditional actuarial literature, see for example Gerber (1997), it is typically assumed (implicitly) that the insurance company invests capital in an account with yearly interest rate i, and that this rate is constant during the term of the insurance contract. Introducing $r = \log(1+i)$, we can alternatively write the one-year *accumulation factor* $1+i$ as e^r. Thus, the t-year accumulation factor is determined as follows:

$$(1+i)^t = e^{rt} = S(t), \qquad (3.4)$$

which clearly satisfies the differential equation

$$\frac{\mathrm{d}}{\mathrm{d}t} S(t) = rS(t), \qquad (3.5)$$

with the initial condition $S(0) = 1$. The quantity r is known as the *force of interest*, and it can be interpreted as the interest per time unit per unit deposited on the account. The t-year *discount factor* is given by

$$v^t = (1+i)^{-t} = e^{-rt} = S(t)^{-1}, \qquad (3.6)$$

where $v = e^{-r}$. How can this be generalized to situations where i is no longer constant? One possibility is to let $i(s)$ represent the annual interest rate for year s. The corresponding force of interest $r(s)$ for year s is then determined from the equation $(1 + i(s)) = e^{r(s)}$, and the t-year accumulation factor is given by

$$S(t) = (1 + i(1)) \cdots (1 + i(t)) = \exp\left(\sum_{s=1}^{t} r(s) \right). \qquad (3.7)$$

If we consider instead the case where the interest rate can change more often than once every year, then the force of interest is the most natural starting point, since it describes the interest per time unit. Letting $r(u)$ be the force of interest at any time u, we can define a new accumulation factor by changing Equation (3.5) such that r depends on time, that is

$$\frac{\mathrm{d}}{\mathrm{d}t} S(t) = r(t) S(t). \tag{3.8}$$

It does not look like a big difference compared to Equation (3.5), but if we solve Equation (3.8) with the initial condition $S(0) = 1$, the accumulation factor becomes

$$S(t) = \exp\left(\int_0^t r(u)\,\mathrm{d}u\right), \tag{3.9}$$

and the corresponding discount factor is given by

$$S(t)^{-1} = \exp\left(-\int_0^t r(u)\,\mathrm{d}u\right). \tag{3.10}$$

Note that the quantity $S(t)$ represents the value at time t of one unit invested at time 0 in the account which bears continuously added interest $r(u)$. In financial mathematics, one refers to this account as a savings account.

We use the accumulation and discount factors from Equations (3.9) and (3.10) in the following. One advantage compared to working with a constant interest rate is that we can now allow interest rates to vary over time by specifying the force of interest as a function of time. In addition, this framework can be used when building models which allow for random changes in the future interest rates. This extension is the basis for more realistic studies of the impact of changes in the interest rates on the balance sheet of an insurance company, an area which is essential within asset-liability management.

3.2.4 The insurer's loss and the principle of equivalence

Now consider a portfolio of l_x pure endowments of one unit expiring at time n paid by a single premium $\pi(0)$ at time 0. Assume moreover that the number of survivors follows the decrement series, i.e. it is deterministic and equal to l_{x+n}. With this contract, each of the survivors at time n receive one unit; the present value at time 0 of this benefit is given by $S(n)^{-1} l_{x+n}$. Since the premiums $l_x \pi(0)$ are payable at time 0, no discounting is needed, and the present value of the premiums is simply equal to the payment $l_x \pi(0)$. Thus, the present value of the insurer's loss associated with the portfolio can be defined as follows:

$$L = l_{x+n} S(n)^{-1} - l_x \pi(0). \tag{3.11}$$

The premium $\pi(0)$ is now said to be fair, if $L = 0$. If $S(n)$ is deterministic (or known at time 0), the fair premium is the well known *equivalence premium*: using the fact that $S(t) = \exp(\int_0^t r(u)\, du)$, we get from Equation (3.11) the following well known result:

$$\pi(0) = \frac{l_{x+n}}{l_x} \exp\left(-\int_0^n r(u)\, du\right) = {}_n p_x \exp\left(-\int_0^n r(u)\, du\right), \qquad (3.12)$$

which is simply the expected present value of the benefit. However, it is important to realize that this argument works only in the situation where the discount factor $S(n)^{-1} = \exp(-\int_0^n r(u)\, du)$ is deterministic. In the case where the future interest rates are unknown at time 0, we cannot charge this premium, since we do not know $S(n)$ at the time of selling of the contract!

Thus, we see from the simple considerations above that mortality risk can essentially be eliminated by increasing the size of the portfolio if the insured lives are independent, i.e. if there is no systematic insurance risk within the model. In this situation, we also say that mortality risk is *diversifiable*. However, we see from (3.12) that we did not get rid of the factor $S(n)^{-1}$ in the case where $S(n)$ is random. We can interpret this by saying that we have eliminated the mortality risk, whereas the financial risk related to the future development of the interest rate could not be eliminated by increasing the size of the portfolio. This is not so surprising, but it is nevertheless worth pointing out, since it raises the question of how we can control or eliminate this risk. The answer is straightforward in the idealized world of our simple example: by trading with financial contracts called *zero coupon bonds*. (Sections 3.3 and 3.5 below are devoted to a more systematic treatment of this topic.) A zero coupon is a contract which pays its holder one unit at a fixed time n (also referred to as an n-bond); the price at time $0 \le t \le n$ is denoted by $P(t, n)$. Clearly, we must have that $P(n, n) = 1$. Before analyzing the company's loss in this setting, we consider the special case where all future zero coupon bond prices are known at time 0, i.e. the situation with deterministic bond prices.

3.2.5 Deterministic bond prices

Let us consider a completely deterministic world, i.e. there is no randomness, where tomorrow's prices for zero coupon bonds are known today. In this setting, we can derive the structure of zero coupon bond prices and give another introduction to the concept of arbitrage.

Fix some times $t \leq n$, where t is today and n is the payment time. If bond prices are deterministic, the price $P(\tau, n)$ at time τ of an n-bond is known already at time t for any $\tau \in [t, n]$. In particular, this implies that

$$P(t, n) = P(t, \tau) P(\tau, n), \qquad (3.13)$$

which says that the value at time t of an n-bond is equal to the value at time t of a τ-bond multiplied by the value at time τ of an n-bond. Thus, one can in this case think of $P(t, \tau)$ and $P(\tau, n)$ as discount factors for $[t, \tau]$ and $[\tau, n]$, respectively. To show that Equation (3.13) is satisfied, recall that $P(t, n)$ is the price at time t of one unit at time n. Under the assumption of deterministic zero coupon bonds, one can alternatively obtain one unit at time n by investing in $P(\tau, n)$ τ-bonds at the price $P(t, \tau) P(\tau, n)$. At time τ, this leads to the payment $P(\tau, n)$, which can be used to buy an n-bond, and this ensures the payment of one unit at time n. This shows that $P(t, \tau)$ and $P(\tau, n)$ can be interpreted as discount factors. However, it is essential to realize that Equation (3.13) is not satisfied in the more realistic situation where $P(\tau, n)$ is not known at time t for $\tau > t$. The reason is again that $P(t, n)$ and $P(t, \tau)$ are known at time t, whereas $P(\tau, n)$ is not known at t, when $\tau > t$.

Assuming in addition that the zero coupon prices are sufficiently nice (smooth) functions, one can actually prove that Equation (3.13) implies the existence of a function r^* such that

$$P(t, n) = \exp\left(-\int_t^n r^*(u)\, du\right). \qquad (3.14)$$

An alternative way of addressing this issue is as follows. Assume that we can buy zero coupon bonds with maturity n at the price given by Equation (3.14) and that we can invest in the savings account with *deterministic interest* $r(u)$ as explained in Section 3.2.3. We have thus constructed a market with two investment possibilities (two assets). It can now be shown that if we insist on prices which do not allow for the possibility of risk-free gains, then there is only one possible price for the zero coupon bond. This type of argument is also called an arbitrage argument. More precisely, we show that the only reasonable price for the bond is given by

$$P(t, n) = \exp\left(-\int_t^n r(u)\, du\right) = \frac{S(t)}{S(n)}, \qquad (3.15)$$

so that $r^*(u)$, which appears in Equation (3.14), must be identical to the interest rate $r(u)$ from the savings account. For reasons of completeness, we give this argument here.

Assume that the price of an n-bond at time t differs from that given in Equation (3.15) and is given by

$$P(t, n) = (1 + \varepsilon) \exp \left(- \int_t^n r(u) \, du \right) = (1 + \varepsilon) \frac{S(t)}{S(n)},$$

for some $\varepsilon \neq 0$. It is now possible to construct a risk-free gain by using the following strategy (if $\varepsilon > 0$).

- Sell one bond at the price $P(t, n)$ at time t. This leads to the liability 1 at time n.
- Invest the amount $P(t, n)$ in the savings account at time t. At time n, the deposit on the savings account is then $P(t, n)S(n)/S(t) = (1 + \varepsilon)$.
- At time n, withdraw the amount $(1 + \varepsilon)$ from the savings account and pay one unit to the buyer of the bond.

This strategy leads to a gain of ε. If $\varepsilon < 0$, a gain of $-\varepsilon$ can be obtained by borrowing money from the bank and buying a bond. The main idea of arbitrage-free pricing is that such possibilities cannot exist in the market, since all investors would want to sell the bond if $\varepsilon > 0$, and there would be no buyers. Consequently, prices would adapt such that it is no longer possible to generate risk-free gains.

We point out that this argument cannot be applied in the situation where $r(u)$ is not deterministic. This can be seen directly by considering Equation (3.15), which involves the future (unknown) interest rate. One alternative idea could be to replace $S(t)/S(n)$ by its expected value. However, as we see below, there is no reasonable argument which supports this idea. Finally, we note that in the case where $r(u)$ is constant and equal to r, Equation (3.15) simplifies to

$$P(t, n) = \exp(-r(n - t)),$$

which is identical to the classical discount factor given in Equation (3.6).

3.2.6 Hedging with zero coupon bonds

In this section, we modify the principle of equivalence to the situation where the insurer can trade zero coupon bonds. This gives a way of *hedging*, i.e. controlling or eliminating, the risk associated with the development of the interest rate. We consider in this section only the guaranteed payments as defined in Chapter 2; the treatment of payments related to bonus is postponed until Chapter 4.

Hedging a portfolio of pure endowments

Assume that the insurer at time 0 invests in $l_x \kappa$ units of an n-bond. The present value of the insurer's loss from the portfolio of l_x pure endowments is then given by

$$\tilde{L} = (l_{x+n} S(n)^{-1} - l_x \pi(0)) + l_x \kappa(P(0, n) - 1 \cdot S(n)^{-1}), \qquad (3.16)$$

where we have assumed that the number of survivors follows the decrement series. In addition, we have discounted payments by using the true interest rate (the market interest rate). The first term in Equation (3.16) corresponds to the present value of the company's loss without investments in n-bonds (but investment in the savings account), and the second term represents the present value of the loss from buying at time 0 exactly $l_x \kappa$ n-bonds at the price $P(0, n)$. This term is the difference between the price $P(0, n)$ of the bond at time 0 and the discounted amount received by the company at time n. By rearranging terms in Equation (3.16), we see that

$$\tilde{L} = (l_{x+n} - l_x \kappa)S(n)^{-1} + l_x(\kappa P(0, n) - \pi(0)).$$

Here, the first term is equal to zero exactly if $\kappa = l_{x+n}/l_x = {}_np_x$, and the second term is zero if, in addition,

$$\pi(0) - {}_np_x P(0, n). \qquad (3.17)$$

Thus we have obtained that $\tilde{L} = 0$, as in the classical situation with deterministic interest. The fair premium given by Equation (3.17) has a very natural form: it is the price at time 0 of a zero coupon bond with maturity n multiplied by the probability of survival to n. In the portfolio with l_x policy holders, the insurer should purchase $l_x {}_np_x = l_{x+n}$ bonds, which is exactly the expected number of survivors.

Note that the arguments leading to Equation (3.17) determine the fair premium (market price) for the guaranteed payments as well as an *investment strategy*: that the insurer should invest the entire premium (the market value) in n-bonds. In this way, the insurer is able to *replicate* the liabilities, since the value at a future time t of the bonds purchased at time 0 is given by

$$l_x {}_np_x P(t, n) = l_{x+n} P(t, n).$$

The argument used for determining the price at time 0 of the guaranteed part of the pure endowment can now be repeated at time t for each of the l_{x+t} remaining policy holders. Hence, the total market value at time t of the guaranteed payments associated with these l_{x+t} pure endowment contracts is given by

$$l_{x+t \; n-t}p_{x+t} \, P(t, n) = l_{x+n} \, P(t, n),$$

which shows that the market value of the liabilities is exactly equal to the value of the investments (the assets) at any time t for any future development of the value of the zero coupon bonds. Any increase or decrease of the bond price leads to exactly the same changes in the value of the assets and liabilities.

Note that the market value of the guaranteed payments does not depend on the company's choice of investment strategy, even though the market value is derived by means of a hedging argument. If it were possible to purchase and sell such contracts at prices which deviated from the market value, it would in fact be possible to generate risk-free gains (arbitrage) by investing in zero coupon bonds. For a more detailed treatment of these aspects, see Møller (2000) and Steffensen (2001).

Hedging a portfolio of term insurances

For completeness, we indicate how this hedging argument can be applied for the pricing and hedging of the guaranteed part of a term insurance. Consider a portfolio of l_x term insurances. The number of deaths in year t predicted at time 0 by the decrement series is given by

$$d_{x+t} = l_{x+t} - l_{x+t+1},$$

where we have used traditional actuarial notation. Consider for simplicity the case where the sum insured (one unit) is payable at the end of the year, i.e. at times $t = 1, 2, \ldots, n$. In this case, the argument used for the pure endowment has to be modified slightly, so that the company now invests in zero coupon bonds with expiration times $t = 1, 2, \ldots, n$. Assume more precisely that the company at time 0 invests in $l_x \kappa(t)$ t-bonds at the price $P(0, t)$. The company's loss at time 0 then becomes

$$\tilde{L} = \left(\sum_{t=1}^{n} d_{x+t-1} \, S(t)^{-1} - l_x \, \pi(0) \right) + l_x \sum_{t=1}^{n} \kappa(t) \left(P(0, t) - 1 \cdot S(t)^{-1} \right), \quad (3.18)$$

which can be interpreted in the same way as for the pure endowment. This expression can be rewritten as follows:

$$\tilde{L} = \sum_{t=1}^{n} (d_{x+t-1} - l_x \kappa(t)) S(t)^{-1} + l_x \left(\sum_{t=1}^{n} \kappa(t) \, P(0, t) - \pi(0) \right).$$

Here, the first term is zero if

$$\kappa(t) = \frac{d_{x+t-1}}{l_x} = {}_{(t-1)|1}q_x = {}_{t-1}p_x \, {}_1q_{x+t-1},$$

which is exactly equal to the probability that a person aged x at time 0 dies in the interval $(t-1, t]$, and the second term is zero if

$$\pi(0) = \sum_{t=1}^{n} {}_{(t-1)|1}q_x \, P(0, t). \tag{3.19}$$

This fair price differs from the classical formulas in that the usual discount factors have been replaced by zero coupon bond prices. Finally, we mention that if the sum insured is payable *immediately* upon death and not at the end of each year as suggested by Equation (3.19), we need a continuous version of (3.19). For example, this can be obtained by considering small time intervals and noting that, for small h,

$$_{t|h}q_x \approx {}_tp_x \, \mu(x+t)h.$$

Thus, Equation (3.19) becomes

$$\pi(0) = \int_0^n {}_tp_x \, \mu(x+t) P(0, t) \, \mathrm{d}t. \tag{3.20}$$

In this situation, it is no longer possible to ensure that $\tilde{L} = 0$, no matter how many different bonds one buys. The reason for this phenomenon is that, in principle, the payments can occur at any time, i.e. there are, in principle, infinitely many possible payment times. However, we can move $\tilde{L}$ arbitrarily close to zero by choosing sufficiently many zero coupon bonds. Another aspect is, of course, that in practice one would work with finitely many different payment times (for example once every day, week or month), which would amount to choosing some discretization of Equation (3.20).

3.2.7 Market values and zero coupon bonds

Consider now the main example from Chapter 2 with an endowment insurance with a continuously payable premium π. Upon survival to n, the policy holder receives the guaranteed amount $b^{\mathrm{a}}(0)$, whereas b^{ad} is payable immediately upon a death before time n. We assume in addition that the contract starts at time 0, where the policy holder is x years old. As in the previous chapter, we assume that bonuses are used to increase the amount payable upon survival only. Accordingly, we denote by $b^{\mathrm{a}}(t)$ the amount guaranteed at time t, so that $b^{\mathrm{a}}(t) \geq b^{\mathrm{a}}(0)$.

The first order basis

Using the notation of Chapter 2, we can determine the premium π calculated under the deterministic first order basis (r^*, μ^*) via

$$\pi a^*_{\overline{xn|}} = b^{\mathrm{a}}(0) \, {}_nE^*_x + b^{\mathrm{ad}} \, A^{1*}_{\overline{xn|}},$$

where

$$_{n-t}E^*_{x+t} = \exp\left(-\int_t^n r^*(\tau)\mathrm{d}\tau\right) {}_{n-t}p^*_{x+t},$$

$$a^*_{\overline{x+t\,n-t|}} = \int_t^n \exp\left(-\int_t^s r^*(\tau)\mathrm{d}\tau\right) {}_{s-t}p^*_{x+t} \, \mathrm{d}s,$$

$$A^{1*}_{\overline{x+t\,n-t|}} = \int_t^n \exp\left(-\int_t^s r^*(\tau)\mathrm{d}\tau\right) {}_{s-t}p^*_{x+t} \, \mu^*(x+s)\mathrm{d}s,$$

and where the survival probability under the first order valuation principle is given by

$${}_{n-t}p^*_{x+t} = \exp\left(-\int_t^n \mu^*(x+\tau)\mathrm{d}\tau\right).$$

Similarly, we can give prospective expressions for the technical reserve under the first order valuation principle. The technical reserve at time t for the payments guaranteed at time t is given by

$$V^*(t) = b^{\mathrm{a}}(t) \, {}_{n-t}E^*_{x+t} + b^{\mathrm{ad}} A^{1*}_{\overline{x+t\,n-t|}} - \pi a^*_{\overline{x+t\,n-t|}}.$$

More generally, the technical reserve at time u for the payments guaranteed at time t is given by

$$V^*(t, u) = b^{\mathrm{a}}(t) \, {}_{n-u}E^*_{x+u} + b^{\mathrm{ad}} A^{1*}_{\overline{x+u\,n-u|}} - \pi a^*_{\overline{x+u\,n-u|}}.$$

For $u \geq t$, we have the following differential equation with side conditions:

$$\frac{\partial}{\partial u} V^*(t, u) = r^*(u) V^*(t, u) + \pi - \mu^*(x+u)R^*(t, u), \qquad (3.21)$$

$$V^*(t, t) = V^*(t),$$

$$V^*(t, n) = b^{\mathrm{a}}(t),$$

where $R^*(t, u)$ is the sum at risk:

$$R^*(t, u) = b^{\mathrm{ad}} - V^*(t, u).$$

Market value of guaranteed payments

In Chapter 2 it was assumed that the mortality intensities μ and μ^* and the interest rates r and r^* were deterministic functions. In fact, all formulas there rely on this assumption. However, by repeating the combined diversification and hedging argument of Section 3.2.6, it follows that the market value (the fair price) at time t of the payments upon survival to n, guaranteed at time 0, is given by

$$b^{\mathrm{a}}(0)\, P(t, n)\, {}_{n-t}p_{x+t},$$

where ${}_{n-t}p_{x+t}$ is the true survival probability. Similarly, the market value at time t for the part of the contract which pays b^{ad} immediately upon a death before time n is given by

$$b^{\mathrm{ad}} \int_t^n P(t, s)\, {}_{s-t}p_{x+t}\, \mu(x+s)\, \mathrm{d}s,$$

where $P(t, s)$ is the price at time t of a zero coupon bond with expiration time s; the market value at time t of the future premiums is given by

$$\pi \int_t^n P(t, s)\, {}_{s-t}p_{x+t}\, \mathrm{d}s.$$

Note that the market value at time t of the future premiums is calculated in the same way as the market value of the benefits. They both involve the zero coupon bond prices at time t instead of the usual discount factors. From a theoretical point of view, the only difference between the benefits and the premiums is the sign. However, the situation becomes much more complicated if one includes the policy holder's possibilities for surrender and for changing the contract into a free policy as indicated in Chapter 2. Combining the three expressions above, we get the following expression for the market value at time t for payments guaranteed at time 0:

$$V^{\mathrm{g}}(0, t) = b^{\mathrm{a}}(0)\, P(t, n)\, {}_{n-t}p_{x+t}$$

$$+ \int_t^n P(t, s)\, {}_{s-t}p_{x+t}\, (\mu(x+s)b^{\mathrm{ad}} - \pi)\, \mathrm{d}s. \qquad (3.22)$$

We denote by $V^{\mathrm{g}}(t)$ the market value at time t for the payments guaranteed at time t. This quantity is obtained from Equation (3.22) by replacing $b^{\mathrm{a}}(0)$ by $b^{\mathrm{a}}(t)$.

When the actual basis (r, μ) is deterministic, i.e. when r and μ are both deterministic functions, Section 3.2.5 shows that the zero coupon bond prices are given by

$$P(t, s) = \exp\left(-\int_t^s r(\tau)\, \mathrm{d}\tau\right). \qquad (3.23)$$

If we insert this expression into Equation (3.22), the market value at time u for the payments guaranteed at time t can be written as follows:

$$V^{\mathrm{g}}(t, u) = b^{\mathrm{a}}(t) \exp\left(-\int_u^n r(\tau)\, \mathrm{d}\tau\right)_{n-u} p_{x+u}$$

$$+ \int_u^n \exp\left(-\int_u^s r(\tau)\, \mathrm{d}\tau\right)_{s-u} p_{x+u} \left(\mu(x+s)b^{\mathrm{ad}} - \pi\right) \mathrm{d}s \quad (3.24)$$

$$= b^{\mathrm{a}}(t)_{n-u} E_{x+u} + b^{\mathrm{ad}} A^1_{x+u\,\overline{n-u}|} - \pi\, a_{x+u\,\overline{n-u}|}, \quad (3.25)$$

which corresponds to the formulas derived in Chapter 2.

What's next?

The above calculations indicate that the market value of the guaranteed payments can be calculated by replacing the usual discount factors with zero coupon bond prices. A natural question is therefore: does this solve the problem of determining market values of the guaranteed payments from a life insurance contract completely? A quick answer is: yes! However, we insist on continuing the discussion here for various reasons. One aspect is that zero coupon bonds are not determined from the true market interest rate r via Equation (3.23) if the market interest rate is stochastic. We can only use this simple formula when the market interest rate is assumed to be deterministic or even constant. In particular, this leads to the question of whether it is possible to construct versions of Thiele's differential equation for the market value of the guaranteed payments. Here, the concept of forward rates proves to be useful. Another aspect is that the majority of bonds on most bond markets are more complicated than zero coupon bonds. This fact requires a more detailed treatment of the relation between the prices of these more general bonds and zero coupon bonds.

3.3 Zero coupon bonds and interest rate theory

In this section, we recall some fundamental concepts related to bond markets. We address questions like: What is the term structure of interest rates? What is a forward rate, and what is the difference between forward rates and the market interest rate? What is credit risk? What is the role of these concepts in the calculation of market values in life and pension insurance? We start by analyzing zero coupon bonds, which can be viewed as the basic building blocks of the bond market. In Section 3.5 below we discuss connections to coupon bonds. In the following, T and T' are fixed (deterministic) finite times.

Definition 3.1 *A zero coupon bond with maturity date T (also called a T-bond) is a contract which pays one unit at time T. The price at time $t \in [0, T]$ is denoted by $P(t, T)$.*

Throughout, we take $P(t, t) = 1$.

Often the contracts defined above are called *default free* zero coupon bonds. This serves to underline that the bonds cannot (or are very unlikely to) default, i.e. that the issuers of the bonds are not likely to go bankrupt. This is in contrast to so-called *defaultable bonds*, which are issued by companies (or countries) which are less credit-worthy. As a consequence, bonds issued by such parties typically give a higher return to the holders, since the bonds may be worthless if the issuer goes bankrupt. This risk is also known as *credit risk*; see Bielecki and Rutkowski (2001), Lando (2004) and Schönbucher (2003). In the following, we focus on default free bonds.

3.3.1 Yield curves

Definition 3.2 *The continuously compounded zero coupon yield (or the continuously compounded spot rate) $R(t, T)$ for the period $[t, T]$ is defined by*

$$R(t, T) = -\frac{1}{T - t} \log P(t, T).$$

It follows directly from this definition that the price of the zero coupon bond can be expressed in terms of the continuously compounded yield as follows:

$$P(t, T) = \exp\left(-R(t, T)(T - t)\right), \tag{3.26}$$

so that Equation (3.26) can be interpreted as a discount factor obtained by using the (constant) interest rate $R(t, T)$ during the interval $[t, T]$. Note that this (constant) interest rate $R(t, T)$ applies for any time $u \in [t, T]$, but that the intensity depends on the price of the zero coupon bond at time t.

Definition 3.3 *The term structure of interest rates at time t (or the zero coupon yield curve) is given by the mapping*

$$h \mapsto R(t, t + h).$$

3.3.2 Forward rates

Now consider times $0 \le t \le T' \le T$. We are interested in finding a *deterministic* rate at time t (today) for a future investment made at time T' and terminated at time T. This quantity is exactly the forward rate. We cannot use the yield $R(T', T)$ since this is defined in terms of $P(T', T)$, which, in general, is not known at time t. Instead, one introduces the concept of forward rates.

Definition 3.4 *The continuously compounded forward rate at time t for the period $[T', T]$ is defined by*

$$f(t, T', T) = -\frac{\log P(t, T) - \log P(t, T')}{T - T'}. \tag{3.27}$$

A better understanding of the concept of forward rates can be obtained by noting that the ratio of the price at time t for a T-bond and a T'-bond is given by

$$\frac{P(t, T)}{P(t, T')} = \exp(-f(t, T', T)(T - T')). \tag{3.28}$$

This can be given the following interpretation:

• at time t, sell one T'-bond and receive $P(t, T')$ (this corresponds to a loan);
• still at time t, use $P(t, T')$ to buy $P(t, T')/P(t, T)$ units of T-bonds;
• at time T' pay one unit on the T'-bond (pay back the loan);
• at time T receive $P(t, T')/P(t, T)$ from the T-bond.

The two transactions at time t are chosen such that the result at time t is exactly 0, since the T-bonds are financed by selling a T'-bond. A result of these transactions is that we have to pay (or invest) one unit at time T'. At time T we receive the result of this investment, $P(t, T')/P(t, T)$. Thus, by trading zero coupon bonds at time t we are, in a sense, able to fix the future return (or interest) for an amount to be invested at a future time T'. Furthermore, from Equation (3.28) we obtain that

$$\frac{P(t, T')}{P(t, T)} = \exp(f(t, T', T)(T - T')).$$

This shows that $f(t, T', T)$ can be interpreted as the constant interest rate, known at time t, which should be used for discounting future payments from time T to time T'.

In our subsequent analysis in Section 3.3.5 of market values in life and pension insurance, it is useful to work with the instantaneous forward rate at time t for a given future time T, i.e. the limit of $f(t, T', T)$ as $T' \nearrow T$. Equation (3.27) shows that this is simply the derivative of $-\log P(t, T)$ with respect to T. So, provided that the mapping $T \mapsto P(t, T)$ is continuously differentiable with respect to the maturity date T, we can state the following definition.

Definition 3.5 *The instantaneous forward rate at time t for time T is defined by*

$$f(t, T) = -\frac{\partial}{\partial T} \log P(t, T).$$ (3.29)

The instantaneous short rate at time t is $r(t) = f(t, t)$.

We show in the following how forward rates appear in a natural way in Thiele's differential equation for the market value of the guaranteed payments from a standard life insurance contract. It follows immediately from the definition above that

$$\int_t^T f(t, \tau) \, d\tau = -\log P(t, T) + \log P(t, t).$$

Since $P(t, t) = 1$, we see that the value at time t of the zero coupon bond is given by

$$P(t, T) = \exp\left(-\int_t^T f(t, \tau) \, d\tau\right).$$ (3.30)

Note, however, that we cannot in general conclude that the zero coupon bond prize is of the form $P(t, T) = \exp(-\int_t^T r(u) \, du)$. To obtain this result, additional assumptions are required. More precisely, it is necessary to assume that *future* bond prices are known at time t, which basically means that the instantaneous short rate is deterministic. This situation was considered in Section 3.2.5.

Equation (3.30) shows that the zero coupon bond prices can in fact be derived directly from the instantaneous forward rates. Thus, there are several possibilities for specifying models for a bond market:

- specify all $P(t, T)$ for $0 \leq t \leq T \leq T^*$, where T^* is some maximum time point;
- specify all $f(t, T)$ for $0 \leq t \leq T \leq T^*$ and derive $P(t, T)$ via Equation (3.30) and the instantaneous short rate $r(t)$ via Definition 3.5;
- specify the development of $r(t)$, for $0 \leq t \leq T \leq T^*$.

We will not go into a treatment of the mathematical aspects associated with these different methods. However, we mention that one has to be careful when using the first two approaches in order to avoid arbitrage possibilities. The last approach also requires some additional work, since it is not clear how r determines the zero coupon bond prices.

3.3.3 Relations between forward rates and spot rates

We have now introduced several quantities, such as zero coupon bond, yield, spot rate and forward rate, and the reader may wonder if all this is really necessary and how all these quantities are related. Some immediate consequences of the above definitions are as follows.

(1) From Equation (3.28) with $T' = t$, it follows that

$$f(t, t, T) = R(t, T),$$

i.e. the forward rate at time t for $[t, T]$ coincides with the spot rate for $[t, T]$.

(2) Combining Equations (3.26) and (3.30), we see that

$$\frac{1}{T-t} \int_t^T f(t, \tau) \, d\tau = R(t, T), \tag{3.31}$$

which shows that the zero coupon yield for $[t, T]$ can be interpreted as the average of the instantaneous forward rates.

3.3.4 Simple rates

As an alternative to the continuously compounded rates introduced above, one can also introduce simple yields (or simple spot rates) and simple forward rates. For completeness, we give a short discussion of this concept, which does not play a further role, however, in our treatment of market values in life and pension insurance in the present chapter. They reappear in our discussion of swap rates in Chapter 7.

Simple rates differ from the usual principle of compounding rates in the sense that past interest is not included in the calculation of the interest for a given period. If we deposit an amount P at time 0 in an account with simple rate L (per time unit), this leads to the interest $PL(t - s)$ for the time period $[s, t]$. With continuously compounding interest under constant interest rate r, the deposit on the savings account would increase from Pe^{rs} at time s to Pe^{rt} at time t. Thus, the interest credited during the interval $[s, t]$ is given by

$$P(e^{rt} - e^{rs}) = Pe^{rs}(e^{r(t-s)} - 1).$$

This can now be formalized via the following definition.

Definition 3.6 *The simple yield (or the simple spot rate or even the LIBOR spot rate) for* $[t, T]$ *is given by*

$$L(t, T) = -\frac{P(t, T) - 1}{(T - t)P(t, T)},$$

and the simple forward rate (or the LIBOR forward rate) for $[T', T]$ *at time* t *is given by*

$$L(t, T', T) = -\frac{P(t, T) - P(t, T')}{(T - T')P(t, T)}.$$

It follows from the definition of the simple spot rate that

$$L(t, T)(T - t)P(t, T) = 1 - P(t, T),$$

which has the following interpretation: $1 - P(t, T)$ is the return or gain during the interval $[t, T]$ from buying the T-bond at time t at the price $P(t, T)$ and cashing the amount 1 at time T. Under the principle of simple interest, the amount

$$P(t, T)L(t, T)(T - t)$$

is exactly the interest which accrues in the interval $[t, T]$ in connection with the investment of $P(t, T)$ under a constant simple interest $L(t, T)$.

3.3.5 Market values and forward rates

In this section we derive a version of Thiele's differential equation for the market values of the guaranteed payments that involves forward rates. In Section 3.3.2 we showed how the instantaneous forward rates $f(t, \tau)$ at time t are related to the price of a zero coupon bond at time t; see Equation (3.30). If we insert this expression into Equation (3.25) for the market value at time $u \geq t$ for the payments guaranteed at time t, we immediately obtain the following expression:

$$V^{\mathrm{g}}(t, u) = b^{\mathrm{a}}(t) \exp\left(-\int_u^n f(u, \tau) \, d\tau\right)_{n-u}p_{x+u}$$

$$+ \int_u^n \exp\left(-\int_u^s f(u, \tau) \, d\tau\right)_{s-u}p_{x+u}(\mu(x+s)b^{\mathrm{ad}} - \pi) \, ds. \quad (3.32)$$

The situation $t = u$ gives the market value $V^{\mathrm{g}}(t)$ at time t of the payments guaranteed at time t. This auxiliary quantity is of importance in situations with stochastic interest, where Equation (3.25) cannot be applied directly. In this situation, we can derive an alternative expression for the market value which is similar to the classical formulas, but where the stochastic interest rate is replaced by the instantaneous forward rates at time u, which are known at time u.

We give here a version of Thiele's differential equation, which also opens up the possibility of deriving a differential equation for the individual bonus potential in a model with stochastic interest rates. It is not possible to derive a differential equation for $V^g(t, u)$ by applying Equation (3.32), since $V^g(t, u)$ is a rather complicated function of u which moreover depends on the interest rate at time u. Instead, we introduce the additional auxiliary function

$$V^{g,\circ}(t, u) = b^a(t) \exp\left(-\int_u^n f(t, \tau)\,d\tau\right)_{n-u}p_{x+u}$$

$$+ \int_u^n \exp\left(-\int_u^s f(t, \tau)\,d\tau\right)_{s-u}p_{x+u}(\mu(x+s)b^{ad} - \pi)\,ds,$$

(3.33)

which may be interpreted as a value at time u for the payments guaranteed at time t, calculated by applying the instantaneous forward rates at time t. Thus, $V^{g,\circ}(t, u)$ is not really a market value. However, the main advantage of this quantity is that it is a very simple function of u, which can be differentiated directly. Hence we obtain the following differential equation for $u \geq t$ with side conditions:

$$\frac{\partial}{\partial u}V^{g,\circ}(t, u) = f(t, u)V^{g,\circ}(t, u) + \pi - \mu(x+u)R^{g,\circ}(t, u),$$ (3.34)

$$V^{g,\circ}(t, t) = V^g(t),$$

$$V^{g,\circ}(t, n) = b^a(t),$$

where $R^{g,\circ}$ is the sum at risk, given by

$$R^{g,\circ}(t, u) = b^{ad} - V^{g,\circ}(t, u).$$

This differential equation provides an alternative method for calculating Equation (3.33) as follows. Given the sum insured $b^a(t)$ guaranteed at time t and the forward rates $f(t, u)$ at time t, the market value $V^g(t)$ can be calculated by solving Equation (3.34) on the interval $[t, n]$ with the terminal condition corresponding to the payment upon survival to n, guaranteed at time t. For a description of the methods for solving differential equations numerically, see, for example, Schwarz (1989).

The individual bonus potential

The forward rates can also be used for deriving an expression for the so-called individual bonus potential V^{ib}. The most simple situation is the case where

$V(t) \geq V^*(t) \geq V^g(t)$, where $V(t)$ is the total reserve for the contract; see Chapter 2. In this case, the individual bonus potential is given by

$$V^{ib}(t) = V^*(t) - V^g(t).$$

By applying the differential equations, Equations (3.21) and (3.34), together with the terminal condition $V^*(t, n) - V^{g,\circ}(t, n) = b^a(t) - b^a(t) = 0$, we find that

$$V^{ib}(t) = \int_t^n \exp\left(-\int_t^s (f(t, \tau) + \mu(x + \tau)) \, d\tau\right) c(t, s) \, ds, \tag{3.35}$$

where

$$c(t, s) = (f(t, s) - r^*(s))V^*(t, s) + (\mu^*(x + s) - \mu(x + s))R^*(t, s). \tag{3.36}$$

Equations (3.35) and (3.36) differ from the corresponding expressions in Chapter 2 (see Equations (2.28) and (2.29)), in that the market interest rate has been replaced by the forward rates. This serves to underline the importance of the forward rates in the situation where the interest rate is stochastic, since the safety loadings $c(t, s)$ for the payments guaranteed at time t now involve the forward rates at time t. The expression in Equation (3.35) has the same interpretation as Equation (2.28) in Chapter 2: the individual bonus potential is the market value of the safety loadings on the guaranteed payments.

3.4 A numerical example

In this section, we illustrate the role of the bonus potentials via a numerical example. We consider an insurance contract, where the benefits have been calculated using a first order mortality intensity of Gompertz–Makeham form as follows:

$$\mu(x + t) = \alpha + \beta c^{x+t}. \tag{3.37}$$

The actual parameters used are listed in Table 3.1. This table also contains Gompertz–Makeham estimates for the Danish population taken from Dahl and Møller (2006) for males and females for 1980 and 2003. The estimated mortality intensities can be found in Figures 3.1 and 3.2, together with the estimates for 1970 and 1990. The estimated mortality intensities are clearly ordered and reveal a decreasing trend from 1970 to 2003. This decrease in the mortality intensity implies that the expected lifetimes have increased during the same period. Figures 3.3 and 3.4 show the expected lifetimes for age 30 and age 65; these figures are also taken from Dahl and Møller (2006).

Table 3.1. *The first order mortality and estimated Gompertz–Makeham parameters for 1980 and 2003.*

	Males			Females		
	α	β	c	α	β	c
First order	0.0005	0.00007586	1.09144	0.0005	0.000053456	1.09144
1980	0.000233	0.0000658	1.0959	0.000220	0.0000197	1.1063
2003	0.000134	0.0000353	1.1020	0.000080	0.0000163	1.1074

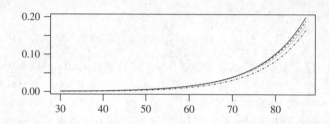

Figure 3.1. Estimated mortality intensities for males. Solid lines are 1970 estimates; dashed lines correspond to 1980; dotted lines to 1990; and dot-dashed lines to 2003.

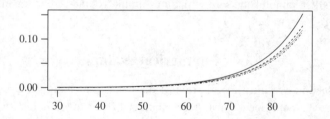

Figure 3.2. Estimated mortality intensities for females. Solid lines are 1970 estimates; dashed lines correspond to 1980; dotted lines to 1990; and dot-dashed lines to 2003.

Figure 3.3 shows that the remaining lifetimes have increased by approximately 2.5 years for males and 1.5 years for females aged 30 from 1980 to 2003. Using this method, the expected lifetime in 2003 is about 75.3 years for 30-year-old males and 79.5 for 30-year-old females. A closer study of the underlying Gompertz–Makeham parameters (α, β, c) indicates that α has decreased during the period from 1960 to 2003 for both males and females. The estimates for β increase from 1960 to 1990, whereas the estimates for c decrease. In contrast, β decreases and c increases in the last part of the period considered (from 1990 to 2003). Table 3.2 shows the expected lifetimes

Table 3.2. *Expected lifetimes with the first order basis and the market-value bases for 1980 and 2003.*

	Age	First order	Est. 1980	Est. 2003	Est. 2003 (longevity 0.5%)	Est. 2003 (longevity 1%)
Males	30	74.1	73.1	75.8	77.8	79.9
	65	78.5	78.9	80.3	80.8	81.2
	90	93.7	93.1	93.4	93.4	93.4
Females	30	77.9	78.8	80.1	82.2	84.5
	65	81.5	82.4	83.3	83.8	84.4
	90	94.9	94.0	94.3	94.3	94.4

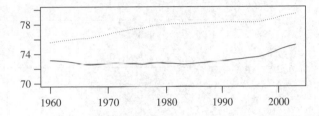

Figure 3.3. Development of the expected lifetime of 30-year-old females (dotted line) and 30-year-old males (solid line) from 1960 to 2003. Estimates are based on the last five years of data available at the given years.

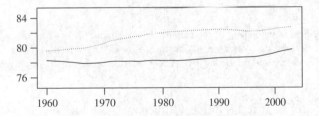

Figure 3.4. Development of the expected lifetime of 65-year-old females (dotted line) and 65-year-old males (solid line) from 1960 to 2003.

calculated for the first order basis and the estimated mortalities for age 30, 65 and 90. With the 2003 estimate, moreover, we have included simple corrections for longevity, i.e. for future reductions in the mortality, by assuming that the mortality in all ages decreases each year by 0.5% and 1%, respectively. In this example, we see that the expected lifetimes calculated under the first order basis are smaller than the expected lifetimes calculated under the 2003 estimate. For males and females aged 30 or 65, the difference is between 1.7 and 2.2 years. If we include a correction for future improvements in the

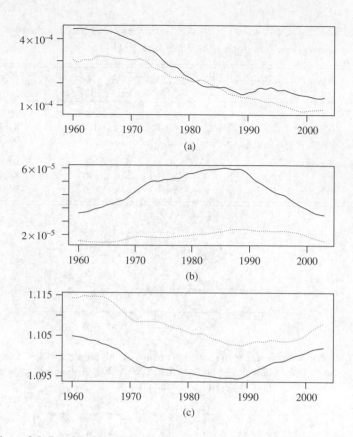

Figure 3.5. Development of the Gompertz–Makeham parameters: (a) α; (b) β; (c) c for females (dotted lines) and males (solid lines) from 1960 to 2003. Estimates are based on the last five years of data available at the given years.

mortality, we see that this difference increases considerably, in particular at low ages. Using a yearly decline of 1%, we see that this difference is now between 2.7 and 6.6 years.

In the example, we have determined market values by using the above 2003 mortality intensity with a yearly 1% correction for future mortality improvements. In addition, we have applied a zero coupon yield curve from 31 December 2005 for discounting the payments. These numbers, which have essentially been adjusted for tax by multiplying the observed yield curve by 0.85, can be found in Table 3.3 for maturity $t = 1, 2, \ldots, 30$; for $t \geq 30$, we use the value for maturity 30. We have used this yield curve for the calculation of all market values below. The expected present values used in the example can be found in Table 3.4 for first order bases with (approximate) interest

Table 3.3. *Zero coupon yields from 31 December 2005 before and after tax.*

Maturity	Yield	Yield after tax	Maturity	Yield	Yield after tax
1	0.02843	0.02422	16	0.03638	0.03100
2	0.02991	0.02548	17	0.03660	0.03120
3	0.03084	0.02627	18	0.03683	0.03139
4	0.03090	0.02632	19	0.03706	0.03159
5	0.03114	0.02653	20	0.03729	0.03178
6	0.03162	0.02694	21	0.03733	0.03182
7	0.03203	0.02729	22	0.03737	0.03185
8	0.03277	0.02792	23	0.03741	0.03189
9	0.03365	0.02867	24	0.03746	0.03193
10	0.03404	0.02901	25	0.03750	0.03196
11	0.03447	0.02937	26	0.03754	0.03200
12	0.03489	0.02973	27	0.03758	0.03203
13	0.03531	0.03009	28	0.03763	0.03207
14	0.03573	0.03045	29	0.03767	0.03211
15	0.03615	0.03081	30	0.03771	0.03214

rates 4.5%, 2.5% and 1.5%, respectively. This table also contains the expected present value calculated by using the zero coupon yield curve of Table 3.3 and the estimated mortality from 2003 with a yearly longevity correction of 1%. We consider now three contracts signed at age 30 with first order interest rate 4.5%, 2.5% and 1.5%, respectively. We set the life annuity payment rate to unity and sum paid at death to five. Premiums are paid continuously at a fixed rate as long as the policy holders are alive and stop at the retirement age of 65. For each of these three contracts, we have determined the equivalence premium at age 30, such that the technical reserves start at zero at time 0. We have then calculated the technical reserve at various ages by rolling forward the policy holders' accounts with the first order assumptions. The fair premiums can be found in Table 3.5 for the three contracts with different technical interest rates. This table shows (not surprisingly) that the premiums and technical reserves increase if the technical interest decreases. (For a study of the dependence of the technical reserve on the interest rate and other parameters, see Kalashnikov and Norberg (2003).) Table 3.5 also includes the so-called free policy factors introduced in Section 2.7.1. These factors are used for calculating the market value V^{f} of the guaranteed free policy benefits. We see that the factors decrease when the technical interest is decreased.

The relevant market values can be found in the lower part of Table 3.5 for the three contracts. At the time of signing these contracts at age 30, we see that the market values of the guaranteed payments are negative for the two contracts with low technical interest rates (2.5% and 1.5%); this leads to

Table 3.4. *Expected present values (for males) under the first order valuation basis and the market-value basis for the premiums, term insurance, pure endowment and the life annuity.*

Premiums are paid continuously and are assumed to stop at age 65, where the term insurance and pure endowment expire. The life annuity is assumed to start at age 65.

	Age	Premiums	Term insurance	Pure endowment	Life annuity
First order	30	17.011	0.086	0.165	1.689
interest 4.5%	40	14.273	0.110	0.262	2.681
	50	10.281	0.122	0.425	4.356
	65	0.000	0.000	1.000	10.239
	90	0.000	0.000	0.000	3.277
First order	30	22.069	0.130	0.323	3.880
interest 2.5%	40	17.406	0.145	0.423	5.080
	50	11.679	0.143	0.568	6.810
	65	0.000	0.000	1.000	11.997
	90	0.000	0.000	0.000	3.460
First order	30	25.519	0.161	0.455	5.952
interest 1.5%	40	19.384	0.168	0.540	7.069
	50	12.492	0.155	0.657	8.595
	65	0.000	0.000	1.000	13.080
	90	0.000	0.000	0.000	3.560
Market values,	30	20.709	0.068	0.278	3.753
1% longevity	40	16.804	0.090	0.384	4.994
	50	11.595	0.103	0.546	6.798
	65	0.000	0.000	1.000	12.188
	90	0.000	0.000	0.000	3.200

bonus potentials at the time of signing the contract. In contrast, the market value is greater than zero at time 0 for the contract with technical interest 4.5%, which implies that the company needs to set aside additional capital for this contract. For the contracts with technical interest 2.5% and 1.5%, we see that the market values of the guaranteed free policy benefits are typically higher than the market values for the guaranteed payments. For the contract with interest rate 4.5%, this is not the case. The individual bonus potentials for this example are listed finally in Table 3.6. We see that the contract with the high technical interest does not lead to any bonus potentials. (At very high ages, however, small bonus potentials arise because the first order mortality is lower than the estimated mortality at high ages.) For the two contracts with technical interest 1.5% and 2.5%, the bonus potentials on the future premiums

Table 3.5. *Fair premiums (equivalence premiums fixed at age 30), technical reserves and free policy factors for the three policies with first order interest 4.5%, 2.5% and 1.5%, respectively (upper part). The market values of guaranteed payments (GP) and market values of guaranteed free policy payments are given in the lower part.*

Contract: term insurance of five units and life annuity of one unit, with continuously paid premiums.

Premiums	0.125	0.205	0.265			
Interest	4.50%	2.50%	1.50%	4.50%	2.50%	1.50%
Age	Technical reserves			Free policy factors		
30	0.000	0.000	0.000	0.000	0.000	0.000
40	1.451	2.235	2.776	0.449	0.385	0.351
50	3.685	5.128	6.062	0.742	0.682	0.647
65	10.239	11.997	13.080	1.000	1.000	1.000
90	3.277	3.460	3.560	1.000	1.000	1.000
Age	Market values, GP			Market values, free policy		
30	1.511	−0.157	−1.393	0.000	0.000	0.000
40	3.347	1.994	0.991	2.445	2.095	1.910
50	5.868	4.934	4.242	5.426	4.984	4.731
65	12.188	12.188	12.188	12.188	12.188	12.188
90	3.200	3.200	3.200	3.200	3.200	3.200

decrease as the age approaches the age of retirement. In contrast, the bonus potentials on the free policy start at zero and increase with the premiums paid. However, at some point, they start to decrease again and eventually vanish as the age increases.

3.5 Bonds, interest and duration

The majority of bonds traded in most bond markets are more general than zero coupon bonds. Typical examples are annuity bonds and bullet bonds. Here, we give a framework that can be used for basically any bond with predetermined payments, which shows how the prices of these more general bonds are related to the prices of zero coupon bonds.

3.5.1 A general bond

Consider a bond issued at time τ_0, say, which specifies payments $c_1, \ldots, c_n$ at given times $\tau_1 < \cdots < \tau_n$. The value of such a bond at time $t \geq \tau_0$ (after

Table 3.6. *The total liability, the additional reserve needed and the two individual bonus potentials (BP): on premiums and on the free policy.*

Interest	4.50%	2.50%	1.50%	4.50%	2.50%	1.50%
Age	Total liability			Additional reserve included		
30	1.511	0.000	0.000	1.511	0.000	0.000
40	3.347	2.235	2.776	1.896	0.000	0.000
50	5.868	5.128	6.062	2.183	0.000	0.000
65	12.188	12.188	13.080	1.949	0.191	0.000
90	3.277	3.460	3.560	0.000	0.000	0.000
Age	Bonus potential, free policy			Bonus potential, premiums		
30	0.000	0.000	0.000	0.000	0.157	1.393
40	0.000	0.140	0.866	0.000	0.100	0.919
50	0.000	0.144	1.331	0.000	0.050	0.489
65	0.000	0.000	0.892	0.000	0.000	0.000
90	0.077	0.260	0.360	0.000	0.000	0.000

possible payments at t) is given by

$$P(t) = \sum_{i:\tau_i > t} P(t, \tau_i)c_i, \tag{3.38}$$

where $P(t, \tau_i)$ is the price at time t of a zero coupon bond with maturity τ_i. Again, a simple arbitrage argument shows that this is the only price that does not lead to the possibility of generating risk-free gains in a market where it is possible to buy and sell the bond in Equation (3.38) as well as zero coupon bonds with maturities $\tau_1, \ldots, \tau_n$. This can be seen by noting that payment streams of the form $c_k, \ldots, c_n$ at times $\tau_k < \cdots < \tau_n$ can be generated by buying exactly c_k τ_k-bonds, c_{k+1} τ_{k+1}-bonds, etc.

Example 3.7 *(Annuity bond) Taking $c_k = c$ for $k = 1, \ldots, n$ gives an annuity bond.* □

Example 3.8 *(Bullet bond) Fix some simple rate L and some amount K (the principal). Consider the situation where*

$$c_k = L(\tau_k - \tau_{k-1})K,$$

for $k = 1, \ldots, n-1$ and

$$c_n = L(\tau_n - \tau_{n-1})K + K.$$

With this bond, the holder receives at time τ_k the simple interest $L(\tau_k - \tau_{k-1})$ on the principal K for the interval $[\tau_{k-1}, \tau_k]$. At time τ_n, the principal K is paid back together with interest for the interval $[\tau_{n-1}, \tau_n]$. □

3.5.2 Yield and duration

In Section 3.3.1, we introduced the zero coupon yield $R(t, T)$, which was defined as the constant intensity for $[t, T]$ which allows the zero coupon bond with maturity T to be expressed as a traditional discounting factor of the following form:

$$P(t, T) = \exp(-R(t, T)(T - t)).$$

A natural generalization of this concept can be given for more general bonds. Here, the yield to maturity $y(t)$ is the constant rate which ensures that the discounted value of all future payments corresponds to the value at time t of the bond. This can be made more precise via the following definition.

Definition 3.9 *The yield to maturity at time t of the bond in Equation (3.38) is the solution $y(t)$ to the following equation:*

$$P(t) = \sum_{i:\tau_i > t} e^{-y(t)(\tau_i - t)} c_i =: F(t, y(t)). \tag{3.39}$$

Note that if all c_i are non-negative and $c_i > 0$ for some i with $\tau_i > t$, then the mapping $y(t) \mapsto F(t, y(t))$ is strictly decreasing, and hence there exists a unique non-negative solution to Equation (3.39). Thus, $y(t)$ is the constant rate of return that the holder receives for the payments during $(t, \tau_n]$.

A natural question is now the following: how sensitive is the price $P(t)$ of the bond to changes in the yield to maturity? Or, more precisely, how will a change in the yield to maturity affect the bond price? It can be relevant to investigate, for example, how sensitive the value of the company's total portfolio of bonds is to changes in the term structure. Similarly, one might be interested in a comparison of the sensitivity of different bonds. The answers to these questions are closely related to the so-called *duration* of the bond, which can be interpreted as the weighted average of the time to the payments $c_i \geq 0$ weighted by the factors $c_i e^{-y(t)(\tau_i - t)}$. These factors represent the values at time t of the payments c_i discounted by using the yield $y(t)$. The precise definition of the concept of duration is given here.

Definition 3.10 *The duration $D(t)$ at time t of the bond in Equation (3.38) with yield to maturity $y(t)$ is defined by*

$$D(t) = \frac{\sum_{i:\tau_i>t}(\tau_i - t)\,e^{-y(t)(\tau_i-t)}c_i}{P(t)}. \qquad (3.40)$$

We see from this definition that the duration at time t for a zero coupon bond with maturity τ is exactly equal to the time to maturity $\tau - t$. If we think of $P(t)$ in Equation (3.39) as a function of the yield to maturity $y(t)$, we obtain, by differentiating Equation (3.39) with respect to $y(t)$, the following:

$$\frac{\mathrm{d}}{\mathrm{d}y(t)}P(t) = -\sum_{i:\tau_i>t}(\tau_i - t)\,e^{-y(t)(\tau_i-t)}\,c_i = -P(t)\,D(t). \qquad (3.41)$$

For more details on duration, see, for example, Hull (2005) and references therein.

3.6 On the estimation of forward rates

In practical situations, one is often confronted with the following problem. Given that we have observed prices of a number of bonds, what can be said about the zero coupon yield curve and the forward rates? It is important to note that so far we have not introduced any model to describe how the price $P(t, T)$ of a given zero coupon bond evolves over time. This will be done later. At this point, we simply think of the prices as given and try to extract as much information from the observations as possible without introducing complicated models.

We consider the most simple situation where we observe the prices at time t of some zero coupon bonds and address the problem of deriving the forward rate curve.

3.6.1 Observing prices of zero coupon bonds

We fix times $\tau_1 < \cdots < \tau_n$ and assume that we have observed at time t the prices $P(t, \tau_i)$ of zero coupon bonds with maturities τ_i, for $i \in J(t)$, where

$$J(t) = \{j \in \{1, \ldots, n\} | \tau_j > t\},$$

i.e. of bonds that have not expired at time t. (We use this notation in order to emphasize the dynamic nature of this problem. Alternatively, we could simply consider one fixed time, $t = 0$, say, and work with a fixed set I of observed bond prices with maturities $\tau_1, \ldots, \tau_n$.) We can now derive the zero coupon yield for the periods $[t, \tau_i]$, $i \in J(t)$, by use of Definition 3.2, which shows that

$$R(t, \tau_i) = -\frac{1}{\tau_i - t} \log P(t, \tau_i), \quad \text{for } i \in J(t).$$

One can visualize this by plotting the points $(\tau_i - t, R(t, \tau_i))$, $i \in J(t)$, which are the pairs of time to maturity and zero coupon yield for the corresponding period.

Definition 3.4 determines the forward rates for the periods $[\tau_{i-1}, \tau_i]$, given by

$$f(t, \tau_{i-1}, \tau_i) = -\frac{\log P(t, \tau_i) - \log P(t, \tau_{i-1})}{\tau_i - \tau_{i-1}}.$$

However, we are also interested in (an estimate for) the entire zero coupon yield curve $h \mapsto R(t, t+h)$ at time t or the curve for the instantaneous forward rates $h \mapsto f(t, t+h)$.

One typical approach to the first problem is to apply some numerical technique to fit the best smooth curve to the observed points. Alternatively, one can fix some parameterized family of possible instantaneous forward rate curves,

$$\{h \mapsto f(t, t+h; \theta) | \theta \in \Theta\},$$

and fit this curve to the estimated zero coupon yields $R(t, \tau_i)$, $i \in J(t)$, by using Equation (3.31), which shows that

$$R(t, \tau_i; \theta) = \frac{1}{\tau_i - t} \int_t^{\tau_i} f(t, u; \theta)\, du.$$

Thus, the problem consists in finding the curve $R(t, t+h; \theta)$ which provides the best fit to the observed quantities $R(t, \tau_i)$, $i \in J(t)$, by using some subjective criterion. This is discussed in more detail below.

3.6.2 The Nelson–Siegel parameterization

In this section, we review the so-called Nelson–Siegel parameterization for the forward rates, suggested by Nelson and Siegel (1987); for an extension and an application to the Swedish Treasury bills and coupon bonds, see Svensson (1995). For simplicity, we fix $t = 0$. Nelson and Siegel (1987) advocated the following parametric family for the forward rates:

$$f(0, \tau) = \beta_0 + \beta_1 e^{-\tau/\delta} + \beta_2 \frac{\tau}{\delta} e^{-\tau/\delta}, \tag{3.42}$$

which is parameterized by $\beta = (\beta_0, \beta_1, \beta_2)$ and δ. The first part, β_0, can be interpreted as a long term component, the part with β_1 is determining the short term forward rate, and the β_2-component is affecting the medium term forward rate. Finally, the parameter δ is determining how "short term," "medium term" and "long term" should be defined. Integrating Equation (3.42) with respect to the maturity τ, we find that the zero coupon yield is given by

$$R(0, \tau) = \frac{1}{\tau} \int_0^\tau f(0, t) \, dt = \beta_0 + (\beta_1 + \beta_2)(1 - e^{-\tau/\delta}) \frac{1}{\tau/\delta} - \beta_2 \, e^{-\tau/\delta}. \quad (3.43)$$

The different components determining the forward rates are depicted in Figure 3.6.

We now discuss a simple way of fitting Equation (3.43) to some observed zero coupon yields for the periods $[0, \tau_1], \ldots, [0, \tau_n]$. In order to simplify notation, we first change the parameterization slightly and introduce the parameter $\vartheta = (\vartheta_1, \vartheta_2, \vartheta_3)^{\text{tr}}$, where tr means "transposed," and

$$R(0, \tau_i; \vartheta, \delta) = \vartheta_1 + \vartheta_2 (1 - e^{-\tau_i/\delta}) \frac{1}{\tau_i/\delta} + \vartheta_3 \, e^{-\tau_i/\delta} =: Y^i(\delta)^{\text{tr}} \vartheta, \quad (3.44)$$

where

$$Y^i(\delta) = \left(1, \; (1 - e^{-\tau_i/\delta}) \frac{1}{\tau_i/\delta}, \; e^{-\tau_i/\delta} \right)^{\text{tr}}.$$

Thus, for given δ, $R(0, \tau_i)$ is linear in ϑ. This special property can be exploited to yield a very simple approach to fitting the model to observed prices using

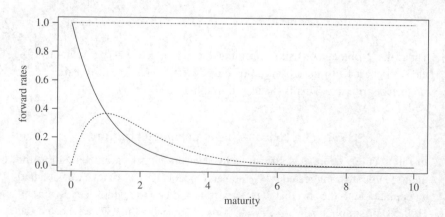

Figure 3.6. Nelson–Siegel parameterization: components determining the forward rates. The horizontal line gives the level for "long term" forward rates; the dashed line affects "medium term" rates, and the exponentially decreasing line affects "short term" forward rates.

the generalized least squares method. This approach can, for example, also be used to fit a Gompertz–Makeham mortality intensity to occurrence-exposure rates; see, for example, Norberg (2000).

Assume that we have observed zero coupon yields $\hat{R}(0, \tau_i)$, for $i = 1, \ldots, n$. (For example, these could be derived from zero coupon bond prices or from some more general bonds as described above.) We then introduce the vector of observed yields $\hat{R} = (\hat{R}(0, \tau_1), \ldots, \hat{R}(0, \tau_n))^{\text{tr}}$ and the $(n \times 3)$-matrix $Y(\delta)$ given by

$$Y(\delta) = \begin{pmatrix} Y^1(\delta)^{\text{tr}} \\ \vdots \\ Y^n(\delta)^{\text{tr}} \end{pmatrix} = \begin{pmatrix} 1 & (1 - e^{-\tau_1/\delta}) \frac{1}{\tau_1/\delta} & e^{-\tau_1/\delta} \\ \vdots & \vdots & \vdots \\ 1 & (1 - e^{-\tau_n/\delta}) \frac{1}{\tau_n/\delta} & e^{-\tau_n/\delta} \end{pmatrix}.$$

One possible way of fitting Equation (3.44) to the observed prices is now to minimize over ϑ, for fixed δ, the quadratic function

$$h(\vartheta) = \frac{1}{2} (Y(\delta)\vartheta - \hat{R})^{\text{tr}} A (Y(\delta)\vartheta - \hat{R}), \tag{3.45}$$

where A is some symmetric, positive definite weight matrix. For example, one could choose A equal to the $(n \times n)$-identity matrix. Alternatively, one could specify A in such a way that the estimated curve is forced to be close to some specific yields; for example, one could use trading volume as a measure or choose to give more weight to yields from specific maturities.

Equation (3.45) is minimized for ϑ solving $(\partial/\partial\vartheta)h(\vartheta) = 0$, i.e.

$$Y(\delta)^{\text{tr}} A (Y(\delta)\vartheta - \hat{R}) = 0, \tag{3.46}$$

which has the following solution:

$$\vartheta(\delta) = (Y(\delta)^{\text{tr}} A Y(\delta))^{-1} Y(\delta)^{\text{tr}} A \hat{R}. \tag{3.47}$$

The optimal choice of δ can then be found by inserting Equation (3.47) into Equation (3.45) and minimizing $h(\vartheta(\delta))$ over δ, i.e.

$$\min_{\delta} h(\vartheta(\delta)).$$

For more details on this approach applied for the estimation of mortality intensities, see Norberg (2000); this method is also applied by Cairns (2004) for the estimation of the yield curve.

3.7 Arbitrage-free pricing in discrete time

What is arbitrage-free pricing? What is hedging? What is a martingale measure? How can these concepts be used for the calculation of market values in life and pension insurance?

This section provides an introduction to the principle of no arbitrage. The main idea is that prices of traded *assets* should be determined in such a way that no risk-less gains arise from trading these assets. The term asset is used for basically any traded securities, such as bonds, stocks and even savings accounts.

The theory presented in this section is particularly useful for explaining how so-called derivatives can be priced. Important examples for life insurance companies are options, swaptions and interest guarantee options. More precisely, it can be shown how these instruments should be priced (within a given model) in order to avoid the possibility of generating risk-free gains. In addition, we see in Section 3.9 how these results can be applied when calculating market values in life and pension insurance.

This section is organized as follows. Section 3.7.1 describes the market of traded assets. In Section 3.7.2 we consider a simple two-period example with two assets, where the interest rate for the last period can attain two different values. Some fundamental results from probability theory that are crucial for a more systematic introduction to arbitrage-free pricing are reviewed in Section A.1 of the Appendix. Readers not familiar with concepts such as filtrations, stochastic processes and martingales may find it helpful to consult this appendix for more details.

Example 3.11 *(An arbitrage) As an example of a risk-less gain or an arbitrage, consider the situation where there exist two traded assets S^0 and S^1 whose prices at time 0 coincide, that is $S^0(0) = S^1(0)$. Assume, furthermore, that we know that with probability 1 (almost surely; see the Appendix, Section A.1) $S^0(T) \geq S^1(T)$ and that $P(S^0(T) > S^1(T)) > 0$. How can this be exploited to make a risk-free gain? Well, it seems intuitively reasonable that there is something wrong with this model, since asset number 0 seems to be to cheap: it has the same price as asset number 1 at time 0, but it will have at least the same value at time T. This observation can be exploited in the following way. At time 0 buy one unit of asset number 0 and sell one unit of asset number 1. (Thus, we assume that we can buy and sell the assets at the given prices, and hence we are not dealing with transaction costs.) At time T this leads to the gain $V = S^0(T) - S^1(T) \geq 0$. By the above assumptions, we have $P(V \geq 0) = 1$ and $P(V > 0) > 0$, which has the following consequences. At*

time T we receive V ≥ 0 without having paid anything at time 0. Basically, this
means that we have received a lottery ticket for free. □

The main assertion in arbitrage-free pricing is that no arbitrage possibilities
(like the one in Example 3.11) should exist. If they existed, all investors would
be interested in following these strategies, and this would imply that there
would only be buyers for the cheap asset (asset 0 in the example) and sellers
for the expensive asset (asset 1 in the example).

3.7.1 Traded assets and information

We consider a financial market consisting of two traded assets, whose prices
at time t are given by $S^0(t)$ and $S^1(t)$, respectively. (It is not difficult to
generalize the model to the case of d traded assets; however, this would only
serve to complicate notation and the presentation in general.) Here we depart
from the previous assumption of deterministic prices as in Section 3.2.5,
and allow for randomness so that future prices are not known in general.
More precisely, the prices at time u are described by the random variables
$(S^0(u), S^1(u))$, which are not observed before time u.

The family of prices for asset i in discrete time, $S^i = (S^i(t))_{t\in\{0,1,\dots,T\}}$, is
an example of a *stochastic process*. To keep track of what is known at time t,
we introduce a so-called *filtration* $\mathbf{F} = (\mathcal{F}(t))_{t\in\{0,1,\dots,T\}}$. Here, $\mathcal{F}(t)$ is the
information available at time t. We assume that the amount of information
is non-decreasing over time (we do not forget), so that $\mathcal{F}(t) \subseteq \mathcal{F}(u)$ for
any $t < u \le T$. (Mathematically, a filtration is an increasing sequence of
σ-algebras.) The price process S^i is said to be *adapted* to the filtration $\mathbf{F}$
if the price of asset i at time t is part of the information $\mathcal{F}(t)$ available at
time t. (Mathematically this means that $S^i(t)$ is $\mathcal{F}(t)$-measurable.) The model
is illustrated in Figure 3.7.

A stochastic process is called *predictable* if its value at time t is already
known at time $t - 1$. Thus, any predictable process is adapted.

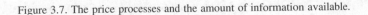

time:	0	1	$t-1$	t	T
prices:	$S^i(0)$	$S^i(1)$	$S^i(t-1)$	$S^i(t)$	$S^i(T)$
information:	$\mathcal{F}(0)$	$\mathcal{F}(1)$	$\mathcal{F}(t-1)$	$\mathcal{F}(t)$	$\mathcal{F}(T)$

Figure 3.7. The price processes and the amount of information available.

We assume that S^0 describes the development of a savings account with periodic interest $i(t)$ for the period $(t-1, t]$, so that

$$S^0(t) = (1+i(1))\cdots(1+i(t)).$$

Typically, $(i(t))_{t\in\{1,\ldots,T\}}$ is also a stochastic process.

For example, one can think of S^1 as the value of a zero coupon bond. As in the previous sections, we apply the process S^0 as a discounting factor (also called a *numeraire*) and we also introduce the *discounted price processes* X and X^0, defined by

$$X(t) = S^1(t)/S^0(t) \quad \text{and} \quad X^0(t) = S^0(t)/S^0(t) = 1.$$

3.7.2 A two-period example

Before we continue our discussion of arbitrage-free pricing, we consider a simple example with two periods. We assume that trading takes place at times $t = 0, 1, 2$. Assume that the interest $i(1)$ for the savings account for the first period is known at time 0, whereas the interest $i(2)$ for the second period is unknown at time 0 and is only revealed at time 1. The value of the savings account at time 0 is given by unity, i.e. $S^0(0) = 1$. Similarly, $S^0(1) = (1+i(1)) = e^{r(1)}$ and $S^0(2) = (1+i(1))(1+i(2)) = e^{r(1)+r(2)}$. We assume, in addition, that the future interest can take two different values only. (For a treatment of such models, see, for example, Jarrow (1996).) An illustration of this model can be found in Figure 3.8, where the interest for the first period is taken to be $i(1) = 5\%$ and where the interest for the second period is either $i(2) = 4\%$ or $i(2) = 6\%$. Let

$$p = P(i(2) = 0.04) = 1 - P(i(2) = 0.06),$$

and assume that $0 < p < 1$, i.e. there is a positive possibility for both events. The example $p = 1/2$ is the case where both events are equally likely.

One can now ask questions such as: is is possible to find the price of a zero coupon bond with maturity $T = 2$ from these assumptions? First, we recall that $P(2, 2) = 1$, independently of the value of the interest. Then, we consider the question of finding the value of the bond at time 1. If interest has increased from 5% to 6%, we are in the upper part of Figure 3.8, where it is possible to deposit money on the savings account and receive an interest of 6% at the end of the period. The usual arbitrage argument now shows that

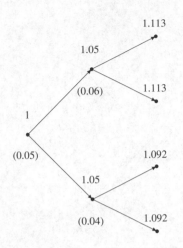

Figure 3.8. Model for the interest (numbers in parentheses) and the savings account S^0.

the value at time 1 of a zero coupon bond with maturity 2 in this situation must be given by

$$P(1,2) = \frac{1}{1.06} \approx 0.943.$$

If interest goes down to 4%, we obtain

$$P(1,2) = \frac{1}{1.04} \approx 0.962.$$

However, we still cannot say precisely what the price $P(0,2)$ at time 0 for the zero coupon bond with maturity 2 should be from the condition of no arbitrage alone. Actually, there are many different prices for the zero coupon bond which are consistent with the condition of no arbitrage. These observations are collected together in Figure 3.9.

In the following we show that the condition of no arbitrage only yields that

$$0.898 \approx \frac{0.943}{1.05} < P(0,2) < \frac{0.962}{1.05} \approx 0.916.$$

However, when the price at time 0 of the zero coupon bond is given, we are able to derive the price of many other contracts. For example, assume that we know already at time 0 that we want to invest one unit at time 1. Is it then possible to ensure that the return does not fall below 4.5%, when the interest in the lower part of Figure 3.9 is 4%? We will introduce some additional concepts before we come back to this question.

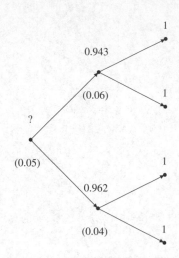

Figure 3.9. Interest (numbers in parentheses) and the price for the zero coupon bond with maturity 2.

3.7.3 Investment strategies and the value process

An *investment strategy* (or simply a *strategy*) is a two-dimensional process $h = (h^0, h^1)$, where h^1 is predictable (i.e. $h^1(t)$ is known/chosen at time $t-1$) and h^0 is adapted (i.e. $h^0(t)$ is known/chosen at time t). This construction is illustrated in Figure 3.10, which describes when the number h^1 of zero coupon bonds purchased and the deposit h^0 on the savings account are chosen.

The quantity $h^1(t)$ represents the total number of units of asset number 1 which are in the portfolio at time $t-1$. In particular, these assets have been a part of the investment portfolio from time $t-1$ to time t. The condition concerning predictability of h^1 ensures that the number of assets held from time $t-1$ to time t is fixed at $t-1$ based on the information available at this time. In contrast, the deposit h^0 on the savings account is only required to be adapted, such that the deposit at time t can be decided based on the additional information which arises from time $t-1$ to time t. The pair $h(t) = (h^0(t), h^1(t))$ is also called the *portfolio* at time t.

At time $t-1$, the insurance company's portfolio is given by

$$h(t-1) = (h^0(t-1), h^1(t-1)),$$

i.e. $h^1(t-1)$ zero coupon bonds and a deposit on the savings account with value $h^0(t-1)S^0(t-1)$. The discounted value of the portfolio $h(t-1)$ at

time:	0	1		$t-1$	t		T
savings account:	$h^0(0)$	$h^0(1)$		$h^0(t-1)$	$h^0(t)$		$h^0(T)$
bonds:		$h^1(1)$	$h^1(2)$	$h^1(t)$	$h^1(t+1)$		.

Figure 3.10. The investment strategy $h = (h^1, h^0)$ and times for changes of investments.

time $t-1$, where we use the savings account S^0 as the discount factor, is defined by

$$V(t-1, h) = S^0(t-1)^{-1} \left(h^1(t-1)S^1(t-1) + h^0(t-1)S^0(t-1) \right)$$
$$= h^1(t-1)X(t-1) + h^0(t-1).$$

The process $(V(t, h))_{t \in \{0, 1, \dots, T\}}$ is also called the (discounted) *value process* of h.

We now turn to an analysis of the flow of capital, which takes place during the time interval $(t-1, t]$; see Figure 3.10. We also refer to the insurance company as *the hedger*.

3.7.4 The cost process

Is is essential to describe changes in the value process and to keep track of whether changes are due to returns on investments or whether new capital has been added. For this purpose, we introduce the so-called *cost process* suggested by Föllmer and Sondermann (1986) and Föllmer and Schweizer (1988); see also Föllmer and Schied (2002). This process can be applied for the construction of risk-minimizing strategies; for applications in insurance, see Chapter 5 or Møller (2002) and references therein.

Consider again the interval $(t-1, t]$. Immediately after time $t-1$, the portfolio $h(t-1)$ is adjusted so that the hedger now holds $h^1(t)$ bonds. This is achieved by buying an additional $h^1(t) - h^1(t-1)$ bonds, and this gives rise to the discounted costs

$$(h^1(t) - h^1(t-1))X(t-1).$$

The new portfolio $(h^0(t), h^1(t-1))$ is held until time t, when new prices $(S^0(t), S^1(t))$ are announced, and thus the hedger receives the following discounted gains:

$$h^1(t)(X(t) - X(t-1)).$$

Finally, the hedger may at time t decide to change the deposit on the savings account from $h^0(t-1)S^0(t)$ to $h^0(t)S^0(t)$ based on the additional information available at time t. This change leads to the additional discounted costs $h^0(t) - h^0(t-1)$. Thus, we have seen that the change in value of the investment portfolio can be written as follows:

$$V(t, h) - V(t-1, h) = (h^1(t) - h^1(t-1))X(t-1)$$
$$+ h^1(t)(X(t) - X(t-1)) + (h^0(t) - h^0(t-1)). \tag{3.48}$$

The first and the last terms on the right hand side of Equation (3.48) represent costs to the hedger, whereas the second term is trading gains obtained from the strategy h during $(t-1, t]$. We now introduce the *cost process* (or the *accumulated cost process*) of the strategy h, given by

$$C(t, h) = V(t, h) - \sum_{s=1}^{t} h^1(s)\Delta X(s), \tag{3.49}$$

where we have used the notation $\Delta X(s) = X(s) - X(s-1)$. The cost process is simply defined as the value of the strategy reduced by trading gains; in particular, the cost process $C(h)$ satisfies the following relation:

$$V(t, h) = V(t-1, h) + h^1(t)(X(t) - X(t-1)) + (C(t, h) - C(t-1, h)),$$

which corresponds to Equation (3.48). It decomposes changes in the value process into trading gains and changes in the accumulated cost process, i.e. additional investments made during $[0, t]$. We note that $C(0, h) = V(0, h)$, which says that the initial costs are exactly equal to the amount invested at time 0.

3.7.5 Self-financing strategies and arbitrage

A strategy is said to be *self-financing* if the change in the value process given by Equation (3.48) is generated by trading gains only, i.e. if the portfolio is not affected by any in- or outflow of capital during the period considered. This means that any changes in the portfolio have to be made in a cost-neutral way, in the sense that the purchase of additional bonds must be financed by reducing the deposit on the savings account by a similar amount. This condition amounts to requiring that

$$V(t, h) = V(0, h) + \sum_{s=1}^{t} h^1(s)\Delta X(s), \tag{3.50}$$

for all t. By inserting Equation (3.50) into Equation (3.49), we see that this corresponds to saying that the cost process is constant and equal to $V(0, h)$, i.e. equal to the value of the initial investment made at time 0. This characterizes the self-financing strategies in terms of the cost process.

An *arbitrage* is a self-financing strategy h such that

$$V(0, h) = 0, P(V(T, h) \geq 0) = 1 \quad \text{and} \quad P(V(T, h) > 0) > 0. \tag{3.51}$$

The interpretation is exactly the same as in Example 3.11; it corresponds to receiving a free lottery ticket. With this strategy, one can invest zero units at time 0 and receive at time T the non-negative amount $V(T, h)$, which is strictly positive with positive probability.

3.7.6 Hedging and attainability

The insurer is assumed to invest on the financial market in order to control the risk associated with some liability H; i.e., the insurer is *hedging* against some risk in order to control or eliminate the risk. In some situations (within certain models) it is possible to determine a self-financing strategy which generates or replicates the liability completely. This is the case if there exists a self-financing strategy h which sets out with some amount $V(0, h)$ and has terminal value $V(T, h) = H$ at time T. In this case, the initial value $V(0, h)$ is the only reasonable price for the liability H; such claims are also said to be *attainable*, and $V(0, h)$ is called the *arbitrage-free price* of H. This is the case in the example considered in Section 3.7.8. However, in many cases the hedger's liabilities cannot be hedged perfectly using a self-financing strategy, and this leaves open the question of how to choose an optimal trading strategy. For a theoretical discussion on the choice of trading strategy for insurance contracts with financial risk, see Møller (2001a, 2002).

3.7.7 Equivalent martingale measures and absence of arbitrage

Typically we would like to verify that a given model does not allow for arbitrage possibilities. Here, the concept of equivalent martingale measures plays a central role.

Equivalent martingale measures

When we specify how the price processes S^0 and S^1 develop, we also have to associate probabilities to the event that prices attain any given value. This fixes the distribution of the future prices and leads to a probability measure P.

More generally, we specify the probabilities for a certain class $\mathcal{F}$ of events A (for example, that tossing a coin leads to "head" as in Section 3.2.1). We write $P(A)$ for the "probability of A under P," where we have added "under P" in order to underline the specific probability and the fact that one could as well speak of the probability of A under another measure Q, say. This situation can, for example, be compared with the way the actuary handles simultaneously various bases for the mortality of a policy holder. Actually, it is possible to formalize this change of mortality intensity by exactly the same method as the one sketched below. For more details, see Section A.1 of the Appendix.

It is essential to introduce another probability measure Q, which associates to events probabilities which might differ from the ones under P. At the moment, we only require that the two probability measures are *equivalent*. Loosely speaking, this means that the measures agree on whether an event is totally unlikely or not, which means that if $P(A) = 0$, we also have that $Q(A) = 0$ (and vice versa). If we again compare with the situation with two different mortality intensities, then it means that the mortality intensity is μ^P if we use the probability measure P and μ^Q if we use the probability measure Q. Basically, the two measures P and Q are now equivalent if we have that μ^P is zero, if and only if μ^Q is zero. In this part, we deal primarily with the development of bond prices over time, and the two different probability measures represent different expectations for the changes in bond prices for a given period. Before we explain why the concept "equivalent martingale measures" appears in the title of this section, we briefly recall what a martingale is.

What is a martingale?

Let us again consider the discounted price process X, which is the ratio between the price of a bond S^1 and the value S^0 of one unit invested at time 0 of the savings account. We can now ask questions such as: what is the expected (discounted) price of the bond at time u? Here, one has to be a little more precise and specify the probability measure that one wishes to use for the calculations – P or Q? If we work with P, the answer is $E^P[X(u)]$, and if we use Q the answer is $E^Q[X(u)]$. We can modify the question slightly and ask: what is the expected discounted price under Q for the bond at time u, given that we take into consideration the amount $\mathcal{F}(t)$ of information available at time $t < u$? This quantity is

$$E^Q[X(u)|\mathcal{F}(t)], \tag{3.52}$$

the conditional expected value under Q of $X(u)$ given the information available at t. The process X is now said to be a *martingale* (under Q), if Equation (3.52) is exactly equal to the discounted price at time t, $X(t)$, i.e.

$$E^Q[X(u)|\mathcal{F}(t)] = X(t), \qquad (3.53)$$

for all $t \leq u$. This condition becomes slightly more transparent in the case where X is a Markov process, since Equation (3.53) then reduces to

$$E^Q[X(u)|X(t)] = X(t). \qquad (3.54)$$

We interpret this as follows. If $X(t)$ and $X(u)$ represent the discounted price at time t (today) and time u (tomorrow) of a bond, and if Q is a martingale measure, the expected discounted price tomorrow (calculated under the probability measure Q) is identical to the price today.

Equivalent martingale measures

An equivalent probability measure Q is said to be an *equivalent martingale measure* if X is a martingale under Q, i.e. if Equation (3.53) is satisfied for all $t < u$. We emphasize that the discounted bond price X is typically not a martingale under the true probability measure P, so that P normally cannot be applied as an equivalent martingale measure. However, the measure P is important since, in particular, it determines the events that are completely unlikely, i.e. if an event has probability zero. The importance of the concept of equivalent martingale measures is illustrated below. Here we introduce the following assumption.

Assumption 3.12 *There exists at least one equivalent martingale measure.*

Martingale measures ensure absence of arbitrage

It is actually not so difficult to show that the existence of an equivalent martingale measure is sufficient to exclude the possibility of arbitrage possibilities in the model, i.e. that there cannot be strategies which satisfy Equation (3.51).

Consider some equivalent martingale measure Q, such that the discounted price process X is a Q-martingale; i.e., for any $t < u \in \{0, 1, \dots, T\}$, we have that $E^Q[X(u)|\mathcal{F}(t)] = X(t)$. We want to show that there cannot exist any self-financing strategies h with $V(0, h) = 0$ and where

$$V(T, h) = V(0, h) + \sum_{s=1}^{T} h^1(s)\Delta X(s) \qquad (3.55)$$

is non-negative and strictly positive with probability 1. To see that such strategies cannot exist, it is sufficient to show that

$$E^Q[V(T, h)] = V(0, h). \tag{3.56}$$

Why does this exclude arbitrage possibilities? Well, if $V(T, h) \geq 0$ and

$$E^Q[V(T, h)] = V(0, h) = 0,$$

we must have that $Q(V(T, h) = 0) = 1$, and hence $P(V(T, h) = 0) = 1$, since P and Q are equivalent.

We still need to show that Equation (3.56) is satisfied for any self-financing strategy h. Here, we need the special construction of the investment strategy h, which ensures that h^1 is predictable, i.e. that the number $h^1(s)$ of bonds in the portfolio during the period $(s-1, s]$ is known at time $s-1$. Using this property, we obtain the following:

$$E^Q\left[h^1(s)\,\Delta X(s)\,\middle|\,\mathcal{F}(s-1)\right] = h^1(s)\,E^Q\left[\Delta X(s)\,\middle|\,\mathcal{F}(s-1)\right] = 0,$$

where we have moved $h^1(s)$ outside the expected value. (Mathematically, we have used that $h^1(s)$ is $\mathcal{F}(s-1)$-measurable.) The second equality follows by noting that X is a Q-martingale, so that

$$E^Q[\Delta X(s)|\mathcal{F}(s-1)] = E^Q[X(s) - X(s-1)|\mathcal{F}(s-1)]$$
$$= X(s-1) - X(s-1) = 0.$$

In fact, this shows that the value process given in Equation (3.50) for a self-financing strategy is also a Q-martingale, i.e.

$$E^Q[V(u, h)|\mathcal{F}(t)] = V(t, h),$$

for all $t \leq u$. If we insert $u = T$ and $t = 0$, we see that

$$E^Q[V(T, h)] = V(0, h).$$

Thus, under Assumption 3.12 there exist no strategies h that satisfy Equation (3.51).

Pricing with an equivalent martingale measure

We now consider some liability which specifies the discounted payoff H, which can be replicated by using a self-financing strategy h, i.e.

$$H = V(T, h) = V(0, h) + \sum_{t=1}^{T} h^1(t)\,\Delta X(t). \tag{3.57}$$

In Section 3.7.6 we introduced the notion of an arbitrage-free price and we explained that this price is equal to $V(0, h)$, the price needed in order to generate H with the self-financing strategy. We can now use the martingale measure Q to compute expected values in Equation (3.57). Since the value process $V(h)$ is a martingale under Q, we see that

$$E^Q[H] = E^Q[V(T, h)] = V(0, h). \qquad (3.58)$$

This very important result shows us that the arbitrage-free price for the liability can actually be calculated as the expected value of the discounted payments, computed under the equivalent martingale measure Q.

3.7.8 The two-period example revisited

Let us return to the example considered in Section 3.7.2 and assume that we have observed the price $P(0, 2)$ at time 0 of the zero coupon bond with maturity 2. The other prices at times 1 and 2 have already been established; see Section 3.7.8. Do there exist martingale measure(s)? How can we determine a martingale measure?

Define a probability measure Q via

$$q = Q(i(2) = 0.04) = 1 - Q(i(2) = 0.06),$$

where $0 \leq q \leq 1$. One can now start to think about whether Q is equivalent to the original measure P, i.e. if the two measures agree about whether an event has probability 0 or a strictly positive probability. Under P, the probability of $i(2)$ attaining the values 0.04 and 0.06 is strictly positive. Hence this should also be the case under Q; this observation gives the condition $0 < q < 1$.

Next, we check if it is possible to choose q in such a way that Q actually becomes a martingale measure. Here, we need to verify that the process

$$X(t) = \frac{P(t, 2)}{S^0(t)}$$

is indeed a martingale under Q. Thus, it should be shown that

$$E^Q\left[\left.\frac{P(u, 2)}{S^0(u)}\right| \mathcal{F}(t)\right] = \frac{P(t, 2)}{S^0(t)}, \qquad (3.59)$$

for $0 \leq t < u \leq 2$. First, consider the case $t = 1$ and $u = 2$, so that $P(u, 2) = 1$ and $S^0(u) = S^0(t)(1 + i(2))$. Since the interest $i(2)$ is assumed to be known at time $t = 1$, Equation (3.59) implies that

$$\frac{1}{1 + i(2)} = P(1, 2),$$

which is exactly the formula that we derived already in Section 3.7.2. For $u = 1$ and $t = 0$, Equation (3.59) states that

$$E^Q \left[\frac{P(1,2)}{S^0(1)} \right] = \frac{P(0,2)}{S^0(0)} = P(0,2). \tag{3.60}$$

In principle, we should include here the information $\mathcal{F}(0)$ available at time 0. However, in our model there is no (non-trivial) information available at time 0, so this can be neglected. In order to be able to calculate the expected value on the left hand side of Equation (3.60), we note that the probability (under Q) that $i(2)$ is equal to 0.04 is q (in this case, $P(1,2) = 0.962$), and that the probability that $i(2)$ is equal to 0.06 is $1 - q$ (in this case, $P(1,2) = 0.943$). Thus we obtain the following condition:

$$P(0,2) = E^Q \left[\frac{P(1,2)}{S^0(1)} \right] = \frac{1}{1.05} (q\,0.962 + (1-q)\,0.943),$$

which has the unique solution

$$q = \frac{1.05P(0,2) - 0.943}{0.962 - 0.943}.$$

In particular, this shows that if $0.943 < 1.05\,P(0,2) < 0.962$, then $0 < q < 1$ and hence Q is indeed an equivalent martingale measure in this case. We see moreover that the martingale measure in this example is uniquely determined from the prices which are given on the market. We can say that the market determines the martingale measure uniquely in this case.

A very simple interest rate guarantee

Consider now the example where we are interested in a protection against the situation where the interest in the second period falls below 4.5%, say. Assume more precisely that we know that we will invest one unit at time 1 (for example because we receive some insurance premiums at this time), and that we want a guarantee which helps us in the scenario where $i(2)$ is 4%. We therefore consider the contract which pays at time 2 the amount $\max(1.045; 1 + i(2))$.

The discounted payment is given by

$$H = \frac{\max(1.045; 1 + i(2))}{S^0(2)} = \frac{1}{1.05\,(1 + i(2))} (1 + i(2) + (0.045 - i(2))^+),$$

$$\tag{3.61}$$

where $()^+$ is the positive part. According to Equation (3.58), the arbitrage-free price at time 0 for this contract is as follows:

$$E^Q[H] = \frac{1}{1.05} + \frac{1}{1.05}\left(q\frac{0.005}{1.04} + (1-q)0\right)$$

$$= \frac{1}{1.05} + q\frac{0.005}{1.04 \cdot 1.05}.$$

We see that the price consists of two terms, where the second term is the price for the guarantee. This price depends on the price of the zero coupon bond; see Figure 3.11.

We end this example by showing how the interest rate risk can alternatively be hedged by buying zero coupon bonds and by using the savings account. More precisely, we construct a self-financing strategy h with a terminal value $V(T, h)$, which coincides with the guarantee part of Equation (3.61); see Equation (3.57). Since the interest rate $i(2)$ is known at time 1, we can construct a figure similar to Figures 3.7 and 3.8 with prices for the interest rate guarantee. This is illustrated in Figure 3.12.

A self-financing strategy which generates the guarantee part of the contract, Equation (3.61), must satisfy the following equation:

$$V(0, h) + h^1(1)\,\Delta X(1) + h^1(2)\,\Delta X(2) = \frac{1}{1.05\,(1+i(2))}(0.045 - i(2))^+.$$

In our simple example, $\Delta X(2) = 0$ and

$$\Delta X(1) = \frac{P(1, 2)}{1.05} - P(0, 2),$$

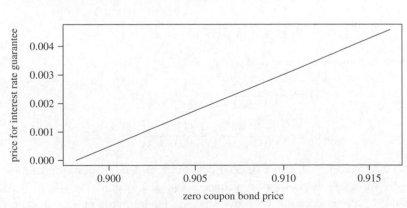

Figure 3.11. The price $q\,(0.005/1.04 \cdot 1.05)$ for the interest guarantee as a function of the price at time 0 of the zero coupon bond with maturity 2.

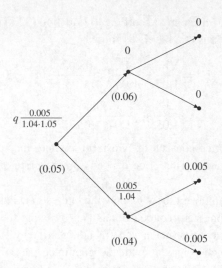

Figure 3.12. Model for the interest $i(t)$ (numbers in parentheses) and the price for the interest rate guarantee.

so that we need to determine $h^1(1)$ and $h^0(0)$ such that

$$V(0, h) + h^1(1)\left(\frac{P(1, 2)}{1.05} - P(0, 2)\right) = \frac{1}{1.05\,(1 + i(2))}(0.045 - i(2))^+.$$

This leads to two equations (one for each of the possible outcomes for the future interest):

$$h^0(0) + h^1(1)P(0, 2) + h^1(1)\left(\frac{0.962}{1.05} - P(0, 2)\right) = \frac{0.005}{1.05 \cdot 1.04};$$

$$h^0(0) + h^1(1)P(0, 2) + h^1(1)\left(\frac{0.943}{1.05} - P(0, 2)\right) = 0.$$

These two equations are solved as follows:

$$h^1(1) = \frac{0.005}{1.04(0.962 - 0.943)} \approx 0.253;$$

$$h^0(0) = -\frac{0.005 \cdot 0.943}{1.05 \cdot 1.04(0.962 - 0.943)} \approx -0.227.$$

The example shows that it is indeed possible to hedge the interest guarantee by buying 0.253 units of the zero coupon bond and by borrowing 0.227 units from the savings account. With this strategy, the insurer is protected against the drop in the interest rate. We point out that the price for the interest rate guarantee, see Figure 3.12, and the investment strategy are both independent of the original probability measure P. The measure P is only used to specify whether an event is completely unlikely (has probability 0) or not.

For a more detailed study of discrete-time bond markets, we refer to Jarrow (1996).

3.8 Models for the spot rate in continuous time

In this section we briefly describe some so-called diffusion models for the spot rate. We assume that the change in spot rate during a small time interval $(t, t + \Delta t]$ can be approximated by

$$r(t + \Delta t) - r(t) = \Delta r(t) \approx \nu(t, r(t)) \Delta t + \sigma(t, r(t)) \Delta \overline{W}(t). \tag{3.62}$$

Here, we have used the notation $\Delta \overline{W}(t) = \overline{W}(t + \Delta t) - \overline{W}(t)$; ν are σ known functions. We assume that the process $\overline{W}$ is a Brownian motion, which means that $\overline{W}$ has independent, normally distributed increments, with $\overline{W}(t) - \overline{W}(s) \sim$ N$(0, t - s)$ (mean 0 and variance $t - s$), and that $\overline{W}$ is continuous. In particular, this means that $\Delta \overline{W}(t) \sim$ N$(0, \Delta t)$.

It is possible to simulate r by choosing some interval length Δt, simulating independent normally distributed random variables $\Delta \overline{W}(t)$, and inserting these into Equation (3.62) for the computation of the increments for r.

To underline that Equation (3.62) is only valid for very small (infinitesimal) time intervals, we also use the following notation:

$$dr(t) = \nu(t, r(t)) \, dt + \sigma(t, r(t)) \, d\overline{W}(t). \tag{3.63}$$

Similarly, we can integrate Equation (3.63) and write r in the following form:

$$r(t) = r(0) + \int_0^t \nu(s, r(s)) \, ds + \int_0^t \sigma(s, r(s)) \, d\overline{W}(s). \tag{3.64}$$

The savings account S^0 is defined by letting $S^0(0) = 1$ and

$$dS^0(t) = r(t) \, S^0(t) \, dt.$$

It is well known that S^0 is then given by

$$S^0(t) = \exp \left(\int_0^t r(\tau) \, d\tau \right).$$

As mentioned above, $\mathcal{F}(t)$ is the information available at time t. We take

$$\mathcal{F}(t) = \sigma\{\overline{W}(u), \ u \le t\},$$

which means that we observe the Brownian motion $\overline{W}$. Typically this corresponds to observing the interest r.

In Section 3.7 we showed that prices of zero coupon bonds and derivatives could be calculated as an expected value under an equivalent martingale measure Q. In particular, prices are not determined by the probability measure P. In addition, we mentioned that the measure Q should be determined from the zero coupon bond prices that are given on the market. We now consider some martingale measure Q and assume that

$$dr(t) = \mu(t, r(t))\, dt + \sigma(t, r(t))\, dW(t), \qquad (3.65)$$

where the function ν has been replaced by another function μ, and where W is a Brownian motion under Q. The function σ appears in both Equations (3.63) and (3.65). We refer to Equation (3.65) as the "dynamics for r under Q." With this martingale measure Q, the price at time t of a zero coupon bond maturing at time T is given by

$$P(t, T) = E^Q\left[\frac{S^0(t)}{S^0(T)} \middle| \mathcal{F}(t) \right] = E^Q\left[\exp\left(-\int_t^T r(\tau)\, d\tau \right) \middle| \mathcal{F}(t) \right]; \qquad (3.66)$$

see, for example, Equation (3.59) for the similar result in discrete time. This ensures that the discounted price process $P(t, T)/S^0(t)$ is indeed a Q-martingale.

Estimation of parameters

The functions ν and σ, which describe the behavior of the spot rate under the probability measure P, are typically specified in such a way that they depend on some parameters. These parameters can be estimated by observing the interest rate over a certain period and then finding the value which describes the observations as well as possible, for example via maximum likelihood estimation. In contrast, the function μ describes how the interest rate evolves under the martingale measure Q, and this function cannot be estimated by observing the interest rate alone. Here one needs to include some observed zero coupon bond prices, compute Equation (3.66) for various choices of parameters, and then find the parameters which give the best description of the observed prices.

Some classical examples of interest rate models of the form in Equation (3.65) are the Vasiček model, Equation (3.67) (see Vasiček (1977)), and the Cox–Ingersoll–Ross model, Equation (3.68) (see Cox, Ingersoll and Ross (1985)):

$$dr(t) = (b - ar(t))dt + \sigma \, dW(t), \tag{3.67}$$

$$dr(t) = a(b - r(t)) \, dt + \sigma \sqrt{r(t)} \, dW(t). \tag{3.68}$$

Both models have the special property that the interest rate returns to a certain level. For the Vasiček model with parameterization, Equation (3.67), this level is given by b/a, and for the Cox–Ingersoll–Ross model, Equation (3.68), this level is b. These two models are examples of so-called affine models, which allow for relatively simple formulas for zero coupon bond prices.

3.8.1 Affine models

What is an affine model? How can prices for zero coupon bonds be calculated in the Vasiček and Cox–Ingersoll–Ross models? Is it possible to determine the instantaneous forward rates in these models?

An interest rate model of the form given in Equation (3.65) is said to be affine if

$$\mu(t, r(t)) = \alpha(t)r(t) + \beta(t),$$

$$\sigma(t, r(t)) = \sqrt{\gamma(t)r(t) + \delta(t)},$$

where α, β, γ and δ are known functions. (Thus, for fixed t, $\mu(t, \cdot)$ and $\sigma^2(t, \cdot)$ are affine functions of r.)

We have the following general result for the price of a zero coupon bond with maturity T (see, for example, Björk (2004, Proposition 17.2) for a proof of this result):

$$P(t, T) = E^Q \left[\exp\left(-\int_t^T r(\tau) \, d\tau \right) \middle| \mathcal{F}(t) \right] = \exp\left(A(t, T) - B(t, T)r(t) \right), \tag{3.69}$$

where A and B solve the following equations:

$$\frac{\partial}{\partial t} B(t, T) + \alpha(t)B(t, T) - \frac{1}{2}\gamma(t)(B(t, T))^2 = -1,$$

$$\frac{\partial}{\partial t} A(t, T) = \beta(t)B(t, T) - \frac{1}{2}\delta(t)(B(t, T))^2,$$

with $B(T, T) = A(T, T) = 0$. The equations can be solved by first determining the function B from the first equation and then inserting this solution in the second equation in order to find A.

The instantaneous forward rates at time t can be found via Equation (3.29) from Definition 3.5:

$$f(t, T) = -\frac{\partial}{\partial T} \log(P(t, T)) = r(t)\frac{\partial}{\partial T}B(t, T) - \frac{\partial}{\partial T}A(t, T). \qquad (3.70)$$

The Vasiček model

With the model given in Equation (3.67), we obtain by solving the differential equations for A and B the following:

$$B(t, T) = \frac{1}{a}\left(1 - e^{-a(T-t)}\right),$$

$$A(t, T) = \frac{(B(t, T) - T + t)(ab - (1/2)\sigma^2)}{a^2} - \frac{\sigma^2(B(t, T))^2}{4a}.$$

The forward rates at time t can be determined by differentiating these expressions with respect to T and then inserting the results into Equation (3.70). In this way, it can be shown that

$$f(t, T) = r(t)e^{-a(T-t)} + \left(\frac{b}{a} - \frac{\sigma^2}{2a^2}\right)\left(1 - e^{-a(T-t)}\right)$$

$$+ e^{-a(T-t)}\frac{2\sigma^2 B(t, T)}{4a}. \qquad (3.71)$$

Since $e^{-a(T-t)} \to 0$ as $T \to \infty$, we see that $B(t, T) \to 1/a$. This shows that the forward rates given by Equation (3.71) converge to

$$\frac{b}{a} - \frac{\sigma^2}{2a^2}, \qquad (3.72)$$

as the maturity goes to infinity. Figure 3.13 presents a few examples of the shape of the forward rate curve. We see that the shape depends crucially on the level of the interest rate $r(t)$ at the time considered, in particular, whether the interest rate $r(t)$ is above or below the level given by Equation (3.72). A couple of simulations for r can be found in Figure 3.14. The Vasiček model has the rather unfortunate property that it allows for negative interest rates. Similarly, the forward rates might become negative, a phenomenon which is most likely for large values of σ. This is not the case for the Cox–Ingersoll–Ross model, which does not allow for negative interest rates.

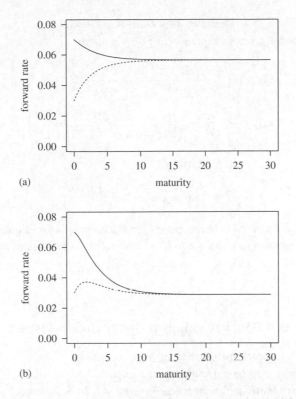

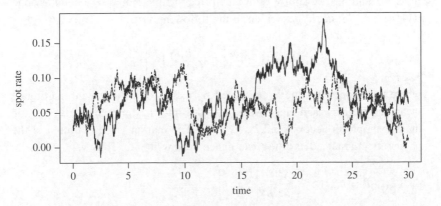

Figure 3.13. Forward rates in the Vasiček model with high initial interest $r(0) = 0.07$ (solid curves) and low initial interest $r(0) = 0.03$ (dashed curves). Parameters used: $a = 0.36$, $b/a = 0.06$. (a) Low standard deviation, $\sigma = 0.03$; (b) high standard deviation, $\sigma = 0.09$.

Figure 3.14. Two possible simulations for r in the Vasiček model with initial interest rate $r(0) = 0.03$. Parameters: $a = 0.36$, $b/a = 0.06$, $\sigma = 0.03$.

The Cox–Ingersoll–Ross model

With the model given in Equation (3.68), we obtain

$$B(t, T) = \frac{2(e^{\xi(T-t)} - 1)}{(\xi + a)(e^{\xi(T-t)} - 1) + 2\xi},$$

$$A(t, T) = \frac{2ab}{\sigma^2} \log\left(\frac{2\xi e^{(a+\xi)\frac{T-t}{2}}}{(\xi + a)(e^{\xi(T-t)} - 1) + 2\xi} \right),$$

where

$$\xi = \sqrt{a^2 + 2\sigma^2}.$$

Again, it is possible to determine the forward rates by using Equation (3.70). However, the formulas turn out to be considerably more complicated than the ones obtained for the Vasiček model.

3.9 Market values in insurance revisited

We end this chapter by illustrating how the market values of the guaranteed payments may be calculated as the expected value under an equivalent martingale measure of the discounted payments. In Sections 3.2 and 3.3 we presented methods for deriving the market value of the guaranteed payments in a model where the interest rate could be stochastic. These results were stated in terms of either prices of zero coupon bonds or forward rates. In Sections 3.7 and 3.8 we showed how the price at time t of a zero coupon bond with maturity n could be written in the following form:

$$P(t, n) = E^Q\left[\frac{S^0(t)}{S^0(n)} \,\middle|\, \mathcal{F}(t) \right],$$

where the expected value is calculated by using some equivalent martingale measure Q. This result can now be inserted into the formulas derived in the main example in Sections 3.2.7 and 3.3.5. The market value at time u of the payments guaranteed at time t can hence be rewritten as follows:

$$V^g(t, u) = b^a(t)\, E^Q\left[\frac{S^0(u)}{S^0(n)} \,\middle|\, \mathcal{F}(u) \right]_{n-u}p_{x+u}$$

$$+ \int_u^n E^Q\left[\frac{S^0(u)}{S^0(s)} \,\middle|\, \mathcal{F}(u) \right]_{s-u}p_{x+u}(\mu(x+s)b^{ad} - \pi)ds, \quad (3.73)$$

which can be recast as

$$V^g(t, u) = E^Q \left[b^a(t) \frac{S^0(u)}{S^0(n)}{}_{n-u}P_{x+u} \right.$$

$$\left. + \int_u^n \frac{S^0(u)}{S^0(s)}{}_{s-u}P_{x+u} \left(\mu(x+s)b^{ad} - \pi \right) ds \, \middle| \, \mathcal{F}(u) \right]. \quad (3.74)$$

In models with a continuously added interest rate, we can use the fact that

$$\frac{S^0(u)}{S^0(s)} = \exp\left(-\int_u^s r(\tau)\,d\tau \right)$$

to rewrite Equation (3.74) as follows:

$$V^g(t, u) = E^Q \left[b^a(t) \exp\left(-\int_u^n r(\tau)\,d\tau \right){}_{n-u}P_{x+u} \right.$$

$$\left. + \int_u^n \exp\left(-\int_u^s r(\tau)\,d\tau \right){}_{s-u}P_{x+u} \left(\mu(x+s)b^{ad} - \pi \right) ds \, \middle| \, \mathcal{F}(u) \right].$$
$$(3.75)$$

This brings to the surface the consequences for the market value, Equation (3.24), of allowing for stochastic interest rates. In these situations, market values are calculated as expected values under the equivalent martingale measure.

The only randomness in Equation (3.75) is that related to the development of the interest rate, i.e. the uncertainty related to the policy holder's lifetime has been averaged out. However, it is possible to work with the payment process $B(t, s)$ introduced in Chapter 2, which described the payments guaranteed at time t. This process is defined by

$$dB(t, s) = -\pi I(s)\,ds + b^{ad}\,dN(s) + b^a(t)\,I(s)\,d\epsilon(s, n),$$

where $I(s)$ is the indicator for the event that the insured is alive at time s, N is a counting process which counts the number of deaths (and hence which is either zero or one) and $\epsilon(s, n) = 1$ if $s \geq n$ and zero otherwise. With this notation, Equation (3.75) can finally be rewritten as follows:

$$V^g(t, u) = E^Q \left[\int_u^n \exp\left(-\int_u^s r(\tau)\,d\tau \right) dB(t, s) \, \middle| \, \mathcal{F}(u) \right]. \quad (3.76)$$

Here, the uncertainty related to the policy holder's lifetime and the uncertainty related to the future development of the interest rate appear simultaneously.

The market value is calculated directly as an expected value under a martingale measure of the random variable

$$\int_u^n \exp\left(-\int_u^s r(\tau)\,\mathrm{d}\tau\right)\,\mathrm{d}B(t,s). \qquad (3.77)$$

From a theoretical point of view, Equation (3.77) is the natural starting point for a discussion of market values in life and pension insurance. This analysis is continued in Chapter 6.

This chapter has focused on determining the market value for the guaranteed payments in situations where the interest rate is stochastic. In this situation, it is natural to replace the usual discount factors by zero coupon bond prices. Moreover, we have shown how forward rates can be applied to derive market values and the individual bonus potential. Finally, it has been demonstrated that the market values can alternatively be computed by using equivalent martingale measures. The next chapter investigates how the market value of the total liability is affected by changes in the interest and in other assets, for example stocks. Such considerations typically rely on a specification of the bonus and investment policy of the insurance company.

4
Bonus, binomial and Black–Scholes

4.1 Introduction

In Chapter 2 we discussed some aspects of valuation assuming only one possible investment with a deterministic interest rate. In Chapter 3 we introduced a stochastic interest rate and a bond market and we discussed the consequences for valuation in general and for valuation of guaranteed payments in particular. In this chapter we again assume a deterministic interest rate, but, in return, we introduce the possibility of investing in stocks and study the total reserve including the reserve for guaranteed payments. In Section 4.6 we comment on the combination of stochastic interest rates and investment in stocks.

The total reserve in connection with a life insurance contract can, under certain conditions, be calculated using a simple retrospective accumulation. The condition is that the total reserve which has been accumulated at the termination of the contract equals the pension sum paid out. We consider the type of insurance where the surplus is accumulated in the technical reserve leading to an increasing pension sum. Here, the condition is that the undistributed reserve, which is the total reserve minus the technical reserve, at the termination of the contract equals zero. The condition and its consequences are formalized and studied in Chapter 2.

One very simple situation in Chapter 2 was the financial market, which consists of one investment possibility only, namely the possibility of investing in the risk-free interest rate. Furthermore, this risk-free interest rate is assumed to be deterministic. In Chapter 3 we introduced a more realistic stochastic model for the interest rate and we discussed the consequences for the entries in the market balance scheme, in particular for the market reserve for guaranteed payments and the individual bonus potential. In this chapter, we introduce investment possibilities in so-called risky assets or stocks and study their consequences for the total reserve. The collective bonus potential is the difference between the total reserve and the larges of either the technical reserve or the market reserve for guaranteed payments. Thus, the collective bonus potential is indirectly determined by calculating the total reserve.

The purpose of this chapter is to develop theoretically substantiated methods for the valuation of the bonus obligations under investment in stocks. The starting point is two classical stock price models in mathematical finance: the binomial model and the Black–Scholes model. The binomial model is the simplest non-trivial stock model one can imagine; pricing in the binomial model is not much more than the solution of two equations with two unknowns. This provides a simple framework for the discussion of the various difficulties arising from a market valuation of insurance liabilities.

The Black–Scholes model is a classical stock price model based on normally distributed returns over small time intervals. The concepts of financial mathematics are mathematically much more involved in the Black–Scholes model than in the binomial model. The power of the Black–Scholes model is that, in spite of its complexity, it has some simple and appealing qualities that provide unique answers to certain pricing problems. This makes it a popular stock price model in practice. The authors of the Black–Scholes model were awarded the 1997 Nobel Prize in Economics.

The Black–Scholes model has been the preferred model for the financial market in literature connecting bonus in life insurance with financial theory. The starting point is typically a Black–Scholes market, within which the authors give a formalization of the special payment streams appearing in life insurance contracts with bonus and possibly other options such as the surrender option. Seminal references are Briys and de Varenne (1994, 1997), which describe the bonus option as a financial derivative within the terminology of financial mathematics. Further important contributions are Grosen and Jørgensen (1997, 2000, 2002), Hansen and Miltersen (2002), Miltersen and Persson (2000, 2003), and also Bacinello (2001) should be mentioned. A complete reference list should also contain Møller (2000) and Steffensen (2001), which deal with the issues on a broader level.

What mainly distinguishes the abovementioned contributions from each other is the way in which the bonus option is formalized, or in another way: precisely how is the value of assets reflected in the bonus that is paid out? This is a fundamental question in this chapter. Furthermore, we go through some calculations for certain relevant formalizations.

As in Chapter 2, we consider an endowment insurance paid by a level premium, in which dividends are used to increase the pension sum. However, we disregard the mortality risk by setting the mortality intensity to zero.

We wish to deal with the financial aspects exclusively. With appropriate arguments and an assumption of diversified mortality risk, all formulas can be adapted to a situation including mortality. The actuarial notation is limited to a discount factor v and a t-year annuity $a_{\overline{t}|}$, which both appear with decorations depending on the underlying interest rate. The same notation is used in discrete and continuous time; the relevant version will be obvious from the context.

In Section 4.2 we describe the relevant quantities in the market balance scheme in a discrete- time model. We calculate the quantities for one formalization of the connection between the bonus and the stock market. In Section 4.3 we describe the binomial model in general. In Section 4.4 the Black–Scholes model is described and the celebrated Black–Scholes equation and Black–Scholes formula are stated and partly derived. In Section 4.5 we show how the Black–Scholes model, the Black–Scholes equation and the Black–Scholes formula may play important roles in the valuation of life insurance contracts with bonus. In Section 4.6 we discuss briefly some generalizations of the considered market models.

The text contains a number of repetitions of definitions and arguments. This emphasizes the cross-sectional similarities. The notions of discrete- and continuous-time financial mathematics contain similarities. Nevertheless, they are introduced in both connections such that both similarities and differences stand out. Correspondingly, the discrete- and continuous-time insurance models are closely connected.

4.2 Discrete-time insurance model

In this section we consider a discrete-time insurance model and the dynamics of various quantities of relevance for valuation within this model. The model is very simple and not very realistic, but it shows a lot of the problems that appear when trying to valuate insurance claims by means of so-called arbitrage arguments. An arbitrage argument is the argument for the value of a claim that if it had any other value, it would be possible, by tactical investments, to obtain risk-free gains beyond what is offered by the financial market.

We formalize the notion of arbitrage and other concepts from mathematical finance in Section 4.3, where we give a systematic introduction to the binomial model. However, we start in this section by studying a relatively complicated example of a product which can be treated within the binomial model. Hereby, the perspectives of the binomial model are emphasized to readers who prefer to think of finance in terms of life insurance and bonus. Møller (2001a) shows some applications of the binomial model to unit-linked insurance.

The insurance contract that we consider in this section is a modification of the main example in Chapter 2, such that it appears as a purely financial product in discrete time and such that investments, on the other hand, take place in a so- called binomial market introduced below. A lot of the quantities relate to quantities in Chapter 2, to which we refer for an interpretation. The insurance sum paid out at time n is paid for by an annuity-due with premium payment π. We speak of the periods as years, but they could cover other time intervals.

The technical reserve V^* and the second order basis that is made up by the second order interest rate r^δ are connected by the following equation which accumulates the technical reserve:

$$V^*(t) = \left(1 + r^\delta(t)\right) V^*(t-1) + \pi 1_{(t<n)}, \tag{4.1}$$

$$V^*(0) = \pi.$$

We also speak of the second order interest rate as the bonus interest rate and a process of bonus interest rates $\left(r^\delta(t)\right)_{t=1,\ldots,n}$ as a bonus strategy.

The technical reserve and the first order basis which is made up by the first order interest rate r^* are connected by the following equation which accumulates the technical reserve:

$$V^*(t) = (1 + r^*) V^*(t-1) + \pi 1_{(t<n)} + \delta(t), \tag{4.2}$$

$$V^*(0) = \pi,$$

where the dividend payment $\delta(t)$ is given by

$$\delta(t) = \left(r^\delta(t) - r^*\right) V^*(t-1),$$

such that the deposits stemming from Equations (4.1) and (4.2) coincide.

The sum $b(t)$ guaranteed at time t is determined for a given technical reserve $V^*(t)$ by the equivalence relation, as follows:

$$V^*(t) = b(t) \left(v^*\right)^{n-t} - \pi a^*_{\overline{n-t}|}.$$

In Chapter 2 we introduced the total reserve U, which is obtained by an accumulation by the real basis:

$$U(t) = (1 + r) U(t-1) + \pi 1_{(t<n)},$$

$$U(0) = \pi.$$

Here, we let r be constant and, in particular, known at time $t-1$. Thus, at time $t-1$, we know which investment gains we have in prospect the following year. We assume that $r \geq r^*$.

The idea now is to generalize this construction such that we have the opportunity to invest part of the money in an asset with risk. The most simple asset with risk is an asset which, given its value at time $t-1$, at time t takes one of two values but such that the value at time t is not known at time $t-1$. This value is not known until time t. We let $S(t)$ denote the price of the risky asset at time t and let the dynamics of S be given by

$$S(t) = (1 + Z(t)) S(t-1).$$

Here, $Z(t)$ is a stochastic variable which takes the value u (for *up*) with the probability $p(u)$ and the value d (for *down*) with the probability $p(d)$. We let the company buy $\eta(t)$ of these assets at time $t-1$. Obviously, $\eta(t)$ must be decided at time $t-1$. The company cannot wait until time t, experience the new asset price and then decide how many assets to buy at time $t-1$. This is the intuitive content of the property *predictable*, which we also require from our investments later on.

The total reserve U at time t is the value U at time $t-1$ plus premiums plus capital gains. The capital gains consist of interest earned on the part of U which was *not* invested in the risky asset at time $t-1$, $U(t-1) - \eta(t)S(t-1)$, and the change of the price of the portfolio of risky assets which follows from changes in asset prices. Thus,

$$U(t) = U(t-1) + r(U(t-1) - \eta(t)S(t-1))$$
$$+ \eta(t)(S(t) - S(t-1)) + \pi 1_{(t<n)}$$
$$= (1+r)U(t-1) + \eta(t)S(t-1)(Z(t) - r) + \pi 1_{(t<n)},$$

$$U(0) = \pi.$$

The undistributed reserve X is given residually by

$$X(t) = U(t) - V^*(t),$$

and we obtain the following:

$$X(t) = (1+r)X(t-1) + \eta(t)S(t-1)(Z(t) - r) + c(t) - \delta(t),$$

where

$$c(t) = (r(t) - r^*(t))V^*(t-1).$$

Thus, the value X at time t is the value of X at time $t-1$ plus capital gains plus the surplus contribution $c(t)$ minus the dividend payment $\delta(t)$.

In Chapter 2, we also introduced the following prospective quantity for the total reserve and for the undistributed reserve:

$$V(t) = b(n) v^{n-t} - \pi a_{\overline{n-t}|}.$$

This reflects the fact that the reserve is set aside to meet future obligations. The problem with this quantity is that, in general, it requires a formalization of the future bonus strategy, and we want to avoid that. Very appropriately, if we arrange the bonus strategy such that $X(n) = 0$, then $V(t) = U(t)$; see Chapter 2. By fulfilment of the $X(n) = 0$, we can work with the retrospective quantities exclusively and disregard the future bonus strategy.

The introduction of risky investments makes the situation more difficult. If the bonus strategy is linked to the gains obtained by risky investments, we do not in general know $b(n)$ at time t.

On one hand, we wish that $b(n)$, in one way or another, is linked to the development in asset prices. On the other hand, if we assume that it is not linked to anything else, in the sense that the development in asset prices determine $b(n)$ completely, then this can be considered as a so-called contingent claim, no matter how complex the link may be. Hereafter, the mathematics of finance concludes a modification of the prospective quantity as follows:

$$V(t) = E_t^Q [b(n)] v^{n-t} - \pi a_{\overline{n-t}|}. \tag{4.3}$$

Here, E_t^Q denotes the expectation given the development in the financial market until time t and under a very special probability measure Q, under which the outcomes that the risky asset goes up and down, respectively, happen with the following probabilities:

$$\begin{aligned} q(u) &= \frac{r-d}{u-d}, \\ q(d) &= \frac{u-r}{u-d}. \end{aligned} \tag{4.4}$$

For now, we pull this probability measure from a hat, but later we discover arguments for its construction.

Finally, we need to define the market value of the payments guaranteed at time t. The following definitions are in correspondence with Equation (4.3). The market value of the guaranteed payments, $V^g(t)$, is given by

$$V^g(t) = b(t) v^{n-t} - \pi a_{\overline{n-t}|}.$$

The market value of the unguaranteed payments, also referred to as the bonus potential $V^b(t)$, is given by

$$V^b(t) = \left(E_t^Q[b(n)] - b(t)\right)v^{n-t}.$$

In correspondence with the valuation formula, Equation (4.3), and the premium paid at time 0, the bonus strategy must obey the equivalence relation:

$$V(0) = \pi.$$

A natural question to ask here is whether there exists a situation such that the constraint $X(n) = 0$ again secures that the prospective quantities coincide with the retrospective quantities, so saving us from a discussion on future bonus strategies. Before we continue, we must ask ourselves whether there exists an investment strategy such that we can construct a bonus strategy leading to $X(n) = 0$? The answer is yes, obviously, since the investment $\eta = 0$ brings us back to the situation in Chapter 2. In the following, we give a sufficient condition on η, less trivial than $\eta = 0$, for a bonus strategy leading to $X(n) = 0$. Let us check the consequence of the constraint. We have that

$$X(n) = 0 \Rightarrow \tag{4.5}$$
$$b(n) = V^*(n) = U(n) \Rightarrow$$
$$V(t) = v^{n-t}E_t^Q[U(n)] - \pi a_{\overline{n-t}|}$$
$$= v^{n-t}\left(v^{-(n-t)}\left(U(t) + \pi a_{\overline{n-t}|}\right)\right) - \pi a_{\overline{n-t}|}$$
$$= U(t).$$

In the third line we use the fact that the interest on $U(t)$ and the premiums paid to U over $(t, n]$ under Q are expected to equal r. This can be seen since Q is exactly constructed such that

$$E^Q[Z] = r;$$

see Equation (4.4). In Chapter 2 we obtained, for risk-free investments, the following:

$$X(n) = 0 \Rightarrow V(t) = U(t).$$

The implications following Equation (4.5) generalize this result to the situation with risky investments.

A sufficient condition on η for $X(n) = 0$ is that we do not risk losing parts of V^g via risky investments, no matter what the outcome of Z. We can write this using an inequality:

$$U(t, d) - V^g(t, d) \geq 0,$$

where the argument d means that the outcome $Z(t) = d$ is plugged in.

If the constraint $X(n) = 0$ is fulfilled, we have seen that $V(t) = U(t)$. If we add the classical solvency rule $X(t) \geq 0$, a sufficient condition on η is that we do not risk losing parts of V^* via risky investments, no matter that the outcome of Z. We can write this using an inequality:

$$X(t, d) \geq 0,$$

where, again, the argument d means that the outcome $Z(t) = d$ is plugged in.

The conditions limit the investments in risky assets. However, one may wish to disregard these conditions. One can formalize a general investment strategy where the proportion of funds invested in risky assets, $\eta(t) S(t-1) / X(t-1)$, is a function Θ of $(t, V^*(t-1), X(t-1))$, i.e.

$$\frac{\eta(t) S(t-1)}{X(t-1)} = \Theta(t, V^*(t-1), X(t-1)).$$

Then,

$$X(t) = (1 + r + \Theta(t, V^*(t-1), X(t-1))(Z(t) - r)) X(t-1)$$
$$+ c(t) - \delta(t).$$

One can for example think of the special case where the value of investments in S is a constant proportion θ of U:

$$\eta(t) S(t-1) = \theta U(t-1) \Leftrightarrow$$

$$\Theta(t, V^*(t-1), X(t-1)) = \frac{\eta(t) S(t-1)}{X(t-1)}$$

$$= \frac{\theta U(t-1)}{X(t-1)}$$

$$= \theta \frac{V^*(t-1) + X(t-1)}{X(t-1)}.$$

If one disregards the condition $X(n) = 0$ in the market with risky assets, the future bonus strategy is inevitably brought into the market values of unguaranteed payments. Then a natural question is: how is the bonus strategy linked to the financial market? One possibility is to suggest an appropriate explicit link which makes sense both from an economical and a mathematical point of view. Many articles on the subject, introducing financial valuation in life insurance with bonus, take as their starting points a certain explicit specification of the link and the authors then consider quantities like that gives in Equation (4.3).

It is important to discuss how the bonus strategy is currently decided, but just as important is to emphasize that there are no true or false answers to the above question. Certainly, there exist answers which do not conform with legislation but, on the other hand, legislation usually gives some degrees of freedom. What we can show is that, given our simple financial market and one qualitative specification of the link between bonus and the financial market, there are no quantitative degrees of freedom if the bonus strategy has to be fair from a financial point of view.

We take as our starting point the fact that the size of X determines the bonus strategy. We let the bonus interest rate be linked to X such that it is determined by

$$r^\delta(t) = r^*(t) + \frac{\Phi(t, X(t-1))}{V^*(t-1)},$$

where Φ is a function specifying how the bonus interest depends on X. Hereby,

$$
\begin{aligned}
c(t) - \delta(t) &= \left(r(t) - r^\delta(t)\right) V^*(t-1) \\
&= \left(r(t) - r^*(t) - \frac{\Phi(t, X(t-1))}{V^*(t-1)}\right) V^*(t-1) \\
&= c(t) - \Phi(t, X(t-1)).
\end{aligned}
$$

One can think of a function Φ in the following form:

$$\Phi(t, x) = (\beta(t) + \alpha(t) x)^+, \tag{4.6}$$

where α and β are deterministic functions of t. In Section 4.2.1 we consider a two-period example with precisely this choice of function Φ. We speak of Φ as the contract function and note that a contract function in the form given by Equation (4.6) contains two interesting constructions as special cases. If $\beta(t) = 0$ and $\alpha(t) = \alpha > 0$, we obtain

$$\Phi(t, X(t-1)) = \alpha(X(t-1))^+,$$

i.e. that the bonus is set as a constant part α of the undistributed reserve if this is positive.

If $\alpha(t) = 1$ and $\beta(t) = -K < 0$, we obtain

$$\Phi(t, X(t-1)) = (X(t-1) - K)^+,$$

i.e. that the bonus is set such that the part of the undistributed reserve which exceeds a constant buffer, K, is paid out.

4.2.1 Two-period model

In this section we consider a contract over two time periods and discuss bonus interest rates and investments. We start out by giving in Figure 4.1 an overview of the different quantities introduced in the previous section in the two periods. Hereafter, we specify the connection between the bonus interest rate and the financial market.

We assume that the company at time 0 decides upon a bonus interest rate for the first year that does not depend on the capital gains in that year. Hereby, $r^\delta(1)$ becomes independent of $Z(1)$. Correspondingly, we let the bonus interest rate in the second year be independent of the capital gains in that year. However, we let the bonus interest rate in the second year depend on the capital gains in the first year. Then we can write that $r^\delta(2)$ becomes dependent on $Z(1)$ but independent of $Z(2)$. The consequence is that (see Figure 4.1) $V^*(1)$ and $b(1)$ are independent of $Z(1)$, whereas $b(2)$ is independent of $Z(2)$.

This accords with the conception of the bonus interest rate as an interest rate which is decided for the subsequent year, independently of the capital gains in that year but dependent on the capital gains in the preceding years. In that sense, the bonus interest rate is always "a year behind" the capital gains. Because of this construction, we need two periods for an illustration: one period to earn capital gains and one period for the redistribution. A construction where the capital gains are redistributed in the same year as they are earned could have been illustrated using a one-period model.

We let the bonus interest rate in the second year depend on the capital gains in the first year through the following formula:

$$r^\delta(2) = r^*(2) + \frac{(\beta + \alpha X(1))^+}{V^*(1)},$$

$$
\begin{bmatrix} S(0) \\ V^*(0) \\ U(0) \\ b(0) \\ V^g(0) \\ V^b(0) \\ V(0) \end{bmatrix}
\rightarrow
\begin{bmatrix} S(1) \\ V^*(1) \\ U(1) \\ b(1) \\ V^g(1) \\ V^b(1) \\ V(1) \end{bmatrix}
\rightarrow
[V^*(2)] = [b(2)]
$$

Figure 4.1. A two-period insurance model.

and we obtain the following expression for the technical reserve after the second year:

$$V^*(2) = \left(2 + r^\delta(1)\right)\left(1 + r^\delta(2)\right)\pi,$$

which only depends on the capital gains in the first year. As a curiosity, we derive the market value of the unguaranteed payments after the first year, the so-called bonus potential, as follows:

$$
\begin{aligned}
V^b(1) &= \frac{E_1^Q[V^*(2)] - b(1)}{1+r} \\
&= \frac{\left(2 + r^\delta(1)\right)\left(1 + r^\delta(2)\right)\pi - b(1)}{1+r} \\
&= \frac{\left(2 + r^\delta(1)\right)\left(1 + r^\delta(2)\right)\pi - V^*(1)\left(1 + r^*(2)\right)}{1+r} \\
&= \frac{\left(2 + r^\delta(1)\right)\left(1 + r^\delta(2)\right)\pi - \left(2 + r^\delta(1)\right)\pi\left(1 + r^*(2)\right)}{1+r} \\
&= \frac{\left(2 + r^\delta(1)\right)\left(r^\delta(2) - r^*(2)\right)}{1+r}\pi \\
&= \frac{\left(\beta + \alpha X(1)\right)^+}{1+r}.
\end{aligned}
$$

We see that this simple construction of bonus interest rates corresponds to a situation where the market value of unguaranteed payments after the first year is simply a part of the undistributed reserve.

Hereafter, we are interested in a connection between a fair investment η and a fair pair of parameters in the bonus strategy (α, β). We determine this connection simply by the equivalence relation

$$V(0) = \pi,$$

which yields

$$\frac{1}{(1+r)^2}E^Q[V^*(2)] - \frac{\pi}{1+r} = \pi \Leftrightarrow$$

$$\left(2 + r^\delta(1)\right)\left(1 + E^Q\left[r^\delta(2)\right]\right) = 1 + r + (1+r)^2 \Leftrightarrow$$

$$\left(2 + r^\delta(1)\right)\left(1 + q(u)r^\delta(2, u) + q(d)r^\delta(2, d)\right) = (1+r)(2+r).$$

Here, $r^\delta(2, u)$ and $r^\delta(2, d)$ are the bonus interest rates in year 2 corresponding to the stock going up and down in year 1, respectively. If

$$\beta + \alpha X(1, d) < 0 < \beta + \alpha X(1, u), \tag{4.7}$$

we have that $r^\delta(2,u) > r^* = r^\delta(2,d)$, such that a bonus is paid out in the second year if and only if the risky asset goes up in the first year, and furthermore we have

$$\left(2+r^\delta(1)\right)\left(1+r^*+q(u)\left(\frac{\beta+\alpha X(1,u)}{V^*(1)}\right)\right)$$

$$= (1+r)(2+r) \Leftrightarrow$$

$$\left(2+r^\delta(1)\right)\left(1+r^*+q(u)\frac{\beta+\alpha\left(r-r^\delta(1)+(\eta s/\pi)(u-r)\right)}{(2+r^\delta(1))}\right)$$

$$= (1+r)(2+r),$$

which implies that

$$q(u)\left(\beta+\alpha\left(r-r^\delta(1)+\frac{\eta s}{\pi}(u-r)\right)\right)$$

$$= (1+r)(2+r)-\left(2+r^\delta(1)\right)(1+r^*). \tag{4.8}$$

Equation (4.8) can determine fair combinations of the three parameters (α, β, η), and we then have to verify Equation (4.7). At least, this is what we claim at this moment because we still have not presented the argument for the application of the artificial probability measure Q, but we shall come back to this later.

In the rest of this section, we consider a numerical example where we let $s = 1$ and $\pi = 1$. We let $\beta = 0$ such that the bonus interest rate is determined exclusively by the parameter α. The interest rate r is 5%, the bonus interest rate in year 1 is also 5%, while the guaranteed interest rate is 3%. The risky asset can raise by 20% or fall by 10%, i.e. $u = 20\%$, $d = -10\%$. With these numbers we find that $q(u) = q(d) = 1/2$, i.e. we determine the market values under a probability measure where the risky asset both rises and falls with probability 1/2. Before determination of α and η, we can readily verify Equation (4.7). Since $r^\delta(1) = r$, we have that $c(1) - \delta(1) = 0$ such that $X(1) = \eta s(Z(t) - r)$. But with $\beta = 0$, Equation (4.7) is then obviously true. Equation (4.8) now gives a fair connection between α and η:

$$\alpha\eta = 0.55.$$

Thus, we have that the redistribution parameter α is a hyperbola as a function of the investment parameter η. We see that if our proportion of the risky asset is less than 55%, we have $\alpha > 1$. A redistribution parameter larger than unity makes sense since there is a bonus potential in the second year which must be redistributed but which is not included in $X(1)$.

In Figure 4.2 we find all quantities for the case where we have placed 60% in the risky asset, i.e. $\eta = 0.6$. This gives a redistribution parameter α

$$\begin{bmatrix} S(1)=1.2 \\ V^*(1)=2.05 \\ X(1)=0.09 \\ b(1)=2.11 \\ V^{\mathrm{g}}(1)=2.01 \\ V^{\mathrm{b}}(1)=0.08 \\ V(1)=2.09 \end{bmatrix} \rightarrow [b(2)=2.19]$$

$$\begin{bmatrix} S(0)=1 \\ V^*(0)=1 \\ X(0)=0 \\ b(0)=2.09 \\ V^{\mathrm{g}}(0)=0.94 \\ V^{\mathrm{b}}(0)=0.06 \\ V(0)=1 \end{bmatrix} \begin{matrix} \nearrow \\ \searrow \end{matrix}$$

$$\begin{bmatrix} S(1)=0.9 \\ V^*(1)=2.05 \\ X(1)=-0.09 \\ b(1)=2.11 \\ V^{\mathrm{g}}(1)=2.01 \\ V^{\mathrm{b}}(1)=0 \\ V(1)=2.01 \end{bmatrix} \rightarrow [b(2)=2.11]$$

Figure 4.2. Two-period insurance model.

of approximately 0.91. Figure 4.2 shows the outcomes of all quantities in Figure 4.1, depending on whether the risky asset goes up or down in the first period.

We see that the technical reserve after the first year is 2.05, independent of the outcome of the risky asset in that year. In contrast, the development of the technical reserve after the second year, and thus the terminal payment, equals 2.19 or 2.11, depending on the outcome of the risky asset. If the risky asset goes up in the first year, the bonus interest rate in the second year becomes 7%. If the risky asset goes down in the first year, the bonus interest rate in the second year equals the first order interest rate, 3%. If the risky asset goes up in the first year, both the individual and the collective bonus potential are 0.04 after the first year. If the risky asset goes down in the first year, all safety margins are lost and both bonus potentials are zero. The difference between the bonus potential after the first year in the two scenarios pays the difference between the two benefits paid out after two years.

So far we have simply claimed how to calculate all values. We now give a brief argument for these values as they look in the example above. The argument simply shows how it is possible, by tactical investments of the premiums, precisely to obtain the benefits that are due after the second year. Hereby, the values above become natural as reserves for future obligations.

We calculate the investment which is required after the first year if the payment after the second year has to be met. There are two cases corresponding to the risky asset going up or down in the first year.

Consider the case where the risky asset goes up. Now, the risky asset can either go up or down in the second year. No matter what happens to the risky asset in the second year, we need 2.19 after the second year. If we let $h^1(2, u)$ denote the number of risky assets and $h^0(2, u)$ denote the investment in the risk-free interest rate, we obtain the following equation system:

$$h^1(2, u)\,1.44 + h^0(2, u)\,1.10 = 2.19,$$

$$h^1(2, u)\,1.08 + h^0(2, u)\,1.10 = 2.19,$$

where 1.44 and 1.08 are the prices of the risky asset after the second year depending on the outcome of the risky asset in the second year and given that the asset goes up in the first year. The number 1.10 is $(1.05)^2$ rounded off, which is the value after two years of one unit at time 0 including accumulated interest rate by 5%. The solution is given by

$$h^1(2, u) = 0,\, h^0(2, u) = 1.99,$$

and we note that the price of this investment is precisely given by

$$1.99 \times 1.05 = 2.09 = V(1, u).$$

A corresponding system is obtained if the asset goes down in the first year:

$$h^1(2, d)\,1.08 + h^0(2, d)\,1.10 = 2.11,$$

$$h^1(2, d)\,0.81 + h^0(2, d)\,1.10 = 2.11,$$

which has the following solution:

$$h^1(2, d) = 0,\, h^0(2, d) = 1.92,$$

and the price for this investment is given by

$$1.92 \times 1.05 = 2.01 = V(1, d).$$

As one would expect, we shall not invest in the risky asset in the second year, no matter its outcome in the first, since the bonus interest rate in the second year is independent of the outcome of the risky asset in that year.

Now we know what to do after the first year no matter the outcome in the first year, but what should we do at time 0? Here again, we can set up a system where we are trying to hit what it takes to establish the required portfolios after the first year, no matter the outcome in the first year. We know, however, that in addition to the capital gains after the first year we also receive a premium payment of one, such that the equation system becomes

$$h^1(1)\,1.20 + h^0(1)\,1.05 + 1 = 2.09,$$
$$h^1(1)\,0.90 + h^0(1)\,1.05 + 1 = 2.01.$$

This system has the following solution:

$$h^0(1) = 0.74,\ h^1(1) = 0.26,$$

and, finally, we see that this investment has exactly the value π:

$$0.74 \times 1 + 0.26 \times 1 = 1 = \pi.$$

The price of this investment is exactly what is paid as a premium at time 0, and we have thus constructed a portfolio strategy with which we can meet our obligations without taking any risk. The arbitrage argument states that the market value of the obligation must be the price of establishing such a portfolio with which we can precisely meet the obligations. Thus, we conclude the numbers in Figure 4.2.

The question is now: was this magic? The boring answer is as follows. For the calculation of all quantities, we used the probabilities $q(u)$ and $q(d)$. These seemed to be drawn from a hat, but we must admit that they were constructed precisely such that the above calculations work out neatly. Hereby, we mean that by calculating expected values with the probability measure Q, we obtain values with which we can meet the obligations without risk. In the next section, we take a closer look at the construction of the measure Q and other concepts in financial mathematics.

4.3 The binomial model

4.3.1 The one-period model

In this section we consider the one-period version of the simplest possible non-trivial financial market, where the stock after one period takes one value out of only two: not because we think that this market is very realistic, but because it is very simple to understand the concepts of financial mathematics in this market. The calculations boil down to two equations with two unknowns and, furthermore, the model is often applied in practice.

The model consists of two investment possibilities: a bond and a stock. The price of the bond is deterministic and takes the following values:

$$S^0(0) = 1,$$

$$S^0(1) = (1+r)S^0(0) = 1+r,$$

where r is a deterministic interest rate for the period 0 to 1. We can also interpret the investment opportunity S^0 as the possibility of saving money on a bank account with interest rate r. The price of the stock is a stochastic process and takes the following values:

$$S^1(0) = s,$$

$$S^1(1) = s(1+Z),$$

$$Z = \begin{cases} u \text{ with probability } p_u, \\ d \text{ with probability } p_d. \end{cases}$$

We study the dynamics of special investment portfolios in the market and define a *portfolio (strategy)* as a vector $h = (h^0, h^1)$ which describes the number of bonds and stocks, respectively, in the portfolio at time 0. We allow for negative components in the portfolio and interpret this as having sold the assets. Such a position is called short-selling. The interpretation of short-selling of bonds is that we borrow money in the bank at interest rate r, whereas the interpretation of short-selling of stocks is that we, against a payment at time 0, oblige ourselves to pay the price of the stock in the future. Linked to a portfolio h, we define a *value process* as follows:

$$V(t, h) = h^0 S^0(t) + h^1 S^1(t), \, t = 0, 1.$$

The notion of arbitrage plays a very important role, and we define an *arbitrage* portfolio as a portfolio obeying the following relations:

$$V(0, h) = 0,$$

$$P(V(1, h) \geq 0) = 1, \tag{4.9}$$

$$P(V(1, h) > 0) > 0.$$

Thus, an arbitrage portfolio is a portfolio which is established at zero price at time 0, has a non-negative value at time 1, but with a chance of being positive. It is important here to emphasize that we usually require from a market that there exist *no* arbitrage portfolios, and we then speak of the market as arbitrage-free. Thus, for a given market one can pose the question, is this market arbitrage-free? It is easy to see that the binomial market is arbitrage-free if

$$d < r < u.$$

The solution $(q(u), q(d))$ to the following system of equations:

$$q(u)u + q(d)d = r, \qquad (4.10)$$

$$q(u) + q(d) = 1, \qquad (4.11)$$

becomes

$$q(u) = \frac{r-d}{u-d},$$
$$q(d) = \frac{u-r}{u-d}. \qquad (4.12)$$

If and only if we have the inequalities $d < r < u$, then $q(u), q(d) > 0$ and the relation $q(u) + q(d) = 1$ in Equation (4.11) assures us that we can interpret $q(u)$ and $q(d)$ as probabilities under a measure that we denote by Q. For this measure we have, according to Equation (4.10), the following:

$$\frac{1}{1+r} E^Q \left[S^1(1) \right] = \frac{1}{1+r} \left(q(u) s (1+u) + q(d) s (1+d) \right)$$

$$= s \frac{1 + q(u)u + q(u)d}{1+r} = s.$$

We see that the expectation of the discounted stock value at time 1 equals the stock price at time 0. A probability measure under which this is the case is called a *martingale measure* (or a *risk-neutral measure* or a *risk-adjusted measure*).

From the reasoning above, we conclude that a binomial model (S^0, S^1) is arbitrage-free if and only if there exists a martingale measure. This is an important result and, in fact, such a link between no arbitrage and the existence of a martingale measure goes far beyond the binomial model.

We assume that the market is arbitrage-free, i.e. $d < r < u$, and we study the valuation problem for so-called contingent claims. It is important to note that whereas arbitrage is a matter of what one *cannot* obtain in the market, valuation is a matter of what one *can* obtain.

A *contingent claim* is a stochastic variable in the form $X = \Phi(Z)$. Thus, it is a stochastic variable since Z is a stochastic variable. Equivalently, it is determined by the outcome of $S^1(1)$ exclusively. The function Φ is called the *contract function*.

A typical example of a contingent claim is a European call option on the stock with strike price K. A European call option gives the right, but not the obligation, to buy a stock at time 1 at price K. In our model this contract is only interesting if $s(1+d) < K < s(1+u)$. If $S^1(1) > K$, the option is exercised, and the owner pays K for the stock and sells it on the market for $s(1+u)$ with a gain equal to $s(1+u) - K$. If $S^1(1) < K$, the owner gives up the option with a gain of 0; i.e.

$$X = \Phi(Z) = (s(1+Z) - K)^+ = \begin{cases} s(1+u) - K, & Z = u, \\ 0, & Z = d. \end{cases} \quad (4.13)$$

Our problem is to find a fair price of this contract if one exists. The price at time t is denoted by $\Pi(t, X)$, and we easily see that in order to avoid arbitrage we must have that $\Pi(1, X) = X$; the problem then is to find $\Pi(0, X)$.

A contingent claim is called *attainable* if there exists a portfolio h such that

$$V(1, h) = X. \quad (4.14)$$

In that case, h is called a *hedging* or *replicating* portfolio. If all contingent claims are attainable, the market is said to be *complete*. If a claim is attainable with the hedging portfolio h, there is in reality no difference between holding the claim and holding the hedging portfolio. Then it is easy to see that in order to avoid arbitrage possibilities in a market including the claim, the price of the claim at time 0 must equal the price of establishing a hedging portfolio at time 0, i.e.

$$\Pi(0, X) = V(0, h).$$

If the market is complete, all claims can be priced by determining the price of the hedging portfolio. A natural question is now whether the one-period binomial market is complete.

According to Equation (4.14), we know that for a portfolio hedging X,

$$\begin{aligned} h^0(1+r) + h^1 s(1+u) &= \Phi(u), \\ h^0(1+r) + h^1 s(1+d) &= \Phi(d). \end{aligned} \quad (4.15)$$

This is a system of two equations with two unknowns (h^0, h^1), the solution of which, under the assumption $d < r < u$, is determined as follows:

$$h^1 = \frac{\Phi(u) - \Phi(d)}{s(u-d)}, \quad (4.16)$$

$$h^0 = \frac{1}{1+r} \frac{(1+u)\Phi(d) - (1+d)\Phi(u)}{u-d}.$$

We can now calculate the price $\Pi(0, X) = V(0, h)$:

$$V(0, h) = h^0 + h^1 s$$

$$= \frac{1}{1+r} \frac{(1+u)\Phi(d) - (1+d)\Phi(u)}{u-d} + \frac{\Phi(u) - \Phi(d)}{(u-d)}$$

$$= \frac{1}{1+r} \frac{(1+u)\Phi(d) - (1+d)\Phi(u) + (1+r)\Phi(u) - (1+r)\Phi(d)}{u-d}$$

$$= \frac{1}{1+r}(q(u)\Phi(u) + q(d)\Phi(d)), \qquad (4.17)$$

where $q(u)$ and $q(d)$ are given by Equation (4.12). We conclude that the one-period binomial model is complete and that $X = \Phi(Z)$ at time 0 has the price given by Equation (4.17) with $(q(u), q(d))$ given by Equation (4.12). We see that the price of a contingent claim X can be calculated by the so-called risk-neutral formula, as follows:

$$\Pi(0, X) = \frac{1}{1+r} E^Q[X],$$

where Q, given by the probabilities $(q(u), q(d))$, is the unique probability measure under which also the price of the risky asset can be calculated using a risk-neutral formula. By risk neutrality we mean the intuitive quality that prices are calculated simply as expected discounted claims. However, it is important to realize that the pricing formula does not assume risk-neutral agents. Risk neutrality is just a notion which shows up naturally when interpreting the quantities $q(u)$ and $q(d)$ as probabilities.

It may be surprising that the probabilities $p(u)$ and $p(d)$ do not play any important role in the pricing formula. After all, if we hold the option, the expected gain is affected by the objective probability measure. On the other hand, by buying the option we give up the possibility of investing the price of the option on the same market with corresponding objective changes in prices. The calculations above show that these two circumstances "level out" and that the disappearance of $p(u)$ and $p(d)$ does not seem that counter-intuitive after all.

We end this section with a numerical example, in which we find the price of a European option, Equation (4.13), with the parameters $r = 5\%$, $u = 20\%$, $d = -10\%$, $K = 110$, $p(u) = 0.6$, $p(d) = 0.4$. The first idea could be to calculate the expected present value under the objective measure to obtain

$$\frac{1}{1.05} E^P[\Phi(Z)] = \frac{1}{1.05}(10p(u) + 0p(d)) = 5.71.$$

$$\begin{bmatrix} S^0(1)=1.05 \\ S^1(1)=120 \\ \Pi(1)=10 \end{bmatrix}$$

$$\begin{bmatrix} S^0(0)=1 \\ S^1(0)=100 \\ \Pi(0)=4.76 \\ h^0=-28.57 \\ h^1=0.33 \end{bmatrix} \quad \begin{smallmatrix} \nearrow \\ \searrow \end{smallmatrix}$$

$$\begin{bmatrix} S^0(1)=1.05 \\ S^1(1)=90 \\ \Pi(1)=0 \end{bmatrix}$$

Figure 4.3. One-period option model.

One may suggest loading that price according to, for example, the variance or the standard deviation. We illustrate the completely different consequences of an arbitrage argument in Figure 4.3.

Figure 4.3 shows how the dynamics of the risk-free asset, the risky asset and the option depend on the outcome of the stochastic variable Z. Firstly, we write S^0 and S^1 for the two time points 0 and 1. Hereafter, we write the price of the option at time 1, which is given by Equation (4.13). Finally, we calculate $\Pi(0)$ and h from Equations (4.17) and (4.16), which in this example are as follows:

$$\Pi(0) = \frac{1}{1.05} E^Q [\Phi(Z)]$$

$$= \frac{1}{1.05} (q(u)\,\Phi(u) + q(d)\,\Phi(d))$$

$$= \frac{1}{1.05} \left(\frac{0.05-(-0.1)}{0.2-(-0.1)}10 + \frac{0.2-0.05}{0.2-(-0.1)}0 \right) = 4.76;$$

$$h^1 = \frac{10-0}{100\,(0.2-(-0.1))} = 0.33;$$

$$h^0 = \frac{1}{1.05} \frac{1.2 \times 0 - 0.9 \times 10}{0.2-(-0.1)} = -28.57.$$

We can now verify that the price for establishing the portfolio h is exactly given by

$$V(0,h) = -28.57 + 0.33 \times 100 = 4.76,$$

whereas the value of the portfolio at time 1 becomes

$$V(1,h) = \begin{cases} -28.57 \times 1.05 + 0.33 \times 120 = 10, & Z = u, \\ -28.57 \times 1.05 + 0.33 \times 90 = 0, & Z = d. \end{cases}$$

4.3.2 The multi-period model

A drawback of the one-period model is, of course, the very simple asset model with only two possible outcomes. If we simply increase the number of outcomes and then search for replicating portfolios, we get into trouble since the number of unknowns in Equation (4.15) will still be two, (h^0, h^1), whereas the number of equations will equal the number of possible outcomes. Thus, the system will only have a solution for special trivial claims such as $\Phi(Z) = S^1(1)$. We can say that the completeness of the binomial model exactly connects to the fact that the number of equations in the system shown in Equation (4.15) equals the number of unknowns.

The answer is to allow for intermediary trading in the two assets. If we put a number of one-period models in a row, the number of outcomes increases with the number of periods. If, on the other hand, we allow agents to change their portfolio after each one-period model, the completeness is maintained. We assume a time horizon n and define the price processes for the risk-free asset and the risky asset as follows:

$$S^0(t) = (1+r) S^0(t-1), t = 1, \ldots, n,$$

$$S^0(0) = 1,$$

$$S^1(t) = (1+Z(t)) S^1(t-1), t-1, \ldots, n,$$

$$S^1(0) = s,$$

where $Z(1), \ldots, Z(n)$ are independent stochastic variables which take one out of two values u and d with the probabilities $p(u)$ and $p(d)$, respectively.

A *portfolio* (*strategy*) is a process

$$h = \{h(t)\}_{t=1,\ldots,n} = \{(h^0(t), h^1(t))\}_{t=1,\ldots,n},$$

such that $h(t)$ is a function of $(S^1(1), \ldots, S^1(t-1))$. The *value process* linked to the portfolio h is defined by

$$V(t, h) = h^0(t) S^0(t) + h^1(t) S^1(t), t = 0, \ldots, n.$$

The portfolio at time t, $h(t)$, is the portfolio held during the period $[t-1, t]$. It is intuitively clear that this portfolio only can depend on the prices until time $t-1$ and not on the future prices from time t and onwards. Otherwise, we would of course take advantage of the future price changes when deciding the portfolio today. We say that the portfolio must be *predictable*. Particularly interesting are the *self-financing* portfolios, for which

$$h^0(t) S^0(t) + h^1(t) S^1(t) = h^0(t+1) S^0(t) + h^1(t+1) S^1(t),$$

$$t = 1, \dots, n-1. \tag{4.18}$$

For a self-financing portfolio, no capital is injected or withdrawn at any of the time points $t = 1, \dots, n-1$, and all new investments at time t are financed by capital gains on old investments. Hereafter, we define an *arbitrage* portfolio as a self-financing portfolio for which Equation (4.9) holds with the time point 1 replaced by n.

The *martingale measure* is now given by the positive probabilities $(q(u),$ $q(d))$ for which the discounted price process for the risky asset is a martingale, i.e.

$$\frac{1}{1+r} E^Q \left[S^1(t+1) \mid S^1(t) = s \right] = s,$$

and we easily see that $(q(u), q(d))$ again is given by Equation (4.12). In order for such a set of probabilities to exist, we must require, as in the one-period model, that $d < r < u$. As in the one-period model, this condition makes sure that it is not possible to construct arbitrage portfolios. Thus, the multi-period model is also arbitrage-free exactly if there exists a martingale measure.

A *simple contingent claim* is a stochastic variable $X = \Phi(S^1(n))$, whereas more general claims are given in the form $X = \Phi(S^1(1), \dots, S^1(n))$. We note here that a claim which is due at time t and which depends on $S^1(t)$ or $S^1(1), \dots, S^1(t)$, respectively, constitutes a simple or a general claim, respectively, in the partial model running from time 0 until time t.

A claim is called *attainable* if there exists a self-financing portfolio h such that $V(n, h) = X$, and h is then called *hedging* or *replicating*. There is, in principle, no difference between holding an attainable claim and the portfolio that hedges the claim, and, thus, the only reasonable price of such a claim is exactly the value of the hedging portfolio, i.e.

$$\Pi(t, X) = V(t, h).$$

By "reasonable price" we mean that if the price is any different, it is possible to construct arbitrage portfolios. We speak, in that case, simply of the arbitrage-free price of the claim. If all claims in a market are attainable, the market is said to be *complete*, and we can ask whether the multi-period model is complete. By copying the argument in the one-period model for each period, one can show that the multi-period model is also complete and that prices and hedging portfolios can be found by solving a number of systems of two equations with two unknowns. We shall not carry out the argument in detail, but instead illustrate the technique for a specific claim, a European call option in a three-period model.

During the rest of this section, we want to find the price of a European option with the parameters $r = 5\%$, $u = 20\%$, $d = -10\%$, $K = 110$. Figure 4.4 shows how the dynamics of the prices of the risk-free asset, the risky asset and the option depend on the outcome of the stochastic variables $Z(1)$, $Z(2)$ and $Z(3)$. We have that $q(u) = q(d) = 1/2$. Firstly, we calculate S^0 and S^1 for the time points 0, 1, 2 and 3. Hereafter, we write the option price at time 3, which is now given by the terminal condition

$$\Pi(3, X) = V(3, h) = X = \left(S^1(3) - K\right)^+.$$

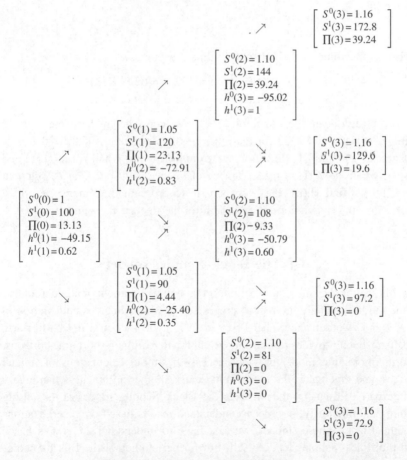

Figure 4.4. Multi-period option model.

Now we calculate $\Pi(2, X)$ and $h(3)$ using Equations (4.17) and (4.16) for each of the three possible outcomes at time 2. For the first outcome, corresponding to the risky asset going up in the two first periods and at time 2 taking the value 144, we obtain

$$\Pi(2, X) = \frac{1}{1.05} E^Q [\Phi(Z)] = \frac{1}{1.05} \left(62.8 \times \frac{1}{2} + 19.6 \times \frac{1}{2} \right) = 39.24,$$

$$h^1(3) = \frac{62.8 - 19.6}{144\,(0.2 - (-0.1))} = 1,$$

$$h^0(3) = \frac{1}{(1.05)^3} \frac{1.2 \times 19.6 - 0.9 \times 62.8}{0.2 - (-0.1)} = -95.02.$$

We can now verify that the price of establishing the portfolio h is exactly given by

$$V(2, h) = -95 \times (1.05)^2 + 1 \times 144 = 39.24,$$

whereas the value of the portfolio at time 3 becomes

$$V(3, h) = \begin{cases} -95.02 \times (1.05)^3 + 1 \times 172.8 = 62.8, & Z(3) = u, \\ -95.02 \times (1.05)^3 + 1 \times 129.6 = 19.6, & Z(3) = d. \end{cases}$$

Now, $V(2, h)$ can substitute for $\Pi(2)$. We continue in the same way by filling in $\Pi(2)$ and $h(3)$ for the other possible outcomes of the risky asset at time 2, 108 and 81. Hereafter, we go to time point 1 and fill in $\Pi(1)$ and $h(2)$, where now $\Pi(2)$ makes up the claim in a new one-year calculation. Finally, we find $\Pi(0)$. It is very simple to program the scheme described here since the calculations at each point in the tree are the same.

4.4 The Black–Scholes model

In this section we study the most important and well known of all continuous-time models, namely the model suggested by Black, Scholes and Merton in 1973 and awarded the Nobel Prize in 1997. The model is not particularly realistic, but it provides a good approximation to reality on short time horizons. Furthermore, the model provides access to simple calculations of unique prices, and this makes the model important. Another argument is that a very large part of financial theory takes the Black–Scholes model as its starting point, and obviously, in order to understand results based on generalizations of the Black–Scholes model, we first have to understand the results based on the Black–Scholes model itself. For further studies of the Black–Scholes model, we refer to Björk (1994, 2004).

The Black–Scholes model consists of two assets with dynamics given by

$$dS^0(t) = rS^0(t)\,dt, \tag{4.19}$$

$$S^0(0) = 1,$$

$$dS^1(t) = \alpha S^1(t)\,dt + \sigma S^1(t)\,dW(t), \tag{4.20}$$

$$S^1(0) = s,$$

where r, α and σ are deterministic constants. It is possible to generalize the model to the situation where r, α and σ are functions of $(t, S^1(t))$, but such a generalization provides no further insight. We briefly mention some other possible generalizations in Section 4.6.

The idea of the dynamics of S^0 is clear since Equation (4.19) simply states that S^0 fulfils a deterministic differential equation with the following solution:

$$\frac{d}{dt}S^0(t) = rS^0(t),\, S_0^0 = 1,$$

$$S^0(t) = e^{rt}.$$

We can interpret investing in S^0 as depositing on a bank account at a constant interest rate. The dynamics of S^1 requires comment. It is based on the assumption that a change of asset price in a "small" time interval $(t, t+\Delta t]$ can be approximated as follows:

$$\Delta S(t) = S(t+\Delta t) - S(t) \tag{4.21}$$

$$\approx \alpha S(t)\,\Delta t + \sigma S(t)\,(W(t+\Delta t) - W(t))$$

$$= \alpha S(t)\,\Delta t + \sigma S(t)\,\Delta W(t),$$

where W is a so-called *standard Brownian motion* or *Wiener process*. Such a Wiener process is characterized by continuity and independent normally distributed increments such that

$$\Delta W(t) \sim N(0, \Delta t).$$

Actually, Equation (4.21) is only assumed for infinitely small time intervals, and this is written in the form given by Equation (4.20). In spite of the fact that W is an extremely complicated process to work with (for example, though continuous it is not differentiable in any point which makes it impossible to illustrate), it plays an important role in various disciplines of applied mathematics, including mathematical finance.

We now continue by defining various concepts in mathematical finance. The content of these concepts correspond, broadly speaking, to the content they were given in the discrete-time models. A *portfolio* (*strategy*) is a process $h = \{h(t)\}_{t\in[0,n]} = \left\{\left(h^0(t), h^1(t)\right)\right\}_{t\in[0,n]}$ such that $h(t)$ is a function of $\left(S^1(s), 0 \le s \le t\right)$. The *value process* linked to the portfolio h is now defined by

$$V(t, h) = h^0(t) S^0(t) + h^1(t) S^1(t), t \in [0, n].$$

The portfolio at a given point in time t, $h(t)$, is interpreted as the portfolio which is held during the period $[t, t+dt)$. It is intuitively clear that this portfolio is allowed to depend on the prices until time t and not on the future prices after time t. Otherwise, one could arrange a portfolio based on future price changes. Of particular interest are the *self-financing* portfolios for which

$$dV(t, h) = h^0(t)\, dS^0(t) + h^1(t)\, dS^1(t) \qquad (4.22)$$

$$= rV(t, h)\, dt + h^1(t) S^1(t)\left((\alpha - r)\, dt + \sigma\, dW(t)\right). \quad (4.23)$$

We do not inject money in or withdraw money from these portfolios at any point in time, and all new investments at time t are financed by capital gains on old investments. It is by no means evident that the idea behind being self-financing is formalized by the definition given in Equation (4.22), but a discrete- time argument and an appropriate content given to Equation (4.20) leads to that result. Hereafter, an *arbitrage* portfolio is defined as a portfolio with the following qualities:

$$V(0, h) = 0,$$

$$P(V(n, h) \ge 0) = 1,$$

$$P(V(n, h) > 0) > 0.$$

As in the discrete-time models, we are interested in prices on derivatives, and again we define a *simple contingent claim* as a stochastic variable $X = \Phi\left(S^1(n)\right)$, whereas more general claims are in the form $X = \Phi\left(S^1(t), t \in [0, n]\right)$. As in the binomial model, it is now natural to discuss concepts such as martingale measures, attainable claims and complete markets. However, a rigorous discussion requires knowledge of the results for stochastic processes which lie beyond the purpose of this material and we refer to Björk (1994). We can, however, take a few steps further, by following the reasoning of Black, Scholes and Merton, who did well with a limited amount of advanced results for Wiener processes.

A claim is called *attainable* if there exists a self- financing portfolio h such that

$$V(n, h) = X, \qquad (4.24)$$

and h is called the *hedging* or *replicating* portfolio. There is no difference between holding an attainable claim and the hedging portfolio. Therefore, the only arbitrage-free price for such a claim is the value of the hedging portfolio, i.e.

$$\Pi(t, X) = V(t, h). \tag{4.25}$$

If all claims in a market are attainable, the market is said to be *complete*, and it is now natural to ask whether the Black–Scholes market model is complete. If the answer is yes, we have found the arbitrage-free price on every claim at any point in time through Equation (4.25), where h is the hedging portfolio.

To show that the Black–Scholes market is complete can, in advance, seem impossible. For the binomial model the task was reduced to counting equations and unknowns and realizing that the system gave us both hedging portfolios and prices. With the introduction of the Wiener process as the stochastic element, this looks difficult. However, in spite of the irregular behavior of the Wiener process, there are a number of quite simple rules of calculation which we use in the following. We shall not go into detail, but just use them as we need them. However, we should emphasize that these rules of calculation are not based on any financial reasoning but are pure mathematical and probability theoretical results about the Wiener process.

Now, we let $\Pi(t)$ denote the price at time t for a simple claim X, for which we seek a hedging portfolio h and an arbitrage-free price Π. Now we assume (a non-trivial assumption) that the price of the claim X can be written as a function of time and the price of the stock, i.e. $\Pi(t) = F(t, S^1(t))$, where $F(t, s)$ is a deterministic function of two variables. We mention that the function F can of course have derivatives with respect to the two variables, and we assume that such derivatives exist to the extent that we need them (another non-trivial assumption).

Thus, we seek a pair (h, Π) such that Equations (4.24) and (4.25) are fulfilled. Here, we need the dynamics of various price processes. The dynamics of the prices S^0 and S^1 are known, but what about the dynamics of Π? Appropriately, there exists a deep result about how the dynamics of S^1, Equation (4.20), is reflected in a sufficiently regular function $F(t, S^1(t))$. The result is called Itô's formula, and its consequence is that Π behaves just like S^1 with specific processes $\alpha^\Pi(t)$ and $\sigma^\Pi(t)$ replacing α and σ. The dynamics of the price process Π is given by

$$d\Pi(t) = \alpha^\Pi(t)\,\Pi(t)\,dt + \sigma^\Pi(t)\,\Pi(t)\,dW(t), \tag{4.26}$$

with

$$\alpha^{\Pi}(t) = \frac{\frac{\partial F}{\partial t}\left(t, S^1(t)\right) + \alpha S^1(t)\frac{\partial F}{\partial s}\left(t, S^1(t)\right)}{F\left(t, S^1(t)\right)}$$

$$+ \frac{\frac{1}{2}\sigma^2\left(S^1(t)\right)^2\frac{\partial^2 F}{\partial s^2}\left(t, S^1(t)\right)}{F\left(t, S^1(t)\right)}, \tag{4.27}$$

$$\sigma^{\Pi}(t) = \frac{\sigma S^1(t)\frac{\partial F}{\partial s}\left(t, S^1(t)\right)}{F\left(t, S^1(t)\right)}. \tag{4.28}$$

On the other hand, we need a portfolio such that the value process equals the price Π, i.e., according to Equation (4.25),

$$\Pi(t) = V(t, h) = h^0(t)S^0(t) + h^1(t)S^1(t), \tag{4.29}$$

and which is self-financing, i.e., according to Equation (4.22),

$$\begin{aligned}
d\Pi(t) &= h^0(t)\, dS^0(t) + h^1(t)\, dS^1(t) \\
&= h^0(t)\, rS^0(t)\, dt + h^1(t)\left(\alpha S^1(t)\, dt + \sigma S^1(t)\, dW(t)\right) \\
&= \frac{h^0(t)\, rS^0(t) + h^1(t)\,\alpha S^1(t)}{\Pi(t)}\Pi(t)\, dt
\end{aligned}$$

$$+ \frac{h^1(t)\,\sigma S^1(t)}{\Pi(t)}\Pi(t)\, dW(t). \tag{4.30}$$

Now we can compare Equations (4.26) and (4.30), and by equating the terms in front of dt and $dW(t)$ we obtain

$$\alpha^{\Pi}(t) = \frac{h^0(t)\, rS^0(t) + h^1(t)\,\alpha S^1(t)}{\Pi(t)},$$

$$\sigma^{\Pi}(t) = \frac{h^1(t)\,\sigma S^1(t)}{\Pi(t)}.$$

By insertion of Equation (4.29), we obtain

$$\frac{\alpha - r}{\sigma} = \frac{\alpha^{\Pi}(t) - r}{\sigma^{\Pi}(t)}, \tag{4.31}$$

$$h^1(t) = \frac{\sigma^{\Pi}(t)\,\Pi(t)}{\sigma S^1(t)} = \frac{\partial F}{\partial s}\left(t, S^1(t)\right), \tag{4.32}$$

$$h^0(t) = \frac{\Pi(t) - h^1(t)S^1(t)}{S^0(t)}. \tag{4.33}$$

Equation (4.31) states that the additional expected gain beyond the risk-free interest rate r per risk measured by the factor in front of the $dW(t)$ term coincides for the stock price and the price Π. This quantity is called the risk premium. If we can find Π using Equation (4.31), then Equations (4.32) and (4.33) specify the hedging portfolio.

Substituting for Equations (4.27) and (4.28) into Equation (4.31) yields

$$0 = \frac{\partial F}{\partial t}\left(t, S^1(t)\right) + rS^1(t)\frac{\partial F}{\partial s}\left(t, S^1(t)\right)$$

$$+ \frac{1}{2}\sigma^2\left(S^1(t)\right)^2\frac{\partial^2 F}{\partial s^2}\left(t, S^1(t)\right) - F\left(t, S^1(t)\right)r. \qquad (4.34)$$

In addition, we have the terminal condition $\Pi(n) = \Phi(S(n))$. This differential equation must be fulfilled at any point in time, no matter the value of $S^1(t)$, and we can instead write down the corresponding deterministic partial differential equation with terminal condition for the function $F(t, s)$. This differential equation triumphs as the *Black–Scholes equation* :

$$\frac{\partial F}{\partial t}(t, s) + rs\frac{\partial F}{\partial s}(t, s) + \frac{1}{2}\sigma^2 s^2\frac{\partial^2 F}{\partial s^2}(t, s) - F(t, s)r = 0, \qquad (4.35)$$

$$F(n, s) = \Phi(s).$$

The Black–Scholes equation is a deterministic partial differential equation which we can solve for every point (t, s). If we need the price of the claim, we simply replace s by $S^1(t)$ in $F(t, s)$. It is important to understand that the Black–Scholes equation is a deterministic tool for determination of the stochastic value $F\left(t, S^1(t)\right)$. If, instead, we wish to carry forward this price in a small time interval, we need the dynamics given in Equation (4.26) again. By insertion of Equations (4.27) and (4.28) and $\partial F\left(t, S^1(t)\right)/\partial t$ isolated in Equations (4.34), we obtain the dynamics which carry forward the price Π, as follows:

$$d\Pi(t) = \left(r\Pi(t) + (\alpha - r)S^1(t)\frac{\partial F}{\partial s}\left(t, S^1(t)\right)\right)dt$$

$$+ \sigma S^1(t)\frac{\partial F}{\partial s}\left(t, S^1(t)\right)dW(t). \qquad (4.36)$$

By comparing Equations (4.23) and (4.36) and using Equation (4.25), we again obtain the hedging portfolio, since $h^1(t) = \partial F\left(t, S^1(t)\right)/\partial s$, and $h^0(t)$ is then determined residually from the following:

$$\Pi(t) = h^0(t)S^0(t) + h^1(t)S^1(t).$$

The solution to a class of deterministic partial differential equations, including Equation (4.35), can be written as a conditional expectation in a so-called stochastic representation formula. We speak of Equation (4.20) as the P-dynamics of S^1, since the dynamics is presented using a process W, which is a Wiener process under the so-called objective probability measure P. This is the measure that relates to the investors' expectations of the future asset prices. Let us instead write the dynamics for S^1 using a process W^Q, which is a Wiener process under a different measure Q, determined such that

$$dS^1(t) = rS^1(t)\,dt + \sigma S^1(t)\,dW^Q(t). \tag{4.37}$$

Under Q, we have that

$$E^Q\left[e^{-r(u-t)}S^1(u)\,\middle|\,S^1(t) = s\right] = s, t \leq u \leq n,$$

where E^Q denotes the expectation under measure Q. We see that, except for the discount factor $e^{-r(u-t)}$, S^1 is a martingale under Q; Q is known as the martingale measure. The solution to the Black–Scholes equation has the following stochastic representation formula:

$$F(t, s) = E^Q\left[e^{-r(n-t)}\Phi\left(S^1(n)\right)\,\middle|\,S^1(t) = s\right]. \tag{4.38}$$

For most contract functions Φ, Equation (4.38) can be calculated by numerical methods or by simulation methods only. However, in a few cases it can be calculated more or less analytically; one example is the European call option, $\Phi\left(S^1(n)\right) = \left(S^1(n) - K\right)^+$. The distribution of S^1 under Q combined with this simple contract function gives, after a number of tedious calculations, a relatively explicit formula for the arbitrage-free price of a European call option in a Black–Scholes market. This formula triumphs as the *Black–Scholes formula*:

$$F(t, s) = sN\left[d_1(t, s)\right] - e^{-r(n-t)}KN\left[d_2(t, s)\right]. \tag{4.39}$$

Here, N is the distribution function for a standard normal distribution, and

$$d_1(t, s) = \frac{1}{\sigma\sqrt{n-t}}\left(\log\left(\frac{s}{K}\right) + \left(r + \frac{1}{2}\sigma^2\right)(n-t)\right),$$

$$d_2(t, s) = d_1(t, s) - \sigma\sqrt{n-t}.$$

In the binomial model, one could wonder what happened to the objective probabilities in the valuation formula. Correspondingly, in the Black–Scholes model one can wonder why the expected return on the asset α does not appear in either the Black–Scholes equation, Equation (4.35), or the Black–Scholes formula, Equation (4.39). However, we can suggest a similar explanation. If we hold an option in a market with a large α, we have a good chance of making capital gains. On the other hand, we give up the possibility of investing the price of the option in the same market with a good chance of capital gains. The results above show that, at the end of the day, we are indifferent to the expected return on the stock when pricing the option.

Disregarding the presence of a martingale measure Q, one should recognize the connection between a deterministic differential equation, a stochastic representation formula and an explicit solution. All this is known from Thiele's differential equation, which is also a deterministic differential equation that corresponds to a conditional expectation of future discounted payments, given that the insured is alive. For most traditional versions of Thiele's differential equation, it is furthermore possible to write an explicit solution which is just the reserve expressed with elementary capital values. The concrete calculations required for realizing more rigorously the connection between Thiele's differential equation and the Black–Scholes formula is based on the theory for stochastic processes. Parts of Steffensen (2001) deal with this subject.

A number of differences between Thiele's differential equation and the Black–Scholes equation are just as important as the similarities. In Thiele's differential equation, we wish to find a conditional expectation under the objective probability measure. We speak of such a conditional expectation as a value by reference to diversification of the risk. Hereafter, we derive a corresponding differential equation and an explicit formula. In the Black–Scholes model, we first derive the differential equation, and we base this derivation on the objective of replicating an attainable claim. Hereafter, it is possible to derive a stochastic representation formula which contains an artificial probability measure on which the explicit solution is also based.

Usually, we use the same Thiele's differential equation for initial backward calculation and for forward accumulation of the reserve. This works because the stochastic element, the indicator for being alive, is constant before and after the insurance event. Hereby, the deterministic backward Thiele's differential equation can be used for accumulation of the reserve in between the insurance events. In the Black–Scholes model, we need to distinguish carefully between the Black–Scholes equation, Equation (4.35), and price accumulation, Equation (4.36). This is because the stochastic element S_t^1 is changing continuously.

4.5 Continuous-time insurance model

In this section, we combine the ideas in Section 4.2 with the Black–Scholes model. More specifically, we consider the continuous-time valuation of the special claims present in a life insurance contract with bonus. We start by modifying the main example in Chapter 2, such that it is a purely financial product and such that investments take place in a Black–Scholes market.

Then the setup becomes a continuous-time version of the discrete-time setup in Section 4.2, with investment in the Black–Scholes market instead of in the binomial market.

The technical reserve V^* relates to the first order and the second order bases, which are made up by the first and second order interest rates r^* and r^δ, through the following differential equation characterizing the technical reserve:

$$\frac{d}{dt} V^* (t) = r^\delta (t) V^* (t) + \pi$$

$$= r^* (t) V^* (t) + \pi + \delta (t), \tag{4.40}$$

$$V^* (0) = 0,$$

where the rate of dividends $\delta (t)$ is given by $\delta (t) = \left(r^\delta (t) - r^* (t) \right) V^* (t)$. We also speak of the second order interest rate and a process of second order interest rates $\left(r^\delta (t) \right)_{0 \le t \le n}$ as the bonus interest rate and the bonus strategy, respectively.

The pension sum $b (t)$ guaranteed at time t is determined, for a given technical reserve, by the equivalence relation,

$$V^* (t) = b (t) (v^*)^{n-t} - \pi a^*_{\overline{n-t}|}.$$

In Chapter 2 we introduced the total reserve U, which appears from an accumulation under the real basis as follows:

$$dU (t) = rU (t) \, dt + \pi dt,$$

$$U (0) = 0,$$

where r is constant. In particular, we know the return over a small time interval. The idea is to generalize this construction such that we have the opportunity to invest a part of the reserve in an asset with risk, and we now allow for investment in the Black–Scholes market. We let the company hold $h^1 (t)$ stocks at time t.

Changes in the total reserve U consist of premiums and capital gains. The capital gains consists of the interest rate return on the part of $U (t)$ that was not invested in stocks, $U (t) - \eta^1 (t) S^1 (t)$, and the price change on the portfolio of stocks. Thus,

$$dU (t) = r \left(U (t) - \eta^1 (t) S^1 (t) \right) dt + \eta^1 (t) \, dS^1 (t) + \pi \, dt$$

$$= rU (t) \, dt + \eta^1 (t) S^1 (t) ((\alpha - r) \, dt + \sigma \, dW (t)) + \pi \, dt,$$

$$U (0) = 0.$$

The undistributed reserve X is determined residually by

$$X(t) = U(t) - V^*(t),$$

and we obtain

$$dX(t) = dU(t) - dV^*(t)$$
$$= rX(t)\,dt + \eta^1(t)\,S^1(t)\,((\alpha - r)\,dt + \sigma\,dW(t))$$
$$+ (c(t) - \delta(t))\,dt,$$

where

$$c(t) = (r(t) - r^*(t))\,V^*(t).$$

The idea now, as in the discrete-time model in Section 4.2, is to introduce prospective quantities for the total and the undistributed reserves, respectively. If $b(n)$ is a contingent claim such that it is uniquely determined by the development of the stock market, the market value of the total payments, the market value of guaranteed payments and the market value of the unguaranteed payments, respectively, are, according to Section 4.4, as follows:

$$V(t) = E_t^Q[b(n)]\,v^{n-t} - \pi a_{\overline{n-t}|}, \tag{4.41}$$
$$V^g(t) = b(t)\,v^{n-t} - \pi a_{\overline{n-t}|},$$
$$V^b(t) = \left(E^Q[b(n)] - b(t)\right)v^{n-t}.$$

Here, E_t^Q denotes the expectation given the development of the financial market up to time t and under a particular probability measure, under which the expected return on investment in the stock is r; see Equation (4.37). In accordance with the valuation (4.41), residual parameters in the bonus strategy must be determined by the equivalence relation,

$$V(0) = 0.$$

As in the discrete-time model in Section 4.2, there exist investment strategies η^1 such that $X(n) = 0$. For example, the investment $\eta^1(t) = 0$ brings us directly back to the situation in Chapter 2. We state a sufficient condition on η^1, less trivial than $\eta^1(t) = 0$, for the existence of a bonus strategy leading to $X(n) = 0$. If this condition is fulfilled, the calculations in Equation (4.5) leading to $V(t) = U(t)$ hold. In these calculations we use the fact that the expected return on $U(t)$ and the premiums paid over $(t, n]$ under Q is r; see Equation (4.37).

A sufficient condition on η for a fulfilment of $X(n) = 0$ is that risky investments are made only if $U(t)$ exceeds $V^g(t)$. Otherwise, investments must give the return r in order to meet the obligations on which $V^g(t)$ is based. We write the condition as follows:

$$U(t) - V^g(t) = 0 \Rightarrow \eta^1(t) = 0.$$

An example where this condition is fulfilled is given by

$$\eta^1(t) S^1(t) = \theta \left(U(t) - V^g(t) \right),$$

for a constant θ whereby a constant part of the bonus potential is invested in stocks. We note that we can allow for $\theta > 1$.

If we add the classical solvency rule $X(t) \geq 0$, a sufficient condition on η is that risky investments are made only if $X(t) \geq 0$. We write the condition as follows:

$$X(t) = 0 \Rightarrow \eta^1(t) = 0.$$

An example where this condition is fulfilled is given by

$$\eta^1(t) S^1(t) = \theta X(t),$$

for a constant θ whereby a constant part of the collective bonus potential is invested in stocks. Again, we can allow for $\theta > 1$.

The conditions on X limit the risk in the portfolio. However, one may wish to disregard these conditions and invest more capital in stocks. One can imagine a general investment where the proportion of funds invested in risky assets, $\eta^1(t) S^1(t) / X(t)$, is a function Θ of $(t, V^*(t), X(t))$, i.e.

$$\frac{\eta^1(t) S^1(t)}{X(t)} = \Theta(t, V^*(t), X(t)). \tag{4.42}$$

Hereby,

$$dX(t) = \left(r\,dt + \Theta(t, V^*(t), X(t)) \left((\alpha - r)\,dt + \sigma\,dW(t) \right) \right) X(t)$$

$$+ \left(c(t) - \delta(t) \right) dt.$$

One can think of an example where a constant part of U is invested in stocks, i.e.

$$\eta^1(t) S^1(t) = \theta U(t) \Leftrightarrow$$

$$\Theta(t, V^*(t), X(t)) = \frac{\eta^1(t) S^1(t)}{X(t)} = \frac{\theta U(t)}{X(t)} = \theta \frac{V^*(t) + X(t)}{X(t)}.$$

If we disregard the condition $X(n) = 0$, one has to discuss, as in the discrete-time insurance model, the question: how is the bonus strategy linked to the stock market? And again, we suggest an explicit connection which is practically meaningful and mathematically tractable. However, we stress that this is only one out of many meaningful constructions. We let the bonus interest rate be linked to $X(n)$ by defining the following:

$$r^\delta(t) = r^*(t) + \frac{\Phi(t, X(t))}{V^*(t)},$$

where Φ is a function specifying the dependence on X. One can think of a function in the form

$$\Phi(t, x) = (\beta(t) + \alpha(t) x)^+, \tag{4.43}$$

where α and β are deterministic functions of t. We now consider valuation under the three bonus forms, terminal bonus, cash bonus and accumulation of benefits, with exactly that choice of function Φ. We still speak of the function Φ as the contract function and recall the two possible constructions included in Equation (4.43): if $\beta(t) = 0$ and $\alpha(t) = \alpha > 0$, we obtain

$$\Phi(t, X(t)) = \alpha(X(t))^+,$$

i.e. the dividend is determined as a constant part of the undistributed reserve, if this is positive.

If $\alpha(t) = 1$ and $\beta(t) = -K < 0$, we obtain

$$\Phi(t, X(t)) = (X(t) - K)^+,$$

i.e. the dividend is determined such that the part of the undistributed reserve that exceeds a constant buffer K is paid out.

4.5.1 Terminal bonus

We start by considering the terminal bonus because this is the bonus form which has most similarities to the European option. This provides us with our first generalization of the Black–Scholes equation. We let the investment be determined by a function Θ, such that $\eta^1(t) S^1(t) / X(t) = \Theta(t, X(t))$. This is not a restriction compared with Equation (4.42) since the technical reserve under terminal bonus is a deterministic function of time. Terminal bonus is given by letting the second order basis coincide with the first order basis throughout the term of the contract and then, at the terminal time n, paying out a bonus sum. Hereby, the dynamics for $X(t)$ becomes

$$dX(t) = (r dt + \Theta(t, X(t)) ((\alpha - r) dt + \sigma dW(t))) X(t) + c(t) dt,$$

$$c(t) = (r(t) - r^*(t)) V^*(t),$$

i.e. the full safety margin makes up the saving rate and is added to the undistributed reserve.

No dividends are added to the technical reserve in the contract period, so we have $b(t) = b(0)$. On the other hand, at termination the company pays out, in addition to $b(0)$, a bonus sum, which we assume can be written as $\Phi(X(n))$ for a deterministic contract function of the form given in Equation (4.43). Note that Φ plays a different role here than in the preceding sections because we now consider a different bonus form. It is now possible to derive, based on arbitrage arguments, a deterministic differential equation for the total reserve V which generalizes the Black–Scholes equation:

$$\frac{\partial}{\partial t} V(t, x) = rV(t, x) + \pi$$

$$-\frac{\partial}{\partial x} V(t, x)\,(rx + c(t))$$

$$-\frac{1}{2}\Theta^2(t, x)\,\sigma^2 x^2 \frac{\partial^2}{\partial x^2} V(t, x), \qquad (4.44)$$

$$V(n, x) = b(0) + \Phi(x),$$

and we can now relate the different terms to the elements of Thiele's differential equation and the Black–Scholes equation. The first line contains the risk-free return on the value and the rate of premiums recognized from Thiele's differential equation. The second line contains the partial derivative with respect to x. This corresponds to the partial derivative with respect to s in the Black–Scholes equation but the factor is modified such that it equals the drift coefficient in the dynamics of X. Here, we remember to replace α by r. The third line contains the second order derivative with respect to x and corresponds to the second order derivative with respect to s in the Black–Scholes equation. The factor equals half of the squared coefficient in front of $dW(t)$ in the dynamics of X. We refer to Steffensen (2000) for details and for the derivation of Equation (4.44).

The differential equation (4.44) is a deterministic tool for the determination of $V(t, X(t))$. A differential equation for accumulating the total reserve, corresponding to the price dynamics, Equation (4.36), can be derived, however, as follows:

$$dV(t, X(t)) = rV(t, X(t))\,dt + \pi\,dt$$

$$+\frac{\partial}{\partial x} V(t, X(t))\,\Theta(t, X(t))\,X(t)\,((\alpha - r)\,dt + \sigma\,dW(t)).$$

Comparing this with the dynamics in Equation (4.23), it is possible, taking into consideration the premium π, to construct a hedging portfolio from the following relation which determines h^1:

$$\frac{\partial}{\partial x} V(t, X(t)) \Theta(t, X(t)) X(t) = h^1(t) S^1(t),$$

and h^0 is then determined residually.

The solution of Equation (4.44) has the following representation formula:

$$V(t, u) = e^{-r(n-t)}\left(b(0) + E_{t,x}^Q[\Phi(X(n))]\right) - \int_t^n e^{-r(s-t)} \pi \, ds,$$

where $E_{t,x}^Q$ denotes the expectation under Q conditioned on $X(t) = x$. For certain specifications of Θ and Φ, it is possible to derive an explicit formula.

Prudent investment

As an example of an explicit formula, we show what happens if we invest so prudently that $X(n) \geq 0$. Then we can assume a contract function in the form $\Phi(x) = \beta + \alpha x$, $\beta \geq 0$, $\alpha \geq 0$, and we can now "guess" a solution of the following form:

$$V(t, x) = f(t) + g(t)x.$$

Substituting this solution into Equation (4.44), we find that $V(t, x)$ fulfils Equation (4.44) if f and g fulfil the following differential equations:

$$f'(t) = rf(t) + \pi - gc(t),$$
$$g'(t) = 0.$$

Together with the terminal conditions $f(n) = b(0) + \beta$ and $g(n) = \alpha$, we obtain the solution to that system as follows:

$$g(t) = \alpha,$$
$$f(t) = \int_t^n e^{-r(s-t)}(\alpha c(s) - \pi)\,ds + e^{-r(n-t)}(b(0) + \beta).$$

We now wish to find a fair combination of the parameters in the contract function, α and β; this is achieved by the fulfilment of the equivalence relation $V(0, 0) = 0$, i.e. $f(0) = 0$, where

$$f(0) = \int_0^n e^{-rs}(\alpha c(s) - \pi)\,ds + e^{-rn}(b(0) + \beta).$$

It is now easy to see that one fair construction (out of many) is given by $(\alpha, \beta) = (1, 0)$, corresponding to paying out the full undistributed reserve as bonus at time n. Thereby,

$$g(t) = 1,$$

$$f(t) = \int_t^n e^{-r(s-t)} (c(s) - \pi) \, ds + e^{-r(n-t)} b(0),$$

and we see how $V(t) = f(t) + X(t)$ consists of $X(t)$ plus the individual bonus potential, $\int_t^n \exp(-r(s-t)) c(s) \, ds$, plus the market value of the guaranteed payments, $e^{-r(n-t)} b(0) - \int_t^n \exp(-r(s-t)) \pi \, ds$. One may argue that the special case $(\alpha, \beta) = (1, 0)$ is uninteresting since then the surplus X appropriately defined at time n, after subtraction of the terminal bonus, equals zero. So, in this case, we actually have that $V(t) = U(t)$, and there is no reason to perform the calculations above. However, the derivation still serves as a demonstration of techniques.

4.5.2 Cash bonus

We now consider the bonus form cash bonus. We let the investment be determined by a function Θ, such that $\eta^1(t) S^1(t) / X(t) = \Theta(t, X(t))$. As was the case for terminal bonus, this is not a restriction compared with Equation (4.42) since the technical reserve is a deterministic function of t. Cash bonus is given by paying out the dividends, according to a second order basis, immediately to the policy holder. Thus, guaranteed payments π and $b(0)$ fall due, but in addition the policy holder receives a cash bonus payment of $(r^\delta(t) - r^*(t)) V^*(t)$. The policy holder can view this as a discount on the premiums. We can link the bonus payments to the undistributed reserve through the contract function Φ by letting

$$r^\delta(t) = r^*(t) + \frac{\Phi(t, X(t))}{V^*(t)}.$$

Thereby, the bonus payments and the dynamics for $X(t)$ become

$$(r^\delta(t) - r^*(t)) V^*(t) = \Phi(t, X(t))$$

and

$$dX(t) = (r \, dt + \Theta(t, X(t)) ((\alpha - r) \, dt + \sigma \, dW(t))) X(t)$$
$$+ c(t) \, dt - \Phi(t, X(t)) \, dt,$$

respectively. One can think of a contract function in the form of Equation (4.43). Again, it is possible to derive a differential equation for the function $V(t, x)$, which becomes

$$\frac{\partial}{\partial t} V(t, x) = rV(t, x) + \pi - \Phi(t, x)$$

$$- \frac{\partial}{\partial x} V(t, x) (rx + c(t) - \Phi(t, x))$$

$$- \frac{1}{2} \Theta^2(t, x) \sigma^2 x^2 \frac{\partial^2}{\partial x^2} V(t, x), \qquad (4.45)$$

$$V(n, x) = b(0),$$

and the elements can be related to those of Thiele's differential equation and the Black–Scholes equation in basically the same way as in Section 4.5.1. Again, we refer to Steffensen (2000) for details and for the derivation of Equation (4.45).

The differential equation for accumulating the total reserve becomes

$$dV(t, X(t)) = rV(t, X(t)) dt + \pi dt - \Phi(t, X(t)) dt$$

$$+ \frac{\partial}{\partial x} V(t, X(t)) (\Theta(t, X(t)) ((\alpha - r) dt + \sigma dW(t)) X(t)),$$

and the hedging portfolio of stocks is, according to (4.22) and taking into consideration the premium payments and cash bonus, determined by

$$\frac{\partial}{\partial x} V(t, X(t)) \Theta(t, X(t)) X(t) = h^1(t) S^1(t).$$

The solution to Equation (4.45) has the following stochastic representation formula:

$$V(t, x) = e^{-r(n-t)} b(0) + \int_t^n e^{-r(s-t)} \left(E_{t,x}^Q [\Phi(s, X(s))] - \pi \right) ds.$$

For certain specifications of Θ and Φ, it is possible to find an explicit formula.

Prudent investment

As an example of an explicit formula, we show what happens if we invest so prudently that $X(t) \geq 0$. Then we can assume a contract function in the form $\Phi(t, x) = \beta(t) + \alpha(t) x$, $\alpha(t) \geq 0$, $\beta(t) \geq 0$, and we can now "guess" a solution of the following form:

$$V(t, x) = f(t) + g(t) x.$$

Substituting this solution into Equation (4.45), we find that $V(t, x)$ fulfils (4.45) if f and g fulfil the following differential equations:

$$f'(t) = rf(t) + \pi - \beta(t) - g(t)c(t) + \beta(t)g(t),$$

$$g'(t) = rg(t) - \alpha(t) + g(t)\alpha(t).$$

Together with the terminal conditions $f(n) = b(0)$ and $g(n) = 0$, we obtain the solution to that system as follows:

$$g(t) = \int_t^n e^{-\int_t^s \alpha(\tau)d\tau}\alpha(s)\,ds,$$

$$f(t) = \int_t^n e^{-r(s-t)}(\beta(s) - \pi + g(s)(c(s) - \beta(s)))\,ds + e^{-r(n-t)}b(0).$$

Now we find a fair contract by determining (α, β) such that the equivalence relation $V(0,0) = 0$ is fulfilled, i.e. $f(0) = 0$.

It is now easy to see that one fair construction (out of many) is given by $(\alpha, \beta) = (0, c)$, corresponding to paying out the contributions as bonus. Thereby,

$$g(t) = 0,$$

$$f(t) = \int_t^n e^{-r(s-t)}(c(s) - \pi)\,ds + e^{-r(n-t)}b(0),$$

and we see how $V(t) = f(t)$ consists of the individual bonus potential given by $\int_t^n \exp(-r(s-t))c(s)\,ds$ plus the market value of the guaranteed payments given by $e^{-r(n-t)}b(0) - \int_t^n \exp(-r(s-t))\pi\,ds$. One may argue that the special case $(\alpha, \beta) = (0, c)$ is uninteresting since then $X(t) = 0$ for all t and, in particular, $X(n) = 0$. So, in this case, we actually have that $V(t) = U(t)$, and there is no reason to perform the calculations above. However, the derivation still serves as a demonstration of techniques.

4.5.3 Additional benefits

Finally, we consider the bonus form accumulation of benefits. This is the bonus form described in Chapter 2 where the dividend payments are added to the technical reserve and where the guaranteed pension sum is increased correspondingly. Thus, the guaranteed payments π and $b(n)$ fall due, where $b(n) = V^*(n)$ is the terminal pension sum, including accumulation of past dividends. We let the investment be determined by a function Θ such that $\eta^1(t)S^1(t)/X(t) = \Theta(t, V^*(t), X(t))$, and again we link the bonus payments to the undistributed reserve through a contract function Φ, i.e. by

$$r^{\delta}(t) = r^{*}(t) + \frac{\Phi(t, V^{*}(t), X(t))}{V^{*}(t)}.$$

Thereby, the dividend payments and the dynamics for X and V^{*} become

$$\left(r^{\delta}(t) - r^{*}(t)\right) V^{*}(t) = \Phi(t, X(t)),$$

$$dX(t) = (r\,dt + \Theta(t, V^{*}(t), X(t))((\alpha - r)\,dt + \sigma dW(t)))\,X(t)$$

$$+ (r(t) - r^{*}(t))\,V^{*}(t)\,dt - \Phi(t, X(t), V^{*}(t))\,dt$$

and

$$dV^{*}(t) = r^{*}V^{*}(t)\,dt + \pi\,dt + \Phi(t, X(t), V^{*}(t))\,dt,$$

respectively. One can think of a contract function in the form of Equation (4.43). It is now possible to derive a differential equation for the function $V(t, v, x)$, which becomes

$$\frac{\partial}{\partial t}V(t, v, x) = rV(t, v, x) + \pi$$

$$-\frac{\partial}{\partial x}V(t, v, x)\,(rx + (r - r^{*})\,v - \Phi(t, v, x))$$

$$-\frac{\partial}{\partial v}V(t, v, x)\,(r^{*}v + \pi + \Phi(t, v, x))$$

$$-\frac{1}{2}\Theta^{2}(t, v, x)\,\sigma^{2}x^{2}\frac{\partial^{2}}{\partial x^{2}}V(t, v, x), \qquad (4.46)$$

$$V(n, v, x) = v.$$

The elements can be related to Thiele's differential equation and the Black–Scholes equation in basically the same way as in Section 4.5.1. Again, we refer to Steffensen (2000) for details and for the derivation of Equation (4.46).

The differential equation for accumulating the total reserve becomes

$$dV(t, V^{*}(t), X(t)) = rV(t, V^{*}(t), X(t))\,dt + \pi\,dt$$

$$+ \frac{\partial}{\partial x}V(t, V^{*}(t), X(t))\,\Theta(t, V^{*}(t), X(t))\,X(t)$$

$$\times ((\alpha - r)\,dt + \sigma dW(t)),$$

and the hedging portfolio of stocks is, according to Equation (4.22) and taking into consideration the premiums, determined by

$$\frac{\partial}{\partial x}V(t, V^{*}(t), X(t))\,\Theta(t, V^{*}(t), X(t))\,X(t) = h^{1}(t)\,S^{1}(t).$$

The solution to Equation (4.46) has the following stochastic representation formula:

$$V(t, v, x) = \int_t^n e^{-r(s-t)} \left(E^Q_{t,v,u} \left[V^*(n) \right] - \pi \right) ds,$$

where $E^Q_{t,v,u}$ denotes the expectation under Q conditioned on $V^*(t) = v$ and $X(t) = x$. For certain specifications of Θ and Φ, it is possible to find an explicit formula.

Prudent investment

As an example of an explicit formula, we show what happens if we invest so prudently that $X(t) \geq 0$. Then we can assume a contract function in the form $\Phi(t, v, x) = \beta(t) + \alpha(t)x$, $\alpha(t) \geq 0$, $\beta(t) \geq 0$, and we can now "guess" a solution of the following form:

$$V(t, v, x) = f(t) + g(t)x + h(t)v.$$

Substituting this solution into Equation (4.46), we find that $V(t, v, x)$ fulfils (4.46) if f, g and h fulfil the following differential equations:

$$f'(t) = rf(t) + \pi + (g(t) - h(t))\beta(t) - h(t)\pi,$$
$$g'(t) = g(t)\alpha(t) - h(t)\alpha(t),$$
$$h'(t) = (r - r^*)h(t) - g(t)(r - r^*).$$

Together with the terminal conditions $f(n) = 0$, $g(n) = 0$, and $h(n) = 1$, the solution to that system becomes

$$g(t) = \int_t^n e^{-\int_t^s \alpha} \alpha(s) h(s) ds,$$

$$h(t) = e^{-(r-r^*)(n-t)} + \int_t^n e^{-(r-r^*)(s-t)} (r - r^*) g(s) ds,$$

$$f(t) = \int_t^n e^{-r(s-t)} (h(s)(\pi + \beta(s)) - g(s)\beta(s) - \pi) ds.$$

The solution to this system can also be written using so-called matrix exponentials. Now we find a fair contract by determining (α, β) such that the equivalence relation $V(0, 0, 0) = 0$ is fulfilled, i.e. $f(0) = 0$.

It is now easy to see that one fair construction (out of many) is given by $(\alpha, \beta) = (0, c)$, corresponding to paying out the contributions as dividends. Thereby,

$$g(t) = 0,$$
$$h(t) = e^{-(r-r^*)(n-t)},$$
$$f(t) = \int_t^n e^{-r(s-t)} \left(h(s) c(s) - \pi (1 - h(s)) \right) ds,$$

and we see how $V(t) = f(t) + h(t) V^*(t)$ consists of two parts. One part, $h(t) V^*(t)$, is actually the market value of the free policy benefits. By differentiation of V with respect to t, one sees that actually $V(t) = U(t)$, and from this we conclude that the other part of V in the representation $V(t) = f(t) + h(t) V^*(t)$, $f(t)$, expresses the bonus potential on the free policy, i.e. $f(t) = V^{\mathrm{bf}}(t)$; see Chapter 2. One may argue that the special case $(\alpha, \beta) = (0, c)$ is uninteresting since $V(t) = U(t)$ and there is no reason to perform the calculations above. However, the derivation still serves as a demonstration of techniques.

4.6 Generalizations of the models

In this chapter the financial market has been modeled by the binomial model and the Black–Scholes model. Often, these models are too simple to cover the effects experienced from the real financial market. In particular, when evaluating life insurance obligations with terms of more than thirty years, these models are far too simple. In this final section we therefore consider some possible generalizations which make the models more realistic.

Stochastic interest in the binomial model

A binomial model for the interest rate was introduced in Chapter 3. It is possible to combine the binomial model introduced in Sections 4.2 and 4.3 with a binomial model for the interest rate. We introduce a sequence of two-dimensional stochastic variables $\left(Z^r(t), Z^S(t) \right)_{t=1,\dots,n}$, where each of the variables $Z^r(t)$ and $Z^S(t)$ assume one of two values and drives the stochastic interest rate and the stock, respectively. Note that $Z^r(t)$ and $Z^S(t)$ may be correlated. One can now put up a pricing formula for the conditional claim X falling due at time n in correspondence with the principle of no arbitrage. Unfortunately, one does not obtain a unique formula but a continuum of formulas, as follows:

$$\Pi^Q(t, X) = E_t^Q \left[\frac{1 + r(t)}{1 + r(n)} X \right], Q \in \mathbf{Q}, \tag{4.47}$$

where $\mathbf{Q}$ is now a set of martingale measures which all give arbitrage-free prices. All martingale measures, i.e. measures under which the discounted stock price,

$$\frac{1}{1+r(1)} \cdots \frac{1}{1+r(t)} S(t),$$

is a martingale, can be used here.

It is indeed a drawback, compared with the binomial model with deterministic interest rate, that we do not obtain unique pricing formulas. However, if we introduce a bond market with observable bond prices, we may again obtain unique prices. This corresponds to pointing out the unique martingale measure under which not only the discounted stock prices, but also the discounted bond prices are martingales. This relates to the situation in Chapter 3, where Q is determined uniquely after the introduction of observable zero coupon bond prices P_t^n. If these are known, and Z^r and Z^S are independent under the measure Q, Equation (4.47) reduces to

$$\Pi(t, X) = P(t, n) E_t^Q [X]. \tag{4.48}$$

Stochastic interest in the Black–Scholes model

As in the binomial model, it would be natural to allow for a stochastic interest rate in the Black–Scholes model. In Chapter 3 a stochastic model is introduced where the dynamics of the interest rate are given by

$$dr(t) = \nu(t, r(t)) dt + \sigma(t, r(t)) dW^r(t),$$

where W^r is a Wiener process. We can now replace the deterministic interest rate in the Black–Scholes model by such an interest rate. Equivalent to the situation in discrete time where the binomial stochastic variables determining the interest rate and the stock could be correlated, we can also let the two Wiener processes, W and W^r, be correlated. The set of arbitrage-free prices of a contingent claim X becomes

$$\Pi^Q(t, X) = E_t^Q \left[e^{-\int_t^n r(s)ds} X \right], Q \in \mathbf{Q}, \tag{4.49}$$

where $\mathbf{Q}$ is the set of martingale measures. As was discussed in Chapter 3, we require a knowledge of the prices at the bond market to determine a unique martingale measure. If we know the zero coupon prices $P(t, n)$ and assume independence between r and S^1 under Q, we obtain the pricing formula given by Equation (4.48) again.

Factor models

The stochastic interest rate process introduced above in a Black–Scholes model belongs to a set of generalized financial models which are called factor models. A K-factor model for a continuous financial market is a model consisting of a K-dimensional factor $Y = (Y^1, \dots, Y^K)$, where the dynamics of Y^k is given by

$$dY^k(t) = \mu^k(t, Y(t))\, dt + \sum_{i=1}^{n} \sigma^{ki}(t, Y(t))\, dW^i(t),$$

where $W = (W^1, \dots, W^n)$ is an n-dimensional Wiener process. These factors determine a risk-free interest rate $r(t, Y(t))$. We are interested in prices and hedging portfolios connected to conditional claims in the form $\Phi(Y)$, where Φ is the contract function. If "a lot" of the factors are prices on traded assets, then we can say "a lot" about prices and hedging portfolios. If only "a few" of the factors are prices on traded assets, then we can say only "a little" about prices and hedging portfolios.

The example with stochastic interest rate in the Black–Scholes model above is a two-factor model where the interest rate itself plays the role of factor. Another popular class of factor models introduces stochastic processes for the volatility $\sigma = (\sigma(t))_{t \geq 0}$ in the Black–Scholes market, the stochastic volatility models. In Chapter 3, a Cox–Ingersoll–Ross process was mentioned as a candidate for the stochastic interest rate. This process is suggested by Heston (1993) for the description of the square of $\sigma(t)$, i.e. $\gamma(t) = \sigma^2(t)$, with the dynamics given by

$$d\gamma(t) = a(b - \gamma(t))\, dt + c\sqrt{\gamma(t)}\, dW^\gamma(t),$$

where W^γ is a Wiener process driving the volatility.

In general, we cannot obtain unique arbitrage-free prices in factor models. This relates to the fact that we cannot determine a unique martingale measure, which again relates to the fact that such models are not, in general, complete. Another important example of an incomplete market appears by introducing life insurance obligations under the consideration of mortality risk which is not to be diversified, such as, For example, by introduction of stochastic mortality intensities. Parts of Møller (2000) and Steffensen (2001) deal with questions arising when dealing with incomplete markets. Chapter 5 gives an introduction to some useful tools in incomplete markets.

5

Integrated actuarial and financial valuation

5.1 Introduction

In the previous chapters it has been assumed that mortality risk is diversifiable. Under this assumption, we have proposed valuation principles which could be derived by working with a big portfolio of insured lives (allowing for deterministic decrement series) or by letting the size of the portfolio converge to infinity. In Chapter 2 the financial market consisted of one single investment possibility, a risk-free asset corresponding to a savings account with a deterministic interest. Chapter 3 considered the case where the interest rate is stochastic and derived formulas for the market value of the guaranteed payments that involved the prices of zero coupon bonds. Finally, Chapter 4 studied a financial market with two investment possibilities, a stock and a savings account, and demonstrated how the market value of the total liabilities (including bonus) could be determined for fixed investment and bonus strategies. This study led to explicit formulas for the market value of the total liabilities in two specific models: the binomial model and the Black–Scholes model under the assumption of no arbitrage and diversifiable mortality risk. In this case, the market value was defined as the amount which was necessary in order to hedge the liabilities perfectly via a self-financing investment strategy.

The main goal of the present chapter is to analyze the combined, or integrated, insurance and financial risk which is present in a life insurance contract, where the benefits are linked to returns on the financial markets. For with-profit insurance contracts, one can model the future investment and bonus strategies of the company in order to obtain a description of the link between future benefits and the development of the traded assets using the setup from Chapter 4. Here, we focus on unit-linked life insurance contracts, where benefits are typically already linked to the returns on certain assets in

146

a specific way, which is stipulated in the insurance contract. Thus, with a unit-linked insurance contract, it is in principle the policy holder who decides where the premiums should be invested and how the benefits should be linked to the actual return on these investments; for example, the policy holder can decide whether or not the contract should include minimum guarantees. Thus, in principle, the contract specifies completely how the benefits and the policy holder's account develops in any financial scenario.

Let us now consider the liabilities from a given portfolio of life insurance contracts as an *integrated risk* or *integrated contingent claim*, i.e. as a contingent claim which depends on some financial risk as well as some insurance risk. In this case, it is no longer possible to derive unique market values for the liability from the assumption of no arbitrage alone. Since we typically cannot trade with mortality in the financial markets, these markets cannot tell how we should price and hedge mortality risk. The consequence of this observation is that we cannot find any self-financing strategies that hedge the liabilities perfectly. For example, how would you hedge a contract which pays one million euros at a future time T, provided that a certain policy holder is alive at this time, and zero otherwise, by trading in a stock and a savings account which evolves independently of the policy holder's lifetime? One possible way of solving this problem is to consider models where there exist traded assets which determine the market's attitude towards mortality risk. For more details on this approach, see Møller (1998) and Steffensen (2001).

An alternative way of solving this problem could be to charge a premium, which, provided that it is invested in the savings account, is sufficient to pay the one million euros whether the policy holder survives or not. One problem with this approach is of course that it essentially corresponds to using a survival probability of 1, and hence completely neglects the element of insurance involved. Another problem is that this method does *not* replicate the liability completely, since it leads to a surplus of one million euros if the policy holder is not alive at time T. Investment strategies which ensure sufficient (but possibly too much) capital in order to cover the liabilities are also called *super-hedging* strategies. The present chapter demonstrates that super-hedging in general leads to unreasonably high prices for life insurance contracts. In addition, we treat various other principles for the pricing and hedging of the total liability. These principles have been developed for so-called *incomplete markets*, that is for markets where there are contingent claims that cannot be hedged perfectly by using a self-financing strategy. The principles are based on some relatively advanced mathematics, which are not covered here; however, some technical details can be found in the

Appendix. The chapter focuses instead on the basic ideas and tries to illustrate the consequences of applying these advanced methods to a portfolio of unit-linked or with-profit life insurance contracts.

The chapter is organized as follows. Section 5.2 gives an introduction to unit-linked life insurance and demonstrates how the liabilities may be viewed as a contingent claim. Section 5.3 proposes a simple system for the modeling of the policy holder's account under unit-linked insurance contracts with guarantees, and Section 5.4 repeats the usual argument for pricing under diversification for a large portfolio. In Section 5.5, we bring to the surface the combined insurance and financial risk inherent in a unit-linked insurance contract by working within a one-period model similar to the one considered in Chapter 4. We then derive strategies that minimize the variance on the company's total costs, defined as the company's liability reduced by premiums and investment gains. In addition, we give examples of models where the mortality risk cannot be eliminated by increasing the size of the portfolio. Section 5.6 is devoted to a review of the multi-period model, which was treated in Chapters 3 and 4, and in Section 5.7 we analyze the combined risk in unit-linked contracts within the multi-period model. We describe principles for valuation that take into account the risk that can be hedged in the financial market as well as the risk that cannot be controlled by trading in these markets. In Section 5.8, comparisons are made between unit-linked and traditional with-profit life insurance contracts. Parts of the present chapter follow Møller (2001a, 2002).

5.2 Unit-linked insurance

A unit-linked life insurance contract differs from traditional life insurance contracts in that benefits (and possibly also premiums) are *linked* directly to the value of a *unit* of some investment portfolio. Other names used for these contracts are *equity-linked*, *equity-based* or *variable-life* (in the USA). This construction allows for a high degree of flexibility in that the policy holder in principle can affect the way premiums are invested. In this way, one can adapt the investment strategy to the policy holder's needs and preferences. One obvious idea is to apply a more aggressive investment strategy for young policy holders than the one used for policy holders which are close to the age of retirement. In addition, it is possible to offer contracts that are linked to certain stock indices, for example world indices, country-specific indices or reference portfolios with more or less clearly defined investment profiles;

examples are stocks from certain lines of businesses, areas or companies with specific ethical codes. Unit-linked insurance contracts seem to have been introduced for the first time in Holland in the beginning of the 1950s. In the USA the first unit-linked insurance contracts were offered around 1954, and in the UK the first contracts appeared in 1957. An overview of the early development of these contracts can be found in Turner (1971).

In this chapter we discuss the development of the policy holder's account and risk management for some of the unit-linked contracts that are offered in practice. However, we first treat some more basic aspects in a simplified framework. In particular, we view portfolios of unit-linked life insurance contracts as integrated risks, which include financial and insurance risk. The financial risk is related to the development of the underlying assets, whereas the insurance risk is related to the uncertain number of survivors. Within this framework, one can ask questions such as: when is it possible to hedge this integrated risk? How big should the portfolio be in order to guarantee that the mortality risk is diversifiable? How can the total risk inherent in a life insurance portfolio be characterized if mortality risk is no longer assumed to be diversifiable?

5.2.1 Unit-linked life insurance as a contingent claim

Consider an insurance company with a portfolio of unit-linked life insurance contracts that are linked to the value of some asset, a stock index or an investment portfolio (henceforth simply called the index). Denote by $S^1(t)$ the value at time t of this index. In the following, we refer to the entire future development of the value of the index until the time of maturity T by simply writing S^1; in principle, we should use the notation $(S^1(t))_{t \in [0,T]}$ in order to underline the fact that we are working with the entire price process. In our example, we consider an idealized portfolio which consists of l_x policy holders with identically distributed lifetimes $T^1, \ldots, T^{l_x}$, who have all purchased the same unit-linked pure endowment paid by a single premium $\pi(0)$ at time 0. We simplify further by assuming that the lifetimes are independent. With the contract considered, the amount $f(S^1)$ is payable upon survival to time T. One can think of f as a function which describes exactly how the sum insured, payable upon survival to T, depends explicitly on the development in the value of the underlying index. We first focus on the problem of valuating the benefits, and hence we do not explicitly deal with relations between benefits and premiums.

The present value at time 0 of the company's liabilities is calculated by discounting the future payments, i.e.

$$H = \sum_{i=1}^{l_x} 1_{\{T^i > T\}} f(S^1) e^{-\int_0^T r(u)du},$$
(5.1)

where we have used the market interest rate r as described in Chapter 3. We can think of Equation (5.1) as a contingent claim, which depends on both the value of the stock index and the number of survivors.

Simple examples are obtained by allowing the amount payable upon survival to T to depend on the terminal value of the stock index only, for example

$$f(S^1) = S^1(T),$$
(5.2)

or the terminal value guaranteed against falling short of some fixed amount K,

$$f(S^1) = \max(S^1(T), K).$$
(5.3)

The contract with Equation (5.2) is also known as a *pure unit-linked* contract, and Equation (5.3) is a *unit-linked contract with terminal guarantee* (the guaranteed benefit is in this case K). However, one can also construct more complicated functions of the process S^1, for example by considering a contract with yearly guarantees with

$$f(S^1) = K \cdot \prod_{t=1}^{T} \max\left(1 + \frac{S^1(t) - S^1(t-1)}{S^1(t-1)}, 1 + \delta(t)\right).$$
(5.4)

Here, the quantity $(S^1(t) - S^1(t-1))/S^1(t-1)$ is the relative return from the index in year t and $\delta(t)$ is the guaranteed return in year t. At time 0, the benefit is guaranteed against falling short of

$$K \cdot \prod_{t=1}^{T} (1 + \delta(t)),$$

but the guarantee is increased during the term of the contract if the yearly relative returns exceed the yearly guaranteed returns.

In other situations, it is relevant to study payment functions of the following form:

$$f(S^1) = \max\left(\sum_{t=0}^{T-1} \frac{S^1(T)}{S^1(t)}, \sum_{t=0}^{T-1} \left(\prod_{s=t+1}^{T} (1 + \delta(s))\right)\right),$$

which arise in the case of periodic premiums, where the policy holder invests one unit at times $t = 0, 1, \dots, T-1$. At time t, this leads to $1/S^1(t)$ units of the underlying index, and the value of this investment changes to $S^1(T)/S^1(t)$

at time T. The benefit at T is now calculated as the maximum of the total value at time T of the premiums invested in the index and the value if all premiums had been invested in an account with periodic return $\delta(t)$.

Unit-linked contracts have been analyzed by actuaries and others since the late 1960s; see, for example, Kahn (1971), Turner (1969) and Wilkie (1978). Kahn (1971) and Wilkie (1978) give simulation studies for an insurance company administrating portfolios of unit-linked insurance contracts. Using modern theories of financial mathematics, Brennan and Schwartz (1979a, b) have suggested new valuation principles and investment strategies for unit-linked insurance contracts with so-called asset value guarantees (minimum guarantees). Their principles essentially consisted in combining traditional (law of large numbers) arguments from life insurance with the methods of Black and Scholes (1973) and Merton (1973). By appealing to the law of large numbers, Brennan and Schwartz (1979a, b) first replaced the uncertain courses of the insured lives by their expected values (see also the argument given in Chapter 3, in particular Section 3.2.4). Thus, the actual insurance claims including mortality risk as well as financial risk were replaced by modified claims, which only contained financial uncertainty. More precisely, instead of considering the claim in Equation (5.1), they looked at

$$H' = l_{x\,T}p_x\,f(S^1)e^{-\int_0^T r(u)du} = l_{x+T}f(S^1)e^{-\int_0^T r(u)du}, \tag{5.5}$$

where we have used standard actuarial notation $_Tp_x = P(T^1 > T)$ and $l_{x+T} = l_{x\,T}p_x$. This modified liability could then essentially be identified with an option (albeit with a very long maturity), which could in principle be priced and hedged using the basic principles of (modern) financial mathematics as described in Chapter 4. (However, the time to maturity of an option is typically less than one year, whereas life insurance contracts often extend to more than fifteen years.) For the pure unit-linked contract in Equation (5.2), i.e. the contract without a guarantee, the liability (5.5) is proportional to the discounted terminal value of the stock $S^1(T)$ at time T. This liability can be hedged by a so-called buy-and-hold strategy, which consists in buying $l_{x\,T}p_x$ units of the stock at time 0 and holding these until T. Thus, in the case of no guarantee, the usual arbitrage argument shows that the unique arbitrage-free price of H' is simply $l_{x+T}S^1(0)$. Consequently, one possible fair premium for each policy holder is $_Tp_xS^1(0)$, the probability of survival to T times the value at time 0 of the stock index. Now consider the contract with benefit $f(S^1) = \max(S^1(T), K) = (S^1(T) - K)^+ + K$. In this case, the pricing of Equation (5.5) involves the pricing of a European call option, since

$$H' = l_{x+T}e^{-\int_0^T r(u)du}K + l_{x+T}e^{-\int_0^T r(u)du}(S^1(T) - K)^+.$$

In the general case, we see that this principle suggests the premium

$$l_{x\,T}p_x V(0, f) = l_{x+T} V(0, f),$$

where $V(0, f)$ is the price at time 0 of the purely financial contract which pays $f(S^1)$ at time T.

More recently, the problem of pricing unit-linked life insurance contracts (under constant interest rates) has been addressed by Aase and Persson (1994), Bacinello and Ortu (1993a) and Delbaen (1986), among others, who combined the so-called martingale approach of Harrison and Kreps (1979) and Harrison and Pliska (1981) with law of large numbers arguments. Bacinello and Ortu (1993b), Bacinello and Persson (1998) and Nielsen and Sandmann (1995), among others, generalized existing results to the case of stochastic interest rates. For a treatment of computational aspects and design of unit-link contracts, see Hardy (2003).

Aase and Persson (1994) worked with continuous survival probabilities (i.e. with death benefits that are payable immediately upon the death of the policy holder and not at the end of the year as would be implied by discrete-time survival probabilities) and suggested investment strategies for unit-linked insurance contracts using methods similar to the ones proposed by Brennan and Schwartz (1979a, b) for discrete-time survival probabilities. Whereas Brennan and Schwartz (1979a, b) considered a large portfolio of policy holders and therefore worked with deterministic mortality, Aase and Persson (1994) considered a portfolio consisting of one policy holder only. However, since the random lifetime had already been replaced by the expected course in order to allow for an application of standard financial valuation techniques for complete markets, the resulting strategies were not able to account for the mortality uncertainty within a portfolio of unit-linked life insurance contracts. This leaves open the question of how to quantify and manage the combined actuarial and financial risk inherent in these contracts. In particular, one can investigate to what extent it is possible to hedge liabilities by trading in the financial market.

5.3 The policy holder's account

This section describes the development (in discrete time) of the policy holder's account associated with a unit-linked insurance contract.

Consider a premium payment plan $\pi(0), \pi(1), \ldots, \pi(T-1)$ (gross premiums), and define the corresponding net premiums by $(1 - \gamma(t))\pi(t)$. Denote by $V^*(t)$ the value at time t of the policy holder's account after payment of the net premium $(1 - \gamma(t))\pi(t)$. The premiums are currently invested in an underlying stock index (or a portfolio) whose value at time t is given by $S^1(t)$. The relative return $\varepsilon(t)$ on this index in the period $(t-1, t]$ is given by

$$\varepsilon(t) = \frac{S^1(t) - S^1(t-1)}{S^1(t-1)}.$$

Our framework allows for contracts with guarantees, which may be changed during the term of the contract as a result of new premiums or as a consequence of the development on the financial markets. The guarantee can be specified in terms of the yearly returns $\varepsilon(t)$ on the index, and hence it may affect not only the sum insured, but also the current value of the account. Alternatively, the guarantee can be formulated directly in terms of the amounts payable at the time of maturity of the contract (at time T). Denote by $b^{ad}(t)$ the sum payable at time t in case of a death during the interval $(t-1, t]$. The basic idea is that the policy holder receives the value $V^*(T)$ of the account upon survival to T. We consider situations where the payment upon survival is guaranteed against falling short of some minimum guarantee $G(T)$.

The development of the policy holder's account during some time interval is in general given as follows:

account, beginning of period + investment returns + premiums

$-$ expenses $-$ payment for guarantee

$-$ risk premiums $=$ account, end of period.

With the notation introduced above, the value of the accounts at time 0 for the portfolio consisting of l_x policy holders is given by

$$V^{*\text{port}}(0) = l_x V^*(0) = l_x(1 - \gamma(0))\pi(0),$$

and the development in the value is taken to be described by the following recursive formula:

$$V^{*\text{port}}(t) = (1 + \tilde{\varepsilon}(t)) V^{*\text{port}}(t-1) + l_{x+t}(1 - \gamma(t))\pi(t)$$

$$-l_{x+t-1}\nu(t) - d_{x+t-1}b^{ad}(t), \qquad (5.6)$$

where $d_{x+t-1} = l_{x+t-1} - l_{x+t}$ is the expected number of deaths in the portfolio between age $x+t-1$ and $x+t$. In the recursion, Equation (5.6), $\nu(t)$ is the price of annual or terminal guarantees and $\tilde{\varepsilon}(t)$ is the return which is actually credited to the policy holders' accounts. The term with the premiums $(1 - \gamma(t))\pi(t)$ involves the current number of survivors at time t, which is given by l_{x+t}. This means that premiums are paid at time t by each of the survivors. In contrast, the term with $\nu(t)$ involves the number of survivors at time $t-1$, which indicates that each of the survivors at the beginning of the period (at time $t-1$) will be charged at time t for the guarantee.

If we divide $V^{*\text{port}}(t)$ by the current number of survivors at time t, l_{x+t}, we can derive a similar recursion for the development of the account $V^*(t) = V^{*\text{port}}(t)/l_{x+t}$ for one policy holder. To see this, note the following:

$$V^*(t) = \frac{V^{*\text{port}}(t)}{l_{x+t}}$$

$$= (1+\widetilde{\varepsilon}(t))\frac{l_{x+t-1}}{l_{x+t}}\frac{V^{*\text{port}}(t-1)}{l_{x+t-1}} + (1-\gamma(t))\pi(t)$$

$$\quad - \frac{l_{x+t-1}}{l_{x+t}}v(t) - \frac{d_{x+t-1}}{l_{x+t}}b^{\text{ad}}(t)$$

$$= (1+\widetilde{\varepsilon}(t))V^*(t-1) + (1-\gamma(t))\pi(t) - \frac{l_{x+t-1}}{l_{x+t}}v(t)$$

$$\quad + (1+\widetilde{\varepsilon}(t))\left(\frac{l_{x+t-1}}{l_{x+t}} - 1\right)V^*(t-1) - \frac{d_{x+t-1}}{l_{x+t}}b^{\text{ad}}(t), \qquad (5.7)$$

where the second equality follows by inserting Equation (5.6), and where the third equality follows by using the definition of $V^*(t-1)$. We now introduce the quantity $\check{\mu}(x+t)$, given by

$$\check{\mu}(x+t) = \frac{d_{x+t-1}}{l_{x+t}}, \qquad (5.8)$$

and the (modified) sum at risk $\check{R}(t)$, which is given by

$$\check{R}(t) = b^{\text{ad}}(t) - (V^*(t-1)(1+\widetilde{\varepsilon}(t)) - v(t)). \qquad (5.9)$$

By inserting Equations (5.8) and (5.9) into Equation (5.7), we obtain the following formula:

$$V^*(t) = (1+\widetilde{\varepsilon}(t))V^*(t-1) + (1-\gamma(t))\pi(t) - v(t) - \check{\mu}(x+t)\check{R}(t). \quad (5.10)$$

This recursive system differs from the system used for traditional with-profit life insurance contracts in that the return $\widetilde{\varepsilon}(t)$ credited in year t to the policy holder's account is directly linked to the actual return from the underlying investment portfolio. It is now essential to describe exactly how $v(t)$ and $\widetilde{\varepsilon}(t)$ should be chosen. We consider two different situations and explain how financial mathematics may be applied when designing these contracts.

For example, a yearly guarantee $\delta(t)$ can be specified by letting

$$\widetilde{\varepsilon}(t) = \max(\varepsilon(t), \delta(t));$$

see also Equation (5.4). In this situation, $\delta(t)$ is interpreted as the guaranteed return between time $t-1$ and time t, and $\nu(t)$ is the payment for this guarantee. In this situation, we can give simple explicit expressions for fair choices of $\nu(t)$; we require that $\nu(t)$ is chosen at time $t-1$. If we alternatively consider a terminal guarantee $G(T)$, which may depend on the premiums paid up to time T, we get a much more complicated product. Denote by $G(t)$ the terminal guarantee at time t, payable upon survival to T; the case $G(t) = -\infty$ corresponds to the situation where there is no terminal guarantee. Nielsen and Sandmann (1996) propose the following guarantee:

$$G(t) = \sum_{j=0}^{t} \pi(j)(1 - \gamma(j))e^{\delta^*(T - t(j))},$$

which means that the guarantee comprises the net premiums accumulated with the inflation rate δ^*. In this situation, it is no longer obvious how $\nu(t)$ should be chosen (or interpreted). The situation becomes more complicated if the customer's possibilities for changing investments or to stop paying premiums are also included.

5.3.1 The financial market

We consider here the usual Black–Scholes model described in Chapter 4, with two traded assets: a stock index S^1 and a savings account S^0. The two assets are given by

$$S^1(t) = \exp\left(\left(\alpha - \frac{1}{2}\sigma^2\right)t + \sigma W(t)\right),$$

$$S^0(t) = e^{rt},$$

where $W = (W(t))_{t \in [0,T]}$ is a standard Brownian motion. We introduce the σ-algebra $\mathcal{F}(t) = \sigma\{S^1(u) | u \leq t\}$ which contains information about the development of the stock up to and including time t. Let Q be a martingale measure for S^1/S^0, so that

$$S^1(t) = \exp\left(\left(r - \frac{1}{2}\sigma^2\right)t + \sigma W^Q(t)\right),$$

where the parameter α has been replaced by r and the Brownian motion W has been replaced by a Q-standard Brownian motion W^Q. Finally, recall that, for $t \leq u$,

$$E^Q[e^{-r(u-t)}S^1(u)|\mathcal{F}(t)] = S^1(t). \tag{5.11}$$

5.3.2 Yearly guarantees and premiums

With the yearly guaranteed return $\delta(t)$, $\widetilde{\varepsilon}(t) = \max(\varepsilon(t), \delta(t))$, and hence the forward recursion of the policy holder's account becomes

$$V^*(t) = V^*(t-1)(1+\varepsilon(t)) + (\delta(t) - \varepsilon(t))^+ V^*(t-1)$$

$$+ (1 - \gamma(t))\pi(t) - \nu(t) - \breve{\mu}(x+t)\breve{R}(t). \tag{5.12}$$

We propose to choose the payment $\nu(t)$ for the guarantee in year t so that

$$V^*(t-1) = e^{-r}E^Q\left[V^*(t) - \pi(t)(1-\gamma(t)) + \breve{\mu}(x+t)\,\breve{R}(t)\big|\,\mathcal{F}(t-1)\right],$$

$$\tag{5.13}$$

where Q is a martingale measure. The interpretation of Equation (5.13) is as follows. The value of the account at time $t-1$ corresponds to the value of the account at time t, reduced by premiums paid at t and added risk premiums $\breve{\mu}(x+t)\,\breve{R}(t)$. By inserting Equation (5.12) into Equation (5.13), we obtain the following condition:

$$e^r V^*(t-1) = V^*(t-1)\left(E^Q\left[(1+\varepsilon(t))\big|\,\mathcal{F}(t-1)\right]\right.$$

$$\left. + E^Q\left[(\delta(t)-\varepsilon(t))^+\big|\,\mathcal{F}(t-1)\right]\right) - \nu(t), \tag{5.14}$$

where we have used that $\nu(t)$ is chosen at time $t-1$, i.e. that $\nu(t)$ is $\mathcal{F}(t-1)$-measurable. Since Q is a martingale measure, and since

$$\varepsilon(t) = [S^1(t) - S^1(t-1)]/S^1(t-1),$$

we see from Equation (5.11) that

$$E^Q\left[(1+\varepsilon(t))\big|\,\mathcal{F}(t-1)\right] = 1 + E^Q\left[\varepsilon(t)\big|\,\mathcal{F}(t-1)\right] = 1 + e^r - 1 = e^r.$$

From Equation (5.14), we now obtain the following expression for $\nu(t)$:

$$\nu(t) = V^*(t-1)E^Q\left[(\delta(t)-\varepsilon(t))^+\big|\,\mathcal{F}(t-1)\right]. \tag{5.15}$$

Explicit expression for the price of the guarantee

The price $\nu(t)$ of the guarantee can be determined explicitly by using the Black–Scholes formula for the price of a European call option. We assume that $\delta(t)$ is chosen based on the information available at time $t-1$, that is $\delta(t)$ is $\mathcal{F}(t-1)$-measurable. Firstly, note that

$$(\delta(t) - \varepsilon(t))^+ = \left((1+\delta(t)) - \frac{S^1(t)}{S^1(t-1)}\right)^+.$$

Using the Black–Scholes formula (see Chapter 4), we then see that

$$E^Q\left[\frac{S^0(t-1)}{S^0(t)}\left((1+\delta(t))-\frac{S^1(t)}{S^1(t-1)}\right)^+\Bigg|S^1(t-1)\right]$$
$$= (1+\delta(t))e^{-r}\Phi(-z_2(t)) - \Phi(-z_1(t)),$$

where Φ is the standard normal distribution function, and where

$$z_1(t) = \frac{-\log(1+\delta(t)) + (r+\frac{1}{2}\sigma^2)}{\sigma},$$

$$z_2(t) = \frac{-\log(1+\delta(t)) + (r-\frac{1}{2}\sigma^2)}{\sigma}.$$

This shows that the fair price for the guarantee for the period $(t-1,t]$ is given by

$$v(t) = V^*(t-1)\left((1+\delta(t))\Phi(-z_2(t)) - e^r\Phi(-z_1(t))\right). \qquad (5.16)$$

We note that this quantity only depends on the past development in the value of the stock index via $V^*(t-1)$, which is the value of the policy holder's account at the beginning of the period $[t-1,t]$. In addition, the above calculations show that the different periods can be considered separately when the price of the guarantee is computed. In particular, this has the advantage that one does not have to work with a model which describes the development of the stock index until the time of maturity for the calculation of prices for the guarantees.

Value of account payable upon death

We consider the special case $\check{R}(t) = 0$, i.e. the situation where

$$b^{\mathrm{ad}}(t) = V^*(t-1)(1+\widetilde{\varepsilon}(t)) - v(t). \qquad (5.17)$$

This is the natural situation, where the value of the account is payable upon death. Under this assumption, the recursion for the value of the account simplifies as follows to:

$$V^*(t) = V^*(t-1)(1+\varepsilon(t)) + (\delta(t)-\varepsilon(t))^+ V^*(t-1)$$
$$+(1-\gamma(t))\pi(t) - v(t). \qquad (5.18)$$

It is not too difficult to see that Equation (5.18) is solved by

$$V^*(t) = \sum_{j=0}^{t} \pi(j)(1-\gamma(j)) \prod_{s=j+1}^{t} (1+\varepsilon(s))$$

$$+ \sum_{j=1}^{t} \left((\delta(j) - \varepsilon(j))^+ V^*(j-1) - \nu(j) \right) \prod_{s=j+1}^{t} (1+\varepsilon(s)), \qquad (5.19)$$

for $t = 1, \ldots, T$. This expression shows how the value of the account can be decomposed into two terms. The first term consists of net premiums accumulated with the actual return on S^1, and the second term is related to the guarantees. One can show that Equation (5.15) implies that

$$\sum_{j=0}^{T-1} e^{-rj} {}_j p_x (1-\gamma(j)) \pi(j)$$

$$= E^Q \left[\sum_{j=1}^{T} {}_{j-1} p_x {}_1 q_{x+j-1} e^{-rj} b^{\mathrm{ad}}(j) + {}_T p_x e^{-rT} V^*(T) \right], \qquad (5.20)$$

where $V^*(T)$ is given by Equation (5.19). This shows that the market value of net premiums is equal to the market value of the benefits, so that the contract is fair.

In more general models with stochastic interest rates, the market value of the premiums appearing on the left hand side of Equation (5.20) would involve the zero coupon bond prices $P(0, j)$ instead of the terms e^{-rj}. In the expression for the market value of the benefits (the right hand side of Equation (5.20)), the factors e^{-rj} and e^{-rT} would have to be replaced by the relevant stochastic discount factors, $1/S^0(j)$ and $1/S^0(T)$.

Account payable upon death under a pure unit-linked contract
We can simplify matters further by omitting the guarantee. Formally, this corresponds to setting $\delta(t) = -1$, but it basically amounts to leaving out the terms with $\nu(t)$ and $(\delta(t) - \varepsilon(t))^+$ in the recursion for the value of the account. This yields the following natural expression for the account:

$$V^*(t) = \sum_{j=0}^{t} \pi(j)(1-\gamma(j)) \prod_{s=j+1}^{t} (1+\varepsilon(s)) = \sum_{j=0}^{t} \pi(j)(1-\gamma(j)) \frac{S^1(t)}{S^1(j)},$$
$$(5.21)$$

i.e. the value of the account is simply the net premiums accumulated with the actual returns from the index S^1. This contract includes no guarantees on the returns and the benefit upon death is the current value of the account. Equation (5.21) indicates that this kind of contract is essentially a "bank product": the value of the account is simply the premiums accumulated with "interest," and this amount is payable at the time of death or at maturity T if the policy holder survives to T.

5.3.3 Terminal guarantees

We now turn to the situation where the return $\varepsilon(t)$ is credited to the policy holder's account, but where the amount payable at time T is given by $\max(V^*(T), G(T))$. For simplicity, we keep the assumption that the value of the account is payable upon death, which ensures that $\check{R}(t) = 0$; see Equation (5.17). The value of the account now satisfies the following equation:

$$V^*(t) = V^*(t-1)(1+\varepsilon(t)) + (1-\gamma(t))\pi(t) - \nu(t). \qquad (5.22)$$

As above, $V^*(t)$ can be written as follows:

$$V^*(t) = \sum_{j=0}^{t} \pi(j)(1-\gamma(j)) \prod_{s=j+1}^{t} (1+\varepsilon(s)) - \sum_{j=1}^{t} \nu(j) \prod_{s=j+1}^{t} (1+\varepsilon(s)),$$

and the question is how $\nu(1), \ldots, \nu(T)$ should be chosen in order to ensure that the contract is fair. More precisely, this amounts to finding $\nu(1), \ldots, \nu(T)$ such that the market values of benefits and premiums balance. Under a terminal guarantee, we obtain the following equation:

$$\sum_{j=0}^{T-1} e^{-rj} {}_{j}p_x(1-\gamma(j))\pi(j)$$

$$= E^Q \left[\sum_{j=1}^{T} {}_{j-1}p_x \, {}_1q_{x+j-1} \, e^{-rj} b^{\mathrm{ad}}(j) + {}_Tp_x \, e^{-rT} \max(V^*(T), G(T)) \right],$$

$$(5.23)$$

which is similar to Equation (5.20) for the case of yearly guarantees. Here, the last term, $\max(V^*(T), G(T))$, can be quite complicated. One possibility is to choose $\nu(t) = \nu$ (constant) and determine

$$E^Q \left[e^{-rT} \max(V^*(T), G(T)) \right]$$

$$= E^Q \left[e^{-rT} \max \left(\sum_{j=0}^{T} (\pi(j)(1-\gamma(j)) - \nu) \prod_{s=j+1}^{T} (1+\varepsilon(s)), G(T) \right) \right],$$

where we use $\pi(T) = 0$. Equation (5.23) can then be solved via simulation. A similar problem is described in Bacinello and Ortu (1993a), who apply fix point theorems in order to find fair parameters.

5.3.4 Pure endowment paid by single premium

A unit-linked pure endowment paid by a single premium at time 0 is obtained by letting $\pi(1) = \cdots = \pi(T-1) = 0$ and $b^{\text{ad}}(1) = \cdots = b^{\text{ad}}(T) = 0$. This contract is fair if the market value of the benefits is equal to the market value of the premiums, i.e. if

$$(1 - \gamma(0))\pi(0) = {}_T p_x E^Q \left[e^{-rT} \max(V^*(T), G(T)) \right],$$

where $V^*(T)$ is defined by the recursion, Equation (5.10). The terminal value $V^*(T)$ depends on the development of the stock index, the net single premium $(1 - \gamma(0))\pi(0)$ and the price ν of the guarantee. Using the notation introduced in Section 5.2, we can rewrite the amount payable at T as follows:

$$f(S^1 | \pi(0), \nu) = \max(V^*(T), G(T)), \tag{5.24}$$

where we have chosen to underline the fact that the benefit depends on the pair $(\pi(0), \nu)$. In the rest of this chapter we study unit-linked pure endowments with benefits of the form given in Equation (5.24) without specifying f explicitly.

5.3.5 On the choice of model

In the previous sections, we have worked with the standard Black–Scholes model. It is well known that this model does not give a perfect description of the development of prices of financial assets. However, the model can still be used to provide an important insight into how premiums, benefits and payment profiles interact. For example, one can apply the model for comparisons of various payment profiles under various contracts with different guarantees. In addition, one can simulate developments of the index and compare the distribution of the benefits for various choices of guarantees.

So what is wrong with the Black–Scholes model? One aspect is the assumption of a constant interest rate on the savings account. For long term considerations, it would certainly seem more natural to include a stochastic interest rate model.

Another aspect is the choice of model for the returns on the underlying stock index. According to the model, the daily changes in the logarithm of the index should be independent and normally distributed with the same variance. Empirical evidence shows that this is typically not the case for financial time series. Firstly, financial time series typically show more heavy tails, which means that there are more large changes in the real world than predicted by the Black–Scholes model. This implies that the assumption of log-normally distributed stock returns underestimates the risk of large losses in the index. Secondly, financial time series typically show changes in the underlying variance (the volatility), such that there are periods with large changes and more quiet periods. This phenomenon, known as stochastic volatility, is also not captured by the Black–Scholes model.

A reference to unit-linked life insurance contracts which investigates these aspects more closely is Hardy (2003). For the modeling of extreme events in finance and insurance in general, see Embrechts, Klüppelberg and Mikosch (1997) and references therein.

5.4 Hedging integrated risks under diversification

A simple valuation formula for unit-linked life insurance contracts of the form in Equation (5.1) can be derived under the assumption that the company can invest in financial instruments (options) which pay $f(S^1)$ at time T by using a diversification argument corresponding to the one used in Section 3.2.6. We repeat this argument here in a slightly modified version which also takes mortality risk into account. Denote by $\pi(0, f)$ the price at time 0 of the option which pays $f(S^1)$ at time T. This contract essentially plays the role of the zero coupon bond from the calculation of the market value of the guaranteed payments on a traditional life insurance contract.

Assume that the insurance company purchases at time 0 exactly κ options for each policy holder, that is $l_x \kappa$ options in total. This investment generates the payoff $l_x \kappa f(S^1)$ at time T, so that the present value at time 0 of the company's net loss (expenses minus income) is given by

$$\widetilde{L} = Y(T) e^{-\int_0^T r(u)\,du} f(S^1) - l_x \pi(0)$$
$$- \left(l_x \kappa f(S^1) e^{-\int_0^T r(u)\,du} - l_x \kappa \pi(0, f) \right), \qquad (5.25)$$

where

$$Y(t) = \sum_{i=1}^{l_x} 1_{\{T^i > t\}}$$

is the actual number of survivors at time $t \in [0, T]$. The first two terms in Equation (5.25) represent the present value at time 0 of the net payment to the policy holders, i.e. the net loss associated with the contract which appears without taking into account the investment side. The last term is exactly the present value of the net loss (or minus the net gain) from investing in options. Thus, $\widetilde{L}$ is the net payment to the policy holders reduced by investment gains.

By rewriting the total net loss as follows:

$$\widetilde{L} = (Y(T) - l_x \kappa)e^{-\int_0^T r(u)\,du} f(S^1) + l_x \left(\kappa \pi(0, f) - \pi(0) \right),$$

and using the independence between the financial market and the insured lives, we see that

$$E[\widetilde{L}] = (l_x \, _T p_x - l_x \kappa) E \left[e^{-\int_0^T r(u)du} f(S^1) \right] + l_x (\kappa \pi(0, f) - \pi(0)).$$

Thus, $E[\widetilde{L}] = 0$ if for example, the single premium $\pi(0)$ is determined such that

$$\pi(0) = \,_T p_x \pi(0, f) \qquad (5.26)$$

and $\kappa = \,_T p_x$. Here, we have calculated the expected value by using the true survival probabilities. In fact, the criterion leads to the fair premium for the pure endowment, which is equal to the option price $\pi(0, f)$ multiplied by the survival probability $_T p_x$.

In the literature, the premium calculation principle from Equation (5.26) is often said to be a consequence of the insurance company being *risk-neutral with respect to mortality*. This notion can, for example, be explained by the fact that the fair premium can be derived by using the law of large numbers and the usual limiting argument, which applies provided that the lifetimes of the policy holders are independent. More precisely, the premium in Equation (5.26) and the corresponding choice of κ are uniquely characterized by the property that the relative loss $(1/l_x)\widetilde{L}$ converges to zero when the size l_x of the portfolio increases (to infinity). Thus, the fair premium is actually derived via an argument which neglects the mortality risk present in any (finite) life insurance portfolio. Another explanation of the notion "risk-neutral with respect to mortality" could be that the factor $_T p_x$ in Equation (5.26) is the true expected value of $1_{\{T^1 > T\}}$, i.e. the true survival probability, whereas the second factor, $\pi(0, f)$, is the price of the option $f(S^1)$ at time 0, which is typically not equal to the expected value under P of the discounted payment. A discussion of this principle and these concepts can also be found in Aase and Persson (1994).

The fair premium $\pi(0)$ has the property that $\lim_{l_x \to \infty} (1/l_x)\widetilde{L} = 0$, if the lifetimes are independent, such that the insurance company (in principle) is able to eliminate the total risk in a portfolio of unit-linked life insurance contract by buying standard options on the stock and by increasing the number of contracts in the portfolio. Similarly, we have that if the premium $\pi'(0)$ is larger than that in Equation (5.26), then, for $\kappa = {}_T p_x$,

$$\lim_{l_x \to \infty} \frac{1}{l_x} \widetilde{L} = {}_T p_x \pi(0, f) - \pi'(0) < 0,$$

and hence $\widetilde{L} \to -\infty$. This leads to an infinitely large surplus, when the size of the portfolio is increased, if the single premium is larger than the product of the option price $\pi(0, f)$ and the probability ${}_T p_x$ of survival to T. Lower premiums lead of course to an infinitely big loss as the size of the portfolio is increased.

In the above analysis, we have obviously simplified matters greatly by disregarding various facts of both theoretical and practical importance. One example is the difference in time horizons between life insurance contracts (typically more than fifteen years) and standard options (typically less than one year), and one can certainly discuss whether it makes sense to work with options with maturities of fifteen years. Another example is the choice of valuation basis for the calculation of premiums of a unit-linked insurance contract, where one might be interested in applying the same first order valuation principle for the insurance risk as the one applied in the pricing of traditional life insurance contracts. However, one can still ask questions like: is it optimal to purchase $l_{x T} p_x$ options which each pay $f(S^1)$ at time T? Does there exist a better investment strategy for issuers of unit-linked insurance contracts? Is it possible to find reasonable investment strategies based on the underlying stock index? Is it possible to currently update the investment strategy as new information from the financial markets and from the portfolio of insured lives becomes available?

In order to be able to address these issues, one has to specify optimization criteria. In the following, we look at several different criteria that can be applied when determining optimal investment strategies.

5.5 Hedging integrated risk in a one-period model

In this section we consider a one-period model, where it is possible to invest in a stock and a bond at two times only: time 0 and time 1. Denote by $S^1(t)$ the value of the stock at time $t \in \{0, 1\}$, and let $S^0(t)$ be the value at t of one unit invested in the savings account at time t. We assume that $S^0(t) = (1 + r)^t$, where $r > 0$ is the annual interest from time 0 to time 1, which is furthermore assumed to be known at time 0. In contrast, the value of the stock $S^1(1)$ at time 1 is known at time 1 only.

Consider now an insurance company facing a liability payable at time 1, with present value H at time 0, and assume that the insurance company is interested in reducing the risk associated with this liability as much as possible. (Here we need to be careful and specify exactly how risk should be measured; we come back to this later.) We start by describing the insurance company's possibilities in the financial market more precisely. This is again formalized by introducing an *investment strategy* h. In the one-period model, an investment strategy consists of a number of stocks h^1, which are bought at time 0 and are a part of the investment portfolio until time 1, where the new price $S^1(1)$ is announced. In addition, the strategy involves the amount $h^0(0)$, which is invested to or borrowed from the savings account at time 0. We work again with discounted prices defined by $X(t) = S^1(t)/S^0(t)$ and $X^0(t) = S^0(t)/S^0(t) = 1$, respectively. The discounted value of the strategy after the purchase of h^1 stocks at time 0 is given by

$$V(0, h) = h^1 X(0) + h^0(0).$$

At time 1, the value of the stocks changes to $h^1 X(1)$. If the insurance company decides to change the deposit on the savings account at time t to $h^0(1)$, the value at time 1 of the investment portfolio becomes

$$V(1, h) = h^1 X(1) + h^0(1).$$

In order to ensure that the company is able to cover the liability H at time 1 by selling the stocks and by withdrawing all capital from the savings account, it might be necessary to add additional capital to the savings account at time 1. Similarly, if the value of the investments exceeds the liabilities, the company may withdraw capital from the investment strategy before covering the liability. More precisely, we require that $h^0(1)$ is chosen at time 1 so that $V(1, h) = H$.

Föllmer and Sondermann (1986) introduced the *cost process* for the strategy h in a model with trading in continuous time, and Föllmer and Schweizer (1988) suggested a similar version in a discrete-time model. In the one-period model considered above, the cost process is defined via $C(0, h) = V(0, h)$ and

$$C(1, h) = V(1, h) - h^1(X(1) - X(0)) = H - h^1 \Delta X(1), \qquad (5.27)$$

where we have used the usual notation $\Delta X(1) := X(1) - X(0)$, and where the second equality is a consequence of the condition $V(1, h) = H$. More precisely, the quantity $C(t, h)$ represents the accumulated costs up to time t. At time 0, the costs are equal to the initial investment $V(0, h)$ corresponding to the portfolio $(h^0(0), h^1)$, and at time 1 the costs are computed as the value

$V(1, h) = H$ of the new portfolio $(h^0(1), h^1)$ reduced by investment gains $h^1 \Delta X(1)$.

The costs given by Equation (5.27) are in fact closely related to $\widetilde{L}$ from Equation (5.25), which we referred to as the company's net loss. The quantity $\widetilde{L}$ was defined as the sum of the net payment to the policy holders (benefits less premiums) and the net financial loss from trading in the financial market. This means that Equation (5.27) essentially differs from the net loss $\widetilde{L}$ only via the premiums paid at time 0.

Variance minimization

A simple measure of the risk associated with the liability H and the investment strategy h is the variance of the accumulated costs at time 1. One idea is therefore to choose an investment strategy, which solves the following problem:

$$\underset{h^1}{\text{minimize}}\; \text{Var}[C(1, h)]. \tag{5.28}$$

One can refer to the solution as the *variance-minimizing* strategy. Problem (5.28) is so simple that it can be solved for a general liability without imposing additional assumptions on the distribution of the discounted value $X(1)$ of the stock as time 1. Direct calculations show that

$$\text{Var}[C(1, h)] = \text{Var}[H - h^1 \Delta X(1)]$$

$$= \text{Var}[H] - 2h^1 \text{Cov}(H, \Delta X(1)) + (h^1)^2 \text{Var}[\Delta X(1)] =: J(h^1),$$

where we have that h^1 is chosen at time 0 so that it is constant. Under the condition $\text{Var}[\Delta X(1)] > 0$, we see that $J''(h^1) > 0$, and hence J is minimized for $\widehat{h}^1$ satisfying $J'(\widehat{h}^1) = 0$; that is

$$\widehat{h}^1 = \frac{\text{Cov}(H, \Delta X(1))}{\text{Var}[\Delta X(1)]}. \tag{5.29}$$

By inserting this solution into the expression for the accumulated costs at time 1, we see that the minimum obtainable variance is given by

$$\text{Var}[H - \widehat{h}^1 \Delta X(1)] = \text{Var}[H] - \frac{\text{Cov}(H, \Delta X(1))^2}{\text{Var}[\Delta X(1)]}$$

$$= \text{Var}[H] \left(1 - \text{Corr}(H, \Delta X(1))^2\right), \tag{5.30}$$

where

$$\text{Corr}(H, \Delta X(1)) = \frac{\text{Cov}(H, \Delta X(1))}{\sqrt{\text{Var}[H] \text{Var}[\Delta X(1)]}}$$

is the correlation coefficient between H and $\Delta X(1)$. The solution, Equation (5.29), and the minimum variance, Equation (5.30), are recognized as the solution to the problem of minimizing the variance on a linear estimator.

Risk minimization

A similar problem is to minimize the expected value of the additional costs, which occur between time 0 and 1, i.e.

$$\underset{(h^0(0),h^1)}{\text{minimize}}\; E[(C(1,h)-C(0,h))^2], \qquad (5.31)$$

as a function of the number of stocks h^1 and the deposit $h^0(0)$ made on the savings account at time 0. Since $C(0,h)$ is constant and equal to $V(0,h)$, we see that this problem is solved by a strategy $\widehat{h}$ with $C(0,\widehat{h}) = E[C(1,\widehat{h})]$, so that the solution to Problem (5.31) is also variance minimizing. This observation could lead to the (wrong) idea that this new problem does not lead to new insight into the risk inherent in H. However, the advantage of the new Problem (5.31) is that it also leads to an optimal initial investment $V(0,\widehat{h})$, which is given by

$$V(0,\widehat{h}) = C(0,\widehat{h}) = E[H - \widehat{h}^1 \Delta X(1)] = E[H] - \widehat{h}^1 E[\Delta X(1)]. \qquad (5.32)$$

Föllmer and Schweizer (1988) refer to this quantity as the *fair premium*; the strategy which solves Problem (5.31) is called the *risk-minimizing strategy*. Under the condition $E[\Delta X(1)] = 0$, which means that the discounted price process X is a martingale, the fair premium is exactly equal to the expected present value of the liability, i.e. $V(0,\widehat{h}) = E[H]$. However, if this condition is not satisfied, the premium typically differs from the expected present value of the liability.

Risk minimization for a unit-linked contract

Consider, for example, a portfolio of pure unit-linked pure endowments, i.e. unit-linked contracts without any guarantees, where the policy holders simply receive the value $S^1(1)$ of one unit of the stock index at time 1 provided that they are still alive at this time. The present value at time 0 of the liability is given by

$$H = Y(1)X(1),$$

where $Y(1) = \sum_{i=1}^{l_x} 1_{\{T^i > 1\}}$ is the actual number of survivors at time 1. At this point, we are not assuming that the insured lifetimes are mutually independent. However, if we assume that the lifetimes $(T^1, \ldots, T^{l_x})$ are independent of the stock X, we obtain, by using standard formulas for conditional covariances, the following:

$$
\begin{aligned}
\text{Cov}(Y(1)X(1), \Delta X(1)) &= E[\text{Cov}(Y(1)X(1), \Delta X(1) \mid X(1))] \\
&\quad + \text{Cov}(E[Y(1)X(1) \mid X(1)], E[\Delta X(1) \mid X(1)]) \\
&= 0 + \text{Cov}(E[Y(1)]X(1), \Delta X(1)) \\
&= E[Y(1)]\text{Var}[\Delta X(1)].
\end{aligned}
$$

By inserting this into the expression for the optimal investment strategy, Equation (5.29), we obtain the optimal number of stocks:

$$
\widehat{h}^1 = E[Y(1)] = l_{x\,1}p_x = l_{x+1}.
$$

Thus, it is optimal to buy a number of stocks that corresponds to the expected number of survivors. The optimal initial investment given by Equation (5.32) is given by

$$
\begin{aligned}
V(0, \widehat{h}) &= E[H] - \widehat{h}^1 E[\Delta X(1)] \\
&= E[Y(1)]E[X(1)] - E[Y(1)]E[X(1) - X(0)] \\
&= F[Y(1)]X(0).
\end{aligned}
$$

This result is similar to the fair premium suggested in Section 5.4, since the price at time 0 of a contract which pays one unit of the stock index at time 1 is exactly $S^1(0) = X(0)$ (buy the stock at time 0 and sell it again at time 1).

The minimum obtainable variance (or the minimal risk) associated with the risk-minimizing strategy can now be easily determined by exploiting the independence between $Y(1)$ and $X(1)$. By using formulas for the calculation of conditional variances, we obtain the following:

$$
\begin{aligned}
\text{Var}[H] &= E[\text{Var}[Y(1)X(1)|X(1)]] + \text{Var}[E[Y(1)X(1)|X(1)]] \\
&= E[X(1)^2]\text{Var}[Y(1)] + (E[Y(1)])^2\text{Var}[X(1)]. \quad\quad (5.33)
\end{aligned}
$$

Now insert this into the expression for the minimum obtainable variance, Equation (5.30), to see that

$$
\text{Var}[C(1, \widehat{h})] = E[X(1)^2]\text{Var}[Y(1)]. \quad\quad (5.34)
$$

When is mortality risk diversifiable?

Let us study the behavior of the minimal risk as l_x increases by considering the standardized liability:

$$H = \frac{1}{l_x} Y(1)X(1) = \frac{1}{l_x} \sum_{i=1}^{l_x} 1_{\{T^i > 1\}} X(1). \tag{5.35}$$

We say that mortality risk is *diversifiable* if the minimum risk for Equation (5.35) converges to zero as l_x converges to infinity. For example, one typically assumes that the policy holders' lifetimes are independent of the stock index. Is this sufficient to ensure that mortality risk is diversifiable? We study this problem in more detail in the following.

Diversifiable mortality risk: independent lifetimes

If, in addition, we assume that the lifetimes $T^1, \ldots, T^{l_x}$ are mutually independent and identically distributed, and that they are independent of the stock index, we see that $Y(1) \sim \mathrm{Bin}(l_x, {}_1p_x)$, and hence

$$\mathrm{Var}[Y(1)] = l_x \, {}_1p_x(1 - {}_1p_x).$$

By replacing $Y(1)$ by $(1/l_x)Y(1)$ in the calculations leading to Equation (5.34), we find that the minimum obtainable risk, Equation (5.30), for Equation (5.35) is given by

$$E[X(1)^2]\frac{1}{l_x}{}_1p_x(1 - {}_1p_x),$$

which indeed converges to zero as l_x converges to infinity. In this situation, mortality risk is diversifiable.

Non-diversifiable mortality risk

It is not difficult to realize that mortality risk is not diversifiable in the general case. To see this, consider as a trivial example the case where all lifetimes are identical, i.e. $T^i = T^1$, $i = 1, 2, \ldots$ In this case, Equation (5.35) is in fact identical to $1_{\{T^1 > 1\}}X(1)$, which does not depend on l_x. A more interesting example is obtained by assuming that the insured lifetimes are independent given some underlying random variable θ, say, which is related to the mortality intensity. For example, one could assume that the true mortality intensity $\widetilde{\mu}(x+t)$ is unknown and is of the form $\theta\mu(x+t)$, where $\mu(x+t)$ is a known function and where θ is a non-observable random variable with some given distribution. One can specify this classical credibility model in the following way.

- Given $\theta = \vartheta$, $T^1, T^2, \ldots$ are independent and identically distributed with survival probability ${}_1p_x^{(\vartheta)} = P_\vartheta(T^1 > 1) = \exp\left(-\int_0^1 \vartheta \mu_{x+s}\, ds\right)$.
- θ and $T^1, T^2, \ldots$ are independent of the stock index X.
- θ follows a non-degenerate distribution U.

This mortality model was used by Norberg (1989) for the analysis of a portfolio of group life insurance contracts. Since the parameter θ is not known at time 0, one could choose to apply the survival probability $E[{}_1p_x^{(\theta)}]$ when valuating life insurance contracts. However, by applying the law of large numbers, we see that

$$\frac{1}{l_x}Y(1) = \frac{1}{l_x}\sum_{i=1}^{l_x} 1_{\{T^i > 1\}} \to P_\theta(T^1 > 1) = \exp\left(-\int_0^1 \theta \mu_{x+s}\, ds\right)$$

as l_x goes to infinity. This limit is no longer constant and typically differs from $E[{}_1p_x^{(\theta)}]$. Thus, the problem is that by using the survival probability $E[{}_1p_x^{(\theta)}]$ one systematically applies a wrong probability, whereas the true conditional (and unknown) probability is given by ${}_1p_x^{(\theta)}$. The financial consequences as the size of the portfolio is increased are obvious and dramatic: if the conditional survival probability exceeds the one used, the insurance company systematically loses money, and if the conditional probability is smaller than the one used, the company will systematically earn money.

By using the fact that $Y(1)$, given $\theta = \vartheta$, is binomially distributed with parameters $(l_x, {}_1p_x^{(\vartheta)})$, and by using the usual formulas for calculation of conditional variances, we see that

$$\mathrm{Var}[Y(1)] = E[\mathrm{Var}[Y(1)|\theta]] + \mathrm{Var}[E[Y(1)|\theta]]$$
$$= l_x E\left[{}_1p_x^{(\theta)}(1 - {}_1p_x^{(\theta)})\right] + l_x^2 \mathrm{Var}\left[{}_1p_x^{(\theta)}\right]. \qquad (5.36)$$

In order to calculate the minimum obtainable risk, Equation (5.30), for the standardized liability given in Equation (5.35), one has to determine $\mathrm{Var}[(1/l_x)Y(1)]$. Here, one sees that the minimum obtainable risk becomes

$$E[X(1)^2]\frac{1}{l_x^2}\mathrm{Var}[Y(1)] = E[X(1)^2]\left(\frac{1}{l_x}E\left[{}_1p_x^{(\theta)}(1 - {}_1p_x^{(\theta)})\right] + \mathrm{Var}\left[{}_1p_x^{(\theta)}\right]\right),$$

which converges to

$$E[X(1)^2]\mathrm{Var}\left[{}_1p_x^{(\theta)}\right] \qquad (5.37)$$

as l_x goes to infinity. Thus, the last term in Equation (5.36) determines the asymptotic behavior of the risk. We see that the company's relative risk does not converge to zero, even if the size of the portfolio increases. This is in line with the observations made above and is of course not surprising, since we are in a situation where θ is unknown. A similar observation can be made from the limit given in Equation (5.37) for the minimal risk, which exactly describes the uncertainty associated with the survival probability. The risk associated with this underlying randomness is also called *systematic mortality risk*, since it cannot be eliminated by increasing the size of the portfolio. This is in contrast to the traditional mortality risk, the *unsystematic mortality risk*, which vanishes when the portfolio is increased.

The example can be generalized further by assuming that the mortality intensity is affected by some process $\theta = (\theta(t))_{t \geq 0}$, such that the mortality intensity at time t is a function of $\theta(t)$. The process θ determines social and economic factors that affect the mortality in the portfolio of insured lives. In the above example, one only needs to change the definition of the conditional survival probability to the following:

$$_t p_x^{(\theta)} = \exp\left(-\int_0^t \mu_{x+s}(\theta(s))\, ds \right).$$

Dahl (2004) analyzes the implications of allowing the mortality intensity to depend on some underlying stochastic processes that are driven by diffusion processes and determines market values for life insurance liabilities in this setting. In Dahl and Møller (2006), this setup is applied for determining risk-minimizing hedging strategies.

Non-diversifiable mortality risk and catastrophes
Further examples with non-diversifiable mortality risk can be constructed by allowing for single events which may cause simultaneous deaths for any fraction of the insured lives (catastrophes). A simple example is the situation where a catastrophe occurs between time 0 and 1 with probability p_0 and where the number of deaths caused by this catastrophe is binomially distributed with parameters (l_x, p), where p is uniformly distributed on $(0, 1)$. If this catastrophe is the only cause of death, it is not difficult to show that the variance of $(1/l_x)Y(1)$ does not go to zero as l_x converges to infinity.

Modeling systematic mortality risk
As pointed out above, the economic consequences of the presence of the systematic mortality risk are indeed dramatic. If, for example, we use survival probabilities that are too low for the pricing of life annuities or pure endowments, we systematically lose money. It is therefore necessary to study models that take into consideration possible changes in the future mortality. However, since the future mortality is affected by many (unpredictable) factors,

one should use models where the future mortality is modeled via stochastic processes.

Various approaches for the modeling of the systematic mortality risk have been studied in the literature. One approach is the so-called Lee–Carter method (see Lee (2000) and Lee and Carter (1992)), where the age-dependent yearly death rates are affected by a time-dependent factor determined from a time series model. Milevsky and Promislow (2001) aimed to model the mortality intensity directly by using a so-called mean-reverting Gompertz model, whereas Olivieri and Pitacco (2002) applied Bayesian methods to model the survival probability. Dahl (2004) focused on an affine diffusion model for the mortality intensity, and Biffis and Millossovich (2006) studied a general affine jump-diffusion model. Further references of interest are Cairns, Blake and Dowd (2006), who applied various methods known from interest rate theory to model the mortality, Olivieri (2001) and Marocco and Pitacco (1998).

Trading with mortality risk

In the presence of systematic mortality risk, we cannot eliminate the risk associated with the mortality by increasing the size of the portfolio. An alternative way of controlling this risk is of course to introduce assets that are linked to the development of the mortality and which can be traded dynamically. One possibility could be to introduce assets that depend explicitly on the behavior of the insured lives in the insurance portfolio. This would be similar to what has been called *dynamic reinsurance markets* proposed by Delbaen and Haezendonck (1989) and Sondermann (1991), and studied more recently by Møller (2004). Applications in life insurance can also be found in Møller (1998) and Steffensen (2001).

So-called *mortality bonds* and *mortality swaps* have been introduced; see, for example, Blake, Cairns and Dowd (2006) for a detailed description of their properties. A mortality bond is essentially a bond whose payments are dependent on the development of the mortality in some specific group. One example is to consider a certain cohort (for example, all individuals of a certain age in a certain country) and let the payments be proportional to the current number of survivors in this group. In this case, the payments to the owner of the bond increase if the underlying individuals live longer than expected. This means that the market value of the mortality bond increases if mortality improves, and hence the mortality bond can provide a hedge against a general decrease in the underlying mortality. A mortality swap provides a similar construction. Here, an insurer can exchange (swap) the uncertain payments within a portfolio of life annuitants with a fixed, certain payment stream by entering a mortality swap directly with a reinsurer.

5.6 The multi-period model revisited

5.6.1 Important concepts

In this section, we briefly review the multi-period model from Chapters 3 and 4 with dynamic investment strategies. This model is used in Section 5.7 for the analysis of the risk inherent in a portfolio of unit-linked life insurance contracts. This section recalls the definitions of a self-financing strategy, the value process, the cost process, arbitrage, martingale measure and attainability. The reader can also consult Chapter 4 for more details. We fix a time horizon T and let $S^1(t)$ be the value of the stock at time $t \in \{0, 1, \ldots, T\}$. The value at time t of one unit deposited in the savings account at time 0 is assumed to be given by $S^0(t) = (1+r)^t$, where r is the annual interest. The discounted prices are defined by $X(t) = S^1(t)/S^0(t)$ and $X^0(t) = S^0(t)/S^0(t) = 1$, respectively. Here, we do not specify a specific model for S^1, but one can, for example, think of the binomial market, where the relative change in the value of the stock can attain two different values. This example is studied further in Section 5.6.3.

An *investment strategy* is a process $h = (h^0, h^1) = (h^0(t), h^1(t))_{t=0,1,\ldots,T}$, where $h^1(t)$ depends on the information available at time $t-1$ and $h^0(t)$ can depend on the information available at t. We let $\mathcal{F}(t)$ represent the information available at t and assume that $\mathcal{F}(s) \subseteq \mathcal{F}(t)$ for $0 \le s \le t \le T$. The quantity $h^1(t)$ denotes the number of stocks in the company's investment portfolio from time $t-1$ to time t, and $h^0(t)$ is the discounted deposit (negative deposit corresponds to a loan) on the savings account at t. The *value process* $V(h)$ describes the value at any time t of the current portfolio $(h^0(t), h^1(t))$; it is given by

$$V(t, h) = (S^0(t))^{-1}(h^1(t)S^1(t) + h^0(t)S^0(t)) = h^1(t)X(t) + h^0(t). \quad (5.38)$$

In Chapters 3 and 4 we introduced the concept of a *self-financing strategy* in two slightly different versions. At first sight, one could perhaps form the impression that there is a difference between these two definitions. Therefore we show here that the two definitions are indeed equivalent. In Chapter 3, an investment strategy was said to be self-financing if its *cost process*,

$$C(t, h) = V(t, h) - \sum_{s=1}^{t} h^1(s)\Delta X(s), \quad (5.39)$$

was constant (and equal to $C(0, h) = V(0, h)$). This amounts to saying that

$$V(t, h) = V(0, h) + \sum_{s=1}^{t} h^1(s)\Delta X(s). \quad (5.40)$$

The interpretation of Equation (5.40) is as follows. If h is self-financing, the discounted value of the portfolio $h(t) = (h^0(t), h^1(t))$ at time t is exactly equal to the initial value $V(0, h)$ at time 0, to which are added the discounted trading gains from the investment in the stocks. For the period $[s-1, s]$, the discounted gains are $h^1(s)\Delta X(s)$, the number $h^1(s)$ of stocks purchased at time $s-1$ multiplied by the change $\Delta X(s) = X(s) - X(s-1)$ in the discounted value of the stock from time $s-1$ to time s. The accumulated costs $C(t, h)$ for the interval $[0, t]$ are the value of the portfolio at t reduced by past investment gains. Thus, the costs represent that part of the total value that has not been generated by investment gains.

We now see that Equation (4.18) is a consequence of this definition. First, note that Equation (5.40) corresponds to

$$\Delta V(t+1, h) = V(t+1, h) - V(t, h) = h^1(t+1)\Delta X(t+1).$$

Using Equation (5.38), we see that

$$V(t+1, h) - V(t, h) = (h^1(t+1) - h^1(t))X(t) + h^1(t+1)(X(t+1) - X(t))$$
$$+ (h^0(t+1) - h^0(t)).$$

By comparing these two expressions for $\Delta V(t+1, h)$, we see that

$$h^1(t+1)X(t) + h^0(t+1) = h^1(t)X(t) + h^0(t),$$

which corresponds to Equation (4.18) if we multiply by $S^0(t)$ on both side of the equality sign.

A self-financing strategy h is said to be an arbitrage strategy if $V(0, h) = 0$, $V(T, h) \geq 0$ P-a.s. (P-almost surely) and $P(V(T, h) > 0) > 0$. A probability measure Q is said to be an *equivalent martingale measure* for X if Q agrees with the probability measure P about whether any event has probability zero or not and if X is a Q-martingale, i.e.

$$E^Q[X(u)|\mathcal{F}(t)] = X(t) \tag{5.41}$$

for $0 \leq t \leq u \leq T$. In Equation (5.41), the term $E^Q[X(u)|\mathcal{F}(t)]$ is the expected discounted value of the stock at time u calculated by using the measure Q and by conditioning on the information available at time t. It was shown in Section 3.7.7 that the existence of a martingale measure ensures the absence of arbitrage possibilities.

An agreement between two parties gives rise to a discounted liability H at time T; we refer to H as a contingent claim. For a given contingent claim, it is important to check if there exists a self-financing strategy h with $V(T, h) = H$. If this is the case, we say that H is *attainable*. This concept is essential in our subsequent discussion on the choice of investment strategies for integrated financial and insurance risks. The requirement of attainability says that there exists a strategy $h = (h^0, h^1)$ such that

$$H = V(T, h) = V(0, h) + \sum_{t=1}^{T} h^1(t)\Delta X(t). \tag{5.42}$$

Here, $V(0, h)$ is the *replication price*, i.e. the amount which has to be invested at time 0. By following the strategy h, the investor can generate sufficient capital at time T in order to pay the liability H. We can see how $V(0, h)$ can be determined by using the martingale measure Q: since X is a Q-martingale, taking expected values (under Q) on both sides in Equation (5.42) shows that

$$E^Q[H] = E^Q[V(T, h)] = V(0, h);$$

see Section 3.7.7 for more details.

5.6.2 Unattainable claims

Attainability is a very special property. As mentioned in Chapter 4, models in which all contingent claims are attainable are also called *complete*. Important examples mentioned in Chapter 4 are the binomial market and the Black–Scholes market. In these two models, any contingent claim is attainable. However, here it is absolutely essential that a contingent claim is defined as a quantity which depends on the risk from the financial market only. For example, a European call option $(S^1(T) - K)^+$ can be hedged in both the binomial and the Black–Scholes markets. In order to be able to distinguish such claims from more complicated claims, we also use the notion *purely financial contingent claim*.

The situation changes drastically if we consider contingent claims that also depend on other sources of uncertainty (risk), for example on the number of surviving policy holders from an insurance portfolio. It seems intuitively reasonable that one cannot hedge such liabilities perfectly by trading in the financial markets only if, for example, the liabilities depend on the number of survivors. We also refer to a claim that depends on both insurance risk and financial risk as an *integrated contingent claim*. Thus, the extension of the set of contingent claims typically leads to a so-called *incomplete market*, i.e. a market which is no longer complete, since these integrated claims are not in general attainable.

The rest of this chapter presents an introduction to methods for determining optimal investment strategies in incomplete markets in the case where the liability H is not attainable, i.e. in situations where it is not possible to find a replicating strategy for the liability. In this case, one cannot use the principle of no arbitrage alone in calculating unique prices or replicating investment strategies for the liability. This means, for example, that we cannot determine a unique price for a unit-linked insurance contract within the present model if we leave out the assumption of diversifiable mortality risk. However, there are several other principles (theories) which can be applied for valuation and hedging in such situations. Here, we give an introduction to these principles and illustrate how they work (and how they do not work) for a portfolio of unit-linked life insurance contracts.

5.6.3 The binomial model

In this section we recall the binomial model, suggested by Cox, Ross and Rubinstein (1979), which is complete such that all purely financial claims are attainable. This model was also described in Chapter 4; see also Baxter and Rennie (1996) and Pliska (1997). For a presentation with emphasis on the mathematical aspects of this model, see Shiryaev *et al.* (1994).

In the binomial model, the dynamics of the stock is given by

$$S^1(t) = (1 + Z(t))S^1(t-1), \qquad (5.43)$$

where $Z(1), \ldots, Z(T)$ is a sequence of i.i.d. random variables with $Z(1) \in \{a, b\}$ and where $0 < P(Z(1) = b) < 1$. The quantity $Z(t)$ is the relative change in the value of the stock during the period $(t-1, t]$, and we assume that this quantity is not known before time t. As mentioned above, the savings account is described by $S^0(t) = (1+r)^t$. A natural condition on the parameters a, b, r is to require that $-1 < a < r < b$, which means that the return on the stock exceeds the interest with positive probability and vice versa. The discounted price process $X(t) = S^1(t)/S^0(t)$ is given by

$$X(t) = X(t-1)\frac{1 + Z(t)}{1 + r}.$$

Introduce now the filtration $\mathbf{G} = (\mathcal{G}(t))_{t \in \{0,1,\ldots,T\}}$ for S^1 given by

$$\mathcal{G}(t) = \sigma\{S^1(1), \ldots, S^1(t)\}$$

where $\mathcal{G}(0)$ is trivial. Again, $\mathcal{G}(t)$ can be interpreted as the information which corresponds to observing the price of the stock S^1 up to time t. We define a new probability measure Q by $Q(Z(1) = b) = (r-a)/(b-a) = q$ and by requiring that $Z(1), \ldots, Z(T)$ are i.i.d. under Q.

The assumption $a < r < b$ ensures that $0 < q < 1$, so that Q is indeed a probability measure equivalent to P. Under Q, we see that

$$E^Q[(1+Z(t))|\mathcal{G}(t-1)] = 1 + E^Q[Z(t)] = 1 + qb + (1-q)a = 1+r,$$

where we used the independence between $Z(t)$ and $(S^1(1), \ldots, S^1(t-1))$ in the first equality. This shows that the discounted price process X is a $(\mathbf{G}, Q)$-martingale, since

$$E^Q[X(t)|\mathcal{G}(t-1)] = X(t-1)\frac{1}{1+r}E^Q[(1+Z(t))|\mathcal{G}(t-1)] = X(t-1).$$

In Chapter 4 it was shown that the binomial model is complete. We can formulate this in the following way.

Theorem 5.1 *Let H be a (discounted) purely financial contingent claim which is payable at time T and assume that the financial market is modeled by the binomial model. Then there exists a process $\alpha(H)$, such that*

$$H = H(0) + \sum_{j=1}^{T} \alpha(j, H)\Delta X(j), \tag{5.44}$$

where $H(0)$ is constant and where $\alpha(j, H)$ depends on the information available at time $j-1$.

Equation (5.44) is also called a *representation formula*, since it allows for H to be represented as the sum of a constant $H(0)$ and some terms of the form $\alpha(j, H)\Delta X(j)$. We underline that this representation property is very special for the binomial model. If, for example, we were to replace the quantities $Z(1), \ldots, Z(T)$ in Equation (5.43) with random variables that could attain three different values (a trinomial model), this result would no longer hold. In the trinomial model it is typically not possible to find a representation of this simple form for a contingent claim. Another important example in which such representation results cannot be established is a contingent claim that depends on an additional source of risk, for example the number of survivors from a portfolio of insured lives.

Theorem 5.1 can be used to derive a self-financing strategy $h = (h^0, h^1)$ which replicates a purely financial contingent claim H. If we let $h^1(t) = \alpha(t, H)$ and define $h^0(t)$ via

$$V(t, h) = h^1(t)X(t) + h^0(t) = H(0) + \sum_{j=1}^{t} \alpha(j, H)\Delta X(j),$$

we see that h is self-financing and that $V(T, h) = H$. Thus, we have constructed a self-financing strategy which replicates H. This self-financing strategy requires an initial investment of $H(0)$ at time 0, that is $H(0)$ is the replication price for H (see Section 5.6.1). In Chapter 4, $\alpha(H)$ was derived for a European call option, i.e. for H:

$$H = \frac{f(S^1(T))}{S^0(T)},$$

with $f(S^1(T)) = (S^1(T) - K)^+$. In the binomial model, $\alpha(t, H)$ can be determined in general by introducing the following process:

$$V^*(t) = E^Q[H \mid \mathcal{G}(t)],$$

and then defining $\alpha(H)$ via

$$\alpha(t, H) = \frac{\mathrm{Cov}^Q(\Delta V^*(t), \Delta X(t) \mid \mathcal{G}(t-1))}{\mathrm{Var}^Q[\Delta X(t) \mid \mathcal{G}(t-1)]}. \qquad (5.45)$$

5.7 Hedging integrated risks

We describe theories for hedging and pricing in incomplete markets and demonstrate how these theories would apply for a portfolio of unit-linked life insurance contracts. All examples build on the binomial market, so that any purely financial contingent claim is attainable, i.e. it can be priced uniquely and hedged perfectly via a self-financing strategy. However, integrated contingent claims which depend on both insurance risk and financial risk are, in general, not attainable, and here we need other methods.

Before describing these various methods, we recall the combined model, which is used in the analysis of the integrated contingent claims. The model is constructed by simply combining the binomial market and the usual actuarial model for the lifetimes of the policy holders. This construction leads to an incomplete market with many different martingale measures, which implies that the choice of martingale measure is no longer a trivial problem. Thus, in such models one cannot derive a unique arbitrage-free price from the assumption of no arbitrage alone. There are typically many different prices that are all consistent with the principle of no arbitrage, and thus one needs to introduce subjective criteria when calculating prices. In the following, we describe several different principles for pricing and hedging in incomplete markets: super-hedging, risk minimization, mean-variance hedging, utility-indifference pricing and quantile hedging. We show how these different principles can be used for valuation and partial hedging/control of the risk in a portfolio of unit-linked life insurance contracts. Our presentation focuses on this application, and we refer the reader to Cont and Tankov (2003) and Föllmer and Schied (2002) for more general treatments of these principles.

5.7.1 The combined model

Consider again the insurance portfolio consisting of l_x policy holders aged x at time 0, and let $Y(t)$ be the number of policy holders that are alive at t. The present value at time 0 of the liabilities from a T-year unit-linked pure endowment is given by

$$H = \frac{Y(T)f(S^1(T))}{S^0(T)}. \tag{5.46}$$

Here, the financial market is described by the binomial market, and the stock price process S^1 is defined via Equation (5.43), that is $S^1(t) = (1 + Z(t))S^1(t-1)$. We assume throughout that f is a non-negative function. The lifetimes for the l_x policy holders are assumed to be independent, identically distributed and independent of the stock index S^1.

Information

The information that is available to the insurance company at time t is now described. It is assumed that the company at time t has access to information concerning the number of deaths each year up to time t and knowledge about the value of the stock at times $0, 1, \ldots, t$. This can be formalized by introducing the filtrations $\mathbf{G} = (\mathcal{G}(t))_{t \in \{0,1,\ldots,T\}}$, defined by $\mathcal{G}(t) = \sigma\{S^1(1), \ldots, S^1(t)\}$, and $\mathbf{H} = (\mathcal{H}(t))_{t \in \{0,1,\ldots,T\}}$, defined by $\mathcal{H}(t) = \sigma\{Y(1), \ldots, Y(t)\}$. The first filtration $\mathbf{G}$ describes the financial market and $\mathcal{G}(t)$ is the information which stems from observing the price of the stock S^1 up to time t. The other filtration $\mathbf{H}$ contains information about the number of survivors and $\mathcal{H}(t)$ is the full knowledge about the number of deaths from time 0 until time t. We are interested in constructing investment strategies $h = (h^0, h^1)$ that depend on both types of information. In order to describe this more precisely, we construct a third filtration $\mathbf{F} = (\mathcal{F}(t))_{t \in \{0,1,\ldots,T\}}$, given by $\mathcal{F}(t) = \mathcal{G}(t) \vee \mathcal{H}(t) = \sigma(\mathcal{G}(t) \cup \mathcal{H}(t))$. This simply means that $\mathcal{F}(t)$ contains the information $\mathcal{G}(t)$ from the financial market and the information $\mathcal{H}(t)$ about the number of survivors. The information structure is illustrated in Figure 5.1. The insurance company can now use the full information $\mathbf{F}$ when determining the investment strategy h.

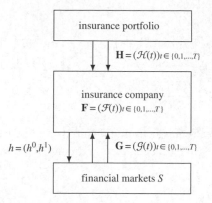

Figure 5.1. Information diagram with the three filtrations **F**, **G** and **H** and the investment strategy h.

Martingale measures

We consider a specific martingale measure Q, which is closely related to the probability measure Q that was introduced for the binomial market in Section 5.6.3. The probability Q considered here has the following properties:

(1) X is a Q-martingale, and under Q, $Z(1), \ldots, Z(T)$ are i.i.d. with $Q(Z(1) = b) = (r - a)/(b - a)$;

(2) $T^1, \ldots, T^{l_x}$ are i.i.d. under Q with $Q(T^1 > t) = P(T^1 > t) = {}_t p_x$;

(3) the lifetimes are independent of the financial market under Q.

The first property says that Q is similar to the probability measure introduced in the section with the binomial market, and the second property says that the probability measure Q corresponds to the true probability P, when we consider the lifetimes only. Finally, the last property says that the lifetimes are independent of the financial market under Q.

One problem with this combined model is that there are (infinitely!) many martingale measures. We can see this by looking more carefully at the properties of the martingale measure Q defined above. In fact, we can construct probability measures Q_n which also satisfy the first condition, so that they are indeed martingale measures, where the financial market is independent of the lifetimes (the third condition), but where the survival probability in the second condition is changed to some value $0 < {}_t p_x^{(n)} < 1$. The details of this construction are given in Section A.1. of the Appendix. Thus, if one aims to calculate the price of the unit-linked life insurance contract as the expected present value under a martingale measure, we obtain for the martingale measure Q_n

the following:

$$E^{Q_n}[H] = E^{Q_n}\left[\frac{Y(T)f(S^1(T))}{S^0(T)}\right] = E^{Q_n}\left[\frac{f(S^1(T))}{S^0(T)}\right]E^{Q_n}[Y(T)]$$

$$= E^Q\left[\frac{f(S^1(T))}{S^0(T)}\right]l_x\,_Tp_x^{(n)}.$$

By choosing different equivalent martingale measures, we can now get any survival probability $_Tp_x^{(n)}$ between zero and unity. This shows that any price in the open interval,

$$\left(0, l_x\,E^Q\left[\frac{f(S^1(T))}{S^0(T)}\right]\right),$$

is in accordance with the assumption of no arbitrage. We can formulate this result alternatively in the following way: *arbitrage-free pricing cannot tell us which survival probability we should use when we can only trade in the stock and the savings account.* The survival probability can, for example, be chosen to be equal to the true survival probability $_Tp_x$, close to (but not equal to) zero, close to (but not equal to) unity, or some other value. This is not very surprising, since we have not introduced the possibility of trading with mortality risk in the financial market. The situation changes when assets that depend on the number of survivors are introduced. If these assets are defined in the right way, it might be possible to reestablish uniqueness of the martingale measure, and arbitrage-free pricing leads again to unique prices also for integrated contingent claims.

We end this section by recalling the result from Theorem 5.1, which shows that the unique arbitrage-free price for the purely financial contingent claim that pays $f(S^1(T))$ at time T is given by

$$\pi(t, f) := E^Q\left[\frac{f(S^1(T))}{S^0(T)}\bigg|\mathcal{G}(t)\right] = E^Q\left[\frac{f(S^1(T))}{S^0(T)}\right] + \sum_{j=1}^t \alpha(j, f)\Delta X(j),$$
$$(5.47)$$

where $\alpha(f)$ determines the *hedge* for $f(S^1(T))$. Thus, one can hedge the option $f(S^1(T))$ by using a self-financing strategy which requires an initial investment of $\pi(0, f) = E^Q[f(S^1(T))/S^0(T)]$ at time 0 and an investment in $\alpha(t, f)$ stocks during the period $(t-1, t]$. Note that we can apply *any* equivalent martingale measure in Equation (5.47) for the calculation of $\pi(t, f)$. Since $f(S^1(T))$ is attainable, we would obtain the same result in Equation (5.47) if we replaced Q by another martingale measure Q_n.

5.7.2 Super-hedging

A very natural suggestion for the choice of investment strategy and premium calculation principle is the idea of super-hedging suggested by El Karoui and Quenez (1995). For a contingent claim, which cannot be hedged perfectly by a self-financing strategy h, such that one cannot ensure that $V(T, h) = H$ in all scenarios, one could look for strategies where

$$V(T, h) \geq H \qquad (5.48)$$

in any scenario. Thus, if the seller of the contract uses a strategy satisfying this condition, and if they can charge the amount necessary as the initial investment, then there is no risk of a loss associated with the liability for the seller. By following the self-financing strategy, the seller generates the capital $V(T, h)$, which by Equation (5.48) exceeds the liability H. We show below that this very natural idea unfortunately leads to unreasonably high prices for unit-linked life insurance contracts.

Definition 5.2 *(Super-hedging) Find the cheapest self-financing strategy h, such that $V(T, h) \geq H$ P-a.s. The minimum initial investment $V(0)$, which allows for a self-financing strategy satisfying Equation (5.48), is called the super-hedging price (or super-replication price), and the associated strategy is called the super-hedging strategy.*

In particular, we are interested in the valuation and hedging of unattainable claims, for example as in the case with the unit-linked life insurance contracts. In such situations there are typically many martingale measures, and we let $\mathbf{Q}$ be the set of all martingale measures. It can be shown that a super-hedging strategy for H exists provided that

$$\sup_{Q' \in \mathbf{Q}} E^{Q'}[H] < \infty, \qquad (5.49)$$

i.e. the expected value of H under all martingale measures is bounded. The solution to the super-hedging problem involves some rather complicated mathematics, see El Karoui and Quenez (1995), and we formulate the result without going into details here. First, it is necessary to study the following process:

$$\overline{V}(t) = \text{ess.sup}_{Q' \in \mathbf{Q}} E^{Q'}[H | \mathcal{F}(t)]. \qquad (5.50)$$

This involves the calculation of the expected value of H given the information available at time t under all martingale measures from the set $\mathbf{Q}$, and $\overline{V}(t)$ is then essentially defined as the supremum of all these different expected values. The next step is to derive a decomposition for the process $\overline{V}$ of the form

$$\overline{V}(t) = \overline{V}(0) + \sum_{j=1}^{t} \overline{h}^1(j)\Delta X(j) - \overline{C}(t), \tag{5.51}$$

where $\overline{C}$ is adapted and non-decreasing and where $\overline{h}^1$ is predictable, i.e. $\overline{h}^1(j)$ is $\mathcal{F}(j-1)$-measurable for $j = 1, \ldots, T$. One of the main results from the theory on super-hedging is given in the following.

Theorem 5.3 *Provided that Equation (5.49) is satisfied, the super-hedging price of H is given by $\overline{V}(0) = \sup_{Q'} E^{Q'}[H]$ and the super-hedging strategy is determined by $h^1(t) = \overline{h}^1(t)$.*

5.7.3 Super-hedging for unit-linked contracts

This section illustrates how super-hedging strategies can be derived for unit-linked contracts of the form given in Equation (5.46) within the market introduced in Section 5.7.1 by using the results from Section 5.7.2. The first step is to check the condition given by Equation (5.49). By noting that the number of survivors at T must be smaller than the number l_x of policy holders at time 0 (no additional contracts are signed), we see that

$$H = \frac{Y(T)f(S^1(T))}{S^0(T)} \leq l_x \frac{f(S^1(T))}{S^0(T)} = H''.$$

This simple inequality is quite useful, since H'' is a purely financial contingent claim, which in the binomial market is attainable, and hence it can be priced uniquely by the principle of no arbitrage. Moreover, we see from Equation (5.47) of $\pi(0, f)$ that the expected value of H'' is the same under all equivalent martingale measures and equal to $l_x E^Q[f(S^1(T))/S^0(T)]$. Thus, we have shown that

$$\sup_{Q' \in Q} E^{Q'}[H] \leq E^Q[H''] = l_x \pi(0, f),$$

which is finite provided that $\pi(0, f)$ is finite (and this is the case here). One might say that this looks like a rather academic discussion. However, this property is actually quite essential. For example, in the situation where $H = N(T)f(S^1(T))/S^0(T)$ and where N is a Poisson process (which is independent of S^1), the condition would no longer be satisfied, and this modified contract cannot be super-hedged. No matter how big the initial capital is and no matter how this capital is invested, there is a (positive) probability of having less capital than needed in order to pay H.

By the above argument, we see that $Y(t) \geq Y(T)$, so that for any martingale measure Q_n:

$$E^{Q_n}\left[\frac{Y(T)f(S^1(T))}{S^0(T)}\bigg|\mathcal{F}(t)\right] \leq Y(t)E^{Q_n}\left[\frac{f(S^1(T))}{S^0(T)}\bigg|\mathcal{F}(t)\right] = Y(t)\pi(t,f),$$

where we have used the fact that $Y(t)$ is known at time t, such that it can be taken outside of the expectation. If we consider a sequence of martingale measures $(Q_n)_{n \in \mathbf{N}}$, where the survival probabilities converge to unity as n goes to infinity, we see that we can get arbitrarily close to $Y(t)\pi(t,f)$. This shows that

$$\overline{V}(t) = Y(t)\pi(t,f),$$

and it remains to find the representation given by Equation (5.51). By noting that

$$\Delta\overline{V}(t) = Y(t-1)(\pi(t,f) - \pi(t-1,f)) + \pi(t,f)(Y(t) - Y(t-1)),$$

and by using Equation (5.47), we see after some rearrangement that

$$\overline{V}(t) = l_x\pi(0,f) + \sum_{j=1}^{t} Y(j-1)\alpha(j,f)\Delta X(j) - \sum_{j=1}^{t}\pi(j,f)(-\Delta Y(j)). \quad (5.52)$$

Here, we see that $Y(j-1)\alpha(j,f)$ is $\mathcal{F}(j-1)$-measurable. The process Y is decreasing since it counts the current number of survivors. This implies that $-\Delta Y(j) \geq 0$, such that the process

$$\sum_{j=1}^{t}\pi(j,f)(-\Delta Y(j))$$

is indeed non-decreasing. Thus, we can now use Theorem 5.3 to obtain the following Proposition.

Proposition 5.4 *The super-hedging price for the unit-linked contract is given by $l_x\,\pi(0,f)$. The cheapest self-financing super-hedging strategy for the unit-linked contract is given by*

$$\overline{h}^1(t) = Y(t-1)\,\alpha(t,f),$$

$$\overline{h}^0(t) = l_x\,\pi(0,f) + \sum_{j=1}^{t}\overline{h}^1(j)\,\Delta X(j) - \overline{h}^1(t)X(t),$$

where $\alpha(f)$ is determined from Equation (5.47).

Let us comment on this result. We see that the price, which is necessary in order to super-hedge the liability associated with the portfolio of unit-linked life insurance contracts, is given by the initial number l_x of policy holders at time 0 multiplied by the price $\pi(0, f)$ of the purely financial contingent claim $f(S^1(T))$. The investment strategy consists in holding from time $t-1$ to time t a number of stocks which is calculated as the current number $Y(t-1)$ of survivors at time $t-1$ multiplied by $\alpha(t, f)$. The latter is exactly the number of stocks needed in order to hedge the claim $f(S^1(T))$. A natural question is now: where did the survival probability go in all these calculations? One answer is that the survival probability has been set to unity. This result illustrates that the natural idea of super-hedging is not the right tool for the handling of the integrated risk in a unit-linked insurance contract. The requirement that the value of the portfolio at time T has to exceed H in any scenario is simply too strong for our applications, since it implies that we must have sufficient capital in order to cover even the case where all policy holders survive to time T. We have to look for alternative criteria.

5.7.4 Risk minimization

Section 5.5 studied risk minimization in a one-period model. Here, we give a version of this criterion in a multi-period model. For $t \in \{0, 1, \ldots, T-1\}$, we define the quantity

$$r(t, h) = E^Q \left[(C(t+1, h) - C(t, h))^2 \,\middle|\, \mathcal{F}(t) \right], \qquad (5.53)$$

the conditional expected value at time t, under the martingale measure Q of the square of the additional costs $C(t+1, h) - C(t, h)$ incurred during the next time interval. In contrast to Section 5.7.3, we here require that $V(T, h) = H$. Since this is not in general possible under a self-financing strategy, we allow for the possibility of adding or withdrawing capital at any time. However, this additional capital is not being priced here.

Definition 5.5 *(Risk minimization) Minimize $r(t, h)$ for all t over h with $V(T, h) = H$. The solution is called the risk-minimizing strategy.*

Minimization of $r(t, h)$ can be viewed as a generalization of Problem (5.31) considered in the one-period model. However, Equation (5.53) is formulated in terms of a specific martingale measure Q, a fact which we address below. The idea of minimizing $r(t, h)$ is in some sense analogous to the calculations for the price in a complete market as described in Chapter 4, in that both problems are solved via a backwards recursion. Here, we start by looking at $r(T-1, h)$.

At time t, $r(t, h)$ is minimized as a function of $h^1(t+1)$ and $h^0(t)$ for given $(h^1(t+2), \ldots, h^1(T))$ and $(h^0(t+1), \ldots, h^0(T))$. This minimization can be performed as in Section 5.5; for more details, see Föllmer and Schweizer (1988). The approach of risk minimization was proposed by Föllmer and Sondermann (1986), who applied a continuous-time setting. Surveys and further references on risk minimization and other quadratic hedging criteria can be found in Pham (2000) and Schweizer (2001a).

The risk-minimizing strategy can also be found by first considering the process V^* defined by

$$V^*(t) = E^Q[H \mid \mathcal{F}(t)]. \tag{5.54}$$

It can be shown that this process has a unique decomposition of the following form:

$$V^*(t) = V^*(0) + \sum_{j=1}^{t} h^1(j, H)\Delta X(j) + L(t, H), \tag{5.55}$$

where $h^1(j, H)$ depends on the information available at time $j-1$, and where $L(H)$ is a Q-martingale, which furthermore has the very special property that the product of X and $L(H)$ is also a Q-martingale, i.e.

$$E^Q[X(u)L(u, H)\mid \mathcal{F}(t)] = X(t)L(t, H)$$

for all $t \leq u$. The decomposition, Equation (5.55), is known as the *Kunita–Watanabe decomposition*; see Föllmer and Schied (2002) for more details. The decomposition can typically be found by first determining Equation (5.54) and then examining the increment $\Delta V^*(t) = V^*(t) - V^*(t-1)$. In Section 5.7.5 we show how this works for a portfolio of unit-linked contracts.

It follows from Föllmer and Schweizer (1988) that the risk-minimizing strategy $\widehat{h} = (\widehat{h}^0, \widehat{h}^1)$ minimizing $r(t, h)$ for all t is given by

$$\widehat{h}^1(t) = h^1(t, H), \tag{5.56}$$

$$\widehat{h}^0(t) = V^*(t) - \widehat{h}^1(t)X(t). \tag{5.57}$$

Thus, the risk-minimizing strategy is determined directly from the decomposition given in Equation (5.55). The proof is recalled in Section A.2. of the Appendix. This strategy has the property that its value at time t is given by

$$V(t, \widehat{h}) = \widehat{h}^1(t)X(t) + \widehat{h}^0(t) = V^*(t),$$

i.e. the value process coincides with the martingale, Equation (5.54). In particular, we see that the investment made at time 0 is $V^*(0) = E^Q[H]$, which can be interpreted as a fair price for H.

Using the definition given in Equation (5.39) of the cost process, we see that the cost process associated with the risk-minimizing strategy is given by

$$C(t,\widehat{h}) = V^*(t) - \sum_{j=1}^{t}\widehat{h}^1(j)\Delta X(j) = V^*(0) + L(t,H) \qquad (5.58)$$

and the minimum obtainable risk is given by

$$r(t,\widehat{h}) = E^Q\left[(\Delta L(t+1,H))^2\,|\,\mathcal{F}(t)\right].$$

Thus, in order to apply the criterion of risk minimization, it is only necessary to derive the decomposition given in Equation (5.55), since this determines the optimal strategy and its associated risk. Since $L(H)$ is a martingale, we see from Equation (5.58) that the cost process associated with the risk-minimizing strategy is also a martingale. As a consequence, the risk-minimizing strategy is also said to be *mean-self-financing* (self-financing in the mean). A self-financing strategy is also mean-self-financing since the cost process of a self-financing strategy is constant and hence, in particular, a martingale. However, a mean-self-financing strategy is not in general self-financing.

Related criteria

The expected value in Equation (5.53) is calculated by applying the equivalent martingale measure Q and not by using the original probability measure P, although it would of course be much more natural to work with the probability measure P. Here one has to be a bit careful, since this can lead to a problem that has no solution; for example, this would be the case if Q is replaced by P in Equation (5.59) below. However, one can show that the solution $\widehat{h}$ also minimizes

$$R(t,h) = E^Q\left[(C(T,h) - C(t,h))^2\,|\,\mathcal{F}(t)\right] \qquad (5.59)$$

for all t, over all strategies h with $V(T,h) = H$. With this formulation, the quantity $C(T,h) - C(t,h)$ can be interpreted as the future costs associated with the strategy, and hence the criterion essentially amounts to minimizing at any time the conditional variance on the total future costs.

An alternative problem is the following optimization problem:

$$\underset{h^1(t),h^0(t),t=0,1,\ldots,T}{\text{minimize}}\quad E^Q\left[\sum_{t=1}^{T}(C(t+1,h) - C(t,h))^2\right]. \qquad (5.60)$$

It can be shown that the solution $h = (h^1, h^0)$ to Equation (5.60) only deviates from $\widehat{h} = (\widehat{h}^0, \widehat{h}^1)$ given by Equations (5.56) and (5.57) via the choice of h^0 and $\widehat{h}^0$, i.e. $h^1 = \widehat{h}^1$.

Alternatively, one could be interested in the strategy that minimizes, for any t,

$$E\left[(C(t+1,h) - C(t,h))^2 \,\middle|\, \mathcal{F}(t) \right],$$ (5.61)

where the expected value under Q in Equation (5.53) has been replaced by the true probability measure P. The solution to Equation (5.61) can be determined via the following recursion formula taken from Föllmer and Schweizer (1988):

$$h^1(t) = \frac{\mathrm{Cov}\left(H - \sum_{j=t+1}^{T} h^1(j)\Delta X(j), \Delta X(t) \,\middle|\, \mathcal{F}(t-1) \right)}{\mathrm{Var}[\Delta X(t) \mid \mathcal{F}(t-1)]},$$

$$h^0(t) = E\left[H - \sum_{j=t+1}^{T} h^1(j)\Delta X(j) \,\middle|\, \mathcal{F}(t) \right] - h^1(t)X(t). \quad \square$$

As mentioned above, the criterion which consists of replacing Q by P in Equation (5.59) does not lead to a well defined problem; see Schweizer (1988, 2001a).

5.7.5 Risk minimization for unit-linked contracts

The main step in determining the risk-minimizing strategy for the unit-linked contract is the derivation of the decomposition, Equation (5.55), within the market introduced in Section 5.7.1. In order to be able to give a better interpretation of our results, we introduce a process M defined by

$$M(t) = E^Q[Y(T)\mid \mathcal{H}(t)] = Y(t)_{T-t}p_{x+t},$$ (5.62)

which keeps track of the conditional expected number of survivors at T given the current number of survivors. The factor $_{T-t}p_{x+t}$ is the probability of surviving to T given survival to t and $Y(t)$ is the actual number of survivors at t. Thus, the process fluctuates over time with the terminal condition $M(T) = Y(T)$, i.e. the terminal value of M coincides with the number of survivors at T. One can express the decomposition given in Equation (5.54) for

$$V^*(t) = E^Q\left[Y(T)\frac{f(S^1(T))}{S^0(T)} \,\middle|\, \mathcal{F}(t) \right]$$

in terms of $\pi(f)$ and M. More precisely, one can show that the decomposition needed is given by

$$V^*(t) = V^*(0) + \sum_{j=1}^{t} M(j-1)\alpha(j,f)\Delta X(j) + \sum_{j=1}^{t} \pi(j,f)\Delta M(j).$$ (5.63)

This follows by first using the independence between Y and (S^0, S^1) to obtain

$$V^*(t) = M(t)\,\pi(t, f),$$

which shows that

$$\Delta V^*(t) = M(t-1)(\pi(t, f) - \pi(t, f-1)) + \pi(t, f)(M(t) - M(t-1)).$$

The decomposition in Equation (5.63) is now obtained by using Equation (5.47) for $\pi(f)$; see Section A.3 of the Appendix for more details. This leads to the following result, which can also be found in Møller (2001a).

Proposition 5.6 *The fair price for the unit-linked contract is* $l_{x\,T}p_x\,\pi(0, f)$. *The risk-minimizing strategy is as follows:*

$$h^1(t) = Y(t-1)_{T-(t-1)}p_{x+(t-1)}\alpha(t, f),$$

$$h^0(t) = Y(t)_{T-t}p_{x+t}\pi(t, f) - Y(t-1)_{T-(t-1)}p_{x+(t-1)}\alpha(t, f)X(t),$$

where $\alpha(f)$ *is determined by Equation (5.47).*

We note the following. The optimal number of stocks $h^1(t)$ for the period $(t-1, t]$ has a very natural form: it is the product of the hedge $\alpha(t, f)$ for the option $f(S^1(T))$ and the conditional expected number of survivors,

$$Y(t-1)_{T-(t-1)}p_{x+(t-1)},$$

calculated at time $t-1$. In addition, we see that the deposit on the savings account is currently being adjusted so that the value of the portfolio at t is equal to $V^*(t)$. This risk-minimizing strategy is not self-financing, and this can be seen by considering the cost process, which, according to Equation (5.58), is given by

$$C(t, h) = V^*(0) + L(t, H) = V^*(0) + \sum_{j=1}^{t}\pi(j, f)\Delta M(j).$$

Thus, the cost process is only constant if the process M defined by Equation (5.62) is constant or if $\pi(t, f) = 0$, which is typically not the case. The quantity $\Delta M(t)$ is the difference between the expected number of survivors calculated at time t and $t-1$, respectively. If the actual number of deaths during the period $(t-1, t]$ is smaller than the expected number of deaths, the expected number of survivors increases, and hence $\Delta M(t) > 0$. This leads to a loss for the insurance company, which must pay the amount $f(S^1(T))$ to each of the survivors at T. The situation $\Delta M(t) < 0$ arises when the expected number of survivors decreases, so that the company may reduce their reserves for these contracts. If we write the survival probability $_{T-(t-1)}p_{x+(t-1)}$ in the form $_1p_{x+(t-1)\ T-t}p_{x+t}$, the loss for the period $(t-1, t]$ can be rewritten as follows:

$$\Delta L(t) = \pi(t, f)_{T-t}p_{x+t}\left(Y(t) - Y(t-1)\,_1p_{x+(t-1)}\right),$$

which has the following interpretation: that the insurance company's loss is proportional to $\pi(t, f)_{T-t}p_{x+t}$, which is exactly the price at t of the option $f(S^1(T))$ multiplied by the survival probability $_{T-t}p_{x+t}$. This quantity is the market value at time t obtained by using the martingale measure Q for each policy holder alive at t. The second factor $(Y(t) - Y(t-1)\,_1p_{x+(t-1)})$ is the difference between the actual number of survivors at t and the expected number of survivors at t, calculated at $t-1$. It only remains to be shown that Equation (5.63) is the decomposition we need, and this is verified in Section A.3 of the Appendix. It was first suggested that risk minimization is applied to unit-linked life insurance contracts by Møller (1998). An extension that allowed for the handling of insurance payment streams was proposed by Møller (2001c).

We end our treatment of risk minimization by assessing the risk which cannot be hedged away, i.e. the minimum obtainable risk. For example, this risk can be quantified by determining the variance under Q of the total costs $C(T, h)$ associated with the risk-minimizing strategy. Here, one can exploit the fact that the increments of the martingales M and $\pi(f)$ are uncorrelated, and that the change of measure from P to Q does not affect the distribution of the lifetimes to show that

$$\text{Var}^Q[C(T, h)] = \sum_{t=1}^{T} E^Q[(\pi(t, f))^2 \Delta M(t)^2]$$

$$= \sum_{t=1}^{T} E^Q[(\pi(t, f))^2] E[\Delta M(t)^2]. \tag{5.64}$$

The term involving $\Delta M(t)$ can be expressed via the following survival probabilities:

$$E[\Delta M(t)^2] = E[\text{Var}[\Delta M(t) \mid \mathcal{F}(t-1)]] + \text{Var}[E[\Delta M(t) \mid \mathcal{F}(t-1)]]$$

$$= E[\text{Var}[_{T-t}p_{x+t}Y(t) \mid \mathcal{F}(t-1)]]$$

$$= l_x\,_Tp_x\,_{T-t}p_{x+t}(1 - {_1p_{x+(t-1)}}), \tag{5.65}$$

where the second equality follows by noting that M is a martingale and the last equality follows by noting that $Y(t) \mid \mathcal{F}(t-1) \sim \text{bin}(Y(t-1), \,_1p_{x+(t-1)})$.

The minimal variance given in Equation (5.64) should be compared with the variance of H, which is given by

$$\text{Var}^Q[Y(T)f(S^1(T))/S^0(T)] = E^Q[\text{Var}^Q[Y(T)\pi(T,f)|\mathcal{G}(T)]]$$
$$+ \text{Var}^Q[E^Q[Y(T)\pi(T,f)|\mathcal{G}(T)]]$$
$$= E^Q[(\pi(T,f))^2]l_{x\,T}p_x(1-{}_Tp_x)$$
$$+ \text{Var}^Q[\pi(T,f)](l_{x\,T}p_x)^2. \qquad (5.66)$$

This quantity is the variance of the company's total loss in the situation with no investment in the stock.

If we compare the risk-minimizing strategy and the super-hedging strategy, we see that the risk-minimizing strategy has a more natural form in that it involves the survival probability. However, one should be a bit careful here, since we have actually made a subjective choice by choosing the martingale measure Q in the calculations. Another martingale measure with an alternative survival probability would lead to different strategies. In addition, one can criticize the fact that the criterion of risk minimization is a quadratic criterion which uses the square of the costs, so that losing 100 euro and earning 100 euro is equally bad! Therefore, it might be more desirable with a criterion which only punished losses. Finally we mention that the criterion of risk minimization leads to strategies that are typically not self-financing, i.e. it is typically necessary currently to add and withdraw capital.

5.7.6 Mean-variance hedging

An alternative criterion is the principle of mean-variance hedging. This criterion does not use a specific martingale measure, and it only uses self-financing strategies. As with the criterion of risk minimization, mean-variance hedging is a symmetric criterion that punishes gains and losses equally.

Definition 5.7 *(Mean-variance hedging) Minimize* $E\left[(H-V(T,h))^2\right]$ *over all self-financing strategies h.*

The principle consists in finding the self-financing strategy that comes as close as possible to the liability H in the $L^2(P)$-sense. Recall that the terminal value at time T of the portfolio for a self-financing strategy is given by

$$V(T,h) = V(0,h) + \sum_{j=1}^{T} h^1(j)\Delta X(j).$$

Thus, the principle of mean-variance hedging can be interpreted as the problem of projecting H on the linear subspace, which consists of all possible values of a self-financing strategy. This can be formulated more precisely by introducing the set of all these possible terminal values:

$$\mathcal{A} = \{ V(T, h) \mid h \text{ self-financing} \}. \qquad (5.67)$$

The solution to the mean-variance problem is exactly the projection of H on $\mathcal{A}$. Mathematically, one can exploit the fact that the problem can be formulated within a Hilbert space $(L^2(P))$, and, from the so-called projection theorem, we know that H can be uniquely written as follows:

$$H = c(H) + \sum_{j=1}^{T} h^1(j, H)\Delta X(j) + N(H) = a(H) + N(H), \qquad (5.68)$$

where $a(H) \in \mathcal{A}$ and where $N(H)$ is orthogonal to $\mathcal{A}$, in the sense that $E[N(H)a] = 0$ for all $a \in \mathcal{A}$. This is illustrated in Figure 5.2. The corresponding initial capital $c(H)$ is called the *approximation price* for H. Together with $h^1(H)$, it determines the *mean-variance strategy*, i.e. the self-financing strategy that minimizes the distance to H. The quantity $N(H)$ is interpreted as the part of the liability H which cannot be hedged. In Sections 5.7.8 and 5.7.9 we examine principles where the non-hedgeable part $N(H)$ of the liability appears in the premium in the form of a safety loading. There is a substantial literature on this topic that involves quite complicated mathematical results; key references are Rheinländer and Schweizer (1997) and Schweizer (2001a). Here, we skip the technical details and formulate the main result directly under some simplifying assumptions which are satisfied in our example of the binomial market. However, even in this situation, we need to introduce

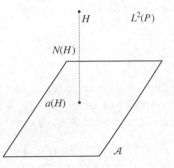

Figure 5.2. Mean-variance hedging. The approximation price and the optimal investment strategy are determined as a projection.

some additional notation in order to be able to give the solution. We define

$$\Delta A(t) = E[\Delta X(t)|\mathcal{F}(t-1)]$$

for $t = 1, \ldots, T$, which is the expected change in X in year t computed under the true probability measure P, and

$$\widetilde{\lambda}(t) = \frac{\Delta A(t)}{E[(\Delta X(t))^2|\mathcal{F}(t-1)]}.$$

We can now define a measure via

$$\frac{\mathrm{d}\widetilde{P}}{\mathrm{d}P} = \prod_{t=1}^{T} \frac{1 - \widetilde{\lambda}(t)\Delta X(t)}{1 - \widetilde{\lambda}(t)\Delta A(t)} = \widetilde{Z}(T), \tag{5.69}$$

and use the notation $\widetilde{E}$ instead of $E^{\widetilde{P}}$. In general, the density given by Equation (5.69) can take negative values, which implies that the measure $\widetilde{P}$ can be a *signed measure*. Note that if X is a martingale under P, $\Delta A(t) = 0$ such that $A(t) = A(0)$ and $\widetilde{\lambda}(t) = 0$. In particular, this implies that $P = \widetilde{P}$ in this case.

We assume here that the quantities $\widetilde{\lambda}(t)\Delta A(t)$ are deterministic, an assumption which is verified for the binomial market in Section A.4 of the Appendix. The calculations there also show that $\widetilde{Z}(T)$ is strictly positive and that $\widetilde{P}$ in this case is in fact identical to the probability measure Q introduced in Section 5.7.1.

Schweizer (1995, Proposition 4.3) shows that the mean-variance hedging strategy $\widetilde{h} = (\widetilde{h}^0, \widetilde{h}^1)$ is determined via

$$\widetilde{h}^1(t) = \widetilde{h}^1(t, H) + \widetilde{\lambda}(t)\left(\widetilde{V}(t-1) - \widetilde{V}(0) - \sum_{j=1}^{t-1}\widetilde{h}^1(j)\Delta X(j)\right), \tag{5.70}$$

which involves processes from the following crucial decomposition:

$$H = \widetilde{H}(0) + \sum_{j=1}^{T}\widetilde{h}^1(j, H)\Delta X(j) + \widetilde{L}(T, H), \tag{5.71}$$

where $\widetilde{L}(H)$ is a martingale (under the true probability measure P), and where $\widetilde{L}(H)$ in addition has the special property that also the product of $\widetilde{L}(H)$ and $(X - A)$ is a P-martingale. The process $\widetilde{V}$ is determined as follows:

$$\widetilde{V}(t) = \widetilde{E}[H|\mathcal{F}(t)].$$

Furthermore, the optimal initial capital (the approximation price) is in this case given by $\widetilde{V}(0) = \widetilde{E}[H] = H(0)$. Finally we mention that the variance of the difference between the optimal investment strategy and the liability H is given by

$$\text{Var}[N(H)] = E[(N(H))^2] = \sum_{t=1}^{T} E[(\Delta \widetilde{L}(t, H))^2] \prod_{j=t+1}^{T} (1 - \widetilde{\lambda}(j)\Delta A(j));$$

(5.72)

see Schweizer (1995, Theorem 4.4). This quantity can be interpreted as a measure for the risk that cannot be hedged away. We show below how Equation (5.72) appears as a safety loading under some alternative premium calculation principles.

5.7.7 Mean-variance hedging for unit-linked contracts

This section gives the mean-variance strategy for the unit-linked contract, Equation (5.46), within the market introduced in Section 5.7.1. Via some tedious calculations, which can be found in Section A.4 of the Appendix, we reach the following result.

Proposition 5.8 *The approximation price for the unit-linked contract is given by $l_{x\,T}p_x\pi(0, f)$. The mean-variance hedging strategy is defined recursively via*

$$\widetilde{h}^1(t) = Y(t-1)_{T-(t-1)}p_{x+(t-1)}\alpha(t, f)$$

$$+ \widetilde{\lambda}(t)\Bigg(Y(t-1)_{T-(t-1)}p_{x+(t-1)}\pi(t-1, f)$$

$$- l_{x\,T}p_0\pi(0, f) - \sum_{j=1}^{t-1}\widetilde{h}^1(j)\Delta X(j) \Bigg),$$

$$\widetilde{h}^0(t) = l_{x\,T}p_x\pi(0, f) + \sum_{j=1}^{t}\widetilde{h}^1(j)\Delta X(j) - \widetilde{h}^1(t)X(t).$$

We comment on this result. The optimal number $\widetilde{h}^1(t)$ of stocks to be held during the interval $(t-1, t]$ is calculated as the number from the risk-minimizing strategy with the addition of a correction term. This correction term is defined recursively, and loosely speaking it compares the change

$$\widetilde{V}(t-1) - \widetilde{V}(0) = Y(t-1)_{T-(t-1)}p_{x+(t-1)}\pi(t-1, f) - l_{x\,T}p_0\pi(0, f)$$

in the fair price and the realized investment gains

$$\sum_{j=1}^{t-1}\widetilde{h}^1(j)\Delta X(j)$$

for the period $[0, t-1]$. If the investment gains do not match the change in $\tilde{V}$, the mean-variance strategy deviates from the risk-minimizing strategy. In addition, we mention that the mean-variance strategy requires an initial investment of $l_{x\,T}p_x\pi(0, f)$ and that the strategy is self-financing.

The two criteria of risk minimization and mean-variance hedging are based on a symmetric criterion that treats gains and losses in the same way (they are to be avoided). Moreover, under these two criteria, the risk that cannot be hedged via a self-financing strategy is *not* part of the premium. It might be more natural if these quantities appeared in the form of a safety loading on the fair premium. This is exactly the case in Section 5.7.8.

5.7.8 Indifference pricing and hedging

We start by considering a so-called mean-variance utility function given by

$$u_\beta(Y) = E[Y] - a\,(\text{Var}[Y])^\beta, \qquad (5.73)$$

where Y is the wealth of the company at time T. (We refer to Dana (1999) for a treatment of mean-variance utility functions.) We focus on the two situations where $\beta = 1/2$ and $\beta = 1$, respectively. Equation (5.73) is considered as a description of the life insurance company's preferences. The classical actuarial variance and standard deviation premium calculation principles can be derived from these utility functions via a so-called *indifference argument*. More precisely, we say that an insurance company with the utility function given by Equation (5.73) prefers the pair (p_β, H) (i.e. selling the contingent claim H and receiving the premium p_β) to the pair (p'_β, H') if

$$u_\beta(p_\beta - H) \geq u_\beta(p'_\beta - H').$$

In particular, the pair $(0, 0)$ corresponds to not selling any contingent claims and not receiving any premium, and the insurance company is now said to be indifferent (with respect to u_β) between selling H at the price p_β and not selling H, provided that

$$u_\beta(p_\beta - H) = u_\beta(0) = 0, \qquad (5.74)$$

i.e. provided that

$$p_\beta = -u_\beta(-H) = E[H] + a(\text{Var}[H])^\beta.$$

This shows that the classical actuarial premium calculation principles can indeed be derived from the mean-variance utility functions given by Equation (5.73).

We now extend the indifference argument by including the insurance company's possibilities for investing in the financial markets. In particular, this involves a more precise description of the company's wealth at a future time T. Assume that the company faces a liability H (payable at T) and that the company has received the premium v_β. Denote by $V(0)$ the company's initial capital at time 0. If the insurance company follows an investment strategy h with the initial investment $V(0, h) = V(0)$, this leads to the wealth at T as follows:

$$V(T, h) + v_\beta - H = V(0) + v_\beta + \sum_{j=1}^{T} h^1(j)\Delta X(j) - H.$$

Alternatively, the insurance company might decide not to accept the liability H and simply follow an investment strategy $\widehat{h}$ with $V(0, \widehat{h}) = V(0)$ and thus obtain the following wealth:

$$V(T, \widehat{h}) = V(0) + \sum_{j=1}^{T} \widehat{h}^1(j)\Delta X(j).$$

One could say that the company is indifferent between these two different possibilities if the premium v_β is determined such that

$$u_\beta\left(V(T, h) + v_\beta - H\right) = u_\beta\left(V(T, \widehat{h})\right).$$

However, we have not yet specified how the insurance company chooses the investment strategies h and $\widehat{h}$, and each choice of strategies could potentially lead to different premiums v_β. A natural way to define the fair premium v_β is instead to compare the utility associated with an optimal strategy in the two cases where the company has accepted the liability and where it has not accepted the liability. This leads to the following definition.

Definition 5.9 *The indifference price $v_\beta(H)$ for H is defined by*

$$\sup_{h:V(0,h)=V(0)} u_\beta(V(T, h) + v_\beta(H) - H) \stackrel{!}{=} \sup_{\widehat{h}:V(0,\widehat{h})=V(0)} u_\beta(V(T, \widehat{h})).$$

The special case with no investments can, for example, be covered by assuming that $V(T, h) = V(0, h)$ for all investment strategies. In this case we recover Equation (5.74) from this definition, and hence the classical actuarial variance and standard deviation principles.

From Møller (2001b) and Schweizer (2001b), we have the following results for the solution to the indifference pricing principles. Under the *variance principle*, i.e. the case where $\beta = 1$, the fair premium is given by

$$v_1(H) = \widetilde{E}[H] + a\mathrm{Var}[N(H)], \tag{5.75}$$

where $N(H)$, defined in Equation (5.68), is the part of H that cannot be hedged away. The investment strategy that maximizes the utility of the company is given by

$$h_1^1(t) = \widetilde{h}^1(t) + \frac{1 + \mathrm{Var}[\widetilde{Z}(T)]}{2a}\widetilde{\beta}(t), \tag{5.76}$$

where

$$\widetilde{\beta}(t) = \widetilde{\lambda}(t)\prod_{j=1}^{t}(1 - \widetilde{\lambda}(j)\Delta X(j)),$$

and where $\widetilde{Z}(T)$ is defined by Equation (5.69). For the *standard-deviation principle*, i.e. the case where $\beta = 1/2$, the fair premium is given by

$$v_{1/2}(H) = \widetilde{E}[H] + \widetilde{a}\sqrt{\mathrm{Var}[N(H)]} \tag{5.77}$$

if $a^2 \geq \mathrm{Var}[\widetilde{Z}(T)]$, where

$$\widetilde{a} = a\sqrt{1 - \frac{\mathrm{Var}[\widetilde{Z}(T)]}{a^2}}.$$

If $a^2 < \mathrm{Var}[\widetilde{Z}(T)]$, then the $u_{1/2}$-indifference price is not defined. The optimal strategy is well defined provided that $a^2 > \mathrm{Var}[\widetilde{Z}(T)]$, and it is in this case given by

$$h_2^1(t) = \widetilde{h}^1(t) + \frac{1 + \mathrm{Var}[\widetilde{Z}(T)]}{\widetilde{a}}\sqrt{\mathrm{Var}[N(H)]}\widetilde{\beta}(t). \tag{5.78}$$

The principles given in Equations (5.75) and (5.77) are also called the *financial variance and standard deviation principles*, respectively. We see that the two fair premiums resemble the classical premium calculation principles in that they consist of two terms: an expected value of H and a safety loading. For the financial counterparts, the expected value of H is calculated under a martingale measure, whereas the safety loading involves the variance of that part of H which cannot be hedged away via a self-financing strategy. Note, moreover, that this variance is calculated with respect to the original probability measure P.

For extensions and further results on the financial variance and standard deviation principles and their applications in insurance, see Møller (2002,

2003a, b). Indifference pricing for insurance contracts under exponential utility functions has been considered by Becherer (2003). For a survey on utility indifference pricing, see the forthcoming book edited by R. Carmona.[†]

5.7.9 Indifference pricing for unit-linked contracts

The results from the previous sections show that the fair premiums and optimal investment strategies are related to the results from mean-variance hedging and risk minimization. Thus, all the hard work has already been done, and it only remains to calculate $\text{Var}[N(H)]$ given by Equation (5.72) for the decomposition in Equation (5.63), i.e. with

$$\widetilde{L}(t, H) = \sum_{j=1}^{t} \pi(j, f)\Delta M(j).$$

The variance of $N(H)$ can be determined via calculations similar to the ones used in Section 5.7.5; see Equations (5.64) and (5.65). In this way, we obtain

$$E[(\Delta\widetilde{L}(t, H))^2] = E[(\pi(t, f))^2]E[\Delta M(t)^2]$$
$$= E[(\pi(t, f))^2]l_x\,_{T}p_x\,_{T-t}p_{x+t}(1 - {}_1p_{x+(t-1)}). \quad (5.79)$$

Thus,

$$\text{Var}[N(H)] = \sum_{t=1}^{T} \left(E[(\pi(t, f))^2]E[\Delta M(t)^2]\right) \prod_{j=t+1}^{T} (1 - \widetilde{\lambda}(j)\Delta A(j)). \quad (5.80)$$

We see from Equation (5.79) that $E[(\Delta\widetilde{L}(t, H))^2]$ and $E[\Delta M(t)^2]$ are proportional to l_x. This implies that the variance of $N(H)$ is proportional to the number l_x of persons insured, whereas the standard deviation of $N(H)$ is proportional to the square root of l_x.

We can now write up the main results as follows.

Proposition 5.10 *The fair premium for the unit-linked contract under the variance principle is given by*

$$v_1(H) = l_x\,_{T}p_x\,\pi(0, f) + a\text{Var}[N(H)],$$

[†] V. Henderson and D. Hobson. Utility indifference pricing – an overview, in R. Carmona (ed.), *Indifference Pricing* (to be published by Princeton University Press).

where $\mathrm{Var}[N(H)]$ *is given by Equation (5.80). The optimal strategy is determined by*

$$h_1^1(t) = Y(t-1)_{T-(t-1)}p_{x+(t-1)}\alpha(t,f)$$
$$+ \widetilde{\lambda}(t)\left(Y(t-1)_{T-(t-1)}p_{x+(t-1)}\,\pi(t-1,f)\right.$$
$$\left. - l_{x\,T}p_0\,\pi(0,f) - \sum_{j=1}^{t-1}\widetilde{h}^1(j)\Delta X(j)\right)$$
$$+ \frac{1+\mathrm{Var}[\widetilde{Z}(T)]}{2a}\,\widetilde{\beta}(t).$$

We note the following. The fair premium under the financial variance principle is the sum of the premium under the criterion of mean-variance hedging and a safety loading, which is proportional to l_x. The optimal strategy consists of two terms: the mean-variance strategy (the second and third lines) and a correction term (the fourth line), where the latter does not depend on the liability H. This last term is closely connected to the variance principle, and it is present even in the case where the company has not accepted any liabilities.

For the standard deviation principle, we get a similar result, which, for completeness, we formulate here.

Proposition 5.11 *The fair premium for the unit-linked contract under the standard deviation principle is given by*

$$v_1(H) = l_{x\,T}p_x\,\pi(0,f) + \widetilde{a}\sqrt{\mathrm{Var}[N(H)]},$$

where $\mathrm{Var}[N(H)]$ *is given by Equation (5.80). The optimal strategy is determined by*

$$h_2^1(t) = Y(t-1)_{T-(t-1)}p_{x+(t-1)}\alpha(t,f)$$
$$+ \widetilde{\lambda}(t)\left(Y(t-1)_{T-(t-1)}p_{x+(t-1)}\,\pi(t-1,f)\right.$$
$$\left. - l_{x\,T}p_0\,\pi(0,f) - \sum_{j=1}^{t-1}\widetilde{h}^1(j)\Delta X(j)\right)$$
$$+ \frac{1+\mathrm{Var}[\widetilde{Z}(T)]}{\widetilde{a}}\,\sqrt{\mathrm{Var}[N(H)]}\,\widetilde{\beta}(t).$$

5.7.10 Quantile hedging

An interesting alternative to the above treated principles is quantile hedging; see, for example, Föllmer and Leukert (1999) and Föllmer and Schied (2002).

Definition 5.12 *(Quantile hedging) Given* $V(0) < \sup_{Q \in \mathbf{Q}} E^Q[H]$,

$$maximize \ P\left(V(0) + \sum_{t=1}^{T} h^1(t)\,\Delta X(t) \geq H\right)$$

over self-financing strategies h with $V(0, h) = V(0)$.

The main idea of quantile hedging is the following. Assume that the company has an initial capital $V(0)$ and is interested in using this amount to reduce the risk associated with the liability H. If the amount is insufficient to super-replicate H, one could alternatively look for the strategy that maximizes the probability that the terminal wealth $V(T, h)$ exceeds the liability H.

The solution is well understood in the complete market case, where there exists a unique equivalent martingale measure. To formulate this result, let Q be the unique martingale measure. It follows from Föllmer and Leukert (1999) that the solution is closely connected to finding an event $\widetilde{A} \in \mathcal{F}(T)$ with

$$P(\widetilde{A}) = \max\{P(A)|A \in \mathcal{F}(T),\ E^Q[H1_A] \leq V(0)\}. \tag{5.81}$$

The main result basically says that quantile hedging for the liability H is similar to performing super-hedging for the modified liability $H1_{\widetilde{A}}$, which is equal to H on the set $\widetilde{A}$ and zero otherwise.

The incomplete market case is less well understood. The main problem is essentially that there are infinitely many martingale measures and that it is not really clear which martingale measure one should choose in Equation (5.81) in the general case. As a consequence, we cannot at this point give the quantile hedging strategy for the unit-linked contract.

5.8 Traditional life insurance

In this chapter, we have focused on the analysis of unit-linked contracts. The main reason for this choice is that these contracts provide a clearly specified connection between benefits and returns on the underlying assets. Once the company's bonus and investment strategy has been specified as in Chapter 4, the company's liability associated with traditional, participating life insurance contracts may also be viewed as an integrated contingent claim. Thus, one can, in principle, apply the same methods for the treatment of this integrated claim if it is possible to determine fairly explicit expressions for the liability.

6

Surplus-linked life insurance

6.1 Introduction

We consider in this chapter the general type of life insurance where premiums and benefits are calculated provisionally at issuance of the policy and later determined according to the performance of the insurance contract or company. The determination of premiums and benefits can take various forms depending on the type of contract. Examples are various types of participating life insurance (in some countries called with-profit life insurance) and various types of pension funding.

The determination of premiums and benefits is based on payment of dividends, which in general may be positive or negative, from the insurance company to the policy holder. It is important to distinguish between two aspects of the determination: the dividend plan and the bonus plan. The dividend plan is the plan for allocation of dividends. However, often the dividends are not paid out immediately in cash but are converted into a stream of future payments. The bonus plan is the plan for how the dividends are eventually turned into payments.

In Steffensen (2000), a framework of securitization is developed where reserves are no longer defined as expected present values but as market prices of streams of payments (which, however, happen to be expressible as expected present values under adjusted measures). An insurance contract is defined as a stream of payments linked to dynamic indices, covering a wide range of insurance contracts including various forms of unit-linked contracts. Securitization is one way of dealing simultaneously with the risk in the insurance policy and the risk in the financial market. It is built on the consideration of the stream of payments stipulated in an insurance contract as a dynamically traded object on the financial market. The insurance company is then considered as a participant in this market that has to adapt prices and

200

strategies to the market conditions. The framework of securitization can be argued for in two different ways.

Firstly, the insurance contracts are indeed in certain ways dynamically traded securities. The insurance company and the policy holder exchange payment streams in a competitive market. The policy holder can typically surrender their contract and hereby give up their position in the security. The insurance company can primarily take the opposite position by reselling (parts of the) risk aggregated in portfolios or sub-portfolios. This happens when the insurance company buys reinsurance cover or sells, for example, non-core business lines to competing insurance companies. Indeed, market prices of risk may be hidden, blurred, ambiguous and hard to obtain due to a non-effective, non-liquid and maybe even obscure market place. They may still be the best source of "best market value estimates," however.

Secondly, even if the market information is found to be inadequate in this respect, the supervisory authorities may implement accounting and solvency standards which are built on this pattern of thinking. By this we mean that such standards could, for example, dictate certain prices of risk for calculation of entries. To this extent the idea of securitization is rather a point of view of the regulators, and one could of course discuss whether such prices of risk should be spoken of as market prices. For a general description of securitization in life insurance, see Cowley and Cummins (2005).

In this chapter we construct a general life and pension insurance contract where we link dividends to a certain notion of surplus within the framework developed in Steffensen (2000). Working with general surplus-linked payments in participating life insurance and pension funding, we go beyond the traditional setup of payments in the existing literature on the emergence of surplus and dividends. However, surplus-linked payments offer a number of appealing setups. The study of such surplus-linked insurance has a three-fold motivation, as we see in the following.

Firstly, it represents a new product, combining properties of participating life insurance, pension funding and unit-linked insurance. In fact, a major Danish life insurance company introduced in 2002 a new product under the name *tidspension* (time pension), which can be analyzed within the framework presented in this chapter.

Secondly, the Danish legislation shows a trend towards a formalization of the participation element of participating life insurance contracts. This trend can be expected to continue world-wide when international rules for market valuation in participating life insurance and pension funding are concretized; see, for example, Jørgensen (2004) for the status of accounting standards and fair valuation. The present chapter serves as an example of such a formalization.

Thirdly, it seems to represent a good imitation of the behavior of managers. As such, it can be used as a management tool as well as a market analysis tool.

Subjugating life and pension insurance to the market conditions, the appropriate tool seems to be mathematical finance or, more specifically, contingent claims analysis. Option pricing theory was introduced as a tool for the analysis and management of unit-linked insurance in the 1970s (see Brennan and Schwartz (1976) and references in Aase and Persson (1994)). The consideration of schemes in pension funding as options also goes back to the 1970s (see, for example, Sharpe (1976) and references in Blake (1998)). In participating life insurance, however, contingent claims analysis as a tool for analysis and management has been long in coming and was, to our knowledge, introduced by Briys and de Varenne (1994). Since then, the framework of Briys and de Varenne (1994) has been developed further and generalized substantially by several financial economists: Grosen and Jørgensen (2000), Hansen and Miltersen (2002) and Miltersen and Persson (2003) are examples of some more recent references.

Contingent claims analysis of participating life insurance has been long in coming mainly for one reason. The link between the payments and the performance of the company in participating life insurance is often laid down by statute so vaguely that it may seem unreasonable to consider dividends as contractual. Working in a framework of securitization, our main objection to this argument is, of course, that the insurance business, and hereby the participation in the performance, takes place in a competitive market. Thus, the insurance company is forced to adapt, for example, its plans for the determination of payments to the market conditions. This objection is, at the same time, the primary argument for applying contingent claims analysis to life and pension insurance at all.

In Grosen and Jørgensen (2000), Hansen and Miltersen (2002) and Miltersen and Persson (2003), the main focus has been on the financial elements of the insurance contracts. In contrast, other authors have contributed to the understanding of the actuarial notion of surplus, including possible insurance risk, and its redistribution in terms of dividends and bonus; see Norberg (1999) and Ramlau-Hansen (1991). Norberg (1999) works with a stochastic economic–demographic environment, though with only one investment opportunity. Steffensen (2001) approaches the actuarial notion of surplus using the methods and terminology of mathematical finance, and hereby links classical (financial) modeling of financial risk and classical (actuarial) modeling of insurance risk. This chapter is very much based on Steffensen (2006b), in which the notion of surplus-linked life insurance is introduced.

The chapter is structured as follows. In Section 6.2 we construct the framework for the insurance contract. In Section 6.3 the notions of surplus are studied and related to previous literature. In Section 6.4 we consider general surplus-linked dividend plans, and the particular situation of a linear link is studied in Section 6.5. Section 6.6 works out a framework for bonus. In section 6.7 we link dividends to the surplus and a certain bonus index, and the particular situation of a linear link is then studied in Section 6.8. At the end of each section we have added a remark which explains how the present section connects to parts of the material presented in Chapters 2 and 4.

6.2 The insurance contract

We take as given a probability space $(\Omega, \mathcal{F}, P)$. On the probability space is defined a process $Z = (Z(t))_{0 \leq t \leq n}$ taking values in a finite set $\mathcal{J} = \{0, \dots, J\}$ of possible states and starting in state 0 at time 0. We define the J-dimensional counting process $N = (N^k)_{k \in \mathcal{J}}$ as follows:

$$N^k(t) = \#\{s \,|\, s \in (0, t], Z(s-) \neq k, Z(s) = k\},$$

counting the number of jumps into state k until time t. Assume that there exist deterministic and sufficiently regular functions $\mu^{jk}(t)$, $j, k \in \mathcal{J}$, such that N^k admits the stochastic intensity process $(\mu^{Z(t)k}(t))_{0 \leq t \leq n}$ for $k \in \mathcal{J}$, i.e.

$$M^k(t) = N^k(t) - \int_0^t \mu^{Z(s)k}(s)\,\mathrm{d}s$$

constitutes a martingale for $k \in \mathcal{J}$. Then Z is a Markov process. The reader should think of Z as a policy state of a life insurance contract; see Hoem (1969) for a motivation for the setup. We let $\mathcal{F}^N = \mathcal{F}^Z$ denote the filtration generated by Z formalizing information about Z, i.e.

$$\mathcal{F}^N(t) = \sigma(Z(s), 0 \leq s \leq t).$$

We emphasize that the intensity process $(\mu^{Z(t)k}(t))_{0 \leq t \leq n}$ is adapted to $\mathcal{F}^N$ such that there is no demographic risk.

Also defined on the probability space is a standard Brownian motion W. We consider a financial market with two assets which are continuously traded. The market prices are described by the following stochastic differential equation:

$$dS^0(t) = rS^0(t)\,dt,$$

$$S^0(0) = 1,$$

$$dS^1(t) = rS^1(t)\,dt + \sigma S^1(t)\,dW(t),$$

$$S^1(0) = s_0,$$

where r and σ are constants. This is the classical Black–Scholes market. We let $\mathcal{F}^W = \mathcal{F}^{S^1}$ denote the filtration generated by S^1 formalizing information about S^1, i.e.

$$\mathcal{F}^W(t) = \sigma\left(S^1(s), 0 \le s \le t\right),$$

and we assume that

$$\mathcal{F} = \mathcal{F}^N \vee \mathcal{F}^W.$$

In the dynamics of S^1 above, we take the short rate of interest r to be the expected infinitesimal return and hereby take P to be the valuation measure not the physical measure. Throughout the chapter we are only interested in valuation, and it is convenient then to specify all dynamics directly under the valuation measure. The same goes for dynamics of Z above in the sense that we take M^k to be a martingale under the valuation measure. Thus, we think of having fixed a market valuation intensity. Whether this intensity has come to our knowledge from prices of other insurance contracts in the market, or from some alternative determination of market attitudes towards insurance (policy) risk, is not important. We follow Steffensen (2000) and speak of conditional expected values under P as arbitrage-free values. The difference in comparison with Steffensen (2000) is that here we have specified the dynamics directly under the valuation measure in the first place.

We consider a standard life insurance payment process; i.e. the accumulated contractual benefits less premiums are described as follows:

$$dB(t) = dB^{Z(t)}(t) + \sum_{k \in \mathcal{J}} b^{Z(t-)k}(t)\,dN^k(t),$$

$$dB^j(t) = b^j(t)\,dt + \Delta B^j(t), j \in \mathcal{J},$$

where $b^j(t)$, $\Delta B^j(t)$ and $b^{jk}(t)$ are deterministic and sufficiently regular functions. The sum $\Delta B^j(t)$ represents a lump sum payment at the deterministic time point t if $Z(t) = j$. The set of deterministic time points with discontinuities in B is given by $\mathcal{D} = \{t_0, t_1, \ldots, t_q\}$.

We consider the deterministic basis (r, μ), which specifies an interest rate and a set of transition intensities. On this basis we introduce the statewise reserves for $j \in \mathcal{J}$ and for $t \in [0, n]$ as follows:

$$V^{Bj}(t) = E_{t,j} \left[\int_t^n e^{-\int_t^s r} dB(s) \right], \tag{6.1}$$

where $E_{t,j}$ denotes the expectation conditioned on $Z(t) = j$ and where $\int_t^n = \int_{(t,n]}$.

Since the expectation in Equation (6.1) is taken under the market valuation measure, we speak of Equation (6.1) as the market value or arbitrage-free value of the payment process B. Financial mathematics teaches us that such a market value can always be written as such a conditional expected present value with an appropriate specification of underlying dynamics. The basis (r, μ) is hereafter spoken of as the market basis.

There is a deep connection between conditional expected values as in Equation (6.1) and solutions to corresponding systems of deterministic differential equations, henceforth spoken of simply as differential equations. This connection is used throughout the chapter, with a reference to Steffensen (2000) where this connection is proved in sufficient generality for all our applications. The differential equation for $V^{Bj}(t)$ is, however, very well known from various other references, since this is the general Thiele differential equation. However, for consistency, we also follow Steffensen (2000) for the following ordinary differential equation for V^{Bj}:

$$V_t^{Bj}(t) = rV^{Bj}(t) - b^j(t) - \sum_{k:k \neq j} \mu^{jk}(t) R^{Bjk}(t), \, t \in [0, n] \setminus \mathcal{D}, \tag{6.2a}$$

$$V^{Bj}(t-) = \Delta B^j(t) + V^{Bj}(t), \, t \in \mathcal{D}, \tag{6.2b}$$

$$R^{Bjk}(t) = b^{jk}(t) + V^{Bk}(t) - V^{Bj}(t), \tag{6.2c}$$

where a subscript denotes (partial) differentiation, i.e. $V_t(t) = (\partial/\partial t) V(t)$. In Equation (6.2a) we have the ordinary differential equation valid for $V^{Bj}(t)$ at all times that are outside $\mathcal{D}$. Differentiability follows from sufficient regularity of the coefficients of Equation (6.2a). This differential equation involves a so-called sum at risk $R^{Bjk}(t)$ given in Equation (6.2c). At the time points of discontinuity, i.e. inside $\mathcal{D}$, the pasting condition, Equation (6.2b), holds. The terminal condition of the differential equation (6.2) is, by definition, $V^{Bj}(n) = 0$. Throughout, we skip the specification of the terminal condition, which will be evident and given by definition.

An important quantity in life insurance is the value of future payments on a so-called technical basis (r^*, μ^*). Which technical basis to use depends on the context or the purpose of the valuation. Given a technical basis, the technical reserve,

$$V^{B*j}(t) = E_{t,j}^* \left[\int_t^n e^{-\int_t^s r^*} dB(s) \right],$$

fulfils the following ordinary differential equation:

$$V_t^{B*j}(t) = r^* V^{B*j}(t) - b^j(t) - \sum_{k:k \neq j} \mu^{*jk}(t) R^{B*jk}(t), t \in [0,n] \setminus \mathcal{D}, \quad (6.3)$$

$$V^{B*j}(t-) = \Delta B^j(t) + V^{B*j}(t), t \in \mathcal{D},$$

$$R^{B*jk}(t) = b^{jk}(t) + V^{B*k}(t) - V^{B*j}(t).$$

Here, E^* denotes the expectation with respect to μ^*.

A special purpose of a special technical basis is the calculation of the payment process B at time 0. The technical basis used for this purpose is called the first order basis. The payment process B is calculated in accordance with the so-called equivalence relation performed under the first order basis. If (r^*, μ^*) is the first order basis, the equivalence relation is as follows:

$$V^{B*0}(0-) = 0. \quad (6.4)$$

We speak of the payment process which results from this equation as the first order payment process. Thus, the first order payment process is simply the payments that are specified in the contract at the time of issue. The equivalence relation given in Equation (6.4) implies a balance between the first order expected present value of the first order premiums and the first order expected present value of the first order benefits.

If the first order basis is chosen as the technical basis, the equivalence relation Equation (6.4) is fulfilled. This relation can then be viewed as an initial condition for V^{B*0}. With this initial condition and the differential equation in Equation (6.3) for the state $j = 0$, one can write down a retrospective (calculated from $0-$ to t) solution $V^{B*0}(t)$ in terms of transition probabilities of Z. This had been spoken of as a retrospective reserve until Norberg (1991) pointed out that this was nothing but a retrospective formula for the prospective value $V^{B*0}(t)$ based on the equivalence relation for V^{B*0}. Norberg (1991) then introduced a different notion of retrospective reserve based on a present valuation of past payments.

In order to rectify the possible non-equivalence of the first order payments under the market basis in the sense of $V^{B0}(0-) \neq 0$, the insurance company adds dividends to the first order payments. We denote by D the process of *accumulated dividend payments*, and we assume that this is described by

$$dD(t) = dD^{Z(t)}(t) + \sum_{k \in \mathcal{J}} \delta^{Z(t-)k}(t) \, dN^k(t), \qquad (6.5)$$

$$dD^j(t) = \delta^j(t) \, dt + \Delta D^j(t), \, j \in \mathcal{J},$$

where $\delta^j(t)$, $\Delta D^j(t)$ and $\delta^{jk}(t)$ are, in general, $\mathcal{F}$-adapted stochastic processes. Note that the coefficients of the payment process D are substantially different from the coefficients of the payment process B. The dividend payments are allowed to depend, in general, on the full history and on the history of capital gains and losses in particular.

We now constrain dividend processes in the form of Equation (6.5) to be fair in some sense. Norberg (1999, 2001) studies fairness constraints on dividends as well in an economic–demographic environment driven by a stochastic market basis. The stochastic interest rate in the stochastic market basis represents the only investment opportunity. The approach by Norberg (1999, 2001) is to constrain dividends to attain ultimate fairness in the sense of equivalence conditional on the economic–demographic history. Formalizing by $\mathcal{F}^{(r,\mu)}$ this history, the fairness constraint by Norberg (1999, 2001) is as follows:

$$E\left[\int_{0-}^{n} e^{-\int_0^t r} \, d(B+D)(t) \,\middle|\, \mathcal{F}^{(r,\mu)}(n)\right] = 0. \qquad (6.6)$$

Note that this fairness constraint prevents the insurance company from taking ultimate economic–demographic risks.

In this chapter we have no demographic uncertainty, while economic uncertainty is contained in $\mathcal{F}^{S^1}$. Thus, a direct translation of Equation (6.6) to our situation is as follows:

$$E\left[\int_{0-}^{n} e^{-\int_0^t r} \, d(B+D)(t) \,\middle|\, \mathcal{F}^{S^1}(n)\right] = 0. \qquad (6.7)$$

From a theoretical point of view, this could work very well as a fairness constraint. In practice, however, the insurance companies do work with dividends which imply ultimate financial risk, indicating that Equation (6.7) is too restrictive. This behavior may be demanded by policy holders. This does not necessarily mean that Equation (6.6) can be said to be too restrictive, though. Recall that Equation (6.6) is introduced in a fundamentally different economic–demographic environment with locally risk-free capital gains.

The question is: which fairness criterion should replace Equation (6.7) (and Equation (6.6)) such that the insurance companies are allowed to take financial risks? From mathematical finance, we inherit the following criterion:

$$E\left[\int_{0-}^{n} e^{-\int_0^t r}\, d\,(B+D)\,(t)\right] = 0. \tag{6.8}$$

This leads to what in Steffensen (2000) is spoken of as an arbitrage-free insurance contract. The fundamental idea is that the constraint given in Equation (6.8) prevents arbitrage opportunities in an (artificial) market where attitudes towards risk conform with the valuation measure P. We refer the reader to Steffensen (2000) for further motivation of Equation (6.8) and matters arising from it.

It is clear, by the tower property, that Equation (6.8) is less restrictive than Equation (6.7) since any dividend process which is fair according to Equation (6.7) is also fair according to Equation (6.8). Since Equation (6.8) says much less about the dividends than Equation (6.7) does, the next important step is to specify further the dividends. Since D is, in general, $\mathcal{F}$-adapted, it is in a sense based on experience, although our experience basis $\mathcal{F}$ differs substantially from the experience basis presented in Norberg (1999, 2001), i.e. $\mathcal{F}^{(r,\mu)}$. The idea of the present chapter is to suggest how the dividends could be based on the experience in order to construct new tractable and relevant insurance products and to imitate (the behavior of managers of) old insurance products. This chapter presents one family of dividend specifications based on this idea.

A major drawback of going from Equation (6.6) to Equation (6.7) and from Equation (6.7) to Equation (6.8) is that realistic modeling of $S = \left(S^0, S^1\right)$ and Z are required. It is doubtful whether one can make realistic assumptions in the long term perspective of a life insurance contract. Both the Black–Scholes market and the Markovian Z applied here seem far too simple. We should here emphasize the purpose of this chapter. It serves to present the concept of surplus-linked life insurance payments and demonstrate the partial differential equation methodology for calculation of reserves based on this concept. It does *not* provide new realistic models for long term financial markets and stochastic intensities.

The idea of surplus-linked life insurance payments generalizes directly to any financial market, and the partial differential equation methodology applies to a wide range of Markovian financial and intensity models. Such markets include popular and well known Gaussian interest rate and volatility models and less popular and less well known Gaussian intensity models. The generalizations follow from appropriate textbooks on mathematical finance (see Björk (2004), for example) and insurance literature proposing stochastic intensity models (see, for example, Steffensen (2000)).

Remark 6.1 *Consider an endowment insurance in the survival model illustrated in Figure 6.1. We can skip the superfluous state specification in this model, and we denote the death counting process by N, the transition intensity by μ, the statewise reserve corresponding to state 0 by V^B and the sum at risk corresponding to transition from 0 to 1 by R^B. Denote by b^{ad} the death sum paid out upon death, by $b^a(0)$ the lump sum paid out upon survival until time n, and by π the continuous level premium paid as long as the insured is alive. Then*

$$\mathrm{d}B(t) = \mathrm{d}B^{Z(t)}(t) + b^{ad}\,\mathrm{d}N(t)$$

$$\mathrm{d}B^0(t) = -\pi\,\mathrm{d}t + b^a(0)\,\mathrm{d}\epsilon_n(t),$$

$$\mathrm{d}B^1(t) = 0,$$

where $\epsilon_n(t) = 1\,[t \geq n]$ indicates that t exceeds n. Noting the general terminal condition $V^B(n) = 0$, Equation (6.2) reduces to the following:

$$V_t^B(t) = rV^B(t) + \pi - \mu(t)R^B(t),$$

$$V^B(n-) = b^a(0),$$

$$R^B(t) = b^{ad} - V^B(t).$$

This is exactly the differential equation for V^g in Equation (2.23) where we put $t = 0$ (and then skip the t argument) since we are here valuating the payments guaranteed at time 0.

Correspondingly, Equation (6.3) reduces to the following:

$$V_t^{B*}(t) = r^*V^{B*}(t) + \pi - \mu^*(t)R^{B*}(t),$$

$$V^{B*}(n-) = b^a(0),$$

$$R^{B*}(t) = b^{ad} - V^{B*}(t).$$

But this is exactly the differential equation for V^* in Equation (2.10) where, again, we put $t = 0$ (and then skip the t argument).

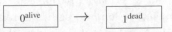

Figure 6.1. Survival model.

6.3 Surplus

In Section 6.2 we introduced the process of dividends. In this section we study a process which, at the same time, is the source of dividends and, in the forthcoming sections, also determines the dividend payments. This process is taken to be a wealth process, denoted by X, with income in the form of a *contribution process*, which we call C, and with consumption in form of the dividend process D. The wealth process is invested in the market described in Section 6.2. The dynamics of this wealth process determines the results in the following sections.

Usually one would speak of the source of dividends as some kind of surplus. The dynamics of the wealth process introduced below is so general that it includes various notions of surplus suggested in the literature. We choose to speak of the wealth process simply as the *surplus*. After having introduced the dynamics of the surplus below, we go through a series of more or less congruent classical surplus definitions which are all special cases.

We consider a surplus X with accumulated income process C and accumulated consumption process D. We take $\sigma^{Z(t)}(t, X(t))/\sigma$ to be the proportion of the surplus invested in S^1, where $\sigma^j(t, x)$ is a deterministic and sufficiently regular function; i.e. if the number of stocks held at time t is denoted by $\eta^1(t)$, then

$$\sigma^{Z(t)}(t, X(t)) X(t) = \sigma \eta^1(t) S^1(t).$$

Recall that σ is the volatility of S^1. Then the surplus satisfies the following stochastic differential equation:

$$dX(t) = rX(t)\,dt + \sigma^{Z(t)}(t, X(t)) X(t)\,dW(t) + d(C - D)(t), \qquad (6.9)$$

$$X(0-) = 0.$$

We assume that the income process C, also spoken of as the contribution process, is described as follows:

$$dC(t) = dC^{Z(t)}(t) + \sum_{k \in \mathcal{J}} c^{Z(t-)k}(t)\,dN^k(t), \qquad (6.10)$$

$$dC^j(t) = c^j(t)\,dt + \Delta C^j(t), j \in \mathcal{J},$$

where $c^j(t)$, $\Delta C^j(t)$ and $c^{jk}(t)$ are deterministic and sufficiently regular functions. For the moment, we have no particular form of these coefficients in mind; this is just a specification of the structure of contributions. Note that this structure is similar to the structure of the payment process B.

This is basically what the reader needs to know about the surplus in the succeeding sections. However, in the rest of this section we relate these surplus dynamics to particular notions of surplus, including the traditional ones. These relations serve as our motivation for working with a surplus in the form given in Equation (6.9).

We first introduce the basic notion of an *individual surplus*. An important part of the individual surplus is the cash balance of past payments including capital gains, which we denote by U. The dynamics of U is given by

$$dU(t) = rU(t)\,dt + \eta^1(t)\,S^1(t)\,dW(t) - d(B+D)(t),$$

$$U(0-) = 0.$$

The individual surplus is now defined as the excess of this cash balance over the technical reserve, i.e.

$$X(t) = U(t) - V^{B*Z(t)}(t), \qquad (6.11)$$

$$X(0-) = 0.$$

We have assumed above that $\sigma^{Z(t)}(t, X(t))/\sigma$ is the proportion of the X invested in S^1. This means that from the cash balance $U(t) = X(t) + V^{B*Z(t)}(t)$, the amount $(\sigma^{Z(t)}(t, X(t))/\sigma) X(t)$ is invested in S^1 such that the capital gains from this investment become $(\sigma^{Z(t)}(t, X(t))/\sigma) X(t)\,dS^1(t)/S^1(t)$ with a diffusion part $\sigma^{Z(t)}(t, X(t)) X(t)\,dW(t)$. The residual amount, given by

$$U(t) - \left(\sigma^{Z(t)}(t, X(t))/\sigma\right) X(t) = V^{B*Z(t)}(t) + X(t)$$

$$\times \left(1 - \left(\sigma^{Z(t)}(t, X(t))/\sigma\right)\right),$$

is invested in S^0. The cash balance is then also seen to follow the dynamics:

$$dU(t) = rU(t)\,dt + \sigma^{Z(t)}(t, X(t)) X(t)\,dW(t) - d(B+D)(t),$$

$$U(0-) = 0.$$

By Ito's formula, we can calculate the dynamics of the individual surplus as follows:

$$dX(t) = rU(t)\,dt + \sigma^{Z(t)}(t, X(t)) X(t)\,dW(t) - d(B+D)(t) \qquad (6.12)$$

$$- V_t^{B*Z(t)}(t)\,dt - \left(V^{B*Z(t)}(t) - V^{B*Z(t)}(t-)\right)$$

$$- \sum_{k \in \mathcal{J}} \left(V^{B*k}(t) - V^{B*Z(t-)}(t-)\right) dN^k(t).$$

Now we can plug in the dynamics of B, D and V^*. After some rearrangements, one finally arrives at the dynamics given in Equation (6.9), with the following specification of the coefficients of C:

$$c^j(t) = (r - r^*) V^{B*j}(t) + \sum_{k:k \neq j} \left(\mu^{*jk}(t) - \mu^{jk}(t) \right) R^{B*jk}(t) \qquad (6.13)$$

$$- \sum_{k:k \neq j} c^{jk}(t) \mu^{jk}(t),$$

$$c^{jk}(t) = - R^{B*jk}(t),$$

$$\Delta C^j(t) = \begin{cases} -\Delta B^j(t) - V^{B*j}(t), & t = 0, \\ 0, & t > 0. \end{cases} \qquad (6.14)$$

The individual surplus shows an application of a technical basis different from the calculation of first order payments. The fact that we allow, in general, the technical basis in the definition of individual surplus to be different from the first order basis is indeed a generalization in comparison with other introductions of surplus in the literature (see below). Note the consequence that $\Delta C^0(0)$ may be different from zero if the first order basis is not used as the technical basis in the surplus. See Norberg and Steffensen (2005) for a detailed study of the connection between a stochastic differential equation of the type given in Equation (6.12) and its solution.

The individual surplus introduced here relates to the notions of surplus introduced by Ramlau-Hansen (1988, 1991) and later by Norberg (1999, 2001). In general, Ramlau-Hansen (1988, 1991) and Norberg (1999, 2001) work with only one investment opportunity, earning interest at a general rate r, and do not account for the dividends on the cash balance. Furthermore, they work with the first order basis as technical basis so that $\Delta C^0(0) = 0$ by the principle of equivalence. The notions of surplus introduced by Ramlau-Hansen (1988, 1991) and Norberg (1999, 2001) can all be written in the following form:

$$dX(t) = rX(t)\, dt + dC(t),$$

$$X(0) = 0.$$

Particular notions of surplus then correspond to particular specifications of the coefficients of $C(t)$.

The *surplus introduced by Ramlau-Hansen* (1988, 1991) corresponds to the specification in Equation (6.13) where the market basis (r, μ) is deterministic, as in this chapter. The *individual surplus introduced by Norberg* (1999, 2001) also corresponds to the specification in Equation (6.13), but with the market basis being stochastic. The *mean surplus introduced by Norberg* (1999, 2001) is obtained by then averaging away insurance risk. The dynamics of the mean surplus is given by the following specification of the coefficients of C:

$$c^j(t) = \sum_j p_{0j}(0,t) \left((r-r^*) V^{B*j}(t) + \sum_{k:k\neq j} \left(\mu^{*jk}(t) - \mu^{jk}(t) \right) R^{B*jk}(t) \right),$$

$$c^{jk}(t) = 0,$$

where we note that $c^j(t)$ does not actually depend on j.

Here we introduce what we call the *systematic surplus*. This is obtained by starting out with the individual surplus and then disregarding the martingale part of C. The systematic surplus then follows the dynamics in Equation (6.9), with coefficients of C given by

$$c^j(t) = (r-r^*) V^{B*j}(t) + \sum_{k:k\neq j} \left(\mu^{*jk}(t) - \mu^{jk}(t) \right) R^{B*jk}(t),$$

$$c^{jk}(t) = 0,$$

$$\Delta C^j(t) = \begin{cases} -\Delta B^j(t) - V^{B*j}(t), & t=0, \\ 0, & t>0. \end{cases}$$

It is important to note that unsystematic financial risk is fully present in the systematic surplus as it was in the individual surplus. Thus, the term "systematic" only applies to the insurance risk, so to speak. It is also important to understand the difference between our systematic surplus and the mean surplus introduced by Norberg (1999, 2001). Indeed, by averaging away insurance risk in the individual surplus, the martingale part vanishes. In addition, however, the insurance risk in the systematic part of the individual surplus is averaged away. The systematic surplus introduced here, where the martingale part of C is disregarded while the systematic part of C is fully present, seems to be the most important concept in practice.

Norberg (1999, 2001) introduces a dividend reserve that only accounts for the systematic part of the individual surplus, but which accounts for the dividends. The dividend reserve based on the individual surplus contributions differs from our systematic surplus only by the economic/financial–demographic model.

We remind the reader that in the rest of the chapter we simply work with the general form, Equation (6.9). The reader can then pick their favorite notion of surplus and plug in the coefficients of the contribution process for further specialization.

Remark 6.2 *Consider again the endowment insurance from Remark 6.1. Assume first that the only investment possibility available is at the constant interest rate r. Assume that dividends are paid out at rate δ. Then the dynamics of the mean surplus for this contract are given by, skipping the superfluous state specification of the surplus contribution,*

$$dX(t) = rX(t)\,dt + p_{00}(0,t)(c(t) - \delta(t))\,dt$$

$$= rX(t)\,dt + e^{-\int_0^t \mu}(c(t) - \delta(t))\,dt,$$

$$X(0) = 0,$$

$$c(t) = (r - r^*)V^{B*}(t) + (\mu^*(t) - \mu(t))R^{B*}(t).$$

This should be compared with the undistributed reserve introduced in Equation (2.15) with the following dynamics:

$$dX^{(2.15)}(t) = (r + \mu(t))X^{(2.15)}(t)\,dt + (c(t) - \delta(t))\,dt,$$

$$X^{(2.15)}(0) = 0.$$

There are two differences which need special attention. Since in this chapter we have not yet introduced the payment of additional benefits for the dividends, the contribution rate c is generated from the reserve $V^{B*}(t)$ and the sum at risk $R^{B*}(t)$ that connects exclusively to the payments guaranteed at time 0. The reserve and the sum at risk appearing in Equation (2.16) are different since they concern all payments guaranteed in the past, not only at time 0. In the context of this chapter, we introduce additional benefits in Sections 6.6–6.8, and the precise connection between surplus here and the undistributed reserve in Section 2.2.3 turns up in Remark 6.6. Furthermore, the mortality intensity comes into play differently. The connection is that the undistributed reserve introduced in Equation (2.15) is actually defined as the mean surplus per expected survivor, i.e.

$$X^{(2.15)}(t) = \frac{X(t)}{E[I(t)]} = X(t)\,e^{\int_0^t \mu},$$

where $I(t) = 1[Z(t) = 0]$ indicates survival until time t. This relation is easily established by differentiation:

$$dX^{(2.15)}(t) = e^{\int_0^t \mu}\,dX(t) + X(t)\,de^{\int_0^t \mu}$$

$$= (r + \mu(t))X^{(2.15)}(t)\,dt + (c(t) - \delta(t))\,dt.$$

6.4 Surplus-linked dividends

In this section we study a particular dividend process, namely a dividend process where the dividend payments are linked to the surplus defined in Section 6.3. We formalize this by defining the processes $\delta^j(t)$, $\delta^{jk}(t)$ and $\Delta D^j(t)$ as functions of $X(t)$:

$$\delta^j(t) = \delta^j(t, X(t)),$$
$$\delta^{jk}(t) = \delta^{jk}(t, X(t)), \tag{6.15}$$
$$\Delta D^j(t) = \Delta D^j(t, X(t)),$$

where we, by abuse of notation, use the same letters for the processes and the functions.

The purpose of this study is two-fold. Firstly, we suggest Equation (6.15) for valuation, management and supervision in participating life insurance and pension funding. In both participating life insurance and pension funding, competition and supervision sees to it that a (positive) surplus generated by policy holders is redistributed in terms of dividends. Traditionally, the legislative formulation of this redistribution leaves degrees of freedom to the insurance company. However, recently insurance companies and supervisory authorities have focused more on measuring redistribution fairness for valuation and management. For this purpose, a formalization of practice is needed which balances practical complexity against mathematical tractability. In Equation (6.15), we suggest such a formalization.

Secondly, we suggest the formalization in Equation (6.15) for general product design in life and pension insurance. Traditional participating life insurance has been criticized for lacking transparency. One could meet this criticism by replacing a (vague) formulation of surplus participation constraints in the legislative environment by a (non-vague) formulation in the contracts. Then Equation (6.15) makes up such a non-ambiguous formulation which captures the main characteristics of present practice. In fact, a major Danish life insurance company has recently introduced a life insurance product where dividends are specified as linear functions of the surplus. Such a construction of dividends is studied in detail in Section 6.5.

We refer to Steffensen (2000, 2001) for the deterministic differential equation that characterizes the reserve V under the specification in Equation (6.15). In Steffensen (2000, 2001) the state process on which all payments depend is required to be Markovian. Here the state process on which all payments depend is $(Z(t), X(t))$. Informally, $(Z(t), X(t))$ is seen to be Markovian since Z is Markovian and since all coefficients of the stochastic differential equation for X depend on $(Z(t), X(t))$ only; see Equations (6.9), (6.10), (6.5) and (6.15). From Steffensen (2000, 2001), we see that the deterministic function given by

$$V^j(t, x) = E\left[\int_t^n e^{-\int_t^s r} d(B+D)(s)\middle| Z(t) = j, X(t) = x\right]$$

is fully characterized by the following differential equation:

$$V_t^j(t, x) = rV^j(t, x) - b^j(t) - \delta^j(t, x) - \sum_{k:k\neq j} R^{jk}(t, x)\mu^{jk}(t)$$

$$- V_x^j(t, x)\left(rx + c^j(t) - \delta^j(t, x)\right)$$

$$- \frac{1}{2}\sigma^j(t, x)^2 x^2 V_{xx}^j(t, x), t \in [0, n]\setminus\mathcal{D}, \qquad (6.16a)$$

$$V^j(t-, x) = \Delta B^j(t) + \Delta D^j(t, x) + V^j(t, x^j), t \in \mathcal{D}, \qquad (6.16b)$$

$$R^{jk}(t, x) = b^{jk}(t) + \delta^{jk}(t, x) + V^k(t, x^{jk}) - V^j(t, x), \qquad (6.16c)$$

$$x^{jk} = x + c^{jk}(t) - \delta^{jk}(t, x),$$

$$x^j = x + \Delta C^j(t) - \Delta D^j(t, x).$$

The differential equations given in Equations (6.16a–c) are similar to Equation (6.2). In Equation (6.16a) we have the partial differential equation valid for $V^j(t, x)$ at all times that are outside $\mathcal{D}$. Differentiability follows from sufficient regularity of the coefficients of Equation (6.16a). This differential equation involves the sum at risk $R^{jk}(t, x)$ given in Equation (6.16c). At the time points of discontinuity, i.e. inside $\mathcal{D}$, the pasting condition in Equation (6.16b) holds.

The differential equation can be used to calculate a set of fair functions, Equations (6.15), leading to equivalence in the sense of

$$V^0(0-, 0) = 0.$$

This corresponds to the equivalence relation, Equation (6.8). In general, the differential equation (6.16a) must be approached by numerical methods. In special cases we can, however, reduce the partial differential equation to a set of ordinary differential equations. Such a special case is studied in Section 6.5.

Remark 6.3 *Assume that we have a purely financial contract such that the process Z is not needed. Then we can also disregard the state specification of all quantities and the risk premia in Equation (6.16a) vanish. Assume that there are no lump sum payments at deterministic points in time except for at termination, i.e.* $\mathcal{D} = \{n\}$*, that the terminal benefit is given by* $b(0)$ *and that the continuous payment is a constant premium rate* π*, i.e.* $b(t) = -\pi$*. Noting the general terminal condition* $V(n, x) = 0$*, Equations (6.16) reduce to the following:*

$$V_t(t, x) = rV(t, x) + \pi - \delta(t, x)$$
$$- V_x(t, x)(rx + c(t) - \delta(t, x))$$
$$- \frac{1}{2}\sigma(t, x)^2 x^2 V_{xx}(t, x),$$

$$V(n-, x) = b(0) + \Delta D(n, x).$$

This partial differential equation can now be compared with the partial differential equations from Sections 4.5.1 and 4.5.2. If no dividends are paid out before termination of the contract, i.e. $\delta(t, x) = 0$*, we recognize Equation (4.44) where the proportion of X invested in* S^1 *(here described by* $\sigma(t, x)/\sigma$*) is denoted by* $\Theta(t, x)$ *and where* $\Delta D(n, x) = \Phi(x)$*. If instead dividends are paid out continuously during the term of the contract, we recognize Equation (4.45) where* $\delta(t, x) = \Phi(t, x)$*.*

6.5 Dividends linear in surplus

In this section we specify further the dividend formalization suggested in Equations (6.15). We derive a semi-explicit solution to Equations (6.16a–c) in the case where the dividend payments are linear functions of the surplus, i.e.

$$\delta^j(t) = q^j(t) X(t),$$
$$\delta^{jk}(t) = q^{jk}(t) X(t), \tag{6.17}$$
$$\Delta D^j(t) = \Delta Q^j(t) X(t),$$

where $q^j(t)$, $q^{jk}(t)$ and $\Delta Q^j(t)$ are deterministic and sufficiently regular functions.

Dividends linear in the surplus are classical in pension funding. In aggregated portfolio models, such dividends were for a long time known to be optimal, adopting a quadratic optimization criteria that punishes deviations from targets of both payments and surplus. See Cairns (2000) for a state of the art exposition of results in this respect. Furthermore, Steffensen (2006a) shows that linear dividends minimize deviations on any sub-portfolio level, and hence even on an individual basis. In addition, Steffensen (2004) shows that in the case of participating life insurance, where dividends are constrained to be positive, linear dividends are optimal, adopting a power utility optimization criterion. This holds at least if $dC(t) = 0$, $t > 0$, which is the case if we work with the systematic surplus and take the technical basis to be equal to the market basis. Thus, there are several motivations for a special study of linear dividends. See also Nielsen (2005, 2006) for further results on utility optimal dividends in life insurance.

With dividends given in the form of Equation (6.17), Equations (6.16a–c) turn into the following:

$$V_t^j(t, x) = rV^j(t, x) - b^j(t) - q^j(t)x - \sum_{k:k\neq j} R^{jk}(t, x)\mu^{jk}(t)$$

$$- V_x^j(t, x)\left(rx + c^j(t) - q^j(t)x\right)$$

$$- \frac{1}{2}\sigma^j(t, x)^2 x^2 V_{xx}^j(t, x), t \in [0, n] \setminus \mathcal{D}, \quad (6.18a)$$

$$V^j(t-, x) = \Delta B^j(t) + \Delta Q^j(t)x + V^j\left(t, x^j\right), t \in \mathcal{D}, \quad (6.18b)$$

$$R^{jk}(t, x) = b^{jk}(t) + q^{jk}(t)x + V^k\left(t, x^{jk}\right) - V^j(t, x), \quad (6.18c)$$

$$x^{jk} = x + c^{jk}(t) - q^{jk}(t)x,$$

$$x^j = x + \Delta C^j(t) - \Delta Q^j(t)x.$$

We now guess that the solution to this differential equation can be written in the following form:

$$V^j(t, x) = f^j(t) + g^j(t)x. \quad (6.19)$$

We can verify this solution and derive ordinary differential equations for f and g by plugging the solution, Equation (6.19), into Equations (6.18a–c). By collecting terms with and without x and dividing the terms including x by x, we arrive at two differential equations characterizing f and g, respectively.
    Introducing

$$\phi^j(t) = g^j(t)c^j(t),$$

$$\phi^{jk}(t) = g^k(t)c^{jk}(t),$$

$$\Delta F^j(t) = g^j(t)\Delta C^j(t),$$

the differential equation for f is as follows:

$$f_t^j(t) = rf^j(t) - b^j(t) - \phi^j(t) - \sum_{k:k \neq j} R^{Fjk}(t) \mu^{jk}(t), t \in [0, n] \setminus \mathcal{D},$$

(6.20)

$$f^j(t-) = \Delta B^j(t) + \Delta F^j(t) + f^j(t), t \in \mathcal{D},$$

$$R^{Fjk}(t) = b^{jk}(t) + \phi^{jk}(t) + f^k(t) - f^j(t).$$

For a given function g, the structure of this differential equation is similar to the structure of Equation (6.2). We can then conclude that f has the following representation:

$$f^j(t) = E_{t,j} \left[\int_t^n e^{-\int_t^s r} d(B+F)(s) \right],$$

(6.21)

$$dF(t) = dF^{Z(t)}(t) + \sum_{k \in \mathcal{J}} \phi^{Z(t-)k} dN^k(t),$$

$$dF^j(t) = \phi^j(t) dt + \Delta F^j(t), j \in \mathcal{J}.$$

The function $f^j(t)$ represented by Equation (6.21) contains two parts. The first part is simply $V^{Bj}(t)$, the market value of first order payments. The second part,

$$E_{t,j} \left[\int_t^n e^{-\int_t^s r} dF(s) \right],$$

represents the part of future contributions to the surplus that are expected to be redistributed. This corresponds to the value of the payment process C, where, however, the coefficients are weighted with the factor g and then lead to coefficients of the artificial payment process F. If, in particular, we work with the systematic surplus and the market basis is used as the technical basis, there are no future contributions and we have the following:

$$V^j(t, x) = V^{Bj}(t) + g^j(t) x.$$

Introducing

$$r^{Gj}(t) = q^j(t) + \sum_{k:k \neq j} q^{jk}(t) \mu^{jk}(t),$$

the differential equation for g is as follows:

$$g_t^j(t) = g^j(t) r^{Gj}(t) - q^j(t)$$

$$- \sum_{k:k \neq j} R^{Gjk}(t) \left(1 - q^{jk}(t)\right) \mu^{jk}(t), t \in [0,n] \setminus \mathcal{D}, \qquad (6.22)$$

$$g^j(t-) = \left(1 - g^j(t)\right) \Delta Q^j(t) + g^j(t), t \in \mathcal{D},$$

$$R^{Gjk}(t) = q^{jk}(t) / \left(1 - q^{jk}(t)\right) + g^k(t) - g^j(t).$$

The structure of this differential equation is also similar to the structure in Equation (6.2). However, we need to deal with two special circumstances when writing down a conditional expected value representation of the solution. Firstly, the intensity appears in Equation (6.22) with the factor $1 - q^{jk}(t)$. This is, however, just a matter of taking the expectation under an appropriately chosen measure. Secondly, the pasting condition specifies the lump sum payment $\left(1 - g^j(t)\right) \Delta Q^j(t)$. Thus, the function g itself appears in the lump sum payment at deterministic points in time. We now conclude that g has the following representation:

$$g^j(t) = E_{t,j}^q \left[\int_t^n e^{-\int_t^s r^g} dG(s) \right], \qquad (6.23)$$

$$dG(t) = dG^{Z(t)}(t) + q^{Z(t-)k}(t) / \left(1 - q^{Z(t-)k}(t)\right) dN^k(t),$$

$$dG^j(t) = q^j(t) dt + \Delta G^j(t),$$

$$\Delta G^j(t) = \left(1 - g^j(t)\right) \Delta Q^j(t),$$

where E^q denotes the expectation with respect to a measure under which N^k admits the intensity process $\left(1 - q^{Z(t)k}(t)\right) \mu^{Z(t)k}(t)$.

Example 6.4 *We consider the survival model with two states corresponding to the policy holder being alive or dead. For simplicity, we restrict ourselves to lump sum payments at deterministic time points at time n only, i.e. $\mathcal{D} = \{n\}$. Furthermore, we think of the realistic situation where no payments fall due after occurrence of death. In this case, it is possible to work with an extensive simplification of notation: $N = N^1$, $\mu = \mu^{01}$ and, for all other quantities and functions, the specification of state 0 is skipped, i.e. $b = b^0$, $b^1 = b^{01}$, $\Delta B = \Delta B^0$, $f = f^0$, $g = g^0$, etc. We assume that all dividends are paid out*

only at the rate $\delta(t) = q(t) X(t)$, *i.e.* $\delta^1(t) = \Delta D(t) = 0$. *Then functions* f
and g *become*

$$f(t) = V^B(t) + \int_t^n e^{-\int_t^s r + \mu} g(s) c(s) \, ds,$$

$$g(t) = \int_t^n e^{-\int_t^s q + \mu} q(s) \, ds.$$

*If, in particular, we work with the systematic surplus and the market basis
and the technical basis coincide, we obtain*

$$f(t) = V^B(t),$$

$$g(t) = \int_t^n e^{-\int_t^s q + \mu} q(s) \, ds.$$

Remark 6.5 *Continuing Remark 6.3, we consider the special case where*
$\delta(t, x) = q(t) x$ *and* $\Delta D(n, x) = \Delta Q(n) x$. *Then the differential equations (6.20) and (6.22) reduce to*

$$f_t(t) = rf(t) + \pi - g(t) c(t),$$

$$f(n-) = b(0),$$

$$g_t(t) = g(t) q(t) - q(t),$$

$$g(n-) = \Delta Q(n).$$

*These differential equations can be recognized from Sections 4.5.1 and 4.5.2.
In those sections these differential equations are given as special cases where
the investment is sufficiently prudent to secure that $X(t) \geq 0$. The reason for
this was that the dividends were considered as something beneficial to the
policy holder. In the present chapter, we have made no such requirements.
The quantities called β in Sections 4.5.1 and 4.5.2 are put to zero since,
in the present chapter, we have chosen to present just linear and not affine
dividends.*

*The differential equations for f and g are presented in Section 4.5.1 for
terminal dividends under "prudent investment" with $q = 0$ and $\Delta Q(n) = \alpha$.
The explicit solution is also presented there. The differential equations f and
g are presented in Section 4.5.2 for continuous dividends under "prudent
investment" with $q(t) = \alpha(t)$ and $\Delta Q(n) = 0$. The explicit solution is also
presented there.*

6.6 Bonus

In this section we consider the situation where dividends are not paid out to the policy holder in cash but are converted into an additional stream of bonus payments. One would typically constrain this conversion to happen on a market basis, i.e. such that the additional insurance added and paid for by the dividend payment is fair in itself. Then, in principle, there is no need to pay special attention to the conversion. Nevertheless, we here present a mathematical framework for handling bonus payments. In the following the additional bonus payments are spoken of as additional first order payments, although they may in practice not necessarily have the same status as the first order payments initiated at time 0.

We now have first order payments and dividends from each insurance contract which has been added in the past. We augment the functions by an additional time argument which specifies the time of initiation. Thus, $B(s, t)$ and $D(s, t)$ are the accumulated first order payments and dividend payments, respectively, at time t stemming from contracts initiated during $[0, s]$. We need to work with the dynamics of $B(s, t)$ in both time dimensions. We use the notation $dB(s, t)$ for the dynamics of $B(s, t)$ in the *time of payment* dimension, i.e.

$$dB(s, t) = B(s, t) - B(s, t-) + b^t(s, t) \, dt,$$

such that $B_t(s, t) = b^t(s, t)$ wherever it exists, and we use the notation $B(ds, t)$ for the dynamics of $B(s, t)$ in the *time of initiation* dimension, i.e.

$$B(ds, t) = B(s, t) - B(s-, t) + b^s(s, t) \, ds,$$

such that $B_s(s, t) = b^s(s, t)$ wherever it exists. Thus, the differential $dB(s, t)$ denotes, conforming with previous sections, the change in accumulated payments over $(t - dt, t]$ for a given fixed time of initiation s. The differential $B(ds, t)$ denotes the change in accumulated payments at time t stemming from initiation of payments over $(s - ds, s]$. The relations in this paragraph indicate that the results in this section are derived for payment processes with the same structure as the payment processes in the preceding sections.

We now denote by $B(t)$ and $D(t)$ the total accumulated first order payments and dividend payments, respectively, at time t, stemming from all insurance contracts initiated in the past. We can then write the following:

$$B(t) = B(0-,t) + \int_{0-}^{t} B(\mathrm{d}s,t),$$

$$D(t) = D(0-,t) + \int_{0-}^{t} D(\mathrm{d}s,t).$$

Here $B(0-,\cdot)$ and $D(0-,\cdot)$ are the payment processes stemming from the original contract, corresponding to the payment processes B and D in the previous sections.

The circumstance that the total dividend payment paid at time t is used as a single premium of an insurance contract initiated at time t can be written as follows:

$$\mathrm{d}D(t) = -B(\mathrm{d}t,t), \tag{6.24}$$

from which we derive the dynamics of the total accumulated payments $B+D$:

$$\mathrm{d}B(t) + \mathrm{d}D(t) = \mathrm{d}B(0-,t) + \mathrm{d}\int_{0-}^{t} B(\mathrm{d}s,t) + \mathrm{d}D(t)$$

$$= \mathrm{d}B(0-,t) + B(\mathrm{d}t,t) + \int_{0}^{t-} \mathrm{d}B(\mathrm{d}s,t) + \mathrm{d}D(t)$$

$$= \mathrm{d}B(0-,t) + \int_{0-}^{t-} \mathrm{d}B(\mathrm{d}s,t). \tag{6.25}$$

This simply shows that the total payments that the policy holder pays and receives are equal to the sum over all first order payments bought until and excluding time t. This is how far we get without specifying further the additional bonus payment. However, we have put some structure on the bonus payment process which allows for substantial mathematical progress.

We now restrict ourselves to the situation where, at any point in time t, the dividends are used to buy a fraction of the part of a given payment process A due over $(t,n]$. The structure of the payment process A is assumed to coincide with the structure of the original first order payment process $B(0-,\cdot)$. Actually, A could be equal to $B(0-,\cdot)$. It could also consist of premiums or benefits of $B(0-,\cdot)$ exclusively. In Steffensen (2001), some calculations are made for $A = B(0-,\cdot)$. In Ramlau-Hansen (1991) and Norberg (1999), some calculations are made for $A = B^{+}(0-,\cdot)$, where the superscript $+$ specifies that only benefits are taken into account. The different possibilities of A are related to the notions of *defined contributions* and *defined benefits* in the sense that A could be the part of B which is not *defined* but is instead adapted to the development of the contract. We introduce $C^B(t)$ and $C^A(t)$ to denote the accumulated surplus contributions based on the payment process A and $B(0-, \cdot)$, respectively.

Denoting by $dY(s)$ the fraction of the payment process A bought at time s, we can formalize the idea explained in the previous paragraph, for $0 < s < t$, as follows:

$$B(ds, t) = B(ds, s) + dY(s)(A(t) - A(s)),$$

or, in differential form,

$$dB(ds, t) = dY(s) \, dA(t). \tag{6.26}$$

By the convention $Y(0-) = 0$, the process Y represents the total proportion of A bought until time t, and using Equation (6.26) we can then continue the calculation in Equation (6.25) as follows:

$$dB(t) + dD(t) = dB(0-, t) + \int_{0-}^{t-} dY(s) \, dA(t)$$

$$= dB(0-, t) + Y(t-) \, dA(t).$$

We also need an extension of notation for the reserves. We let $V^{B*Z(t)}(s, t)$ and $C(s, t)$ denote the technical reserve and the accumulated contributions to the surplus, respectively, at time t for contracts initiated until time s. By application of Equation (6.26), one can now verify the following relations:

$$V^{B*Z(t)}(ds, t) \equiv E\left[\int_t^n e^{-\int_t^s r} dB(ds, t) \middle| \mathcal{F}(t) \right] \tag{6.27}$$

$$= dY(s) V^{A*Z(t)}(t),$$

$$dC(ds, t) = dY(s) \, dC^A(t).$$

Conforming with the notation A and B, we let C denote the total contributions stemming from all contracts initiated in the past. These contributions are as follows:

$$C(t) = C(0-, t) + \int_{0-}^t C(ds, t),$$

$$dC(t) = dC(0-, t) + d\int_{0-}^t C(ds, t)$$

$$= dC^B(t) + C(dt, t) + \int_{0-}^{t-} dC(ds, t)$$

$$= dC^B(t) + C(dt, t) + Y(t-) \, dC^A(t).$$

We now assume that the first order basis on which additional first order payment processes are determined is used as the technical basis in the surplus. Then we have the following two relations from the equivalence principle and Equation (6.14), respectively:

$$V^{B*Z(t)}\left(\mathrm{d}t,t\right) = -B\left(\mathrm{d}t,t\right),\tag{6.28}$$

$$C\left(\mathrm{d}t,t\right) = 0.\tag{6.29}$$

We can now, using Equation (6.27) with $s = t$, Equation (6.28) and Equation (6.24), relate the dynamics of Y and the dynamics of D as follows:

$$\mathrm{d}Y\left(t\right) = \frac{V^{B*Z(t)}\left(\mathrm{d}t,t\right)}{V^{A*Z(t)}\left(t\right)} = -\frac{B\left(\mathrm{d}t,t\right)}{V^{A*Z(t)}\left(t\right)} = \frac{\mathrm{d}D\left(t\right)}{V^{A*Z(t)}\left(t\right)}.\tag{6.30}$$

A particular dividend plan relating to the so-called contribution plan (see Norberg (1999)), specifies that $D = C$. Plugging this plan into Equation (6.30) leads to the following stochastic differential equation for Y:

$$\begin{aligned}\mathrm{d}Y\left(t\right) &= \frac{\mathrm{d}C\left(t\right)}{V^{A*Z(t)}\left(t\right)}\\ &= \frac{\mathrm{d}C^{B}\left(t\right) + Y\left(t-\right)\mathrm{d}C^{A}\left(t\right)}{V^{A*Z(t)}\left(t\right)},\end{aligned}$$

which is a generalized version of corresponding differential equations in Norberg (1999) and Ramlau-Hansen (1991).

Instead, we study in Section 6.7 dividends partly similar to those in Equations (6.15). For this, we need the dynamics of the total surplus, still given by

$$\mathrm{d}X\left(t\right) = rX\left(t\right)\mathrm{d}t + \sigma^{Z(t)}\left(t,X\left(t\right),Y\left(t\right)\right)X\left(t\right)\mathrm{d}W\left(t\right) + \mathrm{d}\left(C - D\right)\left(t\right).$$

Here $\sigma^{Z(t)}\left(t,X\left(t\right),Y\left(t\right)\right)$ is the proportion of X invested in S^{1}, now allowed to depend also on Y. We take $\sigma^{j}\left(t,x,y\right)$ to be a deterministic and sufficiently regular function.

Remark 6.6 *The arrangement of payments presented in this section is a generalization of the arrangement that was presented in Chapter 2. Consider again the endowment insurance from Remarks 6.1 and 6.2. Let the payment process A be given by a pure endowment, i.e.* $\mathrm{d}A(t) = \mathrm{d}A^{Z(t)}(t)$ *and* $\mathrm{d}A^0(t) = \mathrm{d}\epsilon_n(t)$, $\mathrm{d}A^1(t) = 0$. *Then the differential equation for the total technical reserve corresponding to the alive state is, skipping the superfluous state specification, given by*

$$\frac{\mathrm{d}}{\mathrm{d}t} V^{B*}(t) = \frac{\mathrm{d}}{\mathrm{d}t} \left(V^{B*}(0,t) + Y(t) V^{A*}(t) \right)$$

$$\frac{\mathrm{d}}{\mathrm{d}t} V^{B*}(0,t) + \frac{\mathrm{d}}{\mathrm{d}t} Y(t) V^{A*}(t) + Y(t) \frac{\mathrm{d}}{\mathrm{d}t} V^{A*}(t)$$

$$= r^* V^{B*}(0,t) + \pi - \mu^*(t) \left(b^{\mathrm{ad}} - V^{B*}(0,t) \right)$$

$$+ \delta(t) + Y(t) \left(r^* V^{A*}(t) - \mu^*(t) \left(-V^{B*}(0,t) \right) \right)$$

$$= r^* V^{B*}(t) + \pi - \mu^*(t) \left(b^{\mathrm{ad}} - V^{B*}(t) \right) + \delta(t).$$

Due to the equivalence principle, Equation (6.4), and $Y(0) = 0$, $V^{B*}(t)$ *fulfils the initial condition* $V^{B*}(0) = 0$. *Hereafter, the differential equation for* $V^{B*}(t)$ *is recognized as the differential equation for the technical reserve presented in Section 2.2.*

The statewise surplus contribution rate is given by

$$c(t) = c^B(t) + Y(t) c^A(t)$$

$$= (r - r^*) V^*(0,t) + (\mu^*(t) - \mu(t)) \left(b^{\mathrm{ad}} - V^{B*}(0,t) \right)$$

$$+ Y(t) \left((r - r^*) V^{A*}(t) + (\mu^*(t) - \mu(t)) \left(-V^{A*}(t) \right) \right)$$

$$= (r - r^*) V^{B*}(t) + (\mu^*(t) - \mu(t)) \left(b^{\mathrm{ad}} - V^{B*}(t) \right),$$

which is exactly the contribution rate presented in Equation (2.16). The link to the undistributed reserve presented in Section 2.2.3 now boils down to noting that the undistributed reserve is defined as the mean portfolio surplus per expected, as explained in Remark 6.2.

6.7 Surplus- and bonus-linked dividends

In this section we study, within the framework presented in Section 6.6, a particular dividend process, namely a dividend process where the dividend payments are linked to the surplus X and to the process Y defined in Section 6.6.

We formalize this by defining the processes $\delta^j(t)$, $\Delta D^j(t)$ and $\delta^{jk}(t)$ as functions of $(X(t), Y(t))$:

$$\delta^j(t) = \delta^j(t, X(t), Y(t)),$$

$$\delta^{jk}(t) = \delta^{jk}(t, X(t), Y(t)), \tag{6.31}$$

$$\Delta D^j(t) = \Delta D^j(t, X(t), Y(t)),$$

where we, by abuse of notation, use the same letters for the processes and the functions.

The motivation for this study is the same as in Section 6.4. Firstly, we suggest the formalization for valuation, management and supervision in participating life insurance and pension funding. Secondly, we suggest it for product design in life and pension insurance. However, the fact that we allow dividends to depend also on Y requires comment.

The idea is to obtain a stabilizing effect, for example by letting the dividends payments be relatively large when Y is relatively small, all other things being equal. This idea has recently been practised by a major Danish life insurance company in the following extreme sense. Dividends are set in relation to the surplus X, and even negative dividends are allowed to be paid out. However, one is not allowed to violate the first order payments determined at time $0-$, and for this reason one is only allowed to collect negative dividends as long as Y is positive. A formalization of this practice could, for example, be $\delta^j(t) = q^j(t) X(t) I(Y(t) \geq 0)$. The allowance for collecting negative dividends and hereby lowering first order payments can be spoken of as "conditional bonus."

We refer again to Steffensen (2000, 2001) for the deterministic differential equation that characterizes the reserve V under Equations (6.31). The state process on which all payments depend is, in this section, $(Z(t), X(t), Y(t))$. In Section 6.4, we argued that $(Z(t), X(t))$ is Markovian. Informally, $(Z(t), X(t), Y(t))$ is then seen to be Markovian since all coefficients of the stochastic differential equation for Y depend on $(Z(t), X(t), Y(t))$ only; see Equations (6.30), (6.5) and (6.31). From Steffensen (2000, 2001), we see that the deterministic function

$$V^j(t, x) = E\left[\int_t^n e^{-\int_t^s r} dB(s) \,\Big|\, Z(t) = j, X(t) = x, Y(t) = y\right]$$

is fully characterized by the following differential equation:

$$V_t^j(t,x,y) = rV^j(t,x,y) - b^j(t) - ya^j(t) - \sum_{k:k\neq j} R^{jk}(t,x,y)\mu^{jk}(t)$$

$$- V_x^j(t,x,y)\left(rx + c^{Bj}(t) + yc^{Aj}(t) - \delta^j(t,x,y)\right)$$

$$- V_y^j(t,x,y)\left(\frac{\delta^j(t,x,y)}{V^{A*j}(t)}\right)$$

$$- \frac{1}{2}\sigma^j(t,x,y)^2 x^2 V_{xx}^j(t,x,y), t\in[0,n]\setminus\mathcal{D}, \qquad (6.32)$$

$$V^j(t-,x,y) = \Delta B^j(t) + y\Delta A^j(t) + V^j\left(t,x^j,y^j\right), t\in\mathcal{D},$$

$$R^{jk}(t,x,y) = b^{jk}(t) + ya^{jk}(t) + V^k\left(t,x^{jk},y^{jk}\right) - V^j(t,x,y),$$

$$x^{jk} = x + c^{Bjk}(t) + yc^{Ajk}(t) - \delta^{jk}(t,x,y),$$

$$y^{jk} = y + \frac{\delta^{jk}(t,x,y)}{V^{A*k}(t)},$$

$$x^j = x + \Delta C^{Bj}(t) + y\Delta C^{Aj}(t) - \Delta D^j(t,x,y),$$

$$y^j = y + \frac{\Delta D^j(t,x,y)}{V^{A*j}(t)}.$$

The differential equation (6.32) can be used to calculate a set of fair functions, Equations, (6.15) leading to equivalence in the sense of

$$V^0(0-,0,0) = 0.$$

This corresponds to the equivalence relation in Equation (6.8). In general, the differential equation (6.32) must be solved by numerical methods. In special cases we can, however, reduce the partial differential equation to a set of ordinary differential equations. Such a special case is studied in Section 6.8.

Remark 6.7 *Consider again the financial contract studied in Remarks 6.3 and 6.5. We now let dividends be used to buy additional elementary endowment payments. Then Equation (6.32) reduces to*

$$V_t(t,x,y) = rV(t,x,y) + \pi \qquad (6.33)$$

$$- V_x(t,x,y)\left(rx + c^B(t) + yc^A(t) - \delta(t,x,y)\right)$$

$$- V_y(t,x,y)\left(\frac{\delta(t,x,y)}{V^{A*}(t)}\right) - \frac{1}{2}\sigma(t,x,y)^2 x^2 V_{xx}(t,x,y),$$

$$V(n-,x,y) = b(0) + y.$$

We now translate this into a differential equation for another function $\widetilde{V}$, where the reserve is formalized as a function of time, surplus and the total technical reserve. Thus, we put $V(t, X(t), Y(t)) = \widetilde{V}(t, X(t), V^{B*}(t))$. We note first that

$$c^B(t) + yc^A(t) = (r - r^*)V^{B*}(0, t) + (r - r^*)yV^{A*}(t)$$
$$= (r - r^*)\widehat{V}^{B*}(t, y),$$

where

$$\widehat{V}^{B*}(t, y) = V^{B*}(0, t) + yV^{A*}(t),$$

i.e. $V^{B*}(t) = \widehat{V}^{B*}(t, y(t))$. Furthermore, using the following:

$$\widehat{V}_t^{B*}(t, y) = V_t^{B*}(0, t) + yV_t^{A*}(t)$$
$$= r^*V^{B*}(0, t) + \pi + yr^*V^{A*}(t)$$
$$= r^*\widehat{V}^{B*}(t, y) + \pi,$$

we obtain the translation of relevant partial derivatives:

$$V_y = \widetilde{V}_v\widehat{V}_y^{B*}(t, y) = \widetilde{V}_v V^{A*}(t),$$
$$V_t = \widetilde{V}_t + \widetilde{V}_v\widehat{V}_t^{B*}(t, y) = \widetilde{V}_t + \widetilde{V}_v\left(r^*\widehat{V}^{B*}(t, y) + \pi\right).$$

Plugging these relations into Equation (6.33), replacing $\widehat{V}^{B*}(t, y)$ by v and rearranging slightly, we arrive at

$$\widetilde{V}_t(t, x, v) = r\widetilde{V}(t, x, v) + \pi - \widetilde{V}_x(t, x, v)(rx + (r - r^*)v - \delta(t, x, y))$$

$$- \widetilde{V}_v(r^*v + \pi + \delta(t, x, y)) - \frac{1}{2}\sigma(t, x, y)^2 x^2 \widetilde{V}_{xx}(t, x, v),$$

$$\widetilde{V}(n-, x, y) = b(0) + y.$$

It is obvious that this is the partial differential equation given in Section 4.5.3 for the characterization of the reserve.

6.8 Dividends linear in surplus and bonus

In this section, we specify further the dividend formalization suggested in Equations (6.31). We derive a semi-explicit solution to the differential equation (6.32) in the case where the dividend payments are linear functions of the surplus X and the process Y, i.e.

$$\delta^j(t) = q^j(t) X(t) + \rho^j(t) Y(t),$$

$$\delta^{jk}(t) = q^{jk}(t) X(t) + \rho^{jk}(t) Y(t), \tag{6.34}$$

$$\Delta D^j(t) = \Delta Q^j(t) X(t) + \Delta \varrho^j(t) Y(t),$$

where $q^j(t)$, $q^{jk}(t)$, $\Delta Q^j(t)$, $\rho^j(t)$, $\rho^{jk}(t)$ and $\Delta \varrho^j(t)$ are deterministic and sufficiently regular functions. As in Section 6.5, dividends linear in surplus can be motivated by practice and by certain optimization problems. Linking dividends to the process Y is encouraged in Section 6.7, and below we show that a linear link is one construction which leads to a semi-explicit solution.

With dividends given in the form of Equation (6.34), Equation (6.32) turns into the following differential equation:

$$V_t^j(t, x, y) = r V^j(t, x) - b^j(t) - y a^j(t) - \sum_{k: k \neq j} R^{jk}(t, x, y) \mu^{jk}(t)$$

$$- V_x^j(t, x) \left(rx + c^{Bj}(t) + yc^{Aj}(t) - q^j(t) x - \rho^j(t) y \right)$$

$$- V_y^j(t, x, y) \left(\frac{q^j(t) x + \rho^j(t) y}{V^{A*j}(t)} \right)$$

$$- \frac{1}{2} \sigma^j(t, x, y) x^2 V_{xx}^j(t, x, y), t \in [0, n] \setminus \mathcal{D}, \tag{6.35}$$

$$V^j(t-, x, y) = \Delta B^j(t) + y \Delta A^j(t) + V^j(t, x^j, y^j), t \in \mathcal{D},$$

$$R^{jk}(t, x, y) = b^{jk}(t) + y a^{jk}(t) + V^k(t, x^{jk}, y^{jk}) - V^j(t, x, y),$$

$$x^{jk} = x + c^{Bjk}(t) + yc^{Ajk}(t) - q^{jk}(t) x - \rho^{jk}(t) y,$$

$$y^{jk} = y + \frac{q^{jk}(t) x + \rho^{jk}(t) y}{V^{A*k}(t)},$$

$$x^j = x + \Delta C^{Bj}(t) + y \Delta C^{Aj}(t) - \Delta Q^j(t) x - \Delta \varrho^j(t) y,$$

$$y^j = y + \frac{\Delta Q^j(t) x + \Delta \varrho^j(t) y}{V^{A*j}(t)}.$$

We now guess that the solution to this differential equation can be written in the following form:

$$V^j(t, x, y) = f^j(t) + g^j(t) x + h^j(t) y. \tag{6.36}$$

We can verify this solution and derive ordinary differential equations for f, g and h by plugging Equation (6.36) into the differential equation (6.35). By collecting terms with x, with y and without x and y, and dividing terms including x and y by x and y, respectively, we arrive at three differential equations characterizing f, g and h, respectively.

The differential equation for f coincides with Equation (6.20) with $c^j(t)$ and $c^{jk}(t)$ replaced by $c^{Bj}(t)$ and $c^{Bjk}(t)$. With this replacement, the representation in Equation (6.21) also holds true with F replaced by an appropriately defined artificial payment process F^B. The latter part of this representation again represents the part of future contributions to the surplus which belongs to the policy holder, now after conversion into bonus payments.

The differential equation for g is exactly the same as Equation (6.22) with $q^j(t)$ and $q^{jk}(t)$ in the payment process replaced by the fractions $q^j(t) h^j(t)/V^{A*j}(t)$ and $q^{jk}(t) h^k(t)/V^{A*k}(t)$, respectively. In the artificial interest rate $r^{Gj}(t)$, $q^j(t)$ and $q^{jk}(t)$ should not be replaced. With this replacement the representation in Equation (6.23) also holds true, i.e. for

$$\mathrm{d}G(t) = \mathrm{d}G^{Z(t)}(t) + \frac{q^{Z(t-)k}(t) h^k(t)/V^{A*k}(t)}{1 - q^{Z(t-)k}(t)} \mathrm{d}N^k(t),$$

$$\mathrm{d}G^j(t) = q^j(t) h^j(t)/V^{A*j}(t)\,\mathrm{d}t + \Delta G^j(t),$$

$$\Delta G^j(t) = \left(1 - g^j(t)\right) \Delta Q^j(t).$$

Again, the function g specifies the part of the surplus that belongs to the policy holders. However, now the elements in this function are weighted with the fraction $h^{Z(t)}(t)/V^{A*Z(t)}(t)$.

Introducing the following:

$$\eta^j(t) = \phi^{Aj}(t) - g^j(t) \rho^j(t),$$

$$\eta^{jk}(t) = \phi^{Ajk}(t) - g^k(t) \rho^{jk}(t),$$

$$\Delta H^j(t) = \Delta F^{Aj}(t) - g^j(t) \Delta \varrho^j(t) + h^j(t) \frac{\Delta \varrho^j(t)}{V^{A*j}(t)},$$

$$r^{Hj}(t) = r - \frac{\rho^j(t)}{V^{A*j}(t)} + \sum_{k:k \neq j} \frac{\rho^{jk}(t)}{V^{A*k}(t)} \mu^{jk}(t),$$

the differential equation for h is given by

$$h_t^j(t) = r^{Hj}(t) h^j(t) - a^j(t) - \eta^j(t)$$

$$- \sum_{k:k\neq j} R^{Hjk}(t) \frac{V^{A*k}(t) + \rho^{jk}(t)}{V^{A*k}(t)} \mu^{jk}(t), t \in [0,n] \setminus \mathcal{D}, \qquad (6.37)$$

$$h^j(t-) = \Delta A^j(t) + \Delta H^j(t) + h^j(t), t \in \mathcal{D},$$

$$R^{Hjk}(t) = \left(a^{jk}(t) + \eta^{jk}(t)\right) \frac{V^{A*k}(t)}{V^{A*k}(t) + \rho^{jk}(t)} + h^k(t) - h^j(t).$$

The structure in this differential equation is similar to the structure in Equation (6.22). However, as in Equations (6.22) and (6.23) we need to deal with two special circumstances when writing down a conditional expected value representation of the solution. Firstly, the intensity appears in Equation (6.37) with the factor $\left(V^{A*k}(t) + \rho^{jk}(t)\right) / V^{A*k}(t)$, but this is just a matter of taking the expectation under an appropriately chosen measure. Secondly, the pasting condition specifies a lump sum payment that includes $h^j(t) \Delta \varrho^j(t) / V^{A*j}(t)$. Thus, the function h itself appears in the lump sum payment at deterministic points in time. We now conclude that h has the following representation:

$$h^j(t) = E^\rho \left[\int_t^n e^{-\int_t^s r^H} \, d(A+H)(s) \right],$$

$$dH(t) = dH^{Z(t)}(t) + \eta^{Z(t-)k}(t) \frac{V^{A*k}(t)}{V^{A*k}(t) + \rho^{jk}(t)} \, dN^k(t),$$

$$dH^j(t) = \eta^j(t) \, dt + \Delta H^j(t),$$

where E^ρ denotes the expectation with respect to a measure under which N^k admits the intensity process $\left(V^{A*k}(t) + \rho^{Z(t)k}(t)\right) / V^{A*k}(t) \mu^{Z(t)k}(t)$. The function h specifies the part of Y that belongs to the policy holder according to the dividend and the bonus plans. Note that since g appears in the differential equation for h and vice versa, these functions must be calculated simultaneously.

In the special case where dividends are not linked to the process Y, i.e. $\rho^j = \rho^{jk} = \Delta \varrho^j = 0$, we have that $r^{Hj}(t) = r$ and H is similar to F except that B and C^B are replaced by A and C^A, respectively. We conclude that f and h in this case differ by their underlying payment process only.

Example 6.8 *We consider again the survival model introduced in Example 6.4. We consider the same contract, now specified with bonus payments* *proportional to the payment process A. We assume that $\rho^j = \rho^{jk} = \Delta\varrho^j = 0$, leading to the following specialization of the above results:*

$$f(t) = V^B(t) + \int_t^n e^{-\int_t^s r+\mu} g(s) c^B(s) \, ds,$$

$$g(t) = \int_t^n e^{-\int_t^s q+\mu} \frac{h(s)}{V^{A*}(s)} q(s) \, ds,$$

$$h(t) = V^A(t) + \int_t^n e^{-\int_t^s r+\mu} g(s) c^A(s) \, ds.$$

If, in particular, we work with the systematic surplus, and the market basis and the technical basis coincide, we obtain the following:

$$f(t) = V^B(t),$$

$$g(t) = \int_t^n e^{-\int_t^s q+\mu} \frac{h(s)}{V^{A*}(s)} q(s) \, ds,$$

$$h(t) = V^A(t).$$

Remark 6.9 *Continuing Remark 6.7, we consider the special case where $\delta(t, x, y) = q(t) x$ and $\Delta D(n, x) = 0$. Recall that the continuous payment rate $q(t)$ in the differential equation for g, Equation (6.22), should be replaced by $q(t) h(t) / V^{A*}(t)$. Then we obtain the following differential equations for f, g and h from Equations (6.20), (6.22) and (6.37):*

$$f_t(t) = rf(t) + \pi - g(t) c^B(t),$$

$$f(n-) = b(0),$$

$$g_t(t) = g(t) q(t) - q(t) h(t) / V^{A*}(t),$$

$$g(n-) = 0,$$

$$h_t(t) = rh(t) - g(t) c^A(t),$$

$$h(n-) = 1.$$

We now compare these differential equations with the differential equations for the coefficient functions in Section 4.5.3. For this purpose, we write $\widetilde{V}$ from Remark 6.7 as an affine function of the surplus and the total technical *reserve. Using* $V(t, X(t), Y(t)) = \widetilde{V}(t, X(t), V^{B*}(t))$, *we then obtain the following relation between the coefficient functions in the two expositions:*

$$f(t) + g(t) X(t) + h(t) Y(t) = \widetilde{f}(t) + \widetilde{g}(t) X(t) + \widetilde{h}(t) V^{B*}(t, Y(t))$$

$$= \widetilde{f}(t) + \widetilde{h}(t) V^{B*}(0, t)$$

$$+ \widetilde{g}(t) X(t) + \widetilde{h}(t) V^{A*}(t) Y(t).$$

For $X(t) = x$ *and* $Y(t) = y$, *this yields*

$$f(t) + g(t) x + h(t) y = \widetilde{f}(t) + \widetilde{h}(t) V^{B*}(0, t) + g(t) x + \widetilde{h}(t) V^{A*}(t) y.$$

Realizing that $h(t) = \widetilde{h}(t) V^{A*}(t)$, $g(t) = \widetilde{g}(t)$ *and* $f(t) = \widetilde{f}(t) + \widetilde{h}(t) V^{B*}(0, t)$, *we can now find differential equations characterizing* f, g *and* h. *Firstly, we find the equation for* $\widetilde{h}$:

$$\widetilde{h}_t(t) = \frac{V^{A*}(t) h_t(t) - V_t^{A*}(t) h(t)}{(V^{A*}(t))^2}$$

$$= \frac{rh(t) - g(t) c^A(t) - r^* h(t)}{V^{A*}(t)}$$

$$= (r - r^*) \widetilde{h}(t) - g(t) (r - r^*),$$

$$\widetilde{h}(n-) = 1.$$

Secondly, we find the differential equation for $\widetilde{g}$:

$$\widetilde{g}_t(t) = \widetilde{g}(t) q(t) - q(t) \widetilde{h}(t),$$

$$\widetilde{g}(n-) = 0.$$

Thirdly, we find the differential equation for $\widetilde{f}$:

$$\widetilde{f}_t(t) = f_t(t) - \widetilde{h}_t(t) V^{B*}(0, t) - \widetilde{h}(t) V_t^{B*}(0, t)$$

$$= r\widetilde{f}(t) + \pi - \widetilde{h}(t) \pi,$$

$$\widetilde{f}(n-) = f(n-) - \widetilde{h}(n-) b(0) = 0.$$

These differential equations for $\widetilde{f}$, $\widetilde{g}$ *and* $\widetilde{h}$ *can now be recalled from the special case of "prudent investment" in Section 4.5.3, there taking* $\beta = 0$ *in accordance with the linear dividends in this section.*

7

Interest rate derivatives in insurance

7.1 Introduction

This chapter gives an introduction to interest rate derivatives and their use in risk-management for life insurance companies. The first part of the chapter recalls the definitions of swap rates, swaps, swaptions and related products within a setting similar to the one studied in the previous chapters. Then we describe some pricing methods that have been proposed in the literature. There are a vast number of instruments available in the financial markets, and there exist many different models for the pricing of these instruments; see, for example, Brigo and Mercurio (2001), Musiela and Rutkowski (1997) and Rebonato (2002). Our treatment of this area is rather minimal, and our aim is simply to provide a brief introduction to certain developments that seem useful in an analysis of the risk faced by life insurance companies. The reader is therefore referred to the abovementioned references for a more detailed and systematic treatment of the basic theory.

We end the chapter by giving possible applications of these instruments in the area of risk management for a life insurance company facing insurance liabilities that cannot be hedged via bonds in the market due to the very long time horizon associated with the liabilities. Typically, insurance companies are faced by insurance liabilities that extend up to sixty years into the future, whereas the financial markets typically do not offer bonds that extend more than thirty years into the future. In addition, the market for interest rate derivatives (for example, interest rate swaps) has become much more liquid and can therefore be used effectively by insurance companies. Thus, it is relevant to investigate how a combination of investments in bonds of a relatively short maturity and advanced (long term) interest rate derivatives can be used to reduce the risk associated with the liabilities.

7.2 Swaps and beyond in continuous time

What is a swap rate? What is the relationship between swap rates, forward rates and short rates? What are swaps, swaptions and CMS options?

Below we present a discussion of these and other concepts. Our presentation differs slightly from most other presentations of this topic in that we set out by introducing the basic concepts in a continuous-time framework. This has the advantage that it simplifies notation and is more closely related to the previous chapters. We go on to discuss the corresponding quantities in a discrete-time setting, which corresponds to the approach taken in practice.

As in Chapter 3, we denote by $r(\tau)$ the continuously compounding short rate at time τ, and we let $\mathbf{F}$ be some information flow (filtration) related to the bond market. Note that Q is the market measure, i.e. the probability measure used for the pricing of bonds and interest rate derivatives. In particular, the price at time τ of a zero coupon bond expiring at time T is given by

$$P(\tau, T) = E^Q\left[\left. e^{-\int_\tau^T r(s)\,ds} \right| \mathcal{F}(\tau)\right] = e^{-\int_\tau^T f(\tau, s)\,ds},$$

where $(f(\tau, s))_{\tau \le s \le T}$ is the forward rate curve at time τ.

Consider a general bond with payment process C of finite variation, which is adapted to the information flow $\mathbf{F}$. This means that payments during a small time interval $(\tau, \tau + d\tau]$ are given by $dC(\tau)$.

Bonds with continuously paid coupons

As a main example, we study a bond with continuously paid coupons with rate $c(\tau)$ and a possible lump sum payment at time T. This leads to the following payment process:

$$dC(\tau) = c(\tau)\,d\tau + \Delta C(T)\,d\epsilon(\tau, T), \tag{7.1}$$

where $\epsilon(\tau, T) = 1_{\{\tau \ge T\}}$ and where $\Delta C(T)$ is the possible payment at time T. (Recall the notation introduced in Chapter 2.) The present value of all (past and future) payments from C at time $0 \le t \le T$ is given by

$$PV(t, C) = \int_0^T e^{-\int_t^\tau r(s)\,ds}\,dC(\tau) \tag{7.2}$$

$$= \int_0^T e^{-\int_t^\tau r(s)\,ds} c(\tau)\,d\tau + e^{-\int_t^T r(s)\,ds}\Delta C(T),$$

and the market value (or price) at time t of future payments is given by

$$\pi(t, C) = E^Q\left[\left. \int_t^T e^{-\int_t^\tau r(s)\,ds}\,dC(\tau) \right| \mathcal{F}(t)\right].$$

One important example of a payment process of the form in Equation (7.1) is where $c(\tau)$ is identical to the short rate $r(\tau)$ and $\Delta C(T) = 1$. This can be viewed as a continuous-time bullet bond with a variable interest rate similar to the one studied in discrete time in Chapter 3. In this case, the present value at time t of the future payments from C is given by

$$\int_t^T e^{-\int_t^\tau r(s)\,ds} r(\tau)\,d\tau + e^{-\int_t^T r(s)\,ds}. \tag{7.3}$$

Since

$$\int_t^T e^{-\int_t^\tau r(s)\,ds} r(\tau)\,d\tau = -e^{\int_0^t r(s)\,ds} \int_t^T de^{-\int_0^\tau r(s)\,ds} = 1 - e^{-\int_t^T r(s)\,ds},$$

we see that Equation (7.3) is constant and equal to unity. Thus, the payment process with $(c, \Delta C(T)) = (r, 1)$ has the special property that the present value at any time $t < T$ of future payments is constant and equal to unity.

Another important example is where $c(\tau)$ is constant and equal to some value κ and where $\Delta C(T) = 1$. In this case, the present value of future payments becomes

$$\kappa \int_t^T e^{-\int_t^\tau r(s)\,ds}\,d\tau + e^{-\int_t^T r(s)\,ds}. \tag{7.4}$$

The market value at time t of the future payments can be expressed in terms of the zero coupon bond prices $P(t, \tau)$:

$$\kappa \int_t^T P(t, \tau)\,d\tau + P(t, T); \tag{7.5}$$

see Chapters 3 and 5 for similar calculations.

Swaps and swap rates

One can now look for the value of κ which ensures that the prices of the two payment streams coincide at a fixed time t, i.e. the value of κ which ensures that Equation (7.5) is identical to unity. It follows by simple calculations that this is obtained for the following:

$$\kappa(t, T) = \frac{1 - P(t, T)}{\int_t^T P(t, \tau)\,d\tau}. \tag{7.6}$$

We refer to $\kappa(t, T)$ as the *$(T - t)$-year swap rate at time t (under continuous payments)*. For this particular value of κ, market prices at time t of future payments from the two payment streams coincide. This implies that two parties can exchange (swap) these payment streams at time t without making additional payments. The contract which consists in paying the coupons $c = r$ and receiving the coupons $c = \kappa$ is called a *receiver swap*. The contract in which the owner receives $c = r$ and pays $c = \kappa$ is called a *payer swap*.

Relationships between swap rates and forward rates

We can obtain an alternative expression for the swap rate by rewriting the term $1 - P(t, T)$ in Equation (7.6) as follows:

$$1 - P(t, T) = 1 - e^{-\int_t^T f(t, \tau) \, d\tau}$$

$$= \int_t^T f(t, \tau) \, e^{-\int_t^\tau f(t, s) \, ds} \, d\tau = \int_t^T f(t, \tau) P(t, \tau) \, d\tau.$$

By inserting this into Equation (7.6), we obtain the following expression:

$$\kappa(t, T) = \frac{\int_t^T f(t, \tau) P(t, \tau) \, d\tau}{\int_t^T P(t, \tau) \, d\tau}, \tag{7.7}$$

which shows that the swap rate at time t is a weighted average of the forward rates $(f(t, \tau))_{t \leq \tau \leq T}$, weighted by the corresponding zero coupon bond prices. We can now define the swap rate for each $0 \leq t \leq T$ and study the connection between the forward rate curve and the swap curve $(\kappa(t, \tau))_{t \leq \tau \leq T}$ more closely.

Firstly, we use Equation (7.6) to derive a simple recursion for the zero coupon bond prices. If we approximate the integral appearing in the denominator by the following:

$$\int_t^{T-h} P(t, \tau) \, d\tau + P(t, T)h$$

for small h, we see that

$$P(t, T) \approx \frac{1 - \kappa(t, T) \int_t^{T-h} P(t, \tau) \, d\tau}{1 + \kappa(t, T)h}.$$

In this way, zero coupon bond prices may be determined recursively from a given swap curve.

We know from Equation (7.7) that the swap rates are weighted averages of the zero coupon bond prices. It can be seen that the zero coupon bond prices can be expressed alternatively in terms of the swap curve via

$$P(t, T) = 1 - \kappa(t, T) \int_t^T e^{-\int_\tau^T \kappa(t, s) \, ds} \, d\tau.$$

To verify this, insert this expression into Equation (7.6) and change the order of integration in the denominator.

Caps and floors

As described above, the owner of a receiver swap receives the payments $dC(\tau) = (\kappa - r(\tau))\, d\tau$, whereas the owner of the payer swap receives $dC(\tau) = (r(\tau) - \kappa)\, d\tau$. We now define two new contracts, known respectively as a cap and a floor.

The owner of a *cap* receives payments of the form of Equation (7.1), with $c(\tau) = (r(\tau) - \kappa)^+$ and $\Delta C(T) = 0$; κ is called the *strike*. The payments from this contract are similar to the ones from the payer swap if the short rate exceeds the strike, κ, and zero otherwise. Let us modify the situation slightly by considering the case where the payments start at some fixed time $T_0 < T$. At time $t < T_0$, the present value of the payments from the cap is then given by

$$\int_{T_0}^{T} e^{-\int_t^\tau r(s)\, ds} (r(\tau) - \kappa)^+ \, d\tau. \tag{7.8}$$

A *floor* is similar, with $c(\tau) = (\kappa - r(\tau))^+$ and $\Delta C(T) = 0$. In this case, the payments are similar to those from a receiver swap if the short rate is smaller than the strike κ.

Swaptions

Consider as above the payments from a payer swap which starts at time T_0 and stops at time T. The present value at time T_0 of these payments is given by

$$\int_{T_0}^{T} (r(\tau) - \kappa)\, e^{-\int_{T_0}^\tau r(s)\, ds} \, d\tau,$$

which can be rewritten using calculations similar to the ones used above. In particular, this shows that the price at time T_0 of the payer swap is given by

$$1 - P(T_0, T) - \kappa \int_{T_0}^{T} P(T_0, \tau)\, d\tau.$$

A *payer swap option* (or *payer swaption*) is an option to enter a payer swap at time T_0 with strike κ. Thus, the payer swaption gives the holder the right, but not the obligation, to enter the payer swap at time T_0. The price of the payer swaption at time $t < T_0$ can be calculated as follows:

$$E^Q\left[e^{-\int_t^{T_0} r(s)\, ds} \left(1 - P(T_0, T) - \kappa \int_{T_0}^{T} P(T_0, \tau)\, d\tau \right)^+ \middle| \mathcal{F}(t) \right]. \tag{7.9}$$

At time $t < T_0$, we would say that the *maturity* of the swaption is $T_0 - t$, the *tenor* is $T - T_0$ and the *strike* is κ. Similarly, a *receiver swaption* is an option to enter a receiver swap.

Constant maturity swap (CMS) and CMS options

The swaption is really an option exercised at the fixed time T_0 where the holder can enter the swap. At this time, the crucial quantity determining whether or not there is a payoff from the option is the swap rate, $\kappa(T_0, T)$.

A *constant maturity swap (CMS)* differs from the swap in that the payment process involves the current swap rate with a fixed time T_0 to maturity. More precisely, a CMS specifies payments $dC(\tau) = (\kappa(\tau, T_0 + \tau) - \kappa) \, d\tau$ during $[0, T_1]$. The present value at time 0 of these payments is given by

$$\int_0^{T_1} e^{-\int_0^\tau r(s) \, ds} (\kappa(\tau, T_0 + \tau) - \kappa) \, d\tau. \tag{7.10}$$

The parameters are the number of years of payments T_1, maturity of the swap rates T_0 and the strike κ.

A *CMS cap* is now obtained from Equation (7.10) by replacing the payment intensity by $(\kappa(\tau, T_0 + \tau) - \kappa)^+$; a *CMS floor* is the case where the payment intensity is $(\kappa - \kappa(\tau, T_0 + \tau))^+$. Thus, a CMS cap is essentially an integral over call options on the T_0-year swap rates at any time $0 \leq \tau \leq T$. The cap protects its owner against an increase in the T_0-year swap rate during the interval $[0, T]$. Similarly, a CMS floor involves putting options on the T_0-year swap rates and protecting its owner against a decrease in this swap rate.

7.3 Pricing of interest rate derivatives

7.3.1 Change of numeraire and forward measures

In the previous chapters we have been working under a martingale measure Q, which had the special property that price processes discounted by the savings account $S^0(t) = e^{\int_0^t r(\tau) \, d\tau}$ were martingales under Q. In this case, we referred to the savings account S^0 as the numeraire. The measure Q played a key role in the calculation of arbitrage-free prices of derivatives and market values of life insurance contracts, which were defined as expected present values under Q. For the pricing of the various interest rate derivatives introduced above, it is sometimes convenient to work with an alternative numeraire. If, for example, we start by considering the present value of the payments from the continuous-time version of the cap, we see from Equation (7.8) that the integrand is given by

$$e^{-\int_t^\tau r(s) \, ds} (r(\tau) - \kappa)^+.$$

Thus, if we want to calculate the arbitrage-free price of the cap, we need to determine

$$E^Q\left[e^{-\int_t^\tau r(s)\,\mathrm{d}s}(r(\tau)-\kappa)^+\Big|\mathcal{F}(t)\right], \tag{7.11}$$

where we take $t < \tau$. This is not as straightforward as the standard Black–Scholes formula for a European call option on a stock, since it involves the joint distribution of $\int_t^\tau r(s)\,\mathrm{d}s$ and $r(\tau)$. One way of deriving a more simple expression for the price, Equation (7.11), is to introduce another measure Q^τ, which has the special property that all price processes discounted by the zero coupon bond price process $P(t, \tau)$ are martingales. Formally, this measure, *the forward measure*, is defined via its Radon–Nikodym derivative as follows:

$$\frac{\mathrm{d}Q^\tau}{\mathrm{d}Q} = \frac{e^{-\int_0^\tau r(s)\,\mathrm{d}s}}{P(0, \tau)}. \tag{7.12}$$

Equation (7.11) can now be calculated by using the abstract Bayes rule. If, for a moment, we use $t = 0$ and the notation $g(r(\tau)) = (r(\tau)-\kappa)^+$, we can rewrite Equation (7.11) as follows:

$$E^Q\left[e^{-\int_0^\tau r(s)\,\mathrm{d}s}g(r(\tau))\right] = P(0, \tau)\, E^Q\left[\frac{e^{-\int_0^\tau r(s)\,\mathrm{d}s}}{P(0, \tau)}g(r(\tau))\right]$$

$$= P(0, \tau)\, E^{Q^\tau}\left[g(r(\tau))\right],$$

where we have simply divided by $P(0, \tau)$ and multiplied by the same factor in the first equality; in the second equality, we have used Equation (7.12), the definition of the measure Q^τ. Here, it is important to note that the last expected value is calculated under the new measure Q^τ, which typically differs from the original martingale measure Q. This formula can be generalized to values of t not necessarily equal to zero, and this leads to $P(t, \tau)\, E^{Q^\tau}\left[g(r(\tau))|\mathcal{F}(t)\right]$, such that the price of the cap becomes

$$\int_{T_0}^T P(t, \tau)\, E^{Q^\tau}\left[(r(\tau)-\kappa)^+\Big|\mathcal{F}(t)\right]\mathrm{d}\tau.$$

Again, it is important to note that the expected values are to be calculated under the measures Q^τ for $\tau \in [T_0, T]$. The cap price formula is even more complicated, since it involves a new measure for each τ. A similar formula can be put up for the interest rate floor, the only difference being that $(r(\tau)-\kappa)^+$ should be replaced by $(\kappa-r(\tau))^+$.

It is not immediately clear that this is a useful method, since the distribution of $r(\tau)$ under Q^τ could be rather complicated. However, below we present some well known examples for which the forward measure is not more complicated than the risk neutral measure Q. First, recall that the forward rate at time 0 for time τ is defined as $f(0, \tau) = -(\partial/\partial\tau)\log P(0, \tau)$. Using this defining relation, it can be shown that

$$E^{Q^\tau}[r(\tau)] = E^Q\left[\frac{e^{-\int_0^\tau r(s)\,ds}}{P(0, \tau)}r(\tau)\right] = -\frac{\frac{\partial}{\partial\tau}P(0, \tau)}{P(0, \tau)} = -\frac{\partial}{\partial\tau}\log P(0, \tau) = f(0, \tau).$$

Thus, the forward measure can be used to find the forward rates as expected values of the short rates. This result can also be generalized such that $f(t, \tau) = E^{Q^\tau}[r(\tau)|\mathcal{F}(t)]$.

The goal is now to describe in more detail the measures Q^τ, $\tau \in [T_0, T]$, under some specific interest rate models, and to put up a closed formula for the cap and floor prices obtained above. In general, a measure Q^τ is completely determined by its density process:

$$Z^\tau(t) = E^Q\left[\frac{e^{-\int_0^\tau r(s)\,ds}}{P(0, \tau)}\middle| \mathcal{F}(t)\right] = \frac{P(t, \tau)}{P(0, \tau)}e^{-\int_0^t r(s)\,ds}. \tag{7.13}$$

The Vasiček model

Consider the Vasiček model, where the dynamics of r under the market martingale measure Q are given by

$$dr(t) = (b - ar(t))\,dt + \sigma\,dW(t),$$

where W is a standard Brownian motion under Q. The price $P(t, T)$ of a zero coupon bond maturing at time T is given by

$$P(t, T) = e^{A(t,T)-B(t,T)r(t)}, \tag{7.14}$$

where $A(t, T)$ and $B(t, T)$ are determined in Chapter 3. It follows, by a straight-forward application of Itô's formula, that the dynamics of $P(t, T)$ under Q is given by

$$dP(t, T) = r(t)P(t, T)\,dt + v(t, T)P(t, T)\,dW(t), \tag{7.15}$$

where $v(t, T) = -\sigma B(t, T)$. In this model, we have a very simple structure for the forward rates (see Chapter 3):

$$f(t, T) = r(t)e^{-a(T-t)} + \left(\frac{b}{a} - \frac{\sigma^2}{2a^2}\right)\left(1 - e^{-a(T-t)}\right) + e^{-a(T-t)}\frac{2\sigma^2 B(t, T)}{4a}.$$

Thus, the entire forward rate curve is determined from the short rate r. Using Equation (7.7), we can now calculate the swap rate curve for a given forward

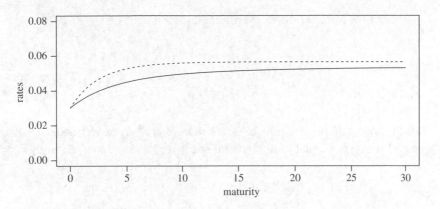

Figure 7.1. Forward rate curve (dashed line) and the corresponding swap rate curve (solid line). Calculations for the Vasiček model with $r(0) = 0.03$, $\sigma = 0.03$, $a = 0.36$ and $b/a = 0.06$.

rate curve. In Figure 7.1, the swap rate curve and the forward rate curve can be found for the Vasiček model with the same parameters as in Chapter 3. We see from Figure 7.1, that the swap curve in our situation is below the forward rate curve. This can be explained by the fact that the forward rate curve is increasing in this example.

In order to determine the behavior of r under the forward measure Q^T, we need to examine the density process $Z^T(t)$ and derive its dynamics. Using the above expression for the zero coupon bond price, we see that

$$dZ^T(t) = v(t, T)Z^T(t)\, dW(t),$$

such that

$$\frac{dQ^T}{dQ} = \exp\left(\int_0^T v(t, T)\, dW(t) - \frac{1}{2}\int_0^T (v(t, T))^2\, dt\right).$$

Girsanov's theorem now yields that the dynamics of r under Q^T is given by

$$dr(t) = (b + \sigma v(t, T) - ar(t))\, dt + \sigma\, dW^T(t), \tag{7.16}$$

where W^T is a standard Brownian motion under Q^T. Thus, the equation with the dynamics under Q^T is similar to the one for the dynamics under our usual martingale measure Q. One difference is that the drift term in Equation (7.16) now involves the function $v(t, T)$. This new type of dynamics should now be used when calculating expected values like the ones appearing in the prices for caps and floors.

Using Itô's formula, we can verify the following:

$$r(T) = r(t)\,e^{-a(T-t)} + \int_t^T e^{-a(T-s)}(b + \sigma v(s, T))\,ds$$

$$+ \int_t^T e^{-a(T-s)}\sigma\,dW^T(s), \tag{7.17}$$

which shows that the conditional distribution of $r(\tau)$ given $r(t)$ under Q^τ is normal with mean equal to the forward rate $f(t, \tau)$ and variance given by

$$\sigma^2 \int_t^\tau e^{-2a(\tau-s)}\,ds = \frac{\sigma^2}{2a}\left(1 - e^{-2a(\tau-t)}\right) = \Sigma_r(t, \tau).$$

Thus, we have a very simple structure for the conditional distribution of the short rate. However, even though the short rate is normally distributed, we are not able to arrive at closed form expressions for the caps, floors and swaptions introduced above. Instead, we can put up simple expressions for the prices, which may be evaluated numerically.

For the cap, the price given in Equation (7.11) appearing under the integral sign in the cap price can be written as follows:

$$P(t, \tau)E^{Q^\tau}\left[g(r(\tau))|\,\mathcal{F}(t)\right] = P(t, \tau)\frac{1}{\sqrt{2\pi\Sigma_r(t, \tau)}}$$

$$\times \int_{-\infty}^\infty g(u)\exp\left(-\frac{(u - f(t, \tau))^2}{2\Sigma_r(t, \tau)}\right)du, \tag{7.18}$$

with $g(u) = (u - \kappa)^+$. This integral has to be evaluated numerically.

Similarly, the price given in Equation (7.9) of the payer swaption can be determined as follows:

$$P(t, T_0)\,E^{Q^{T_0}}\left[\left(1 - P(T_0, T) - \kappa \int_{T_0}^T P(T_0, \tau)\,d\tau\right)^+\middle|\mathcal{F}(t)\right],$$

where one can insert Equation (7.14) to obtain an expression similar to Equation (7.18) and evaluate the integral numerically.

Finally, the price of the CMS floor can also be calculated numerically via the following expression:

$$\int_0^{T_1} P(0, \tau)\,E^{Q^\tau}\left[(\kappa - \kappa(\tau, T_0 + \tau))^+\right]d\tau,$$

where $\kappa(\tau, T_0 + \tau)$ is given by either Equations (7.6) or (7.7).

Bond options in the Vasiček model

We finally provide a formula for call options on zero coupon bonds. We want to calculate the price at time t of a call option maturing at time T_1 on a zero coupon bond with maturity T_2. This contract has the following price process:

$$
\begin{aligned}
\Pi_{\text{call}}(t) &= E^Q \left[e^{-\int_t^{T_1} r(s)\,ds} \left(P(T_1, T_2) - K \right)^+ \middle| \mathcal{F}(t) \right] \\
&= E^Q \left[e^{-\int_t^{T_1} r(s)\,ds} P(T_1, T_2) 1_{\{P(T_1,T_2) \geq K\}} \middle| \mathcal{F}(t) \right] \\
&\quad - E^Q \left[e^{-\int_t^{T_1} r(s)\,ds} K 1_{\{P(T_1,T_2) \geq K\}} \middle| \mathcal{F}(t) \right].
\end{aligned}
$$

Using the forward measure techniques introduced above, this can be rewritten as follows:

$$
\begin{aligned}
\Pi_{\text{call}}(t) = {}& P(t, T_2) Q^{T_2} \left(P(T_1, T_2) \geq K \middle| \mathcal{F}(t) \right) \\
&- K P(t, T_1) Q^{T_1} \left(P(T_1, T_2) \geq K \middle| \mathcal{F}(t) \right),
\end{aligned} \tag{7.19}
$$

where we are using the forward measures Q^{T_1} and Q^{T_2}. Under Q^{T_1}, we have that $P(t, T_2)/P(t, T_1)$ is a Q^{T_1}-martingale, and similarly $P(t, T_1)/P(t, T_2)$ is a martingale under the measures Q^{T_2}. Moreover, it follows from the dynamics for the option price process, Equation (7.15), that

$$
\begin{aligned}
\frac{P(\tau, T_1)}{P(\tau, T_2)} = {}& \frac{P(t, T_1)}{P(t, T_2)} \times \exp\left(\int_t^\tau \left(v(s, T_1) - v(s, T_2) \right) dW(s) \right. \\
&\left. - \frac{1}{2} \int_t^\tau \left(v(s, T_1)^2 - v(s, T_2)^2 \right) ds \right),
\end{aligned} \tag{7.20}
$$

which involves W, a standard Brownian motion under Q. Alternatively, we may use the relations between the dynamics under Q and under the forward measures Q^{T_i}, which imply that $dW(t) = dW^{T_i}(t) + v(t, T_i)\,dt$, where W^{T_i} are standard Brownian motions under Q^{T_i}. This can be used to show that

$$
\begin{aligned}
\frac{P(\tau, T_1)}{P(\tau, T_2)} = {}& \frac{P(t, T_1)}{P(t, T_2)} \exp\left(\int_t^\tau \left(v(s, T_1) - v(s, T_2) \right) dW^{T_2}(s) \right. \\
&\left. - \frac{1}{2} \int_t^\tau \left(v(s, T_1) - v(s, T_2) \right)^2 ds \right)
\end{aligned}
$$

under Q^{T_2} and

$$
\begin{aligned}
\frac{P(\tau, T_2)}{P(\tau, T_1)} = {}& \frac{P(t, T_2)}{P(t, T_1)} \exp\left(\int_t^\tau \left(v(s, T_2) - v(s, T_1) \right) dW^{T_1}(s) \right. \\
&\left. - \frac{1}{2} \int_t^\tau \left(v(s, T_2) - v(s, T_1) \right)^2 ds \right)
\end{aligned}
$$

under Q^{T_1}. These two ways of writing the ratios between $P(\tau, T_2)$ and $P(\tau, T_1)$ differ from Equation (7.20) in that they involve standard Brownian motions under the new measures Q^{T_1} and Q^{T_2}, respectively. The two probabilities appearing in Equation (7.19) can now be calculated by using these two formulas. In fact, it follows that

$$Q^{T_1}\left(P(T_1, T_2) \geq K \mid \mathcal{F}(t)\right) = \Phi\left(z_1(t, T_1, T_2, K)\right),$$

where

$$z_1(t, T_1, T_2, K) = \frac{\log\left(\frac{P(t, T_2)}{KP(t, T_1)} - \frac{1}{2}\int_t^{T_1} \left(v(s, T_2) - v(s, T_1)\right)^2 \, ds\right)}{\sqrt{\int_t^{T_1} \left(v(s, T_2) - v(s, T_1)\right)^2 \, ds}}. \qquad (7.21)$$

Similarly, one can show that

$$Q^{T_2}\left(P(T_1, T_2) \geq K \mid \mathcal{F}(t)\right) = \Phi\left(z_2(t, T_1, T_2, K)\right),$$

where

$$z_2(t, T_1, T_2, K) = z_1(t, T_1, T_2, K) + \sqrt{\int_t^{T_1} \left(v(s, T_2) - v(s, T_1)\right)^2 \, ds}. \quad (7.22)$$

Putting everything together, we obtain the following formula:

$$\begin{aligned}
\Pi_{\text{call}}(t, T_1, T_2, K) = {}& P(t, T_2)\Phi\left(z_2(t, T_1, T_2, K)\right) \\
& - KP(t, T_1)\Phi\left(z_1(t, T_1, T_2, K)\right), \qquad (7.23)
\end{aligned}$$

for the price at time t of the call option on the zero coupon bond price. Here, z_1 and z_2 are given by Equations (7.21) and (7.22), respectively.

7.4 Swaps and beyond in discrete time

In a discrete-time setting, we can introduce quantities similar to the ones introduced in the continuous-time framework. However, here one has to specify further when the actual payments take place, and there are several ways of defining these payments. Recall the definition of the LIBOR rate $L(t, T)$, which is a simple rate for the interval $[t, T]$ defined by

$$L(t, T) = \frac{1 - P(t, T)}{(T - t)P(t, T)}. \qquad (7.24)$$

Similarly, the forward LIBOR rate for the interval $[T', T]$ is defined by

$$L(t, T', T) = \frac{P(t, T') - P(t, T)}{(T - T')P(t, T)}. \qquad (7.25)$$

Swaps and swap rates

We start by describing a so-called *payer interest rate swap* settled in arrears in the discrete-time setting under simple interest. Our specification involves a set of future dates $T_0 < T_1 < \cdots < T_n$, where, for simplicity, we assume that the time intervals are of equal length, i.e. that $T_i - T_{i-1} = \delta$. We refer to T_n as the maturity of the contract. In addition, we consider some fixed, simple rate K and a nominal value N of the contract. The times $T_1 < \cdots < T_n$ are the payment times and T_0 is the starting time for the measurement of the payments. At time T_i the holder of the contract pays the fixed amount $K\delta N$, which is the simple interest on the nominal value N at the simple rate K during an interval of length δ. In return, the holder receives $L(T_{i-1}, T_i)\delta N$, which is the deterministic return available at time T_{i-1} for the interval from T_{i-1} to T_i. Thus, the net payment to the holder of the contract is given by

$$(L(T_{i-1}, T_i) - K)\delta N, \qquad (7.26)$$

and we want to find its value at time t. To do this, we first determine the value at time T_{i-1}. This is simple, since the size of the payment is already known at time T_{i-1}. By inserting the definition of the LIBOR rate and by discounting the payments to time T_{i-1} via the zero coupon bond, we get the value at time T_{i-1}:

$$(1 - (1 + K\delta)P(T_{i-1}, T_i))N, \qquad (7.27)$$

which at time $t \le T_{i-1}$ has the value

$$(P(t, T_{i-1}) - (1 + K\delta)P(t, T_i))N.$$

This can be seen via a simple hedging argument as follows. Simply invest in the corresponding bonds at time t and calculate the value at time T_{i-1} of this investment to see that this is identical to Equation (7.27).

By adding together the value of all these payments at times $T_1, \ldots, T_n$, we obtain the value at time $t < T_0$ of the payer swap as follows:

$$\Pi_{\text{payer swap}}(t, K) = \sum_{i=1}^{n}(P(t, T_{i-1}) - (1 + K\delta)P(t, T_i))N$$

$$= N\left(P(t, T_0) - P(t, T_n) - K\delta\sum_{i=1}^{n}P(t, T_i)\right). \qquad (7.28)$$

If we change the signs on the cash flow, so that the holder pays at time T_i the amount in Equation (7.26), we obtain a so-called *receiver interest rate swap* settled in arrears. The value of this contract is obtained by multiplying Equation (7.28) by -1. We can consider contracts with the payments given in

Equation (7.26) for basically any value of K; however, it is particularly interesting to find the value of K such that the value of the contract at time t is zero. As in the continuous-time case, this implies that two parties can enter this agreement at time t without making any additional payments. It follows from Equation (7.28) that this is obtained by setting K equal to

$$R_{\text{swap}}(t, T_0, T_n) = \frac{P(t, T_0) - P(t, T_n)}{\delta \sum_{i=1}^{n} P(t, T_i)}, \tag{7.29}$$

which we also refer to as the *forward swap rate* at time t. We note that the forward swap rate depends on the time t as well as on the chosen set of dates $T_0, \ldots, T_n$. For $t = T_0$, the formula for the forward swap rate, Equation (7.29), reduces to

$$\frac{1 - P(t, T_n)}{\delta \sum_{i=1}^{n} P(t, T_i)}, \tag{7.30}$$

which is then simply called the the *swap rate*. Note the resemblance between Equation (7.30) and the continuous-time version of the swap rate, Equation (7.6).

Typical shapes for the swap rate curves can be found in Figure 7.2.

Relations between swap rates and LIBOR forward rates
As in the continuous-time case, we can represent the swap rate as a weighted average of forward rates. Here, in the discrete-time setting with simple interest,

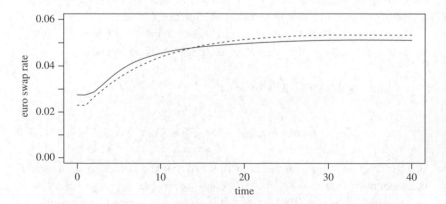

Figure 7.2. Euro swap rate curves.

the relevant forward rates are the LIBOR forward rates. To obtain this representation, we rewrite the left side of Equation (7.28) as follows:

$$\sum_{i=1}^{n}(P(t, T_{i-1}) - (1 + K\delta)P(t, T_i))N$$

$$= N\delta \sum_{i=1}^{n} P(t, T_i) \left(\frac{P(t, T_{i-1}) - P(t, T_i)}{(T_i - T_{i-1})P(t, T_i)} - K \right)$$

$$= N\delta \sum_{i=1}^{n} P(t, T_i) \left(L(t, T_{i-1}, T_i) - K \right), \qquad (7.31)$$

where the second equality follows by using Equation (7.25), the definition of the forward LIBOR rate with $T' = T_{i-1}$ and $T = T_i$, for $i = 1, \ldots, n$. This shows that the value at t of the payer swap is zero provided that K is given by

$$\frac{\sum_{i=1}^{n} P(t, T_i)L(t, T_{i-1}, T_i)}{\sum_{i=1}^{n} P(t, T_i)}. \qquad (7.32)$$

Thus, the forward swap rate can alternatively be written in the form given in Equation (7.32), which is the discrete-time version of Equation (7.7).

Caps and floors

We have already discussed caps and floors in the continuous-time setting. The floor is a contract which provides payments at times $T_1, \ldots T_n$, where the payment at time T_i is of the following form:

$$(K - L(T_{i-1}, T_i))^+ \delta N. \qquad (7.33)$$

Thus, the holder of the floor receives the difference between the fixed level K and the LIBOR rate, provided that this difference is positive. In this way, the floor provides a protection against low interest rates. The contract which only prescribes one payment of the form given in Equation (7.33) is called a *floorlet*. The cap is similar to the floor, with payments $(L(T_{i-1}, T_i) - K)^+ \delta N$, and it provides a protection against high interest rates.

By the definition of $()^+$, we have, for any $x, K \in \mathbf{R}$, $(x - K) = (x - K)^+ - (K - x)^+$. Thus, the payments from the payer swap can, for any $K > 0$, be expressed in terms of the payments from the cap and the floor via the following:

$$(L(T_{i-1}, T_i) - K) = (L(T_{i-1}, T_i) - K)^+ - (K - L(T_{i-1}, T_i))^+,$$

which shows that the payer swap is the difference between the cap and the floor. This implies also that the value at t of the payer swap is the difference between the values of the cap and the floor, i.e.

$$\Pi_{\text{payer swap}}(t, K) = \Pi_{\text{cap}}(t, K) - \Pi_{\text{floor}}(t, K).$$

In particular, if

$$K = R_{\text{swap}}(0, T_0, T_n) = \frac{P(0, T_0) - P(0, T_n)}{\delta \sum_{i=1}^{n} P(0, T_i)},$$

then we have, by definition of the forward swap rate, that $\Pi_{\text{payer swap}}(t, K) = 0$ and hence $\Pi_{\text{cap}}(t, K) = \Pi_{\text{floor}}(t, K)$. Furthermore, it follows that

$$\Pi_{\text{cap}}(t, K) < \Pi_{\text{floor}}(t, K)$$

if $K > R_{\text{swap}}(0, T_0, T_n)$. Similarly,

$$\Pi_{\text{cap}}(t, K) > \Pi_{\text{floor}}(t, K)$$

if $K < R_{\text{swap}}(0, T_0, T_n)$. Consequently, the floor at time 0 is said to be *at-the-money* if $K = R_{\text{swap}}(0, T_0, T_n)$, *in-the-money* if $K > R_{\text{swap}}(0, T_0, T_n)$ and *out-of-the-money* if $K < R_{\text{swap}}(0, T_0, T_n)$.

By using Equation (7.24), the definition of the LIBOR rate $L(T_{i-1}, T_i)$, we can rewrite the payments given in Equation (7.33) under the floor as follows:

$$\frac{1}{P(T_{i-1}, T_i)} (1 + K\delta) \left(P(T_{i-1}, T_i) - \frac{1}{1 + K\delta} \right)^+ N. \qquad (7.34)$$

This payment takes place at time T_i, but it is known in full already at time T_{i-1}. Thus, its value at time T_{i-1} is obtained by simply multiplying Equation (7.34) by the zero coupon bond price $P(T_{i-1}, T_i)$, which shows that the value at time T_{i-1} of the payment at time T_i, Equation (7.33), is given by

$$(1 + K\delta) \left(P(T_{i-1}, T_i) - \frac{1}{1 + K\delta} \right)^+ N. \qquad (7.35)$$

This is recognized as the payoff at time T_{i-1} of $(1 + K\delta)$ call options on the zero coupon bond price $P(T_{i-1}, T_i)$ with strike $1/(1 + K\delta)$. This result can be used to obtain closed form solutions for the price of the floor, in terms of prices on bond options.

Pricing via bond options in the Vasiček model

The alternative expression given by Equation (7.35) for the value at time T_{i-1} of the payment at time T_i allows for simple closed form solutions for the price of the discrete-time version of caps and floors in the Vasiček model. For the floor, the value is given by

$$\Pi_{\text{floor}}^{V}(t, K) = (1 + K\delta)N \sum_{i=1}^{n} E^{Q}\left[e^{-\int_{t}^{T_{i-1}} r(s)\,\mathrm{d}s} \left(P(T_{i-1}, T_i) - \frac{1}{1 + K\delta} \right)^{+} \middle| \mathcal{F}(t) \right]$$

$$= (1 + K\delta)N \sum_{i=1}^{n} \Pi_{\text{call}}^{V}\left(t, T_{i-1}, T_i, \frac{1}{1 + K\delta} \right),$$

where $\Pi_{\text{call}}^{V}(t, T_{i-1}, T_i, 1/(1 + K\delta))$ is defined by Equation (7.23).

Black's formula for caps and floors

The floor is typically priced in the market by using the so-called Black's formula, which can be derived by assuming that forward LIBOR rates are lognormally distributed under a certain measure. For the payment at T_i from the floor (the floorlet at T_i), Black's formula yields the price as follows:

$$\Pi_{\text{floorlet } T_i}(t, K) = \delta N P(t, T_i) \left(K\Phi(-d_2(T_i, t)) - L(t, T_{i-1}, T_i)\Phi(-d_1(T_i, t)) \right),$$
$$(7.36)$$

where

$$d_1(T_i, t) = \frac{\log\left(L(t, T_{i-1}, T_i)/K \right) + \frac{1}{2}\sigma(t)^2(T_{i-1} - t)}{\sigma(t)\sqrt{T_{i-1} - t}},$$

$$d_2(T_i, t) = d_1(T_i, t) - \sigma(t)\sqrt{T_{i-1} - t}.$$

For the caplet at T_i, we obtain, similarly,

$$\Pi_{\text{caplet } T_i}(t, K) = \delta N P(t, T_i) \left(L(t, T_{i-1}, T_i)\Phi(d_1(T_i, t)) - K\Phi(d_2(T_i, t)) \right).$$

This means that the price at time t of the floor is given by

$$\Pi_{\text{floor}}(t, K) = \sum_{i=1}^{n} \Pi_{\text{floorlet } T_i}(t, K).$$

The crucial parameter is the volatility $\sigma(t)$ used at time t. The volatility typically depends on whether we are pricing a cap or a floor and on whether the contracts are at-the-money or not. Moreover, the volatility depends on the maturity T_n of the caps and floors.

Swaptions

The *payer swaption* gives its holder the right to enter a payer swap at a given date, which is also called the maturity of the swaption, at a fixed rate K, which is called the strike rate. As above, we let $T_1, \ldots, T_n$ be the payment dates of the swap and denote by T_0 its reset date. The payoff of the swaption with nominal value N and maturity T_0 thus becomes:

$$\left(\Pi_{\text{payer swap}}(T_0, K)\right)^+ = N\delta \left(\sum_{i=1}^{n} P(T_0, T_i) \left(L(T_0, T_{i-1}, T_i) - K\right)\right)^+, \quad (7.37)$$

where we have used the alternative expression, Equation (7.31), for the price at time T_0 of the payer swap. The problem now consists in finding the value at time $t < T_0$ of the contract, which pays the payoff given in Equation (7.37) at time T_0. This is more complicated than for the caps and floors, since the positive part $()^+$ of a sum does not split into the sum of the positive parts. However, since by definition of the swap rate $R_{\text{swap}}(T_0, T_0, T_n)$ we have that

$$\Pi_{\text{payer swap}}(T_0, R_{\text{swap}}(T_0, T_0, T_n)) = 0,$$

Equation (7.37) can be rewritten as follows:

$$\left(\Pi_{\text{payer swap}}(T_0, K) - \Pi_{\text{payer swap}}(T_0, R_{\text{swap}}(T_0, T_0, T_n))\right)^+$$

$$= N\delta \left(\sum_{i=1}^{n} P(T_0, T_i)\Big(\big(L(T_0, T_0, T_i) - K\big) - \big(L(T_0, T_0, T_i)\right.$$

$$\left. - R_{\text{swap}}(T_0, T_0, T_n)\big)\Big)\right)^+ = N\delta \sum_{i=1}^{n} P(T_0, T_i) \left(R_{\text{swap}}(T_0, T_0, T_n) - K\right)^+.$$

$$(7.38)$$

As with caps and floors, we say that the payer swaption is at-the-money if $K = R_{\text{swap}}(t, T_0, T_n)$, in-the-money if $R_{\text{swap}}(t, T_0, T_n) > K$ and out-of-the-money if we have that $R_{\text{swap}}(t, T_0, T_n) < K$. This illustrates that the swap rate $R_{\text{swap}}(T_0, T_0, T_n)$ determines whether or not there is a payment from the swaption.

Black's formula for swaptions

Similar to the pricing of caps and floors, the market uses Black's formula for the pricing of swaptions. For the payer swaption, the formula reads as follows:

$$N\delta \left(R_{\text{swap}}(t, T_0, T_n)\Phi(d_1(t)) - K\Phi(d_2(t))\right) \sum_{i=1}^{n} P(t, T_i),$$

where

$$d_1(t) = \frac{\log\left(R_{\text{swap}}(t, T_0, T_n)/K\right) + \frac{1}{2}\sigma(t)^2(T_0 - t)}{\sigma(t)\sqrt{T_0 - t}},$$

$$d_2(t) = d_1(t) - \sigma(t)\sqrt{T_0 - t}.$$

The volatility parameter σ used for swaptions in the market typically differs from the one used for the pricing of caps and floors.

Constant maturity swap (CMS) and CMS options

We end this section by describing CMS options in the current setting. We consider times $T_0 < T_1 < \cdots < T_n < T_{n+1} < \cdots T_{n+m}$, where $T_1, \ldots, T_n$ are payment times and $T_{n+1}, \ldots, T_{n+m}$ are times used for determining the size of the payments. We assume throughout that $T_i - T_{i-1} = \delta$. More precisely, the payment at time T_i, $i = 1, \ldots, n$, is defined in terms of a certain swap rate with a fixed maturity. As usual, we have the following swap rate:

$$R_{\text{swap}}(T_i, T_i, T_{i+m}) = \frac{1 - P(T_i, T_{i+m})}{\delta \sum_{j=i+1}^{m} P(T_i, T_j)}.$$

The payment at time T_i from the constant maturity swap (CMS) is now defined as $(R_{\text{swap}}(T_i, T_i, T_{i+m}) - K)\delta$. With a CMS cap, the payments are changed to $(R_{\text{swap}}(T_i, T_i, T_{i+m}) - K)^+\delta$, and a CMS floor pays $(K - R_{\text{swap}}(T_i, T_i, T_{i+m}))^+\delta$ at time T_i, $i = 1, \ldots, n$. Thus, the individual payments resemble the payoff from a swaption, and hence one could suggest a Black-type formula for valuation to obtain

$$\Pi_{\text{CMS cap}}(t) = \delta \sum_{i=1}^{n} P(t, T_i) \left(R_{\text{swap}}(t, T_i, T_{i+m})\Phi(d_1(t, T_i)) - K\Phi(d_2(t, T_i))\right),$$

where

$$d_1(t, T_i) = \frac{\log\left(R_{\text{swap}}(t, T_i, T_{i+m})/K\right) + \frac{1}{2}\sigma(t, T_i)^2(T_i - t)}{\sigma(t, T_i)\sqrt{T_i - t}},$$

$$d_2(t, T_i) = d_1(t, T_i) - \sigma(t, T_i)\sqrt{T_i - t}.$$

Similarly, the value of the CMS floor could be calculated as follows:

$$\Pi_{\text{CMS floor}}(t) = \delta \sum_{i=1}^{n} P(t, T_i) \left(K\Phi(-d_2(t, T_i)) - R_{\text{swap}}(t, T_i, T_{i+m})\right.$$

$$\left. \times \Phi(-d_1(t, T_i))\right).$$

However, it is important to realize that the discounting for the CMS floors and caps is completely different from the one that appears for the swaptions. In practice, one would therefore modify these formulas by applying a so-called convexity-correction; see, for example, Brigo and Mercurio (2001, Sect. 10.7).

7.5 A brief introduction to market models

This section briefly describes some so-called market models that can be used to obtain Black's formula for caps, floors and swaptions. In order to obtain the formula for the price of the cap, one essentially needs to assume that the forward LIBOR rates are lognormally distributed. Similarly, one assumes that the swap rates are lognormally distributed in order to obtain Black's formula for the swaptions. Unfortunately, these two models are not consistent in the sense that the LIBOR model does not lead to lognormal swap rates. For more complete presentations of this topic, we refer again to textbooks such as Brigo and Mercurio (2001) and Rebonato (2002).

In this section, we use again the change of numeraire techniques and forward measures introduced in Section 7.3.

We fix times $T_0 < T_1 < \cdots < T_n$ and assume an equal distance δ between the time points. For valuation purposes, we introduce the so-called implied savings account, which is obtained by investing at time T_{i-1} in bonds maturing at times T_i, etc. Using this strategy from time t to T_k, $t < T_k$, for an investment of one unit at time t, where $T_j < t < T_{j+1}$, yields

$$B(t, T_k) = \frac{1}{P(t, T_{j+1})} \frac{1}{P(T_{j+1}, T_{j+2})} \cdots \frac{1}{P(T_{k-1}, T_k)}$$

$$= \frac{1}{P(t, T_{j+1})} \prod_{i=j+2}^{k} \frac{1}{P(T_{i-1}, T_i)}.$$

(Here, the product over an empty set is defined as unity.) Thus, we can use $(B(t, T_k))^{-1}$ as a (stochastic) discount factor. This factor plays the same role as the usual discount factor, $\exp\left(-\int_t^{T_k} r(s)\, ds\right)$, which is defined in terms of the short rate process r. However, in the present setting, the short rate process is not defined; we simply take as given the bonds with maturities $T_1, \ldots, T_n$.

7.5.1 A market model for pricing a floorlet

In order to introduce the main ideas, we first consider the problem of pricing a floorlet with payoff given in Equation (7.33) at time T_i. Thus, the present value at time t of the payment at time T_i is given by

$$(B(t, T_i))^{-1} (K - L(T_{i-1}, T_i))^{+} \delta N,$$

and its market price at time t is given by

$$E^Q\left[(B(t,T_i))^{-1}(K - L(T_{i-1},T_i))^+\delta N\,\middle|\,\mathcal{F}(t)\right], \tag{7.39}$$

where Q is the market measure, which has the property that all traded assets divided by the implied savings account are Q-martingales, and where $\mathcal{F}(t)$ is the information available at time t. In particular, we have that

$$P(t,T_i) = E^Q\left[(B(t,T_i))^{-1}\,\middle|\,\mathcal{F}(t)\right].$$

Using the forward measure technique introduced in Section 7.3.1, we can simplify this formula further. To see this, introduce a T_i-forward measure defined by

$$\frac{\mathrm{d}Q^{T_i}}{\mathrm{d}Q} = \frac{(B(0,T_i))^{-1}}{P(0,T_i)}.$$

Via the usual calculations, we can now rewrite the market price of the floorlet in terms of the T_i-forward measure:

$$P(t,T_i)E^{Q^{T_i}}\left[(K - L(T_{i-1},T_i))^+\delta N\,\middle|\,\mathcal{F}(t)\right], \tag{7.40}$$

which is much more simple than the previous expression given in Equation (7.39). To calculate the conditional expected value under Q^{T_i}, we only need the conditional distribution of $L(T_{i-1},T_i)$ given $\mathcal{F}(t)$ under Q^{T_i}. To obtain this, one idea is to introduce a model for the development of the forward swap rate $L(t,T_{i-1},T_i)$ directly under the T_i-forward measure Q^{T_i}. Firstly, recall that the T_i-forward measure has the special property that the ratio between a traded asset and the T_i-bond prize process is a Q^{T_i}-martingale. Secondly, we reexamine the definition for the forward LIBOR rate $L(t,T_{i-1},T_i)$, Equation (7.25), to see that it is essentially defined as the ratio between $P(t,T_{i-1})$ and $P(t,T_i)$, which should be a Q^{T_i}-martingale. Thus, one possible model would be to assume that the dynamics for $L(t,T_{i-1},T_i)$ under Q^{T_i} is given by

$$\mathrm{d}L(\tau,T_{i-1},T_i) = \lambda(\tau,T_{i-1})L(\tau,T_{i-1},T_i)\,\mathrm{d}W^{T_i}(\tau), \tag{7.41}$$

for $\tau \le T_{i-1}$, where W^{T_i} is a standard Brownian motion under Q^{T_i} and where $\lambda(\tau,T_{i-1})$ is a deterministic function. We could assume that λ is itself a stochastic process; however, if λ is deterministic the distribution of the LIBOR rate,

$$L(T_{i-1}, T_i) = L(T_{i-1}, T_{i-1}, T_i),$$

becomes lognormal, which allows for a simple closed form expression for the market price of the floorlet. It follows, by using Itô's formula, that the solution to Equation (7.41) is given by

$$L(T_{i-1}, T_i) = L(t, T_{i-1}, T_i) \times$$

$$\exp\left(\int_t^{T_{i-1}} \lambda(s, T_{i-1})\, dW^{T_i}(s) - \frac{1}{2}\int_t^{T_{i-1}} \lambda(s, T_{i-1})^2\, ds\right).$$

$$(7.42)$$

Since we have assumed that λ is a deterministic function, this shows that the conditional distribution under Q^{T_i} of $\log(L(T_{i-1}, T_i))$, given $\mathcal{F}(t)$, is normal, with variance given by

$$\Sigma(t, T_{i-1}) := \int_t^{T_{i-1}} \lambda(s, T_{i-1})^2\, ds,$$

and mean given by

$$\log(L(t, T_{i-1}, T_i)) - \frac{1}{2}\Sigma(t, T_{i-1}).$$

Thus, calculations similar to the ones used for the derivation of the Black–Scholes formula show that the price of the floorlet, Equation (7.40), can be written as follows:

$$\widehat{\Pi}_{\text{floorlet } T_i}(t, K) = P(t, T_i)\left(K\Phi(-\widehat{d}_2(t, T_{i-1}))\right.$$

$$\left. -L(t, T_{i-1}, T_i)\Phi(-\widehat{d}_1(t, T_{i-1}))\right), \qquad (7.43)$$

where

$$\widehat{d}_1(t, T_{i-1}) = \frac{\log\left(\frac{L(t, T_{i-1}, T_i)}{K}\right) + \frac{1}{2}\Sigma(t, T_{i-1})}{\sqrt{\Sigma(t, T_{i-1})}}$$

and

$$\widehat{d}_2(t, T_{i-1}) = \widehat{d}_1(t, T_{i-1}) - \frac{1}{2}\sqrt{\Sigma(t, T_{i-1})}.$$

It is worth mentioning that the valuation formula, Equation (7.43), differs from the market formula, Equation (7.36), only via the variance term $\Sigma(t, T_{i-1})$. In fact, if we choose $\lambda(\tau, T_{i-1})$ independent of T_{i-1}, then the two formulas are identical.

The floor consisting of floorlets at times $T_1, \dots, T_n$ can now be valued by modelling forward LIBOR rates $L(t, T_{i-1}, T_i)$ for any $i = 1, \dots, n$ under the corresponding forward measures $Q^{T_1}, \dots, Q^{T_n}$.

As mentioned above, Black's formula for swaptions cannot be obtained within this model, since swap rates are not log-normally distributed.

7.6 Interest rate derivatives in insurance

We recall the basic example introduced in Chapter 2 of an endowment with a continuously paid premium. It was demonstrated in Chapter 3 how the guaranteed payments from this contract could (in principle) be hedged perfectly by investing in zero coupon bonds. Here we address the more realistic situation, where the insurance company does not have access to the zero coupon bonds that are necessary for this perfect hedge. In this situation, the market for long term interest rate derivatives provides additional possibilities for reducing the risk inherent in the insurance contract.

Here, one has to be a little more precise and specify in more detail the optimization criteria used by the company. There are several different possibilities, which we describe vaguely here.

One idea is to require that the total reserves at any time exceed the market value of the guaranteed payments. This can be viewed as the minimal requirement, i.e. this condition cannot be relaxed. One of the main current problems to life insurers seems to be handling of policies with a high first order rate, which have been issued in periods with very high (nominal) rates and which have not been fully hedged. Firstly, the guarantees were originally not taken seriously, since the guarantees (of say 4.5%) were substantially lower than the nominal rates (say 15%). Secondly, a perfect hedge was not really possible in the bond market, due to the extremely long time horizons associated with life and pension insurance contracts. Today, these contracts represent a major risk to life insurance companies and pension funds, since they essentially guarantee policy holders yearly returns which exceed current short rates.

7.7 A portfolio of contracts

We analyze the impact of interest rate derivatives by considering some simple examples. We restrict the analysis to the continuous-time framework presented in Section 7.2.

Pure endowment repeated

Consider as a simple example the pure endowment paid by single premium, which was also analyzed as an introductory example in Chapters 3 and 5. We assume that premiums are fixed using some deterministic interest rate r^*, which is chosen on the safe side, such that the premium payable at time 0 for a T-year pure endowment contracts with sum insured 1 is given by

$$\pi(0) = {}_Tp_x\, e^{-\int_0^T r^*(s)\,ds},$$

which can also be written in terms of a decrement series by using the formula ${}_Tp_x = l_{x+T}/l_x$; see Section 3.2.4 for more details. As in the previous chapters, we consider a portfolio of l_x identical contracts, such that the present value at time 0 of benefits less premiums is given by

$$l_{x+T}\, e^{-\int_0^T r(s)\,ds} - l_x\,\pi(0).$$

Note that we are here discounting the payments by using the market interest rate r, which is a stochastic process; one possibility is to use the Vasiček model for r, which was discussed in Chapter 3. As mentioned in Chapter 3, the insurer's liability can be hedged perfectly by investing in a certain amount of T-bonds (zero coupon bonds). Since this bond might not be available in the market, we investigate here the effect of using a swap instead of the T-bond. More precisely, we assume that the company invests premiums in the savings account (which we can think of as the result of investing in bonds with very short time to maturity). If we put the premiums into an account which bears interest r, the value at time t becomes

$$\Pi_{\text{premium}}(t) = l_x\,\pi(0)\, e^{\int_0^t r(s)\,ds}.$$

Finally, the market value of the guaranteed future payments at time t is given by

$$V^g(t) = l_{x+t}\,{}_{T-t}p_{x+t}P(t,T), \tag{7.44}$$

where we have assumed that the market mortality intensity is equal to the mortality intensity used for calculation of the premium.

7.7.1 Hedging via a static swap position

The swap account

We assume now that the company enters $N = l_x\,\pi(0)(1+\varepsilon)$ receiver swaps with strike κ, which in the continuous-time formulation means that the company receives fixed interest κ and pays floating interest r. (We refer to N as the face value.) The present value at time 0 of the payments from one unit of the swap is given by

$$\int_0^T e^{-\int_0^\tau r(s)} (\kappa - r(\tau)) \, d\tau, \qquad (7.45)$$

and we assume that the strike κ is the T-year swap rate at time 0, $\kappa(0, T)$, which is defined by Equation (7.6). This means that the company can enter the contract at time 0 without paying anything to the other party. The disadvantage of this contract is, of course, that the company has to pay coupons $(r(\tau) - \kappa)$ to the other party if the interest exceeds the strike κ. Let us imagine that we create an account in the company which consists of the market value of the swap to which are added past incomes and from which are subtracted past outgoes, and that everything is accumulated with the market interest r. We denote by $\Pi_{swap}(t)$ the value of this account at time t. Since $\kappa = \kappa(0, T)$, we have $\Pi_{swap}(0) = 0$. At time t, the value is given by

$$\Pi_{swap}(t) = N \int_0^t e^{\int_\tau^t r(s) \, ds} (\kappa - r(\tau)) \, d\tau$$

$$+ NE^Q \left[\int_t^T e^{-\int_t^\tau r(s)} (\kappa - r(\tau)) \, d\tau \, \middle| \, \mathcal{F}(t) \right],$$

which is past incomes less outgoes added to the market value of future payments. By using calculations similar to the ones following Equation (7.3), we can rewrite the first term on the right as follows:

$$N\kappa \int_0^t e^{\int_\tau^t r(s) \, ds} \, d\tau - N(e^{\int_0^t r(s) \, ds} - 1).$$

For the second part, we obtain

$$N\kappa \int_t^T P(t, \tau) \, d\tau - N(1 - P(t, T)).$$

Putting everything together, we obtain

$$\Pi_{swap}(t) = N\kappa \left(\int_0^t e^{\int_\tau^t r(s) \, ds} \, d\tau + \int_t^T P(t, \tau) \, d\tau \right)$$

$$- N(e^{\int_0^t r(s) \, ds} - P(t, T)).$$

The total account
We can now compare the value of the investments (the accounts for the paid premiums and the swap account) with the market value of the liabilities. Thus,

we study the process defined as the difference between these quantities in more detail, and let

$$U(t) = \Pi_{\text{premium}}(t) + \Pi_{\text{swap}}(t) - V^{\text{g}}(t)$$

$$= l_x\,\pi(0)\,e^{\int_0^t r(s)\,ds} + N\kappa\left(\int_0^t e^{\int_\tau^t r(s)\,ds}\,d\tau + \int_t^T P(t,\tau)\,d\tau\right)$$

$$- N\left(e^{\int_0^t r(s)\,ds} - P(t,T)\right) - l_{x+t\,T-t}\,p_{x+t}\,P(t,T).$$

The investments should ensure that assets exceed liabilities, i.e. it is desirable that this account is non-negative. Note that if we take $\varepsilon = 0$, such that $N = l_x\,\pi(0)$, we obtain the following more simple equation:

$$U(t) = l_x\,\pi(0)\,P(t,T) - l_{x+t\,T-t}\,p_{x+t}\,P(t,T)$$

$$+ l_x\,\pi(0)\,\kappa\left(\int_0^t e^{\int_\tau^t r(s)\,ds}\,d\tau + \int_t^T P(t,\tau)\,d\tau\right)$$

$$= \kappa\,l_{x+T}\,e^{-\int_0^T r^*(s)\,ds}\left(\int_0^t e^{\int_\tau^t r(s)\,ds}\,d\tau + \int_t^T P(t,\tau)\,d\tau\right)$$

$$- l_{x+T}\,P(t,T)\left(1 - e^{-\int_0^T r^*(s)\,ds}\right),$$

where, in particular,

$$U(0) = l_x\,\pi(0) - l_{x\,T}\,p_x\,P(0,T) = l_{x+T}\left(e^{-\int_0^T r^*(s)\,ds} - P(0,T)\right),$$

which is recognized as the individual bonus potential at time t; see Section 3.3.5. At time T, the value of the total account is given by

$$U(T) = l_{x+T}\left(\kappa\,e^{-\int_0^T r^*(s)\,ds}\int_0^T e^{\int_\tau^T r(s)\,ds}\,d\tau - \left(1 - e^{-\int_0^T r^*(s)\,ds}\right)\right).$$

It is interesting to compare the distribution of $U(t)$ with that of $\Pi_{\text{premium}}(t) - V^{\text{g}}(t)$, which corresponds to the situation where the company has not entered any swaps. In addition, one can study the sensitivity of $U(t)$ to changes in the current short rate $r(t)$. A more refined version of the present study is to modify the company's investment strategy such that the company invests premiums in bonds with a longer maturity.

We present here a simple simulation study and compare the distribution of $U(T)$ with that of

$$\Pi_{\text{premium}}(T) - V^{\text{g}}(T-) = l_{x+T}\left(e^{\int_0^T (r(s)-r^*(s))\,ds} - 1\right),$$

which is the terminal value of the account if we are not investing in any swaps, but only using the savings account (a roll-over strategy in bonds with very short maturity).

Numerical example

We present some simulation results for the Vasiček model with the parameters $r(0) = 0.03$, $\sigma = 0.03$, $a = 0.36$ and $b/a = 0.06$, which were also used in Chapter 3 and in Section 7.3.1. We take $l_{x+T} = 1$.

Figures 7.3 and 7.4 show histograms for the terminal values of the total accounts without and with swaps, respectively. The figures indicate how the swap can be used to center the distribution of the terminal value of the account, so that the impact of very low interest rates is reduced. The cost is that in situations with high interest, the account is reduced with the swap,

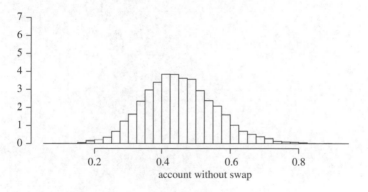

Figure 7.3. Histogram for the total account without swaps.

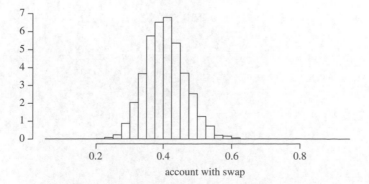

Figure 7.4. Histogram for the total account with swaps.

since the insurance company has to make a net payment when the short rate exceeds the swap rate κ.

We end the analysis here. Obviously, these calculations could be performed for the other types of interest rate derivatives described in this chapter. Similarly, one could include the mortality aspect and introduce optimality criteria for determining the optimal number of interest rate derivatives that should be included in order to control the combined mortality and financial risk inherent in these contracts.

Appendix

A.1 Some results from probability theory

We recall some well known concepts from probability theory that might be helpful when reading the introduction to arbitrage theory.

Probability spaces and random variables

When we talk about random variables, X and Y, say, they are typically defined on some probability space $(\Omega, \mathcal{F}, P)$; Ω is a set which can be interpreted as all states of the world; $\mathcal{F}$ is a σ-algebra of subsets of Ω; P is a probability measure, which, in particular, describes the joint distribution of the pair (X, Y). The measure P will be called the *true measure* or the *physical measure*, since it describes the true nature of the random variables. We use the phrase *almost surely* (abbreviated a.s. or P-a.s.) when describing properties for random variables which hold for (almost) all $\omega \in \Omega$, except for ω's in some negligible subset $N \in \mathcal{F}$ with $P(N) = 0$. For example, we say that "X is constant a.s." if there exists some real number K and some set $N \in \mathcal{F}$ with $P(N) = 0$ such that $X = K$ for all $\omega \in \Omega \setminus N$.

Random phenomena over time

We are interested in modeling the evolution of bond prices and other prices over a certain fixed time interval $[0, T]$. For example, it is natural to require that the price $P(t, \tau)$ at time t of a zero coupon bond with maturity τ, see Chapter 3, is a random variable which is not revealed before time t. The family of prices up to time T, $(P(t, \tau))_{t \in [0, T]}$, is an example of a *stochastic process*. More generally, a stochastic process is a family of random variables $X = (X(t))_{t \in [0, T]}$. In order to model more precisely what is known and what is not known at time t, one introduces a so-called *filtration* **F**, which describes the amount of information available at any time during the time interval $[0, T]$. Mathematically, a filtration is an increasing sequence of sub-σ-algebras of $\mathcal{F}$, also written $\mathbf{F} = (\mathcal{F}(t))_{t \in [0,T]}$, indexed by time t. This means that $\mathcal{F}(s) \subseteq \mathcal{F}(t) \subseteq \mathcal{F}$ for any $s < t \leq T$. The σ-algebra $\mathcal{F}(t)$ includes all the information that is available at time t. The stochastic process X is now said to be *adapted* (to the filtration **F**) if $X(t)$ can be determined from the σ-algebra $\mathcal{F}(t)$ for any $t \in [0, T]$, i.e. if $X(t)$ is observed at time t; mathematically this means that $X(t)$ is $\mathcal{F}(t)$-measurable. An adapted process is called *predictable* if the process X satisfies some additional measurability conditions. In particular, an adapted process X is predictable if it is deterministic (completely known at time 0) or if it is left-continuous. In discrete time, the concept of predictability is more simple; see Section 3.7.

Martingales

A stochastic process X is said to be a martingale if for any $t < u$ we have that $E[X(u)|\mathcal{F}(t)] = X(t)$. In particular, if X is a Markov process with respect to the filtration **F**, then the condition simplifies to $E[X(u)|X(t)] = X(t)$. This has the following interpretation. If $X(t)$ and $X(u)$ represent the price of a bond at time t (today) and u (tomorrow), respectively, then we see that, if X is a martingale, then the average price for tomorrow, given today's price, is exactly equal to the price today.

Change of measure

It will be necessary to introduce probability measures that are different from the true measure, or, in other words, to change the probability measure. For any non-negative random variable $Z \geq 0$ with $E^P[Z] = \int_\Omega Z(\omega) \, dP(\omega) = 1$, we can define a new probability measure Q as follows:

$$Q(A) = E^P[1_A \, Z] = \int_A Z(\omega) \, dP(\omega), \qquad (A.1)$$

for $A \in \mathcal{F}$. In particular, if $Z > 0 \, P$-a.s., then $\forall A \in \mathcal{F} \colon P(A) = 0 \Leftrightarrow Q(A) = 0$. In this case, P and Q are said to be *equivalent*, and Z is called the *density* for Q with respect to P.

Change of measure for remaining lifetimes

Actuaries in life insurance are in fact used to work with several different equivalent probability measures at the same time! Consider, for example, a group of insured individuals whose true mortality intensity is given by

$\mu(x+t)$, i.e. this is the mortality intensity under the true probability measure P. The true survival probability for an individual with remaining lifetime T_x is then given by

$$P(T_x > t) = \exp\left(-\int_0^t \mu(x+u)\,du\right) = {}_t p_x.$$

For the computation of premiums, actuaries would then introduce a first order mortality intensity $\mu^*(t+x)$, which means that, under some other probability measure P^*, the survival probability is $P^*(T_x > t) = \exp(-\int_0^t \mu^*(x+u)\,du) = {}_t p_x^*$. Provided that μ and μ^* are sufficiently regular and provided that $\mu^*(x+t)$ is only equal to zero if and only if $\mu(x+t)$ is, then one can actually define P^* via Equation (A.1) by using the following:

$$Z = \exp\left(-\int_0^T (\mu^*(x+s) - \mu(x+s))1_{\{T_x > s\}}\,ds\right)\left(\frac{\mu^*(x+T_x)}{\mu(x+T_x)}\right)^{1_{\{T_x < T\}}}.$$
$$(A.2)$$

Since this type of argument is not given in typical textbooks on life insurance mathematics, we give the proof in some detail here. It should be proved that $E^P[Z] = 1$ and that the measure P^* defined by $dP^*/dP = Z$ satisfies $P^*(T_x > t) = \exp(-\int_0^t \mu^*(x+u)\,du)$. It follows immediately by integrating with respect to the distribution of T_x, whose density is given by ${}_t p_x\, \mu(x+t)$, that

$$E^P[Z] = \int_0^T {}_t p_x\, \mu(x+t)\left(e^{-\int_0^t (\mu^*(x+s) - \mu(x+s))\,ds}\,\frac{\mu^*(x+t)}{\mu(x+t)}\right)\,dt$$

$$+ \int_T^\infty {}_t p_x\, \mu(x+t)\left(e^{-\int_0^T (\mu^*(x+s) - \mu(x+s))\,ds}\right)\,dt$$

$$= \int_0^T e^{-\int_0^t \mu^*(x+s)\,ds}\mu^*(x+t)\,dt$$

$$+ e^{-\int_0^T (\mu^*(x+s) - \mu(x+s))\,ds} \int_T^\infty {}_t p_x \mu(x+t)\,dt$$

$$= (1 - e^{-\int_0^T \mu^*(x+s)\,ds}) + e^{-\int_0^T (\mu^*(x+s) - \mu(x+s))\,ds}\, e^{-\int_0^T \mu(x+s)\,ds}$$

$$= 1.$$

For $t < T$, we find from similar calculations the following:

$$P^*(T_x > t) = E^P \left[1_{\{T_x > t\}} Z \right]$$

$$= \int_t^T {}_u p_x \mu(x+u) \left(e^{-\int_0^u (\mu^*(x+s) - \mu(x+s)) \, ds} \frac{\mu^*(x+u)}{\mu(x+u)} \right) du$$

$$+ \int_T^\infty {}_u p_x \mu(x+u) \left(e^{-\int_0^T (\mu^*(x+s) - \mu(x+s)) \, ds} \right) du$$

$$= e^{-\int_0^t \mu^*(x+s) \, ds} = {}_t p_x^*,$$

so that μ^* is indeed the mortality intensity under the measure P^* with density given in Equation (A.2). More on this subject can be found in Møller (1998) and Steffensen (2000).

A.2 The risk-minimizing strategy

In this appendix we give the direct construction of the risk-minimizing strategy outlined in Equations (5.56) and (5.57) proposed by Föllmer and Schweizer (1988). The cost process is defined by

$$C(t, h) = V(t, h) - \sum_{j=1}^t h^1(j) \Delta X(j), \qquad (A.3)$$

and we consider the problem of minimizing:

$$r(t, h) = E^Q[(C(t+1, h) - C(t, h))^2 \mid \mathcal{F}(t)], \qquad (A.4)$$

considered as a function of $(h^1(t+1), h^0(t))$ under the side condition $V(T, h) = H$. Since H is assumed to be $\mathcal{F}(T)$-measurable, we see from the decomposition in Equation (5.55) that

$$H = E^Q[H \mid \mathcal{F}(T)] = V^*(0) + \sum_{j=1}^T h^1(j, H) \Delta X(j) + L(T, H). \qquad (A.5)$$

It now follows via standard arguments, similar to those given in Section 5.5, that the minimum for Equation (A.4) is obtained for a strategy $\widetilde{h}$, where $\widetilde{h}^0$ is chosen such that

$$C(t, \widetilde{h}) = E^Q[C(t+1, \widetilde{h}) \mid \mathcal{F}(t)],$$

i.e. such that $C(\widetilde{h})$ is a Q-martingale. By using Equation (A.3), we see that the value process $V(\widetilde{h})$ is also a Q-martingale. Since, furthermore, $V(T, \widetilde{h}) = H$,

Equation (A.5) shows that

$$V(t, \widetilde{h}) = V^*(0) + \sum_{j=1}^{t} h^1(j, H)\Delta X(j) + L(t, H), \qquad (A.6)$$

and hence $\widetilde{h}^0(t) = V^*(t) - \widetilde{h}^1(t)X(t)$. This fixes $\widetilde{h}^0$ in terms of $\widetilde{h}^1$. Our next step is to insert Equations (A.3) and (A.6) into Equation (A.4), which leads to the following:

$$r(t, \widetilde{h}) = E^Q \left[\left((h^1(t+1, H) - \widetilde{h}^1(t+1))\Delta X(t+1) + \Delta L(t+1, H) \right)^2 \Big| \mathcal{F}(t) \right].$$
$$(A.7)$$

Since $\widetilde{h}^1(t+1)$ and $h^1(t+1, H)$ are $\mathcal{F}(t)$-measurable, and since

$$E^Q[\Delta X(t+1)\Delta L(t+1, H) \mid \mathcal{F}(t)] = 0,$$

by the orthogonality between X and L^H, we can rewrite Equation (A.7) as follows:

$$(h^1(t+1, H) - \widetilde{h}^1(t+1))^2 E^Q \left[(\Delta X(t+1))^2 \big| \mathcal{F}(t) \right]$$
$$+ E^Q \left[(\Delta L(t+1, H))^2 \big| \mathcal{F}(t) \right],$$

which is minimized for $\widetilde{h}^1(t+1) = h^1(t+1, H)$. This shows that the risk-minimizing strategy is given by

$$(\widehat{h}^1(t), \widehat{h}^0(t)) = (h^1(t, H), V^*(t) - h^1(t, H)X(t)).$$

A.3 Risk minimization for unit-linked contracts

Since Y and S are assumed to be independent, we obtain the following:

$$V^*(t) := E^Q \left[Y(T)\frac{f(S^1(T))}{S^0(T)} \Big| \mathcal{F}(t) \right]$$

$$= E^Q \left[\frac{f(S^1(T))}{S^0(T)} \Big| \mathcal{F}(t) \right] E^Q[Y(T)| \mathcal{F}(t)]$$

$$= E^Q \left[\frac{f(S^1(T))}{S^0(T)} \Big| \mathcal{G}(t) \right] E^Q[Y(T)| \mathcal{H}(t)]$$

$$= \pi(t, f)M(t).$$

In the second equality, we have used the independence between $Y(T)$ and $S^1(T)$, and in the third equality we have used the definition of the σ-algebra

$\mathcal{F}(t)$ as well as the independence between the two sources of risk. The last equality follows from the definitions of $\pi(f)$ and M. Now, note that

$$\Delta V^*(t) = V^*(t) - V^*(t-1) = \pi(t, f)M(t) - \pi(t-1, f)M(t-1)$$
$$= (\pi(t, f) - \pi(t-1, f))M(t-1) + \pi(t, f)(M(t) - M(t-1))$$
$$= M(t-1)\alpha(t, f)\Delta X(t) + \pi(t, f)\Delta M(t),$$

where we have used the representation given in Equation (5.47) for $\pi(f)$ in the last equality. The term $M(t-1)\alpha(t, f)$ is $\mathcal{F}(t-1)$-measurable, such that the process $h^1(H)$ defined by

$$h^1(t, H) = M(t-1)\alpha(t, f)$$

is predictable. If we can show that the process $L(H)$ defined by

$$L(t, H) = \sum_{j=1}^{t} \pi(j, f)\Delta M(j)$$

is a Q-martingale, and that the product $L(H)X$ is also a Q-martingale, then we have actually verified that the decomposition in Equation (5.55) is indeed given by

$$V^*(t) = V^*(0) + \sum_{j=1}^{t} M(j-1)\alpha^f(j)\Delta X(j) + \sum_{j=1}^{t} \pi(j, f)\Delta M(j). \qquad (A.8)$$

To see that $L(H)$ is a martingale, we apply the rule of iterated expectations and the independence between the two sources of risk, or, more precisely, between the two filtrations $\mathbf{G}$ and $\mathbf{H}$. Using these ingredients, we obtain

$$E^Q[\Delta L(t, H)| \mathcal{F}(t-1)] = E^Q[\pi(t, f)\Delta M(t)| \mathcal{F}(t-1)]$$
$$= E^Q[\pi(t, f)E^Q[\Delta M(t)|\mathcal{G}(t) \vee \mathcal{H}(t-1)]|\mathcal{F}(t-1)]$$
$$= 0,$$

since M is a martingale and since M is independent of the filtration $\mathbf{G}$. Similar calculations show that $L(H)X$ is also a martingale. Since

$$\Delta(L(H)X)(t) = L(t, H)X(t) - L(t-1, H)X(t-1)$$
$$= \Delta L(t, H)\Delta X(t) + L(t-1, H)\Delta X(t) + X(t-1)\Delta L(t, H),$$

it is sufficient to show that

$$E^Q[\Delta L(t, H)\Delta X(t)| \mathcal{F}(t-1)] = 0.$$

This now follows by using calculations similar to the ones used to show that $L(H)$ is a martingale, so that Equation (A.8) is indeed the desired decomposition. From the results in Section A.2 it now follows that the risk-minimizing strategy is as follows:

$$h^1(t) = Y(t-1)_{T-(t-1)}p_{x+(t-1)}\alpha(t, f),$$

$$h^0(t) = Y(t)_{T-t}p_{x+t}\pi(t, f) - Y(t-1)_{T-(t-1)}p_{x+(t-1)}\alpha(t, f)X(t).$$

A.4 Mean-variance hedging for unit-linked contracts

In this section, we derive the mean-variance hedging strategy of Proposition 5.8 for the unit-linked contract given in Equation (5.46). Firstly, we examine the structure of the probability measures $\widetilde{P}$. In the binomial model, the increments of the discounted stock price process are given by

$$\Delta X(t) = X(t-1)\frac{Z(t)-r}{1+r},$$

and hence the (conditional) expected return is as follows:

$$\Delta A(t) = E[\Delta X(t)|\mathcal{F}(t-1)] = X(t-1)\frac{E[Z(t)]-r}{1+r}.$$

Similarly, the (conditional) variance on the return in year t is given by

$$\text{Var}[\Delta X(t)|\mathcal{F}(t-1)] = \frac{X(t-1)^2}{(1+r)^2}\text{Var}[Z(t)-r].$$

In addition, we have that

$$\widetilde{\lambda}(t) = \frac{\Delta A(t)}{E[(\Delta X(t))^2|\mathcal{F}(t-1)]}$$

$$= \frac{X(t-1)\frac{E[Z(t)]-r}{1+r}}{X(t-1)^2 E\left[\left(\frac{Z(t)-r}{1+r}\right)^2\right]}$$

$$= \frac{1+r}{X(t-1)}\frac{E[Z(t)]-r}{E[(Z(t)-r)^2]},$$

so that $\widetilde{\lambda}(t)\Delta A(t)$ is deterministic. We can now describe more precisely the properties of $\widetilde{P}$. In particular, we see that $\widetilde{P}$ is indeed a martingale measure, i.e. X is a $\widetilde{P}$-martingale. To see this, note that

$$\frac{1-\widetilde{\lambda}(t)\Delta X(t)}{1-\widetilde{\lambda}(t)\Delta A(t)} = \frac{E[(Z(t)-r)^2] - (Z(t)-r)(E[Z(t)]-r)}{E[(Z(t)-r)^2] - (E[Z(t)]-r)^2},$$

such that the factors in the definition of $\widetilde{P}$ are independent. One can use this independence to show that $Z(1), \ldots, Z(t)$ are i.i.d. under $\widetilde{P}$, and that

$$\widetilde{E}[\Delta X(t)|\mathcal{F}(t-1)] = E\left[\left.\frac{d\widetilde{P}}{dP}\Delta X(t)\right|\mathcal{F}(t-1)\right] = 0. \qquad (A.9)$$

Thus, $\widetilde{P}$ is actually identical to the probability measure Q that was already introduced in Section 5.7.1.

It is now relatively easy to show that the decomposition given in Equation (5.71) is identical to the representation given in Equation (5.63) which was derived for the risk-minimizing strategy. The proposition now follows directly by using Equation (5.70) and by choosing the deposit $\widetilde{h}^0$ in the savings account such that the strategy is self-financing. For completeness, these calculations are included here.

In Section 5.7.5, we worked with the martingale measure Q which was obtained as the product measure of the unique martingale measure for the binomial market and the physical measure for the insured lifetimes. Under this measure, we derived the Kunita–Watanabe decomposition for the Q-martingale $V^*(t) = E^Q[H|\mathcal{F}(t)]$ and showed that it was given by

$$V^*(t) = V^*(0) + \sum_{j=1}^{t} h^1(j, H)\Delta X(j) + L(t, H),$$

where

$$h^1(j, H) = M(j-1)\alpha(j, f),$$

$$L(t, H) = \sum_{j=1}^{t} \pi(j, f)\Delta M(j).$$

Here, $L(H)$ is a Q-martingale which is orthogonal to the Q-martingale, i.e.

$$E^Q[L(u, H)X(u)|\mathcal{F}(t)] = L(t, H)X(t)$$

for all $u \geq t$. In order to solve the mean-variance hedging problem, we need the decomposition from Equation (5.71) given by

$$H = \widetilde{H}(0) + \sum_{j=1}^{T} \widetilde{h}^1(j, H)\Delta X(j) + \widetilde{L}(T, H), \qquad (A.10)$$

where $\widetilde{L}(H)$ is a P-martingale which is orthogonal to the P-martingale $X - A$. This implies that one cannot conclude directly that the decomposition in Equation (A.10) can be obtained from the Kunita–Watanabe decomposition for the Q-martingale V^*. However, we claim that the decomposition in Equation (A.10) is given by

$$\widetilde{H}(0) = V^*(0),$$

$$\widetilde{h}^1(t, H) = h^1(t, H),$$

$$\widetilde{L}(t, H) = L(t, H).$$

To see this, one has to check that $\widetilde{L}(H)$ is a P-martingale (we only know that it is a Q-martingale) and that $\widetilde{L}(H)$ is orthogonal to $X - A$. We note that

$$\widetilde{L}(t, H) = \sum_{j=1}^{t} \pi(j, f)\Delta M(j)$$

is indeed a P-martingale, since M is a P-martingale and since $\pi(j, f)$ is stochastically independent of $\Delta M(j)$. To see that $\widetilde{L}(H)$ is orthogonal to $X - A$, it is sufficient to verify that

$$E\left[(\Delta X(t) - \Delta A(t))\Delta L(t, H)\vert \mathcal{F}(t-1)\right] = 0,$$

and this follows via calculations similar to the ones used in Section A.3. By conditioning on $\mathcal{G}(t) \vee \mathcal{H}(t-1)$ and by using the independence between $\mathcal{G}(T)$ and $\mathcal{H}(T)$ and the fact that M is a P-martingale, we see that

$$E\left[(\Delta X(t) - \Delta A(t))\Delta \widetilde{L}(H, t)\Big\vert \mathcal{F}(t-1)\right]$$

$$= E\left[(\Delta X(t) - \Delta A(t))E\left[\pi(t, f)\Delta M(t)\vert \mathcal{G}(t) \vee \mathcal{H}(t-1)\right]\vert \mathcal{F}(t-1)\right]$$

$$= E\left[(\Delta X(t) - \Delta A(t))\pi(t, f)E\left[\Delta M(t)\vert \mathcal{G}(t) \vee \mathcal{H}(t-1)\right]\vert \mathcal{F}(t-1)\right]$$

$$= 0.$$

Here, the last equality follows by exploiting the fact that M is a P-martingale.

References

Aase, K. K. and Persson, S. A. (1994). Pricing of unit-linked life insurance policies, *Scandinavian Actuarial Journal*, pp. 26–52.

Bacinello, A. R. (2001). Fair pricing of life insurance participating policies with a minimum interest rate guaranteed, *ASTIN Bulletin* **31**, 275–297.

Bacinello, A. R. and Ortu, F. (1993a). Pricing equity-linked life insurance with endogenous minimum guarantees, *Insurance: Mathematics and Economics* **12**, 245–257.

Bacinello, A. R. and Ortu, F. (1993b). *Pricing Guaranteed Securities-Linked Life Insurance under Interest-Rate Risk*. Proceedings of the 3rd AFIR Colloquium, Rome, Vol. I, pp. 35–55.

Bacinello, A. R. and Persson, S. A. (1998). *Design and Pricing of Equity-Linked Life Insurance under Stochastic Interest Rates*. Preprint, Institute of Finance and Management Science, The Norwegian School of Economics and Business Administration.

Baxter, M. and Rennie, A. (1996). *Financial Calculus. An Introduction to Derivative Pricing* (Cambridge: Cambridge University Press).

Becherer, D. (2003). Rational hedging and valuation of integrated risks under constant absolute risk aversion, *Insurance: Mathematics and Economics* **33**, 1–28.

Bielecki, T. R. and Rutkowski, M. (2001). *Credit Risk: Modelling, Valuation and Hedging* (Berlin: Springer).

Biffis, E. and Millossovich, P. (2006). The fair value of guaranteed annuity options, *Scandinavian Actuarial Journal*, pp. 23–41.

Björk, T. (1994). *Stokastisk Kalkyl och Kapitalmarknadsteori*. Lecture notes, Kungl. Tekniska Högskolan, Stockholm.

Björk, T. (1997). Interest rate theory, in Runggaldier, W. J. (ed.), *Financial Mathematics*, Springer Lecture Notes in Mathematics, Vol. 1656 (Berlin: Springer Verlag).

Björk, T. (2004). *Arbitrage Theory in Continuous Time*, 2nd edn (Oxford: Oxford University Press).

Black, F. and Scholes, M. (1973). The pricing of options and corporate liabilities, *Journal of Political Economy* **81**, 637–654.

Blake, D. (1998). Pension schemes as options on pension fund assets: implications for pension fund management, *Insurance: Mathematics and Economics* **23**, 263–286.

Blake, D., Cairns, A. J. G. and Dowd, K. (2006). Living with mortality: longevity bonds and other mortality-linked securities. Preprint, Actuarial Mathematics and Statistics, School of Mathematical and Computer Sciences, Heriot-Watt University, Edinburgh.

Brennan, M. J. and Schwartz, E. S. (1976). The pricing of equity-linked life insurance policies with an asset value guarantee, *Journal of Financial Economics* **3**, 195–213.

Brennan, M. J. and Schwartz, E. S. (1979a). Alternative investment strategies for the issuers of equity-linked life insurance with an asset value guarantee, *Journal of Business* **52**, 63–93.

Brennan, M. J. and Schwartz, E. S. (1979b). *Pricing and Investment Strategies for Guaranteed Equity-Linked Life Insurance*. Monograph no. 7. The S. S. Huebner Foundation for Insurance Education, Wharton School, University of Pennsylvania, Philadelphia.

Brigo, D. and Mercurio, F. (2001). *Interest Rate Models: Theory and Practice*, (Berlin: Springer).

Briys, E. and de Varenne, F. (1994). Life insurance in a contingent claim framework: pricing and regulatory implications, *The Geneva Papers on Risk and Insurance Theory* **19**, 53–72.

Briys, E. and de Varenne, F. (1997). On the risk of life insurance liabilities: debunking some common pitfalls, *Journal of Risk and Insurance* **64**, 673–694.

Cairns, A. J. G. (2000). Some notes on the dynamics and optimal control of stochastic pension fund models in continuous time, *ASTIN Bulletin* **30**, 19–55.

Cairns, A. J. G. (2004). *Interest Rate Models: An Introduction* (Princeton: Princeton University Press).

Cairns, A. J. G., Blake, D. and Dowd, K. (2006). Pricing death: frameworks for the valuation and securitization of mortality risk. *ASTIN Bulletin* **36**, 79–120.

Cont, R. and Tankov, P. (2003). *Financial Modelling with Jump Processes* (Boca Raton: Chapman & Hall/CRC Press).

Cowley, A. and Cummins, J. D. (2005). Securitization of life insurance assets and liabilities, *The Journal of Risk and Insurance* **72**, 193–226.

Cox, J., Ingersoll, J. and Ross, S. (1985). A theory of the term-structure of interest rates, *Econometrica* **53**, 385–408.

Cox, J., Ross, S. and Rubinstein, M. (1979). Option pricing: a simplified approach, *Journal of Financial Economics* **7**, 229–263.

Dahl, M. (2004). Stochastic mortality in life insurance: market reserves and mortality-linked insurance contracts, *Insurance: Mathematics and Economics* **35**, 113–136.

Dahl, M. and Møller, T. (2006). Valuation and Hedging of Life Insurance Liabilities with Systematic Mortality Risk, *Insurance: Mathematics and Economics*, **39**, 193–217.

Dana, R. A. (1999). Existence, uniqueness and determinacy of equilibrium in C.A.P.M. with a riskless asset, *Journal of Mathematical Economics* **32**, 167–175.

Delbaen, F. (1986). Equity linked policies, *Bulletin de l'Association Royale des Actuaires Belges*, pp. 33–52.

Delbaen, F. and Haezendonck, J. (1989). A martingale approach to premium calculation principles in an arbitrage-free market, *Insurance: Mathematics and Economics* **8**, 269–277.

El Karoui, N. and Quenez, M. C. (1995). Dynamic programming and pricing of contingent claims in an incomplete market, *SIAM Journal on Control and Optimization* **33**, 29–66.

Embrechts, P., Klüppelberg, C. and Mikosch, T. (1997). *Modelling Extremal Events in Insurance and Finance* (Berlin: Springer-Verlag).

Föllmer, H. and Leukert, P. (1999). Quantile hedging, *Finance and Stochastics* **3**, 251–273.

Föllmer, H. and Schied, A. (2002). *Stochastic Finance: An Introduction in Discrete Time*, de Gruyter Series in Mathematics 27 (Berlin: Walter de Gruyter).

Föllmer, H. and Schweizer, M. (1988). Hedging by sequential regression: an introduction to the mathematics of option trading, *ASTIN Bulletin* **18**, 147–160.

Föllmer, H. and Sondermann, D. (1986). Hedging of non-redundant contingent claims, in W. Hildenbrand and A. Mas-Colell (eds), *Contributions to Mathematical Economics* (Amsterdam: North-Holland), pp. 205–223.

Gerber, H. U. (1997). *Life Insurance Mathematics* (Berlin: Springer-Verlag).

Grosen, A. and Jørgensen, P. L. (1997). Valuation of early exercisable interest rate guarantees, *Journal of Risk and Insurance* **64**, 481–503.

Grosen, A. and Jørgensen, P. L. (2000). Fair valuation of life insurance liabilities: the impact of interest rate guarantees, surrender options, and bonus policies, *Insurance: Mathematics and Economics* **26**, 37–57.

Grosen, A. and Jørgensen, P. L. (2002). Life insurance liabilities at market values: an analysis of insolvency risk, bonus policy, and regulatory intervention rules in a barrier option framework, *Journal of Risk and Insurance* **69**, 63–91.

Hansen, M. and Miltersen, K. (2002). Minimum rate of return guarantees: the Danish case, *Scandinavian Actuarial Journal*, pp. 280–318.

Hardy, M. (2003). *Investment Guarantees: Modeling and Risk Management for Equity-Linked Life Insurance* (Hoboken, NJ: Wiley).

Harrison, J. M. and Kreps, D. M. (1979). Martingales and arbitrage in multiperiod securities markets, *Journal of Economic Theory* **20**, 381–408.

Harrison, J. M. and Pliska, S. R. (1981). Martingales and stochastic integrals in the theory of continuous trading, *Stochastic Processes and their Applications* **11**, 215–260.

Heston, S. L. (1993). A closed-form solution for options with stochastic volatility with applications to bond and currency options, *The Review of Financial Studies* **6**, 327–343.

Hoem, J. (1969). Markov chain models in life insurance, *Blätter der Deutschen Gesellschaft für Versicherungsmathematik* **9**, 91–107.

Hull, J. C. (2005). *Options, Futures, and other Derivatives*, 6th edn. (Upper Saddle River, NJ: Prentice-Hall).

Jarrow, R. (1996). *Modelling Fixed Income Securities and Interest Rate Options* (New York: McGraw-Hill).

Jørgensen, P. L. (2004). On accounting standards and fair valuation of life insurance and pension liabilities, *Scandinavian Actuarial Journal*, pp. 372–394.

Kahn, P. M. (1971). Projections of variable life insurance operations, with discussion, *Transactions of the Society of Actuaries*, **XXIII**, 335–366.

Kalashnikov, V. and Norberg, R. (2003). On the sensitivity of premiums and reserves to changes in valuation elements, *Scandinavian Actuarial Journal*, pp. 238–256.

Lamberton, D. and Lapeyre, B. (1996). *Introduction to Stochastic Calculus Applied to Finance* (Boca Raton: Chapman & Hall).

Lando, D. (2004). *Credit Risk Modeling – Theory and Applications* (Princeton: Princeton University Press).

Lee, R. D. (2000). The Lee–Carter method for forecasting mortality, with various extensions and application, *North American Actuarial Journal* **4**, 80–93.

Lee, R. D. and Carter, L. (1992). Modeling and forecasting the time series of US mortality, *Journal of the American Statistical Association* **87**, 659–671.

Marocco, P. and Pitacco, E. (1998). *Longevity Risk and Life Annuity Reinsurance*. Transactions of the 26th International Congress of Actuaries, Birmingham, England, Vol. 6, 453–479.

Merton, R. C. (1973). Theory of rational option pricing, *Bell Journal of Economics and Management Science* **4**, 141–183.

Milevsky, M. A. and Promislow, S. D. (2001). Mortality derivatives and the option to annuitise, *Insurance: Mathematics and Economics* **29**, 299–318.

Miltersen, K. R. and Persson, S. A. (2000). *A Note on Interest Rate Guarantees and Bonus: The Norwegian Case*. Proceedings of the 10th AFIR Colloquium, Tromsø, pp. 507–516.

Miltersen, K. R. and Persson, S. A. (2003). Guaranteed investment contracts: distributed and undistributed excess return, *Scandinavian Actuarial Journal*, pp. 257–279.

Møller, T. (1998). Risk-minimizing hedging strategies for unit-linked life insurance contracts, *ASTIN Bulletin* **28**, 17–47.

Møller, T. (2000). Quadratic hedging approaches and indifference pricing in insurance, Ph.D. thesis, University of Copenhagen.

Møller, T. (2001a). Hedging equity-linked life insurance contracts, *North American Actuarial Journal* **5**, 79–95.

Møller, T. (2001b). On transformations of actuarial valuation principles, *Insurance: Mathematics and Economics* **28**, 281–303.

Møller, T. (2001c). Risk-minimizing hedging strategies for insurance payment processes, *Finance and Stochastics* **5**, 419–446.

Møller, T. (2002). On valuation and risk management at the interface of insurance and finance, *British Actuarial Journal* **8**, 787–828.

Møller, T. (2003a). Indifference pricing of insurance contracts in a product space model, *Finance and Stochastics* **7**, 197–217.

Møller, T. (2003b). Indifference pricing of insurance contracts in a product space model: applications, *Insurance: Mathematics and Economics* **32**, 295–315.

Møller, T. (2004). Stochastic orders in dynamic reinsurance markets, *Finance and Stochastics* **8**, 479–499.

Musiela, M. and Rutkowski, M. (1997). *Martingale Methods in Financial Modelling* (Berlin: Springer-Verlag).

Nelson, C. R. and Siegel, A. F. (1987). Parsimonious modeling of yield curves, *Journal of Business* **60**, 473–489.

Nielsen, J. and Sandmann, K. (1995). Equity-linked life insurance: a model with stochastic interest rates, *Insurance: Mathematics and Economics* **16**, 225–253.

Nielsen, J. and Sandmann, K. (1996). Uniqueness of the fair premium for equity-linked life contracts, *The Geneva Papers on Risk and Insurance Theory* **21**, 65–102.

Nielsen, L. T. (1999). *Pricing and Hedging of Derivative Securities* (New York: Oxford University Press).

Nielsen, P. H. (2005). Optimal bonus strategies in life insurance: the Markov chain interest case, *Scandinavian Actuarial Journal*, pp. 81–102.

Nielsen, P. H. (2006). Utility maximization and risk minimization in life and pension insurance, *Finance and Stochastics* **10**, 75–97.

Norberg, R. (1989). Experience rating in group life insurance, *Scandinavian Actuarial Journal*, pp. 194–224.

Norberg, R. (1991). Reserves in life and pension insurance, *Scandinavian Actuarial Journal*, pp. 3–24.

Norberg, R. (1999). A theory of bonus in life insurance, *Finance and Stochastics* **3**, 373–390.

Norberg, R. (2000). *Basic Life Insurance Mathematics*. Lecture notes, Laboratory of Actuarial Mathematics, University of Copenhagen.

Norberg, R. (2001). On bonus and bonus prognoses in life insurance, *Scandinavian Actuarial Journal* **2**, 126–147.

Norberg, R. and Steffensen, M. (2005). What is the time value of a stream of investments?, *Journal of Applied Probability* **42**, 861–866.

Olivieri, A. (2001). Uncertainty in mortality projections: an actuarial perspective, *Insurance: Mathematics and Economics* **29**, 231–245.

Olivieri, A. and Pitacco, E. (2002). *Inference about Mortality Improvements in Life Annuity Portfolios*. Proceedings of the Transactions of the 27th International Congress of Actuaries, Cancun, Mexico.

Pham, H. (2000). On quadratic hedging in continuous time, *Mathematical Methods of Operations Research* **51**, 315–339.

Pliska, S. R. (1997). *Introduction to Mathematical Finance: Discrete Time Models* (Oxford: Blackwell Publishers).

Ramlau-Hansen, H. (1988). The emergence of profit in life insurance, *Insurance: Mathematics and Economics* **7**, 225–236.

Ramlau-Hansen, H. (1991). Distribution of surplus in life insurance, *ASTIN Bulletin* **21**, 57–71.

Rebonato, R. (2002). *Modern Pricing of Interest-Rate Derivatives: The LIBOR Market and Beyond* (Princeton: Princeton University Press).

Rheinländer, T. and Schweizer, M. (1997). On L^2-projections on a space of stochastic integrals, *Annals of Probability* **25**, 1810–1831.

Schönbucher, P. J. (2003). *Credit Derivatives Pricing Models: Models, Pricing and Implementation* (Chichester: John Wiley & Sons Ltd).

Schwarz, H. R. (1989). *Numerical Analysis. A Comprehensive Introduction* (New York: John Wiley & Sons Ltd.)

Schweizer, M. (1988). Hedging of options in a general semimartingale model. Dissertation, ETH Zurich, no. 8615.

Schweizer, M. (1995). Variance-optimal hedging in discrete time, *Mathematics of Operations Research* **20**, 1–32.

Schweizer, M. (2001a). A guided tour through quadratic hedging approaches, in Jouini, E., Cvitanić, J. and Musiela, M. (eds), *Option Pricing, Interest Rates and Risk Management* (Cambridge: Cambridge University Press), pp. 538–574.

Schweizer, M. (2001b). From actuarial to financial valuation principles, *Insurance: Mathematics and Economics* **28**, 31–47.

Sharpe, W. F. (1976). Corporate pension funding policy, *Journal of Financial Economics* **3**, 183–193.

Shiryaev, A. N., Kabanov, Y. M., Kramkov, D. D. and Melnikov, A. V. (1994). Towards the theory of options of both European and American types. I. Discrete time, *Theory of Probability and its Applications* **39**, 14–60.

Sondermann, D. (1991). Reinsurance in arbitrage-free markets, *Insurance: Mathematics and Economics* **10**, 191–202.

Steffensen, M. (2000). A no arbitrage approach to Thiele's differential equation, *Insurance: Mathematics and Economics* **27**, 201–214.

Steffensen, M. (2001). On valuation and control in life and pension insurance, Ph.D. thesis, University of Copenhagen.

Steffensen, M. (2002). Intervention options in life insurance, *Insurance: Mathematics and Economics* **31**, 71–85.

Steffensen, M. (2004). On Merton's problem for life insurers, *ASTIN Bulletin* **34**, 5–25.

Steffensen, M. (2006a). Quadratic optimization of life and pension insurance payments, *ASTIN Bulletin* **36**, 245–267.

Steffensen, M. (2006b). Surplus-linked life insurance, *Scandinavian Actuarial Journal*, pp. 1–22.

Svensson, L. E. O. (1995). Estimating forward interest rates with the extended Nelson & Siegel method, *Penning- & Valutapolitik* **1995**(3), 13–26.

Turner, S. H. (1969). Asset value guarantees under equity-based products, with discussion, *Transactions of the Society of Actuaries* **XXI**, 459–493.

Turner, S. H. (1971). Equity-based life insurance in the United Kingdom, with discussion, *Transactions of the Society of Actuaries* **XXIII**, 273–324.

Vasiček, O. (1977). An equilibrium characterization of the term structure, *Journal of Financial Economics* **5**, 177–188.

Wilkie, A. D. (1978). Maturity (and other) guarantees under unit linked policies, *Transactions of the Faculty of Actuaries* **36**, 27–41.

Index